Asia-Europe Industrial Connectivity in Times of Crisis

Innovation and Technology Set

coordinated by
Chantal Ammi

Volume 16

Asia-Europe Industrial Connectivity in Times of Crisis

Edited by

Lucía Morales
Sam Dzever
Robert Taylor

iSTE

WILEY

First published 2022 in Great Britain and the United States by ISTE Ltd and John Wiley & Sons, Inc.

ISTE Ltd
27-37 St George's Road
London SW19 4EU
UK

www.iste.co.uk

John Wiley & Sons, Inc.
111 River Street
Hoboken, NJ 07030
USA

www.wiley.com

Library of Congress Control Number: 2022941227

British Library Cataloguing-in-Publication Data
A CIP record for this book is available from the British Library
ISBN 978-1-78630-862-7

Contents

Introduction: Connectivity in Euro-Asian Business

The topics discussed in the following chapters highlight the acceleration of trends in international business already apparent before the Covid-19 pandemic, notably the reaction against globalisation and the revolution in connectivity, with the growing incidence of cyber warfare, especially between China and the United States. China's emergence as a global economic player is especially in evidence in Asia, as the latter's trade and investment increases in a context of regional economic integration, where the Chinese are set to play a major role in digital and physical infrastructural connectivity. There are nevertheless concerns that authoritarian controls by the Chinese state have adverse implications for personal privacy.

I.1. The Chinese conception of a new world order

The Covid-19 pandemic has accelerated trends already in evidence in international business prior to the outbreak. Three factors can be highlighted: China's growing global role in conflict with the United States, the revolution in digital connectivity and the reaction against globalisation accompanied by moves towards economic integration, especially in Asia. Global rivalry will increasingly focus on acquisition of new technologies. The main protagonists in cyber competition are China and the United States, with rivalry being played out globally but especially in Europe and Asia, where it is manifested by market competition, thus affecting both trade and investment. These issues informed the subjects of the 25th International Euro-Asia Roundtable and Research Conference held in 2020 and 2021. The following chapters are mainly revised versions of those contributions.

Introduction written by Robert TAYLOR.

China's emergence as a global player reflects its leader's articulation of a new world order. This is based largely on a search for economic pre-eminence. When, on the country's economic opening up in 1978, China's leaders appeared to abandon their call for revolution in developing countries, Western governments adopted a policy of engagement, whereby Chinese accession to such bodies as the World Trade Organisation (WTO) would mean adherence by China to the values and norms underpinning commitment to those institutions. However, since 2021 China's leader Xi Jinping has adopted a more proactive stance, whereby China seeks not to overturn the international order by force but create their own brand of economic interdependence, especially among developing countries, the aim being to supplant liberal democratic values by encouraging particularly developing countries to mirror Chinese domestic political norms and values via influence exerted, for instance, through the One Belt One Road (OBOR) initiative as the basis of a new world order. The means are thus economic, although military force may never be procluded. Here we can see the implications of Chinese-built 5G networks, as commented on by Nadège Rolland. There is thus a sense in which any military moves could threaten China's ascent as a global economic player (Rolland 2020; Pantucci 2020).

I.2. China as a global economic player in Europe

China's outreach is indicated by trade and investment in European countries but this is nevertheless accompanied by suspicion over Huawei's participation in the British 5G system, suspicion fuelled by American fears that the adoption of Huawei's hardware will provide a back door into British telecommunications, in other words, a security risk. Members of the European Union (EU) are, however, ambivalent about the United States' fears; in late 2020 the Union was negotiating a deal that would give EU firms better access to the Chinese market, improving competitiveness and protecting investment, even though it was later reported in May 2021 that the European Parliament had failed to ratify the agreement because of China's record on human rights and its sanctions against Europeans critical of the Chinese government (Ivens 2020; US-China Business Council News Overview 2020e). In fact, China became the main trading partner of the EU in 2020. The bloc's imports from China grew by 5.6% year on year to £383.5 billion and exports grew by 2.2% to £202.5 billion (US $465 billion) (US-China Business Council News Overview 2020a). The United Kingdom (UK) exported £23.4 billion worth of goods and services to China in 2019, with Chinese imports totalling £44.9 billion. China accounted for 7% of UK imports and 4% of its exports in 2020 (Collingridge 2020; Ivens 2020). The Chinese have invested heavily in UK utilities and infrastructure, buying stakes in Thames Water, Heathrow Airport, North Sea oil production and National Gas pipelines (Pogrund *et al.* 2020).

I.3. Sino-American rivalry in Asia

In geopolitical terms Sino-American competition has a higher profile in Asia, where countries do not, in contrast with the United States, see US-China conflict in zero sum terms. Such people live in Asia and may be attracted by China's state-led economic development and apparent commitment to sustainable green growth (Armstrong 2021a).

In spite of China's growing global power, there are emerging weaknesses in China's economy which the 14th Five Year Plan is designed to address. The course charted for the next 15 years is to reach the level of moderately developed countries, to expand the size of the country's middle income group, to provide equitable access to public services and to reduce urban–rural and regional disparities. The 14th Five Year Plan could be said to have elevated China's commitment to self-reliance into a national strategic pillar, even though to date the Chinese have been accused of state directed cyber theft. Accordingly, R&D investment will be increased and innovation emphasised, while development of advanced technologies like artificial intelligence, biotechnology, blockchain, neuroscience, quantum computing and robotics will be furthered. Digital connectivity through internal infrastructure, 5G networks and data centres is to be continually strengthened. The objective is to address the lingering productivity challenge. In terms of output per worker and unit of capital, productivity is a gauge of overall economic efficiency and China's economy is only 30% as productive as the world's best-performing economies like the United States, Japan and Germany. This strategy in general could help guarantee the projected rise in the size of private consumption expected to double in the next decade, with the share of services expected to overtake that of goods (US-China Business Council News Overview 2020c; US-China Business Council News Overview 2020b; US-China Business Council News Overview 2021d; US-China Business Council News Overview 2021b; US-China Business Council News Overview 2021c).

Thus a premium will be placed on the training of skilled manpower. Significantly, the Chinese government has also pledged to raise the retirement age, given the potential shortage of skills, induced in part by China's former but now abandoned one child policy.

Commitment to increasing domestic consumption and higher productivity does not, however, suggest self-sufficiency or autarky, since the Chinese economy is still heavily dependent on foreign trade. A key feature of China's current economic policy is the dual circulation strategy, where China still remains part of international circulation, involving competitive global exports and trade with a concomitant effort to improve domestic circulation. This involves building a vibrant domestic economy with less, though continuing, dependence on imports (Yu 2021). Because of supply chains there can be no complete decoupling among major economies like China and the United States. Nevertheless, given restrictions imposed by the United States during the Trump presidency, the Chinese company, Huawei, has responded by investing in semiconductor producers like Nikkei Asia Data (US-China Business Council News Overview 2021a).

China will remain a rival of the United States in Southeast Asia, and the above projections of Chinese growth will necessarily affect foreign trade and investment in the region.

I.4. China's trade and investment in Asia

Ever since their accession to power in 1949 successive Chinese leaders have expressed anti-Western commonality with developing countries, conceiving human rights in terms of a nation's right to economic development rather than the liberal view of individual freedoms espoused by Western democracies. In short, the Chinese strategy is to mould a Southeast Asian identity through proselytising Chinese values, norms and discourse. Asian regional leaders, including in China, have come to believe that international institutions like the International Monetary Fund (IMF) and the World Bank need to be reformed or replaced, as they are seen to be increasingly out of touch with the needs and aspirations of developing countries. Alternatives include the Chiang Mai Initiative, the Asian Development Bank and the Asian Infrastructure Investment Bank (Armstrong 2021b). These institutions in turn contribute to economic integration.

A further example of such institution building in Southeast Asia is the Regional Comprehensive Economic Partnership (RCEP), ratified by China and also including the 10 ASEAN nations, in addition to Japan, South Korea, Australia and New Zealand. The RCEP can potentially function as a rule-setting institution for the region, at a time when the WTO is struggling to govern adequately as an anchor of global multilateral trade. As a regional bloc which already covers about a third of global GDP, the body's objectives are to boost regional trade, increase the competitiveness of member countries' products and strengthen supply chains. Through the organisation the Chinese leaders seek to gain regional influence by involving Southeast Asian countries in economic relationships, thus forcing them to defer to China's wishes and thereby countering their ability to challenge Chinese power. In contrast, countries like Japan and the United States desire a freer and open Indo-Pacific, without Chinese dominance (Boustany 2021; Sahoo 2021; Rolland 2020).

Thus trade is undoubtedly an ingredient in China's regional strategy but as yet there is a lack of complementarity in the China-ASEAN trading structure; categories of commodities with the largest amount of imports and exports remain the same, for example, electro-mechanical and audio-visual equipment. China could increase exports of more value-added products to ASEAN, even though China's investment strategy in the region, as discussed below, is to prioritise innovation led production (Bi 2021).

An extension of the Chinese trading outreach in Southeast Asia is investment, outlined in the China-ASEAN Strategic Partnership Vision 2030, with major priorities being technological innovation, particularly in telecommunications and e-commerce, in addition to the development of physical infrastructure. China may prove a mentor through past experience in a number of these areas (ibid).

I.5. China's digitalization strategy in Asia

Undoubtedly, the Covid-19 lockdown in Southeast Asia, as elsewhere, has accelerated moves towards digitalization and this has serious implications for international commerce and exchange, given that in future, physical distance may matter less. In fact, digitalization raises a whole host of issues beyond trade, notably access to data and protection of privacy, particularly in relation to financial transactions or fintech. Nevertheless, although these issues are yet to be adequately addressed, in the wake of the interruption of supply chains and social distress like unemployment caused by the Covid-19 crisis, digital trade will be integral to Asia's recovery and growth (Armstrong 2021c).

Because of its advanced technologies China is set to play a major role in the digital governance of Asian countries through its digital road projects. It has been a major driver in formulating provisions regarding e-commerce within a trade agreement reached by RCEP. Such Chinese policies form part of China's Digital Silk Road which, as well as being integral to the One Belt One Road Initiative, is designed to use new communications technologies, especially 5G, to build a regional and ultimately global information highway with China as its centre. Through this medium the Chinese will be able to promote their own digital standards, their own companies and their own digital highway. This has enormous implications for security and privacy, as it could offer captive markets for Chinese tech firms, give them rich sources of data for analysis and consequently facilitate leverage over Asian political and business elites. Consequently, the Chinese state and also the country's private firms can both control physical infrastructural development like fibre-optic cable construction as well as set legal frameworks. In short, building a backbone of communications infrastructure in Asian countries will allow the Chinese government to access the huge data systems of Asian countries. Implicitly, the Chinese are exporting their surveillance system to observe recipients, even though it might be added that such authoritarian controls are not necessarily alien to Asian leaders. These are practices which threaten personal privacy. While China's private firms like Alibaba, Baidu and Tencent, for example, have been active in Malaysia, there is no doubt that Chinese state partnership is paramount and this conceivably adds to the perception of threat by countries like Japan and the United States. Japan, for instance, is alert to the need to enhance consumer awareness regarding risks to privacy presented by surveillance (Moynihan and Patel 2021; Holleyman 2021; Dutta 2020).

So far this introduction has stated in general terms the potential risk to privacy and security presented by China's digitalization policy. In fact, the Chinese especially aim to replicate the domestic success of financial inclusion and integration at home and transfer it to Southeast Asian countries. Geographical proximity and ethnic/cultural connections could facilitate Chinese fintech company access to the region. Significantly, such firms which have a poor record regarding security and privacy at home could potentially be subject to pressure from the Chinese government, with implications regarding data protection (ibid).

China's influence is being wielded not only through digital but physical infrastructure like transportation in Southeast Asia which has the potential to speed supply chain mobility. This is especially pertinent since, because of the pandemic, many regional companies have been compelled to reduce the length of supply chains in order to avoid future product shortages and transportation delays. Digital and physical infrastructure is thus crucial. China, in concert with other regional countries, is promoting the China-Myanmar Economic Corridor, an initiative also sponsored by the Asian Development Bank and the OBOR Initiative. In general, it can be said that physical infrastructural connections among Asian countries are very backward; China, through experience of building high speed rail, roads, bridges and ports, could prove a valuable mentor, examples being Chinese investment in Indonesia's Jakarta-Bandung high speed railway and a Malaysian rail project. In conclusion, China and ASEAN have formulated strategies to meet the challenges of the fourth industrial revolution via both digitalization and the creation of physical infrastructure (US-China Business Council News Overview 2020d; Igarashi 2021; Bi 2021; US-China Business Council News Overview 2021e).

I.6. Summary and conclusion

In conclusion, this overview has in a sense produced an optimistic scenario, on the assumption that Euro-Asian trade and investment will continue to expand, as the world recovers from the effects of the lockdown caused by the Covid-19 pandemic which has wrought havoc on the lives of the disadvantaged and those least able to face emerging challenges. Nevertheless the lockdowns have accelerated changes already in evidence.

China, in rivalry with the United States, has emerged in recent years as a global economic player and its leaders have sought to articulate a new world order; their concept of international relations offers developing countries a state-directed model of development contrasting with that of Western liberal democracies. China's outreach is demonstrated by its growing trade and investment, whether with the EU, the United States or the developing countries of Asia. American suspicions of China's cyber warfare are not necessarily shared by all EU countries; the latter's stance is ambivalent.

Sino-American competition has a higher profile in Asia, even though regional states do not always see rivalry between the two powers in zero-sum terms. Chinese ambitions in Asia are reflected in China's 14th Five Year Plan which stresses innovation and advanced technologies like artificial intelligence. China's economic problems include declining productivity and a low birth rate. Prioritised domestic production in China does not, however, suggest autarky since there remains heavy Chinese dependence on foreign trade.

As rivals of the United States the Chinese leaders seek to mould an Asian identity through proselytising Chinese values, norms and discourse. In common with Chinese leaders, other Asian regional rulers believe institutions like the IMF and the World Bank reflect Western interests. Instead Asian leaders confer legitimacy on local institutions like the Chiang Mai Initiative and the Asian Infrastructure Bank. Economic integration is to be furthered by the RCEP, boosting intraregional trade and product competitiveness in addition to strengthening supply chains. There are, however, anomalies in China's trading relations with Asian countries, because of similar reciprocal imports and exports. Significantly, China's investment in Asia focuses heavily on both digital and physical infrastructure, and its Digital Silk Road is designed to develop a regional information highway, with China as its centre. But for local regional elites there are enormous implications for privacy and security, concerns often also raised by Japan and the United States.

Given the great potential of digitalization, any great power rivalry will very likely be increasingly played out, whether regionally or globally, via cyber warfare. While the pandemic has demonstrated the impact of digitalization, particularly on employment practices, it will remain indispensable in all avenues of life, even after the current crisis has passed.

This overall theme of connectivity underlies the discussion of Euro-Asian trade and investment in the following chapters, which are summarised below.

In the first section of this volume which concerns foreign direct investment, (FDI), innovation and the digital age, the first contribution by Grzeszkowiak discusses the achievement to date of Japan's latest Science and Technology Basic Plan in its quest for innovation.

With a broader focus, Remanda's topic in Chapter 2 is the Economic Partnership Agreement between the European Union and Japan, providing an overview of the European and Japanese business systems framework.

Similarly, O'Mahony and Dao show in Chapter 3 how Ireland, Japan and Vietnam display both similarities and differences in their respective experiences with inward foreign direct investment (FDI).

In Chapter 4, Li and Andreosso-O'Callaghan's cover the EU-China agricultural products trade relationship, utilising the trade gravity model as an instrument of international trade analysis.

Tang, in Chapter 5, considers the United States action against Huawei as a serious setback to globalisation in the advanced technology field, given implications for 5G development internationally.

In Chapter 6, Xu and Dzever stress the importance of online product reviews regarding consumer purchase decisions. Two antecedents, product type and monetary incentives, are investigated through empirical research.

The second set of chapters in this book has two foci, leadership and internationalisation. Chapter 7, written by Zavadska, Morales, Zimmermannová and Pászto, examines these global concerns and, through spatial analysis, highlights the challenge of balancing environmental protection with economic growth in China, given implications for that nation's human health.

With a broader political economic perspective, Hänle, Weil and Cambré consider in Chapter 8 the organisational and fostering mechanisms employed by the Chinese government in providing overseas foreign direct investment (OFDI) support mechanisms for small and medium sized enterprises (SMES) going to Germany.

Nivoix and Rey adopt an original approach in Chapter 9, studying stock market patterns in Japan, China and South Korea, suggesting that Hofstede's model provides the most accurate means of understanding the relationship between cultural dimensions and financial behaviour.

In Chapter 10, Morales, Rajmil and Andreosso-O'Callaghan underline the importance of China's Belt and Road Initiative (BRI) and the roles of Iran and Pakistan regarding the economic integration objectives of the Chinese Silk Road.

Likewise, Kettunen and Alvstam explore China's New Silk Road but from a Nordic perspective in Chapter 11, one focus being the development of container train transportation on two routes between Finland and China.

This overall context informs the following chapters.

I.7. References

Armstrong, S. (2021a). How Biden will shape the US-China relationship. *East Asia Forum Weekly Digest*, 15 February.

Armstrong, S. (2021b). How can Biden win over a still sceptical Asia. *East Asia Forum Weekly Digest*, 22 February.

Armstrong, S. (2021c). Global digital governance can start in Asia. *East Asia Forum Weekly Digest*, 12 April.

Bi, S.H. (2021). Between China and ASEAN under the building of the ASEAN economic community. *Journal of Contemporary East Asian Studies*, 22 February.

Boustany, C.W. (2021). Prospects for US trade engagement in the Indo-Pacific and options for the Biden administration. *National Bureau of Asian Research*, 6 April.

Collingridge, J. (2020). The great China dilemma. *Sunday Times*, 24 May.

Dutta, A. (2020). Introduction to China's Silk Road: Economic and technological implications, discussing contributions by Hemmings, J., Naughton, B., Mochinaga, D. and Kshetri, N., during the Roundtable in Asia Policy 15.1. *The National Bureau of Asian Research*, 28 January.

Holleyman, R. (2021). Data governance and trade: The Asia-Pacific leads the way. *National Bureau of Asian Research*, 9 January.

Igarashi, S. (2021). Possibility of building a new architecture in the Mekong region. *The Council on East Asia Community (CEAC) E-Letter*, 14(2), (Issue 84), 10 March.

Ivens, M. (2020). Beast from the East. *Sunday Times Magazine*, 31 May.

Moynihan, H. and Patel, C. (2021). Restrictions on online freedom of expression in China. Chatham House Research Paper, China-Pacific Programme Newsletter, 17 March.

National Bureau of Asian Research (2021a). Testimony by Nadège Rolland on America's way forward in the Indo-Pacific. 19 March.

National Bureau of Asian Research (2021b). Interview with Pravakar Sahoo. India's economic future: Charting a course towards renewed growth. 13 April.

Pantucci, R. (2020). Beijing aims to avoid battle but wins war with new dark arts. *Sunday Times*, 27 December.

Pogrund, G., Shipman, T., Collingridge, J. (2020). Universities face "wipeout" if Beijing bans students. *Sunday Times*, 19 July.

Rolland, N. (2020). China's vision of a new world order: Implications for the United States. *National Bureau of Asian Research*, 2 October.

US-China Business Council News Overview (2020a). China becomes EU's biggest trade partner in 2020. *Xinhua*, 17 February.

US-China Business Council News Overview (2020b). China pledges quality growth, tech powerhouse in 5 year plan. *Financial Post*, 29 October.

US-China Business Council News Overview (2020c). Key CPC Session draws 15 year roadmap for China's modernization. *People's Daily*, 30 October.

US-China Business Council News Overview (2020d). Firms want to adjust supply chains post-pandemic but changes take time. *WSJ*, 28 December.

US-China Business Council News Overview (2020e). EU-China investment deal likely this week. *EU Reporter*, 29 December.

US-China Business Council News Overview (2021a). Huawei ramps up chip investment in fight for survival. *Nikkei Asia*, 13 January.

US-China Business Council News Overview (2021b). China's economic recovery belies a lingering productivity challenge. *WSJ*, 18 January.

US-China Business Council News Overview (2021c). China's private consumption to more than double by 2030: Report. *Xinhua*, 28 January.

US-China Business Council News Overview (2021d). Why China worries about losing manufacturing: Keep manufacturing as a percentage of the economy basically stable. *WSJ*, 9 March.

US-China Business Council News Overview (2021e). Malaysia accepts 14% cost increase in China-led rail project taking longer route. *Reuters*, 5 April.

Yu, J. (2021). Beijing sets new course. *The World Today, Chatham House*, 5 February.

1

Japan's Plans for Society 5.0 – A Global Concept, an Isolated Solution or Utopia?

In 2016, following global trends, the government of Japan announced its idea for a new growth engine, named Society 5.0, in its 5th Science and Technology Basic Plan. Society 5.0 is advertized as the vision of a human-centric, super smart society created by fusing the cyber space and the real world, and by leveraging technologies and innovation to the fullest, with the intention of fostering economic development, while solving social challenges and finally becoming a globally applicable conception. As the 5th Science and Technology Basic Plan expires in 2020 and will be revised in 2021, the first half of 2020 is a good time to assess the achievements so far. The question whether Society 5.0 is a reconceptualization of society or just another policy concept will be examined in this research. Therefore, the implementation process is investigated, potential problems are examined and the applicability to other nations is considered.

1.1. Introduction

With Shinzo Abe's second inauguration in 2012 as prime minister, a comprehensive policy package, including fiscal, monetary and growth policies was launched to end deflation in Japan and achieve sustainable economic growth, while solving the Japanese demographic problems. The policy package has become known as "Abenomics". The Prime Minister officially announced the second stage of Abenomics in October 2015, when the "Plan for Dynamic Engagement of All Citizens" (Government of Japan 2015) was launched. With this step, the government of Japan has shifted the focus to growth strategies. (Abe 2015) In January 2016, in the "5th Science and Technology Basic Plan" (Government of Japan 2016a), the

Chapter written by Jana-Larissa GRZESZKOWIAK.

government of Japan introduced its idea for a new growth engine called "Society 5.0" (Government of Japan 2016a). It is said to be Japan's answer to "Industry 4.0" (Government of Japan 2016a), but goes one step further. Society 5.0 is a vision of a human-centric, super smart society intending to foster economic development while solving social challenges.

By the fusion of the cyber space and the real world and leveraging information and communication technologies (ICT) to the fullest, Japan has the means to build a perfectly connected, highly efficient and inclusive society, serving the individual needs of its members, regardless of age, sex, etc. (Fukuyama 2018). The government considers Society 5.0 as the key to Japan's severe demographic challenges, its ageing population, the depopulation of rural areas, its shrinking labour force, as well as its energy and environmental issues (Waldenberger 2018).

For several reasons, Japan sees itself in a very good position to build this future society by mastering the challenges of digitalization and connectivity. In particular, Japan had the second largest IT sector in the World at the time of announcing Society 5.0 (OECD 2015) and previously declared that it would become "the world's most advanced IT Nation" in 2013 (Government of Japan 2013). Japanese investments in its ICT and Research and Development (R&D) sectors are high and its products are highly in demand on the global market. Additionally, Japan has one of the highest penetration rates of mobile broadband in the world (Waldenberger 2018). The evolution of digital technologies, such as the Internet of Things (IoT), artificial intelligence (AI), big data, blockchain technologies and robotics, in combination with increasing globalization, is seen as an opportunity to make a change in society (Keidanren 2018a). Nevertheless, Japan is aware of the risks that will come along with the digital transformation, such as security and privacy issues (Fukuyama 2018). Being aware that an "all at once" approach cannot be realistically implemented, the government of Japan has defined 11 systems that are to be given precedence in their development, as they are seen to have the ability to accelerate the coordination of multiple systems and bring industrial advantages, thus increasing global competitiveness (Government of Japan 2016a). To achieve this ambitious goal, the close co-operation between the government, including the cabinet, the relevant ministries (especially to be mentioned the Ministry of Economy, Trade and Innovation (METI)), the industry (especially Keidanren), the Japan Business Federation and the academia will be enhanced by sharing problematic issues and successful cases across the initiatives via a common platform, thus, allowing for cross-application (Ibid; Waldenberger 2018). Here, the Keidanren (2016) names "five walls" as the biggest obstacles to overcome. In the eyes of Keidanren, these are the areas with the highest probabilities for disruptions. As ideas for overcoming these five walls are only qualitative ones that not quantifiable yet, their investigation in detail is not part of this contribution. Moreover, there are more obstacles which are not in the focus of the institutions yet, such as a lack of a vibrant start-up eco-system or building a good testing field for new explorations (Joh 2017). It remains to be seen whether the government will be able to turn its ambitious plans into reality (Waldenberger 2018).

Although Society 5.0 is a growth strategy for Japan assimilated to Japanese features, its goals have much in common with the "Sustainable Development Goals" (SDGs) (UN 2020) of the United Nations and thus could be used as a global attempt (Fukuyama 2018). As Society 5.0 is something to be created (Keidanren 2018b), it may have the opportunity to become a global solution that is individually adapted to each nation's needs.

This research intends to look at the progress in the implementation of Society 5.0 in Japan until the first half of 2020 in the next section by the examination of indicators for the 11 prioritized systems. The following section highlights the intention of Society 5.0, its main objectives and possible obstacles and risks, as well as the global applicability of the concept.

1.2. Achievements in the implementation process

Although Society 5.0 was officially announced with the "5th Science and Technology Basic Plan" (Government of Japan 2016a) in January 2016, there were no particular measures given as the plan is a qualitative description of the idea of "Society 5.0" and how to realize it. As Society 5.0 is meant to become the beating heart of Japan's growth strategy (Government of Japan 2016a), generally these measures are specified in the annually revised growth strategy. Unfortunately, this is not the case for the 2016 growth strategy. Although Society 5.0 is incorporated into the policy plan, the introduction of the according measures remains qualitative (Government of Japan 2016b).

For this reason, a later growth strategy has to be evaluated for quantitative achievements. The "5th Science and Technology Basic Plan" (Government of Japan 2016a) states that to achieve improvements, more visible measures to implement Society 5.0 are to be set into specific timeframes. The first timeframe lasted from 2015 to 2020 (Government of Japan 2016a).

As evaluating all of the growth strategies released in that period is beyond the scope of this work, the growth strategy closest to the targeted time is investigated. Thus, the first section of Japan's "Growth Strategy 2019" (Government of Japan 2019) is chosen, since it is the one relating to Society 5.0, and is checked is for the major "key performance indicators" (KPIs) as these are quantitative indicators defined by the government.

The first section, named "Realization of Society 5.0" (Government of Japan 2019) consists of 11 subsections, each having several subparts. These subsections relate to the "11 pillars" of the initial Science and Technology Basic Plan and name the areas that are particularly focused on.

The first subsection deals with "The Development of Rules for the Digital Market" (Government of Japan 2019). Its first major KPI proposes to create at least 20 venture companies with more than US$1 billion in corporate values by 2023. According to the "Japan Startup Finance Report 2018" (Ministry of Finance 2018) and data by the Cabinet Office (Government of Japan 2019), seven of these venture companies were set up by the end of 2018, in contrast to only one in 2015. So, achieving the targeted number remains attainable yet appears somewhat unrealistic. The second KPI states the aim of establishing 5G services in all prefectures by the end of FY2020. Until April 2020, there were four main operators for 5G services in Japan. The first already operates 29 out of 47 prefectures, the second 15, the third 7 and the fourth none. All operators are working on extending their services (European 5G Observatory 2020). So, this KPI remains attainable, albeit the 5G service coverage concentrates in urban, particularly metropolitan, areas and leaves behind rural regions (nPerf 2020). The last KPI announces the creation of 30 projects for cross-industrial/operator data sharing by 2020. As of March 2019, there were already 25 cases and, thus, the goal appears to remain achievable.

The second subsection deals with "Fintech/Finance" (Government of Japan 2019) and has two KPIs. The first one proposes the implementation of open Application Programming Interfaces (APIs) in at least 80 banks by June 2020. As of March 2019, 95 banks had already deployed APIs (Osawa 2020). Thus, this KPI was achieved before time. The second KPI proposes to increase the percentage of cashless payment to 40% by 2025. In 2018, cashless payment already accounted for 24.1%. To promote this kind of transaction, the government introduced a rebate programme on cashless purchases and in November 2019, in a survey, almost 90% stated that they intended to continue cashless payment. Nevertheless, the majority of the elderly does not feel comfortable with this type of transaction. (Kajimoto and Nakagawa 2019). The KPI remains achievable. The Covid-19 pandemic may contribute to the promotion of cashless payments.

The third subsection deals with "Mobility" (Government of Japan 2019). The first KPI proposes the launch of autonomous driving in certain areas in 2020 and the second KPI is an extension to 100 locations by 2030. The government announced that they would present self-driving services for Olympia 2020, which was postponed due to the Covid-19 pandemic (Tsukimori 2020). Thus, the first indicator was achieved even if this appears rather limited. Hence, the second indicator remains attainable, too. By the third KPI, more than 90% of all newly purchased cars should be equipped with an automatic braking system. Although the share was already at almost 85% in 2018 and annually rising, the government made such a system mandatory for all cars sold from the end of 2021. This implies the missing of the indicator, but may be due to the introduction of a unified certification, which was lacking previously (Niekawa 2019). The fourth KPI announces a share of 20% of domestic vehicles equipped with safe driving support systems, which would result in a rate of 30% of the global market. The latest data available is from 2017 and states an installation rate for domestic vehicle of 14.1%, accounting for a 16.2% substitution rate in the global market (Government of Japan 2019). The last KPI is an extension to 100% of all domestic vehicles having such a system by 2030. It remains to be seen whether this can be achieved.

The fourth subsection contains only one KPI on "Corporate Governance" (Government of Japan 2019), which proposes to raise the Returns on Assets (ROA) of large Japanese incorporated companies, included in the Tokyo Stock Price Index (TOPIX500), to levels similar to the US and EU by 2025. The calculations from late May 2019 for the previous year (April 2018–March 2019) show that Japan accounts for 4.0%, in contrast to EU with 4.2% and the US with 6.2% (Government of Japan 2019). Hence, the KPI remains attainable.

The fifth subsection deals with "Smart Public Services" (Government of Japan 2019). Its first KPI announces a reduction of lower system upgrading costs by 30% by 2025, but as it is integrated in the growth strategy for the first time (Ibid), it will not be investigated in this research. The second KPI states that Japan should rank in at least third place among developed economies in the World Bank's "Doing Business Report" by 2020. In the "Doing Business 2020" report (World Bank 2019) of October 2019, Japan ranked place 29. The first 28 positions are several developed economies. When comparing it with the previous year's report, Japan advanced from rank 39 (World Bank 2018), but it appears doubtful if Japan can make up more than 25 positions within one year. The last KPI in this section notes a reduction in administrative costs in priority areas by at least 20% by March 2020. As no reference point is given, neither in initial point in time nor in values, the indicator is unavailable for investigation. Nevertheless, the additional declaration to this KPI (Government of Japan 2019) states that certain areas may be given more time until 2022. This implies that the KPI was not achieved in all areas.

Subsection six deals with the topic of "Next Generation Infrastructure" (Government of Japan 2019). The first KPI states a target for improvement in construction site productivity by 20% by 2025. Again, this KPI is not available for investigation as no reference points are given. The next KPI is not investigable due to a lack of data. It states that there should be a rise in the share of new technology using facility managers in domestic critical as well as in aging infrastructure to 20% by 2020, and to 100% by 2030. The third KPI announced that Tokyo should rank among top three in the "Global Power City Index" by 2020 and this was already achieved in the 2019's report, as well as in the previous one (Mori Memorial Foundation 2019). Thus, this indicator is likely to be achieved. The last KPI reports an expansion of Public Private Partnerships (PPP) and Private Finance Initiative (PFI) business scale up to 21 trillion yen by FY2022, including 7 trillion yen stemming from PFI business utilizing the confession method. According to projection, the indicators are likely to be achieved (OECD 2019a).

The seventh subsection is "Aiming for Realization of a Decarbonized Society" (Government of Japan 2019). The first KPI states that the power system reforms should be finalized by implementing the legal separation of the power transmission and distribution sectors on April 1 2020. This was achieved as it was implemented into the "Electricity Business Act" (Ministry of Justice 2020). The second KPI aims for a share of 50–70% of next generation vehicles of new passenger car sales by 2030. As the share was already 36.7% in FY2017 (Government of Japan 2019), the indicator may be attainable. The last KPI set the target of 160 commercial hydrogen stations by FY2020, and 320 by FY2025. As of March 2019, there were 103 stations installed (Government of Japan 2019). Hence, the indicator seems hard to achieve as the number has to multiply by more than 1.5 within one year.

The eighth subsection deals with the "Construction of Innovation Ecosystem for Realizing Society" (Government of Japan 2019). The first KPI states that the corporate investment in universities and national research institutes will triple. Once more, as no reference value is given, the indicator is unattainable for checking. The second KPI announces a ratio on public-private R&D investment of at least 4% of GDP by FY2020. In FY2017, it already accounted for 3.48% (Ibid) and thus, the indicator appears realistic to be achieved. The next KPI targets the creation of at least 20 Unicorns[1] by 2023. As of March 2020, there were three Unicorns in Japan (CBInsights 2020). Thus, the indicator appears unrealistic to be attained. The fourth KPI reports a reduction of the time required for acquisition to average 14 months by 2023. Since the average of FY2017 was already 14.1 months (Government of Japan 2019), the indicator appears to be achievable. The fifth and sixth KPI are identical in meaning and state an annual improvement of labour productivity in the manufacturing industry by more than 2%. According to the OECD this indicator was already above 3% on average from 2014–2016 (OECD 2019b), but according to the government of Japan, it was under 2% until 2017, but ever rising (Government of Japan 2019). So, the indicator is probably achievable. By the seventh KPI the government wants to achieve a share of 80% of companies collecting data at their production plants and 40% of them to link the data for solving specific management issues by 2020. In 2018, the shares were 58% and 26% (Ibid). Thus, the achievement of this indicator seems somewhat unrealistic. The last KPI says to

1 Unicorn: private (start-up) company with an initial value of more than US$1 billion, mostly realized through venture capital.

increase the size of domestic robot production in manufacturing, as well as in non-manufacturing areas, to 1.2 trillion yen each in 2020. In 2017, the manufacturing sector accounted for around 900 billion yen, whereas the non-manufacturing one accounted for only 180 billion yen (Ibid). Hence, the indicator seems unrealistic to be obtained in time.

The ninth subsection focuses on "Human Resources Development for the Society 5.0 Era" (Government of Japan 2019). The first KPI states that wireless LAN should be installed in 100% of classrooms by FY2020. In FY2017, the coverage was about 40% (Ibid). So, the KPI may be achievable, but what is more important than the availability of wireless LAN is the actual incorporation of digital technologies and their usage in lessons. Until 2020, schooling still mainly relied on analog technologies and paper based resources, mostly due to concerns about equality, with 80% of students stating that they do not use digital technologies in the classroom at all in the latest PISA survey of 2018 (Obe and Okutsu 2020). The second KPI reports that there should be at least one computer among three students. According to FY2017, there was one computer available for 5.6 children (Government of Japan 2019). Moreover, the government launched a programme to provide all students with tablets by 2023 and the Covid-19 pandemic may fuel this development (Obe and Okutsu 2020). Hence, the KPI seems achievable. The third KPI is the introduction of 500,000 IT passports for exam takers by 2023 and is unattainable for investigation as the planned testing phase was scheduled for FY2019, which ended March 2020, and there are no data available yet. The fourth KPI reports that there should be 100 certified Fourth Industrial Revolution skill acquisition courses by FY2020. As there were 54 courses available in April 2019 (Government of Japan 2019), the indicator's achievement appears somewhat unrealistic to be obtained in time. The last KPI proposes to increase the number of adult students in universities and professional schools to one million people by FY2022. For FY2016, the stated number is about 500,000 people (Ibid). The indicator is unprecise as there is neither the definition of adult student nor the source of data given. That makes this figure hard to compare to other official values. Nevertheless, the OECD reports a share of about 50% participation of 25–64-year olds in some kind of training, but states that adult education is highly job-related (OECD 2019c). At least, the numbers are related to the same year. Mainly due to the long period, the KPI may thus remain achievable.

The tenth subsection gives insight into "Taking the Overseas Growing Markets" (Government of Japan 2019). The first KPI proposes to conclude Regional Comprehensive Economic Partnership (RCEP) negotiations as soon as possible to reach a Free Trade Agreement (FTA) coverage ratio of more than 70%. As end of FY2018, according to the government (Ibid) the ratio was 51.6% and would rise to 78.7% with all RCEP agreements in force based on the trade volume of 2018, which was a very prosperous year. In contrast, other official projections, as of June 2019, are much lower, stating that the current ratio was at 36.7% and would increase to 63.8% with all RCEP agreements in force (JETRO 2019a). Thus, the indicator appears somewhat unrealistic to achieve, particularly as the timeframe for the enforcements of the agreements is very vague. The second KPI announces the doubling of inward foreign direct investment (FDI) to 35 trillion yen by 2020. In 2018, inward FDI already accounted for 30.7 trillion yen (JETRO 2019b), but, according to other official data, inward FDI stocks to Japan only accounted for slightly above US$200 billion in 2017 and 2018 (OECD 2020), which is approx. less than 25 trillion yen, and thus, the indicator may not be achieved in time. The third KPI contains the doubling of the export value and the overseas subsidiary sales by small and medium enterprises (SMEs) compared to the 2010's level by 2020. Since the export values and overseas subsidiary sales have increased to 20.6 trillion yen in FY2016 from initially 12.8 trillion yen in FY2010 (Government of Japan 2019), the indicator is likely to be achieved. The fourth KPI reports to reach foreign infrastructure system orders of about 30 trillion yen. In 2017, the value was already 23 trillion yen (Ibid), thus more than double within seven years. Hence, the indicator is presumably achievable, especially as different amounts are additionally included into the KPI, such as "the amount of income from business investment" (Ibid). The last KPI states to increase overseas sales of broadcast contents to 50 billion yen by FY2020. The indicator is probable to be attained as the sales already had a volume of 44.5 billion yen in FY2017 (Ibid).

The last subsection deals with the "Promotion of Active Participation by Highly-Skilled Foreign Professionals" (Government of Japan 2019). The first KPI aims for the recognition of 10,000 highly skilled foreign professionals, referring to the point-based immigration system introduced in May 2012, by 2020 and increase this number to 20,000 people by 2022. Since more than 15,000 people matching this criterion, were recognized as of December 2018 (Ibid), the indicator for 2020 was already achieved and is likely to be achieved for 2022, too. The second and last KPI states a number of 300,000 foreign students by 2020. According to the Japanese Student Service Association's (JASSO) survey of 2019, Japan had already achieved its target in 2019 (JIJI 2020), but the number of students learning Japanese in language school is included in this (Government of Japan 2019). Additionally, it should be mentioned that the majority of 95% are from Asian countries, with students from Vietnam, Nepal and China already making up approximately half of all students (Sawa 2019). If the indicator can may not be attainable in 2020 due to travel restrictions following the Covid-19 pandemic (Ministry of Education, Culture, Sports, Science and Technology 2020).

In summary, there is visible progress in the development of the 11 systems prioritized until the first half of 2020. Although some indicators are unprecise or vague in expression and thus, not investigable, and others may appear unlikely to be achieved in the scheduled time, the conception in general does not seem unrealistic to attain. Thus, it appears like a sound and sensible strategy for the start of the implementation of Society 5.0.

1.3. Society 5.0 – a science, technology and innovation policy

Although it appears that Society 5.0 is advertized as a new conception for a future society, Society 5.0 remains at the core feature of the "5th Science and Technology Basic Plan" (Government of Japan 2016a), thus, it is a science, technology and innovation (STI) policy. Society 5.0 is Japan's STI policy shift from its traditionally technology-driven STI policy to a society-centred and more challenge-driven one, adapting to globally expected changes in economic structures due to digitalization, the availability of big data and increasing the connectivity of research institutions. As the goal of solving social challenges is not a solely technological one, the policy aims to give more weight to society in the innovation process (Carraz and Harayama 2019).

In general, Japan put emphasis on STI policy since the 1990s, as the economic stagnation due to the burst of the Japanese bubble economy urged Japan to search for a new growth engine. With the enactment of the "Science and Technology Basic Law" in 1995, the Japanese government committed itself to promote R&D by increasing public investment and compiling a quinquennial "Science and Technology Basic Plan" (hereinafter referred to as the "Basic Plan"). These successive Basic Plans were meant as broad governmental identifications of prior research issues and framing expectations of stakeholders, rather than being a detailed action plan. Nevertheless, they built the foundations and evolved to the fifth Basic Plan, introducing Society 5.0. The first Basic Plan (1996–2000) purely focused on the development of a novel R&D system for the economy, whereas the second Basic Plan (2001–2005) already contained visions for societal changes through technology by focusing more on research areas related to political and social concerns, such as environmental sustainability and global competitiveness. The third Basic Plans (2006–2010) aimed to create a globally highly competitive research environment, whereas the fourth Basic Plan (2011–2015) emphasized the importance of innovation over technology and laid ground for challenge-driven research, particularly related to social and economic issues.

In 2001, the "Council for Science and Technology Policy" (CSTP) was founded and placed above individual ministries as part of the cabinet. It was in force in the formulation and coordination of all national STI policies. Under the second Abe administration, the CSTP became responsible for the "Science, Technology and Innovation Comprehensive Strategy" in 2013, which was meant as a policy recommendation providing complement to the Basic Plans. With this, the CSTP gained new competences as it allowed the implementation as well as budgeting of programmes, and was transformed into the "Council for Science, Technology and Innovation" (CSTI) in 2014. Because of these new competences, the CSTI were then able to implement the novel "Cross-Ministerial Strategic Innovation Promotion Programme" (SIP), dealing with big challenges through networking ideas, increasing the mobility of people and creating innovation hubs. In addition, the CSTI set up the "Impulsing Paradigm Change through Disruptive Technologies Programme" (ImPACT) and allowed itself to invest in high risk, high impact R&D to facilitate the generation of ground-breaking innovation. These two programmes in particular, enabled the CSTI to conduct policy experimentation, helping with the development of innovation-based and human-centred Society 5.0, which was finally introduced in the fifth Basic Plan, which links STI policies to growth policies directly (Carraz and Harayama 2019).

The idea for Society 5.0 is a systemic approach to create an ecosystem of innovation and has two main objectives at its heart. Firstly, the introduction of an "super smart society service platform", interconnecting big data, IoT and other technologies and facilitating knowledge transfer and collaboration of the academia, the industry and the government, is enacted in the fifth Basic Plan (Government of Japan 2016a). As the Basic Plans are not precise action plans, no schedule is given for this goal, but the "Connected Industries Tokyo Initiative 2017" was released in 2017 to give a more detailed plan (Ministry of Economy, Trade and Industry 2017). To achieve the ambitious target of a common platform, a stepwise approach is sensible. For this reason, a first IoT service platform should have been developed to be ready to have first test-runs at Olympia 2020 (Keidanren 2017). But as Olympia has been delayed to 2021 due to the Covid-19 pandemic, it remains to be seen how developed this system is in the future. The second main objective is that the public investment in R&D should be raised to 1% of GDP (Keidanren 2017). This target is seen as crucial by the business federation to overcome "the Wall of technology", one of the five walls. It is the only quantifiable statement on the five walls so far, but there is no time scheduled yet. In FY2018, the overall expenditures on R&D were 19.53 trillion yen, equalling 3.56% of GDP (Statistics Bureau 2019). As expenditures of business enterprises accounted for 14.23 trillion yen, non-business expenditures accounted for 0.97% of GDP (own calculation based on Statistics Bureau (2019)). Since these non-business expenditures are composed of non-profit institutions and public organisations investments, as well as universities and colleges expenses, they are not equal to public expenditures. Thus, the public investment in R&D to GPD ratio is well below 1%. At least the R&D expenditures increased for two consecutive years and were higher than they have ever been before (Statistics Bureau 2019).

Because Society 5.0 is in line with the SDGs (Keidanren 2018c), Japan sees it as a globally usable conception (Nakanishi 2019). Despite these common goals, Society 5.0 is tailored for the Japanese economy. First, the required close co-operation of industry and government without threatening liberalism has a long tradition in Japan, but is not a common characteristic for economies. Second, Japan is in the position to draw on well-documented physical data to feed big data systems (Carraz and Harayama 2019). Third, Japan has a high broadband coverage (nPerf 2020) and its population makes use of this, as one can see from high penetration rates of mobile broadband (Waldenberger 2018). Next, Japan has a big IT sector and holds a leading position in robotics and human interface technology (Carraz and Harayama 2019). As whole, these points only relate to advanced economies and thus, Society 5.0 is not applicable globally. The last point to be mentioned, Japan is under severe social pressure due to its very high public debt and demographic challenges, and thus may push harder for a solution and may be more willing to take risks than other countries, even if the match the other criteria.

This willingness to accept high risk, as proven by the ImPACT programme, may cause concerns about the already high public debt and fiscal sustainability, as this high risk technology investment may turn out to be a bottomless pit. In addition, there is a probability that innovation may result in creative destruction dynamics, the interruption of other fields or increasing unemployment rate. It even may generate dystopian changes in technology and society or bring up unforeseeable unintended scientific consequences (Carraz and Harayama 2019). Even if these dark scenarios are unlikely, there is a realistic probability that such a transformation of society can cause an increase in social and regional divergence. Social divergence may occur because of income disparities, with some people being able to participate better and take more advantages from it, or due to different attitudes towards risk. Some people may exclude themselves from participating and thus from society. Regional divergence may increase because already advanced regions are easier to develop and thus, bring more profits for companies. In addition, these areas bring more profits because most of the time they are higher populated and so, have more users or customers. Hence, it is likely that companies focus on them. Another reason could be that in these areas more entities with influence may be located and push harder for these new technologies than other areas, e.g. rural ones. The government is in charge to avoid a widening gap of social and regional differences, but may be biased by the close co-operation with the industry. All of these issues directly point towards the biggest obstacle, which is social acceptance. In addition to the just mentioned issues, which could easily result in fear, there are many other reasons for society's non-acceptance, such as too fast implementation speed, too many sacrifices for individuals or too many habits and manner changes at once, resulting in people just feeling uncomfortable about it.

1.4. Conclusion

In summary, Society 5.0 is Japan's attempt to master the unforeseeable changes in the structure for future economies. As in many other nations, like the EU with

Europe's "Industry 4.0" or Japan's neighbour China with its "Made in China 2025" incentives, Japan tries to integrate new technologies, such as the IoT, AI, Robotics and big data, and enhance innovation to gain global advantages. In that case, Japan is not an exception. Society 5.0 originates from the necessity to master the new challenges of digitalization and connectivity across the world. In combination with the social challenges Japan has been struggling with for the past few years, the digital transformation of society itself has become the aim. Nevertheless, Society 5.0 is a STI policy rather than a reconceptualization of society. The big ideas behind the policy remain qualitative and thus are not quantifiable yet. However, as the 5th Science and Technology Basic Plan's 5-year duration ends with 2020, the stepwise implementation process has its first quantifiable aims so far. The assessment shows that many of the indicators are likely to be achieved in time and others are at least not unrealistic to be achieved at all, albeit some indicators are formulated in an unprecise or vague manner and thus, are not investigable. Yet, these are only the first steps of the implementation of Society 5.0, and although they are rather successful for the most part, there is still a long way to go. The biggest obstacle may be the full acceptance and adaption by society, and the incorporation of all its members and thus the avoidance of the increase of social divergence. Finally, although Society 5.0 has some aims in common with the UN's SDGs, it appears that Japan's concept is not globally applicable in general, as only developed nations match similar preconditions, and even it is only comparable to advanced economies in particular cases.

1.5. References

Abe, S. (2015). Prime Minister in Action: National Council for Promoting the Dynamic Engagement of All Citizens [Online]. Available at: https://japan.kantei.go.jp/97_abe/actions/201510/29article5.html [Accessed 31 May 2020].

Carraz, R. and Harayama, Y. (2019). Japan's innovation system at the crossroads: Society 5.0. *Panorama: Insight into Asian and European Affairs*, Konrad-Adenauer-Stiftung, Singapore, 33–45 [Online]. Available at: https://www.kas.de/documents/288143/4843367/panorama_digital_asia_v3a_Carraz_Harayama.pdf/b57f6b67-f317-cfc5-010c4ee501c3a398 [Accessed 31 May 2020].

CBInsights (2020). The Complete List Of Unicorn Companies [Online]. Available at: https://www.cbinsights.com/research-unicorn-companies [Accessed 31 May 2020].

European 5G Observatory (2020). Announcement of commercial launches. *European Commission* [Online]. Available at: https://5gobservatory.eu/market-developments/5g-services/ [Accessed 31 May 2020].

Fukuyama, M. (2018). Society 5.0: Aiming for a new human-centered society. *Japan Economic Foundation*, Japan SPOTLIGHT, July/August, 47–50 [Online]. Available at: https://www.jef.or.jp/journal/pdf/220th_Special_Article_02.pdf [Accessed 31 May 2020].

Government of Japan (2013). Declaration to be the World's Most Advanced IT Nation. *Strategic Headquarters for the Promotion of an Advanced Information and Telecommunications Network Society*, June 14 [Online]. Available at: https://japan.kantei.go.jp/policy/it/2013/0614_declaration.pdf [Accessed 31 May 2020].

Government of Japan (2015). Japan's Plan for Dynamic Engagement of All Citizens. [Online]. Available at: https://www.kantei.go.jp/jp/singi/ichiokusoukatsuyaku/pdf/plan2.pdf [Accessed 31 May 2020].

Government of Japan (2016a). The 5th Science and Technology Basic Plan. January 22 [Online]. Available at: https://www8.cao.go.jp/cstp/english/basic/5thbasicplan.pdf [Accessed 31 May 2020].

Government of Japan (2016b). Japan Revitalization Strategy 2016 [Online]. Available at: https://www.kantei.go.jp/jp/singi/keizaisaisei/pdf/hombun1_160602_en.pdf [Accessed 31 May 2020].

Government of Japan (2019). Follow-up on the Growth Strategy. June 21 [Online]. Available at: https://www.kantei.go.jp/jp/singi/keizaisaisei/pdf/fu2019en.pdf [Accessed 31 May 2020].

JETRO (2019a). JETRO Global Trade and Investment Report 2019: The fluctuating international economic order and global business in the future [Online]. Available at: https://www.jetro.go.jp/en/reports/white_paper.html [Accessed 31 May 2020].

JETRO (2019b). JETRO Invest Japan Report 2019. [Online]. Available at: https://www.jetro.go.jp/en/invest/reports/ [Accessed 31 May 2020].

JIJI (2020). Number of foreign students in Japan reaches record high. *The Japan Times* [Online]. Available at: https://www.japantimes.co.jp/news/2020/04/23/national/foreign-students-record/#.XtOKwMDgpPY [Accessed 31 May 2020].

Joh, A. (2017). Tokyo-based podcaster explains Japan's declining startup scene and its future. *Tech in Asia* [Online]. Available at: https://www.techinasia.com/talk/japan-declining-startup-scene-future [Accessed 31 May 2020].

Kajimoto, T. and Nakagawa, I. (2019). Japan wants to go cashless, but elderly aren't so keen. *Reuters Business News* [Online]. Available at: https://www.reuters.com/article/us-japan-economy-cashless/japan-wants-to-go-cashless-but-elderly-arent-so-keen-idUSKBN1XF0BT [Accessed 31 May 2020].

Keidanren (2016). Toward realization of the new economy and society: Reform of the economy and society by the deepening of "Society 5.0". April 19 [Online]. Available at: www.keidanren.or.jp/en/policy/2016/029_outline.pdf [Accessed 31 May 2020].

Keidanren (2017). Revitalizing Japan by Realizing Society 5.0: Action Plan for Creating the Society of the Future [Online]. Available at: www.keidanren.or.jp/en/policy/2017/010_overview.pdf [Accessed 31 May 2020].

Keidanren (2018a). Society 5.0: Co-creating the future [Online]. Available at: https://www.keidanren.or.jp/en/policy/2018/095_booklet.pdf [Accessed 31 May 2020].

Keidanren (2018b). Society 5.0: Co-creating the future [Online]. Available at: https://www.keidanren.or.jp/en/policy/2018/095_summary.pdf [Accessed 31 May 2020].

Keidanren (2018c). Society 5.0 for SDGs. [Online]. Available at: https://www.keidanren.or.jp/en/policy/2018/095_outline.pdf [Accessed 31 May 2020].

Ministry of Economy, Trade and Industry (2017). "Connected Industries" Tokyo Initiative 2017' Released. *The Government of Japan* [Online]. Available at: https://www.meti.go.jp/english/press/2017/1002_004.html [Accessed 31 May 2020].

Ministry of Education, Culture, Sports, Science and Technology (2020). [Covid-19] Information about MEXT's measures. *The Government of Japan* [Online]. Available at: https://www.mext.go.jp/en/mext_00006.html [Accessed 31 May 2020].

Ministry of Finance (2018). Japan Startup Finance Report 2018. *The Government of Japan* [Online]. Available at: https://initial.inc/enterprise/report/jsf2018/ [Accessed 31 May 2020].

Ministry of Justice (2020). Electricity Business Act: Supplementary Provisions, Article 1. *The Government of Japan* [Online]. Available at: http://www.japaneselawtranslation.go.jp/law/detail/?id=3355&vm=04&re=02 [Accessed 31 May 2020].

Mori Memorial Foundation (2019). Global Power City Index 2019. *Institute for Urban Strategies, The Mori Memorial Foundation* [Online]. Available at: http://mori-m-foundation.or.jp/english/ius2/gpci2/index.shtml [Accessed 31 May 2020].

Nakanishi, H. (2019). Toward the Realization of Society 5.0 for SDGs. Speech by Chairman of Keidanren [Online]. Available at: https://www.keidanren.or.jp/en/speech/2019/0101.html [Accessed 31 May 2020].

Niekawa, S. (2019). Japan to require automatic brake systems in all new car models. *The Asahi Shimbun* [Online]. Available at: http://www.asahi.com/ajw/articles/AJ201911270035.html [Accessed 31 May 2020].

nPerf (2020). SoftBank Mobile 3G / 4G / 5G coverage map, Japan [Online]. Available at: https://www.nperf.com/en/map/JP/-/27305.SoftBank-Mobile/signal/?ll=54.77534585936449&lg=140.27343750000003&zoom=2 [Accessed 31 May 2020].

Obe, M. and Okutsu, A. (2020). Coronavirus forces Japan schools to grapple with online education. *Nikkei Asia* [Online]. Available at: https://asia.nikkei.com/Business/Technology/Coronavirus-forces-Japan-schools-to-grapple-with-online-education [Accessed 31 May 2020].

OECD (2015). *OECD Digital Economy Outlook.* OECD Publishing, Paris [Online]. Available at: https://www.oecd.org/internet/oecd-digital-economy-outlook-2015-9789264232440-en.htm [Accessed 31 May 2020].

OECD (2019a). *OECD Economic Survey: Japan 2019.* OECD Publishing, Paris [Online]. Available at: https://www.oecd-ilibrary.org/economics/oecd-economic-surveys-japan-2019_fd63f374-en [Accessed 31 May 2020].

OECD (2019b). *OECD Compendium of Productivity Indicators 2019.* OECD Publishing, Paris [Online]. Available at: https://www.oecd-ilibrary.org/industry-and-services/oecd-compendium-of-productivity-indicators-2019_1e1087a0-en [Accessed 31 May 2020].

OECD (2019c). *Education at a Glance 2019*. OECD Publishing, Paris [Online]. Available at: https://www.oecd-ilibrary.org/education/education-at-a-glance-2019_f8d7880d-en [Accessed 31 May 2020].

OECD (2020). FDI stocks. OECD Data [Online]. Available at: https://data.oecd.org/fdi/fdi-stocks.htm [Accessed 31 May 2020].

Osawa, H. (2020). Open APIs are essential to Japanese banking innovation. *lakyara, Nomura Research Institute*, 310, January 24 [Online]. Available at: https://www.nri.com/en/knowledge/publication/fis/lakyara/lst/2020/01/01 [Accessed 31 May 2020].

Sawa, T. (2019). Foreign student number don't tell whole tale. *The Japan Times* [Online]. Available at: https://www.japantimes.co.jp/opinion/2019/04/12/commentary/japan-commentary/foreign-student-numbers-dont-tell-whole-tale/#.XtOFisDgpPY [Accessed 31 May 2020].

Statistics Bureau (2019). Summary of results: Results of the survey of research and development. *Ministry of Internal Affairs and Communication, the Government of Japan* [Online]. Available at: https://www.stat.go.jp/english/data/kagaku/1546.html [Accessed 31 May 2020].

Tsukimori, O. (2020). 2020 Olympics fuel race to monetize autonomous driving. *The Japan Times* [Online]. Available at: https://www.japantimes.co.jp/news/2020/01/05/business/2020-tokyo-olympics-monetize-autonomous-driving/#.XtAy7sDgpPY [Accessed 31 May 2020].

UN (2020). Sustainable development goals [Online]. Available at: https://sustainabledevelopment.un.org/?menu=1300 [Accessed 31 May 2020].

Waldenberger, F. (2018). Society 5.0: Japanese ambitions and initiatives. *Konrad-Adenauer-Stiftung & Deutsches Institut für Japanstudien, The Digital Future*, International report 1, 48–55 [Online]. Available at: https://www.kas.de/de/web/auslandsinformationen/artikel/detail/-/content/society-5.0 [Accessed 31 May 2020].

World Bank (2018). Doing business 2019 [Online]. Available at: https://www.doingbusiness.org/en/reports/global-reports/doing-business-2019 [Accessed 31 May 2020].

World Bank (2019). Doing business 2020 [Online]. Available at: https://www.doingbusiness.org/en/reports/global-reports/doing-business-2020 [Accessed 31 May 2020].

2

European Union–Japan Relations: A Business System Overview of Free Trade Agreements (FTAs)

2.1. Introduction

After initiating an Economic Partnership Agreement (EPA) in 2013, the European Union and Japan succeeded in completing negotiations to finalize it in July 2018. The purposes of this partnership are to increase productivity of goods and services between them, while reducing taxes related to borders; to define the rules of international trade in accordance with their high standards and common values; and to send strong signals that two of the world's largest economies are rejecting protectionism.

The aim of this chapter is to analyze the relationship between two economic and political entities through the negotiation of their latest agreement from a Management Sciences standpoint. A Free Trade Agreement (FTA) is often described by economics scholars *as "an equilibrium agreement if and only if R = F is a unilateral stance in both countries*" (Grossman and Helpman 1993). The decision to form a written consent is essentially a binary choice by the government of two countries since, according to the General Agreement on Tariffs and Trade's (GATT) Article XXIV, only complete (no partial) FTAs can be formed between two countries (Baier and Bergstrand 2004). For that reason, governments respond by increasing their large trade flows, even though their outcomes are expected to

---

Chapter written by Louis-Caleb REMANDA.

mainly benefit actors that take part in respective economies, meaning organizations. One must not ignore the value of the other.

In the case of the Japanese and European economic systems, even though corresponding companies benefit from that partnership – and manage to attain a combined export value of more than €9.4 trillion – they still face obstacles, which can make them less competitive. These hurdles led political and economic entities – the Government of Japan and the European Commission – to initiate a Strategic Partnership Agreement (SPA) in 2018, a legally binding pact that covers not only political dialogue and policy cooperation, but also cooperation on regional and global challenges, including the environment and climate change, development policy, disaster relief and security policy.

Considering the implementation of these various agreements, this chapter focuses on two theoretical concepts: *Business Systems* and *Marketcraft*. These two concepts will be thoroughly developed. The chapter also identifies concepts related to the emergence of internationalization in these countries, perceived as dynamic process allowing organizations to operate.

After a literature review, the chapter highlights the benefactors of the FTA mentioned above, the players in charge of its implementation and the initiatives taken by each stakeholder to make it a success. We will review actions from two institutions that have been mandated as intermediaries for the Free Trade Agreement between Japan and the European Union, from 2013 to 2020. These two distinctive institutions represent both sides of the establishment of the EPA for state-owned companies and SMEs: Japan External Trade Organization (JETRO) a government-related organization; and the EU-Japan Centre of Industrial Cooperation (EU-Japan Centre), a non-profit venture between the European Commission and the Japanese Government.

2.2. Literature review

In this chapter, we focus our attention on the relationship between two economic entities with regard to the construction of their business relations. Three major research areas, often borrowed from multidisciplinary strands, but mostly used in Management Sciences allow us to understand this relation: International relations (IR), Public Administration (PA) and Organizational Theory (OT). IR is more concerned with the role and power played by the entities in the political world, what motivates them being set up and how to nurture them. PA remains a fertile ground because it allows to study behaviors of bureaucratic staff, representativeness, and the socialization of international officials. However, OT responds to the approaches mentioned above by identifying the institution as an organization, a structure that is "either complex or formal".

With these three disciplines in mind, two main concepts embody our research: *Business Systems* and *Marketcraft*. *Business systems* is a concept introduced by Richard Whitley, to define an institutional structure of organizations, which in turn is derived from the societal institutional structure in which organizations are embedded. Organizations are incorporated entities that coordinate economic activities through market relations. They exercise a great deal of discretion, and use a disposition of human and material resources, integrated, coordinated and controlled through the authority system. Theory surrounding the concept has been seen as a comparative analysis of hierarchical market relations arrangements that become institutionalized in societies, combining preferences of activities and capabilities to coordinate economic activities and resources authoritatively by organizations in the field (Whitley 1992, 1999, 2008). *Marketcraft* is, in essence, the idea in which "the free market has become irrelevant". According to Vogel (2016), they need rules, not simply to protect people and the environment from collateral damage, but also to function effectively in the first place.

We also take interest in the structural process of regionalization. Described as a dynamic process, regionalization expresses a more restricted form of internationalization. Stemming from the phenomenon of globalization, this form of internationalization responds to the accessibility of foreign markets without fixed barriers and poses as an institutional arrangement that allows organizations to use their products or services beyond their borders of origin. All these aspects will be extensively covered in the literature review. Nevertheless, assessing the relationship between Japan and the European Union remains a priority.

2.2.1. *The relationship between Japan and the European Union in context*

According to De Prado (2017), the relationship between Japan and the European Union can be explained in two phases: the first period was from the 1960s to 1980s, when economic frictions emerged despite slow political relations, because of the absence of common strategic vision. The second period (1990s to 2010s) was characterized by a "normalization of economic dialogs while attempting to establish a more strategic framework for cooperation in trade and security underpinned by converging values". Since then, Japan and the EU undertook multiple summits to firmly formalize their relations.

Regardless, Japan not only increased the total amount of foreign direct investment in the 1980s, but it also significantly changed its industrial, manufacturing, and non-manufacturing structure, especially in the commercial sector (46% according to a study set up by the Ministry of Economy (METI) in 1989). Its development policies enable large companies to become major suppliers to the national sector, first, and then to the world sector, after reflection. Since 2018, the number of subsidiaries in Europe has risen to around 2,859, i.e., 11.4% of the worldwide distribution of these units, of which 908 are in the European Economic Area, representing a workforce of around 630,000 employees. Of these units in the 26 countries of the European Union, approximately 51% are non-manufacturing. Their main operational challenges remain "the security of human resources, high labor costs and the social/political situation", according to JETRO[1]. The need for human resources is mainly focused on personnel management (57%).

For Taylor *et al.* (2000), the choice of the mode of entry into foreign markets for Japanese multinationals can be summarized in five factors:

– The host country's interest in attracting investment.

– The tendency of multinationals to opt for high-control entry modes in high-risk countries.

– The level of entry is equivalent to the number of resources invested by Japanese companies.

– Government restrictions that influence the choice of entry mode based on local content, foreign exchange, or level of ownership.

– Finally, the importance of supervising production, marketing, and distribution operations where a local contribution is required.

As far as the European region is concerned, Europe and Japan have always had a strong cultural attraction. Despite trade frictions in the 1970s and 80s, they signed a Joint Declaration in 1991 with the sole purpose of exploring areas of possible cooperation together. Japanese organizations have tended to take the "oligopolistic matching" model that characterizes their competitive behavior in their domestic market into their geographic model of international expansion. In other words, when a Japanese firm sets up in a country, its competitors tend to follow suit, creating a sudden surge in Japanese investment that gives it much greater visibility.

For Hamada (2007), the interactions between Japan and the European Union are revealed in three major elements: the use of business associations, the intensive use of personalized networks and the emphasis on harmony. Business associations

1 According to the Japan External Trade Organization, a government agency attached to the Ministry of Economy of Japan (METI), in Japan External Trade Organization (2018b).

remain key political channels for business interests and have shaped many large companies into independent political players in the market. Being part of a long tradition of business activism or lobbying is part of the daily life of Japanese multinationals to strengthen their collective action in the economic sector. We recognize the strong influence of the Keidanren (Japan Business Federation) or the European Automobile Manufacturers Association (ACEA), in which the representation of corporate interests is for the benefit of the whole economy.

But for Nitsch and Beamish (1995), Japanese organizations' tendency to invest in Europe has varied over time, but the Japanese understanding of globalization should be interpreted from their perspective, rather than from the European perspective. The globalization strategies of Japanese manufacturing organizations in the late 1980s, which consisted in simply moving production and sales facilities abroad, evolved towards the establishment of a system of collaborative management abroad that included finance, distribution, and R&D in addition to production. And the intensity of these investments is linked to the need to catch up with its main competitors, resulting in a degree of internationalization which is considered low (Sachwald 1993).

The aim was therefore to normalize the local economy to rebalance flows between major nations.

2.2.2. *Understanding the business systems overview*

Whitley thus defines *business systems* as "arrangements of hierarchical-market relationships that become institutionalized and are relatively successful contexts" (Whitley 1992, p. 5). These arrangements combine preferences for activities and skills to be coordinated in an authoritarian manner, with variations in the degree of discretion exercised by managers or owners of shareholding rights. The unit of analysis in this comparative study of systems is therefore organizations, in the sense that they coordinate economic activities through authoritative relationships in the market; that they exercise a high degree of discretion over the acquisition, use and disposal of human and material resources; and that they integrate, coordinate and control these resources through the authoritative system and its direction of authoritative economic activities, adding value to these resources and functions, which are generally regarded as separate units in the decision-making process.

Marketcraft as the idea of "free market" has become irrelevant. For Vogel (2016), markets need rules, not simply to protect people and the environment from collateral damage, but to function effectively in the first place. They may appear as exogenous societal constraints on behavioral choices to individual agents but are endogenously created and confirmed through agents' strategic interactions (Aoki

2011). Much of their social and relational construction is therefore part of the institutional paradigm. These key social institutions influence the business systems established in different and varied market economies and can be distinguished between those that structure the general patterns of trust, cooperation, identity, and subordination in a society and those that are more directly involved in shaping the economic system and the immediate business environment.

We distinguish background institutions which are processes of reproduction of primary institutions (family, religion, education) (North 1990) supporting the organization of all economic systems and shaping industrialization from the development of modern market economies (Whitley 1992). When markets become institutionalized, they generate considerable trust between trading partners, coordinate economic activities between organizations and organize work within them. We also distinguish between proximate institutions that are products of the process of industrialization from development parallel to the formation of the modern state. Proximate institutions affect the forms of organization of the enterprise and deal with the availability of financial resources and all types of manpower that ensure the stability and security of the system and vary according to the degree and type of support for private business activities (Whitley 1992). To distinguish markets from Japan and the European Union, we must then refer to institutions. Institutions contribute to the development of the state, which is referred to herein as the "institutional regime".

An institutional regime refers to the ability of the state to establish rules in coordinating its development (rules of governance and decision-making) and in encouraging organizations to contribute to this development through intermediary associations, representing the interests of the different groups that will participate in policy formulation and implementation (Whitley 2008).

Developmentalist regimes are structures in which the state plays a role as a provider of competitive goods in the market. It delimits its direct provision of competitive goods to privileged organizations and reinforces their expansion of the internally generated funds allow it to do so. Organizations will rely on the political–bureaucratic alliances they have formed with the dominant classes of the country's political system (Whitley 2008).

This is somewhat like the case of Japan (Figure 2.1), where the government plays a discreet but strategic role in supplying markets, with the aim of bringing together all types of organization. The post-war market model is supported by intermediary associations between the state and business; banks, unions and inter-company groups called "keiretsu"[2]. This will influence the organizations in their decision making for national and even global activities.

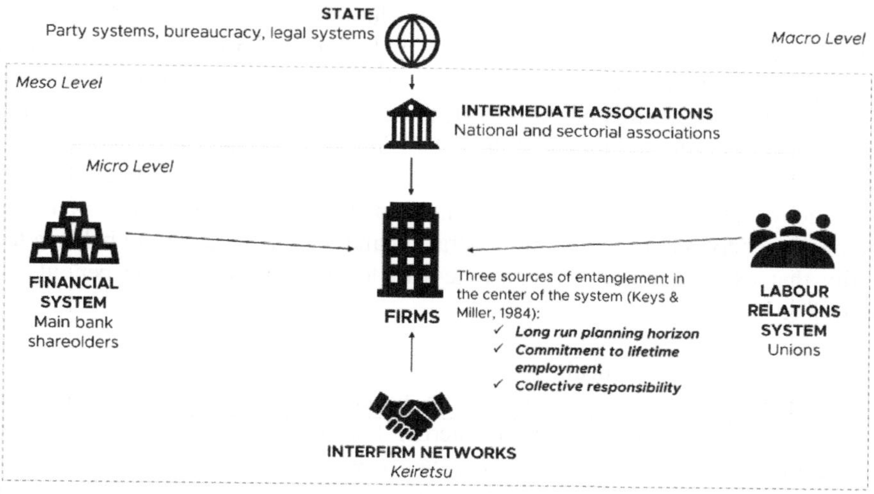

Figure 2.1. *The Japanese Business System (adapted from Vogel 2016)*

The European Union is a different animal from Japan, not only in its structure but also in its position. IR, PA, and OT approaches refer to the European Union as a "public and heterodox structure" in which mandates and functions are its key elements of survival. Rational choices from members of the European Union allow supranational institutions such as the European Commission (EC) to control the economic performance of the region, despite the lack of historical mechanisms within. The EU's compliance system works by using a combination of mechanisms of "enforcement" – that deals with coercive strategies of monitoring, sanctions and "management" – adopting an approach to solve problems based on capacity reinforcement, interpretation of rules and transparency (Remanda 2017).

2.2.3. *Regionalization and Europeanization*

Literature on International Management drives our research on the concept of Regionalization. Regionalization, based on the research of Alan Rugman (2000, 2004, 2005), reflects a form of internationalization circumscribed on a more

2 Keiretsu are sets of business networks locked together by business relationships, embedded with formal and informal links between companies, customers and suppliers, and financial institutions that reduce agency costs and provide financial and strategic flexibility.

affordable framework – a region – that presents itself for multinational organizations as a re-evaluation of their strategies to strengthen regional competitiveness, rather than developing global organizational responses to international competition. As Internationalization takes a turn in its evolution, while the world economy experiments with significant reductions in trade barriers through the creation of "trading blocs", trade blocs ultimately converge to free trade agreements such as NAFTA in 1994 or MERCOSUR in 1991; these follow the example of the European Union project (1990), previously of the GATT in 1947 and later of the World Trade Organization. Contributions from several authors, namely Siddiqi (2000), Seno-Alday (2009), and Khan (2010), emphasize a process that offers an intermediary between a multidomestic strategy and a global strategy, to balance the duality that exists between responsiveness to local markets with the benefits of controlling integration.

Many studies also deal with the concept of "Europeanization" as a regionalization dimension framed on the European continent. Europe is often understood as an entity with poor internal borders, which is its strength. Its heterogeneity has been difficult to conceive of, which means that human resource management in this case is at the crossroads of national differences, influenced by value systems, social welfare, and labor legislation (Hermel 1996).

According to Sachwald (1993), "Europeanization" motivations are discussed in relation to three dimensions: the strong growth of foreign direct investment in certain sectors of European industry, the choice of the country in which to set up and the way in which European units are organized. This model also assumes that production must begin in developed countries and then spread to developing countries. For Rouet (2016), European integration allows for questions about the nationality and citizenship of the organizations that reside within it. As the European community attempts to build an identity, the economic logic which sees companies only as multinationals is no longer sufficient. The company integrates an environment in which it becomes a citizen, and its citizenship is not only a cultural element, less important than the structure of the company. Multinationals also have identities, drawn from their place of origin

The European market is an interesting contextual framework for examining the direct influence of the autonomy of the subsidiary in its links with its parent company, for several reasons. First, Europe appears to be attractive to both domestic and foreign organizations because of the size of its goods and services market. Second, despite the progress of European economic and political integration over the past two decades, different European countries remain relatively varied in terms of institutional quality, technological development, consumer preferences, business potential, educational systems, and ethnicity. Therefore, the expansion of the European Economic Area towards new markets, mainly in Eastern Europe, is also a factor in motivating and increasing Japanese FDI. The last ten countries to enter the European space (EU-10) have experienced a radical transformation, particularly in their corporate governance policies, which have been of interest to Japan. Corporate governance is important and has a positive association that attracts Japanese direct investment (Petric 2010).

The relationship between Japan and the EU is therefore a bridge to understanding the motivation of FDI. Partners for more than 25 years, the Invest Japan Report conducted by JETRO (2016), shows that Japan is the 4th largest investor in the European Union, and that direct investment inflows into Japan from Europe are €9,354 billion, according to the Japan Electronics and Information's Technology industries Association (JEITA). As of today, Japan and the EU occupy important positions in the world economy (30% share of global GDP). Even if Japan is no longer considered as a "superpower" as it was in the 1980s, it is still economically ranked #3 in terms of Nominal GDP[3], with nearly 60% of the population aged over 65[4], 63% of Japanese SMEs not globalized and 43% interested in globalizing (Arima 2015).

2.3. Research propositions and methodology

Approaching the topic from a purely structural perspective it is important to remember the fact that Japan is a single country and the European Union is a community of countries. The two entities work on different systems; economic and political influence is not the same with regard to their respective economic strategies. We assume that, on the one hand, Japan is a highly coordinated economy, dominantly developed by political and business elites (government, banks, organizational networks) that provide collective competitivity goods, keeping a distant eye on governance structure of companies, and playing a major role in interfirm alliances. On the other hand, the European Union is a market based on national public policies, where individual countries' markets vary between coordinated and highly coordinated. The European Union internal market has become quite liberalized over several decades services increasingly so since the 1990s, and competition among businesses assured by the European Commission. Ultimately, intermediary institutions must play a go-between role to coordinate exchange between the entities.

The objective of this research was first, thanks to the literature review, to give insight on potential success in this FTA that is the Japan-EU Economic Partnership Agreement (EPA), whether at the macro-level, meso-level, but also at the

3 IMF World Economy Outlook 2018.

4 Aizawa Yuko, *NHK News*, March 2019.

micro-level, and expectations from respective stakeholders involved in the agreement, namely the European Commission and the Japanese government. In this comprehensive analysis, two distinct institutions representing the two sides played a major role in explaining and implementing the establishment of the EPA for state-owned companies and SMEs:

– The *Japan External Trade Organization (JETRO)*, a government-related organization, whose core focus is to promote foreign direct investment into Japan and to help small to medium size Japanese organizations maximize their global export potential.

– The *EU-Japan Centre of Industrial Cooperation (EU-Japan Centre)*, a non-profit venture between the European Commission and the Japanese Government that aims to promote all forms of industrial, trade and investment cooperation between the EU and Japan.

Data collection consisting of *semi-structured interviews* were considered for both organizations. These interviews mainly deal with their implication in the EPA, what the value added from their work to the agreement is and whether they have received any support from the respective governments and/or multinational corporations regarding this question. Data collection also envisaged *secondary data*, with the ability from both entities to express their opinion on the development of the EPA thanks to activity reports, press releases and survey results. Website content from both institutions has also been explored. Finally, *non-participant observation* was conducted, as we took part in numerous events, promoting the partnership between the economic entities. These events were organized by the actors that will follow.

Data was collected during the 2018–2020 academic period, from immediately after the completion of the deal to its entry into force in February 2019, and one year after this entry. Thematical analysis from all this data is applied to get an internal view of the business synopsis of the Economic Partnership Agreement.

We finally conducted two semi-structured interviews with members of the EU-Japan Centre (the first in 2018 and the second in 2019). JETRO was unavailable at the time to give any interviews. Nevertheless, the whole secondary database is mostly provided by JETRO. It is important to mention that JETRO is quite well established in Europe. They operate within 13 countries in Europe, 11 of them members of the European Union[5]. Most of their data (survey results) is directed towards Japanese organizations operating in Europe. Both JETRO and the EU-Japan Centre have at their disposal well-furnished websites with information about their contribution to the EPA. We also participated in the

5 Considering the recent withdrawal of the United Kingdom from the European Union and Switzerland, which is part of the Schengen Area.

EU-Japan Forum that took place in April 2018, in Copenhagen (Denmark). This event, dedicated to the EPA, brought together more than 250 stakeholders, policy makers, regulatory experts, leaders of major companies and international trade and investment experts. Organized by JETRO, the European Commission, the Japanese Ministry of Foreign Affairs and the Danish Chamber of Commerce, the theme of the forum was "*Regulatory issues for companies and new business opportunities*".

2.4. Case of Japan – European Union Economic Partnership Agreement

2.4.1. *The targets of the Free Trade Agreement*

As part of the Abenomics growth strategy, the Japanese government initiated a series of Free Trade Agreements (FTAs) in 2009. The one with the European Union was set up in March 2013. The goal of this agreement is to favor economic exchanges between the two entities from trade philosophy to an FDI perspective. As mentioned above, the EU is one of the largest investors in Japan in terms of FDI and Japan is the third largest investor in the EU. Trading has always been the "link" between the two economic entities (Schweisgut 2012). Japanese companies have contributed to creating employment representing more than 460,000 jobs in Europe (Tanaka 2014). According to the Ministry of Foreign Affairs in Japan (2019), the objective is to promote the liberalization of trade by reducing protectionist movements and market-distorting measures, like those implemented by emerging countries.

A model of economic order in the 21st century based on free and fair rules (state-owned enterprises, intellectual property and regulatory cooperation, etc.):

- 30% of world GDP
- 40% of world trade
- 290,000 jobs estimated for Japan (Japan Cabinet Secretariat)
- 500,000 jobs for EU (European Commission)

What market is concerned about EPA:

- Industrial products
- Agriculture, forestry, fishery products
- Services, e-commerce

Figure 2.2. *A summary of the Japan-European Union Economic Partnership Agreement*

Since March 2013, the two parties had been negotiating an FTA aimed at increasing economic stakes (GDP, exports). The fact remains that this agreement has so far been subject to several political and institutional ratifications. Even if the motivation for Japanese companies to set up in Europe has always been a spirit of globalization, this FTA remains difficult to interpret in the theoretical sphere, since it embodies several factors, such as sociological protectionism and economic intelligence, but also structural differences in terms of sectors of activity. This agreement came at the right time, since 52.1% of Japanese organizations exporting to Europe are in favor of it (JETRO 2017). It took 6 years to be signed, and came into force in February 2019, to help the two entities counter the protectionist market movements implemented by emerging governments.

2.4.2. *The organizations in charge of the implementation*

In Japan, one institution has always overseen promoting external trade and investment abroad. Originally established in 1958, JETRO is a government-related organization that directly reports to the Ministry of Foreign Affairs (MOFA) and the Ministry of Economy, Trade, and Industry (METI). Its core focus has changed over the centuries, as they shifted from exports only in the 1960s toward promoting foreign direct investment into Japan and helping small to medium size Japanese organizations maximize their global export potential. With its global headquarters in Tokyo, it controls 51 regionals offices, and 74 overseas (with a total of 732 employees overseas). Its main activities are dedicated to promoting FDI, trade and business between Japan and the rest of the world, assisting business expansion of developing countries and contributing to trade policies and economic partnerships. It also invests in Research to understand potential investors in developing economies with the help of the Institute of Developing Economies (IDE-JETRO).

From the EU's perspective, the mission is carried out in a form of a joint venture called the EU-Japan Centre for Industrial Cooperation (EU-Japan Centre). Established in 1987, the EU-Japan Centre is a unique venture between the European Commission and the Japanese Government comprising 30 people; it is an established non-profit organization that aims to promote all forms of industrial, trade and investment cooperation between the EU and Japan and improving EU and Japanese companies' competitiveness and cooperation by facilitating exchanges of experience and know-how between EU and Japanese businesses. It is jointly funded and managed by the two sides. With their main offices in Tokyo and Brussels, bringing together around 100 people, they focus on training (Japanese Business Culture, Cross-cultural Issues, Japanese Manufacturing Expertise, Industrial Internships in Japan), developing business services (EPA Helpdesk, Business Partnership, Office Opportunity, Cluster Cooperation, etc.) and formulating intelligence and policies (Policies, fellowship, Business dialogues).

We can already perceive, through the structure of each institution, that management in the two institutions is widely different. As JETRO is a public organization and acts as the intermediary between the state and the targeted companies, it has guaranteed support from the Japanese government, it also takes incentive directly from them. Let us look at the initiatives implemented by the two institutions to make the Japan-EU EPA a successful agreement.

2.4.3. *Initiatives taken for the success of the EPA*

As mentioned above, due to its structural organization, initiatives from the EU-Japan Centre are less profitable, even if they support European and Japanese SMEs, clusters, business executives, researchers and even students. As the Economic Partnership Agreement took an explicit form in 2018, they started to launch action to "raise awareness of the opportunities this agreement offers and to help European SMEs take advantage of them".

The EPA Helpdesk is a guideline that publishes factsheets covering information about the changes brought by the EPA. The EU-Japan Centre also organizes related webinars on the main topics covered by the agreement. For each webinar, it provides free post-recordings and a PowerPoint presentation, freely accessible on its website. Yet, the biggest initiative taken by the Centre existed long before negotiations started for the EPA. In 1999, the institution established the Business Roundtable (EU-Japan BRT) to foster cohesive communication between Japanese and European industry. It is an annual meeting between members from 55 leading European and Japanese companies and various business federations whose main objectives are to provide recommendations to the Japanese and European authorities so as to help develop trade and investment between the EU and Japan, and to encourage industrial cooperation in fields of common interest such as innovation, climate change, or industrial standards. These recommendations take two forms: one a collective view from the BRT members on certain topics (Positions Statements), and the second a set of recommendations (Working Parties).

JETRO has also contributed to the comprehension of the EPA from a practical perspective. In 2013, they released a compilation from their own data to show the "openness" of the Japanese market to world[6]. They co-organized and partnered with local trade organizations on numerous events about the benefits of the agreement between Europe and Japan. In 2014, JETRO held seminars in three cities in Europe, Frankfurt, Berlin, and Paris, under the theme of the *Japan-EU Economic Partnership Agreement (EPA)*. In 2015, they co-organized with the Konrad

6 Japan's market is open to the world: https://www.jetro.go.jp/ext_images/en/eu-japan/pdf/EN201310rev.pdf.

Adenauer Foundation (KAS), a seminar in Berlin, under the theme of "*what impact the EU-Japan economic partnership agreement (EPA) has on the further globalization of small and medium-sized enterprises (SMEs)*" aiming to promote negotiations related to the EPA. In 2016, The *Invest Japan Seminar* in Brussels was about encouraging Japanese companies to further local investments, with strong messages from Japanese Prime Minister Shinzo Abe and Belgian Deputy Prime Minister Kris Peeters.

The same exercise was repeated in Dublin and Munich in 2017; Brussels, Berlin, Helsinki, Stockholm, and Madrid in 2018; and Fürth and Dusseldorf in 2019. From 2018 to the present day, they have co-organized the EU-Japan EPA Forum with the European Commission and The Ministry of Foreign Affairs of Japan (MOFA), a business summit that brought together key policymakers behind the EU-Japan Economic Partnership Agreement and a high-level international audience of 200+ senior business leaders together. They prolonged the initiative in Milan in 2019 and one livestream event in December 2020, where they discussed the mergers and acquisitions landscape and the blueprint of effective integration with stakeholders in the light of the Covid-19 crisis.

2.4.4. *JETRO and the EU-Japan Centre as bridges between authorities*

The EU-Japan BRT plays a major role in being the advisor for leadership organizations in the EU-Japan Summit. This major role was so well carried out that "*Summit leaders recognized the important contribution of the Japan-EU Business Round Table (BRT) to the development of bilateral economic relationships and reaffirmed their determination to continue cooperation with the business communities on both sides, notably through the BRT, in order to strengthen relations further*"[7].

Even before formal negotiations began, the EU-Japan BRT was already in favor of a high-level, comprehensive, equitable partnership agreement. "*The Japanese government and the European Commission possess political and governmental capacities, and even when they set up policies like the EPA. [...] The BRT was a way for the industry to raise a voice as the agreement opens the floor to them, without knowing what is going on in the market*" said Simon Craig Gray[8], Deputy Director of the EU-Japan Centre in charge of BRT.

---

7 Retrieved from the 21st Japan-EU Summit Tokyo – Joint Press Statement (19 November 2013): https://ec.europa.eu/commission/presscorner/detail/en/MEMO_13_1015.

8 Retrieved from an interview conducted in Brussels with EU-Japan Centre of Industrial Cooperation on March 4th, 2019.

They launched, in total, 18 formal rounds of negotiations from March 2013, and countless other formal and informal contacts and exchanges between the EU and Japanese Authorities. In July 2017, they announced an "agreement in principle", and the successful conclusion of negotiations on December 8, 2017. Despite the presence of other lobbies and business associations, the BRT has reached a position in which they can be consulted by both the Japanese Government and the European Commission, on certain crises. For example, "the Japanese government did not understand what was going on with the Brexit crisis. For them, United Kingdom was always a gateway to foster the economy. Many Japanese companies operate there", said Simon Craig Gray.

As for JETRO, the organization opened a dedicated website that provided resources for the EPA, including a Japanese guide on the agreement preferential tariff, rules of origin and basic procedures for Japanese companies to obtain tariff reductions[9].

It also publishes a survey report on the "Business Conditions of Japanese Companies in Europe" each year, a survey that analyses the activities of Japanese affiliated companies operating in Europe, to comprise an understanding of operating challenges that could be directly impacting their business performance. These surveys were used to assist companies in developing overseas operation strategies and policy planning, but they also served as a basis of information for governmental agencies on providing sufficient support for Japanese-affiliated companies based in Europe. They further served as a basis of information for European companies regarding the conditions of business in Japan.

In 2018, the response from EU-based companies in favor of the EPA was positive by 42% despite a lower figure from the year before. Companies in favor were mostly from the Netherlands (73.3%), Czechia (68.4%), Denmark (66.7%), Spain (62.5%), Romania (58.3%) and Poland (56.0%). The "Tariff reduction/abolition on imports from Japan" was a reason for this impact, part of which came from the manufacturing sector. The problematic issues were "In-house system improvements" (47.4%), "Cooperation with supplier/business partners e.g., completion of certificate of origin documentation" (43.1%) and "Proof of origin procedures by self-certification" (34.6%). Despite those issues and the Brexit crisis, they planned on continuing to utilize the agreements for Import/Export (70%) (Japan External Trade Organization 2018).

9 Japan-EU Economic Partnership Agreement (EPA) - 日EU経済連携協定（EPA）について: https://www.jetro.go.jp/world/europe/eu/epa.html#about.

2.5. Conclusion

Ten months after the implementation of the EPA, both European Union and Japan observed an increase in exports of around 6%, an increase that "outperforms the growth of European Union for the past three years". The EPA seems to have created new opportunities, especially for European farmers and food producers. Indeed, 211 high-quality food and drink products from the EU can now be sold under their own name in Japan and are protected from imitation.

According to the "2019 survey on business conditions of Japanese companies in Europe" (Japan External Trade Organization 2020), the utilization rate of the EPA for import was high in industries such as fabricated metal products (80.0%), textiles (80.0%), transportation equipment parts (79.5%), sales companies (72.1%), and food/processed food, agricultural or fishery products (70.0%). For exports from the EU to Japan, higher utilization rates came from sectors such as transport activities (88.9%), transportation equipment parts (76.5%), and sales companies (72.7%)[10]. But it has a few drawbacks: While Japan struggles with the clarification and the consistency of the applications of the agreement (rules and procedures), the European Union wishes to relax rules around customs and clearance (rules and certification of origin, practical cooperation, visas, etc.).

As of today, and based on the success achieved around the Economic Partnership Agreement, the Ministry of Foreign Affairs of Japan in collaboration with the European Commission wishes to open a new agreement – this time strategic – which will serve as a legal basis to promote cooperation on matters of mutual interest in a wide range of areas, between Japan and the European Union and its Member States that share the values and principles of democracy, the rule of law, human rights and fundamental freedoms, and to strengthen their enduring strategic partnership (MOFA 2018). But how long will it take to reach a conclusion, especially considering the full withdrawal of the United Kingdom from the EU, still under negotiation; the global Covid-19 crisis, and the resignation of the Prime Minister of Japan, Shinzo Abe, who was at the forefront of these agreements, agreements considered as tools for so-called "Abenomics" (Nagata 2020).

2.6. References

Aoki, M. (2011). Institutions as cognitive media between strategic interactions and individual beliefs. *Journal of Economic Behavior & Organization*, 79(1–2), 20–34.

10 The survey was addressed to 842 Japanese companies, including affiliated companies where the ratio of direct or indirect investment from Japanese companies is 10% or more in the EU. Among them, 65% have used the EU-Japan EPA.

Arima, J. (2015). EU-Japan FTA/EPA: JETRO's perspective [Online]. Available at: https://www.jetro.go.jp/ext_images/jetro/topics/pdf/1501_topics3_annex3.pdf.

CEFJ-JETRO (2014). Japan-EU Economic Partnership Agreement: Japan's political views [Online]. Available at: https://www.jetro.go.jp/ext_images/france/missions/pdf/english_report_forum140314.pdf.

De Prado, C. (2017). Towards a substantial EU-Japan partnership. *European Foreign Affairs Review*, 22(4), 435–454.

EU-Japan Centre for Industrial Cooperation (2019). A new era for the EU and Japan starts today. Press release. [Online]. Available at: https://www.eu-japan-brt.eu/system/files/recommendations/2018_EPAstatement.pdf.

European Commission (2018a). Key elements of the EU-Japan Economic Partnership Agreement. Press release. [Online]. Available at: https://ec.europa.eu/commission/presscorner/detail/en/MEMO_18_6784.

European Commission (2018b). Opening up Japan's market to European exports: An introduction to the EU-Japan Economic Partnership Agreement. Report, European Commission.

European Commission (2019). EU-Japan trade agreement enters into force. Press release. [Online]. Available at: https://ec.europa.eu/commission/presscorner/detail/en/IP_19_785.

European Commission (2020). First year of EU-Japan Economic Partnership Agreement shows growth in EU exports. Press release. [Online]. Available at: https://trade.ec.europa.eu/doclib/press/index.cfm?id=2107.

Grossman, G.M. and Helpman, E. (1993). *The Politics of Free Trade Agreements*. National Bureau of Economic Research, Cambridge, MA.

Hermel, P. (1996). European and International Management. Georgetown University, Washington, DC.

Heydemann, S. (2008). Institutions and economic performance: The use and abuse of culture in new institutional economics. *Studies in Comparative International Development*, 43(1), doi:10.1007/s12116-007-9015-3.

Japan External Trade Organization (2013). Le marché japonais est ouvert sur le monde [Online]. Available at: https://www.jetro.go.jp/ext_images/en/eujapan/pdf/FR201307rev.pdf.

Japan External Trade Organization (2018a). 2018 survey on business conditions of Japanese companies in Europe [Online]. Available at: https://www.jetro.go.jp/ext_images/en/reports/survey/pdf/rp_firms_euro201812.pdf.

Japan External Trade Organization (2018b). FY2017 survey on the international operations of Japanese firms. Press release. [Online]. Available at: https://www.jetro.go.jp/en/news/releases/2018/86aeedf1557c1864.html.

Japan External Trade Organization. (2020). 2019 survey on business conditions of Japanese companies in Europe [Online]. Available at: https://www.jetro.go.jp/ext_images/en/reports/survey/pdf/rp_firms_EU2019en.pdf.

Khan, O.J. (2010). The regionalization vs. globalization debate on internationalization: An analysis and direction for future research. *Global Partnership Management Journal*, 1.

MOFA (2016). Japan-EU relations [Online]. Available at: https://www.mofa.go.jp/files/000033265.pdf.

MOFA (2018). Japan-EU Strategic Partnership Agreement (SPA) [Online]. Available at: https://www.mofa.go.jp/files/000381944.pdf.

MOFA (2022). Japan-EU Economic Partnership Agreement outline [Online]. Available at: https://www.mofa.go.jp/files/000013835.pdf.

Nagata, K. (2020). Abenomics here to stay despite Japan PM's looming departure. *Japan Times* [Online]. Available at: https://www.japantimes.co.jp/news/2020/08/29/business/economy-business/abenomics-japan-shinzo-abe-economy/.

Razeen, S. (2007). Looking east: The European Union's new FTA negotiations in Asia. *Jan Tumlir Policy Essays*, 3(03/2007), 5–27.

Remanda, L.-C. (2017). Understand the European identity through the institutional embeddedness theory: The case of the crisis of migrants/refugees. *Politické vedy*, 20(4), 153–173.

Rouet, G. (2016). Les entreprises, acteurs d'intégration européenne. In *Les Entreprises et l'intégration européenne*, Raytcheva, S. and Rouet, G. (eds). C.L. Global, L'Harmattan.

Rugman, A.M. and Verbeke, A. (2004). A perspective on regional and global strategies of multinational enterprises. *Journal of International Business Studies*, 35(1), 3–18.

Rugman, A.M. and Verbeke A. (2005). Towards a theory of regional multinationals: A transaction cost economics approach. *MIR: Management International Review*, 45, 1.

Schweisgut, H.D. (2012). The EU and Japan: The way forward of two likeminded strategic partners. *EU Studies in Japan*, 2012(32), 1–17, doi:10.5135/eusj.2012.1.

Seno-Alday, S. (2009). Market characteristics and regionalisation patterns. *European Management Journal*, 27(5), 366–376.

Siddiqi, S. (2000). Customizing core competencies: The regional challenge. *International Journal of Commerce Management Decision*, 10(1), 91.

Tallberg, J. (2002). Delegation to supranational institutions: Why, how, and with what consequences? *West European Politics*, 25(1), 23–46.

Vogel, S.K. (2018). *Marketcraft: How Governments Make Markets Work*. Oxford University Press, Oxford.

Whitley, R. (ed.) (1992). *European Business Systems: Firms and Markets in their National Contexts*. SAGE, Thousand Oaks, CA.

Whitley, R. (2008). *Business Systems and Organizational Capabilities: The Institutional Structuring of Competitive Competences*. Oxford University Press, Oxford.

3

The Evolving Foreign Direct Investment Landscape: Evidence from Europe and Asia

Foreign direct investment (FDI), one of the main indicators of globalization, has increased substantially in recent decades.

FDI is long-term investment involving a management interest in an enterprise located abroad. The common perception is of investment by large multinational enterprises (MNEs) in the productive capacity of a foreign country. The expected economic benefits to the host economy are higher output, employment and exports, as well as various spill-over advantages such as productivity increases and technological transfer. Governments therefore often seek to attract FDI to boost economic development and growth.

However, the large increase in FDI observed worldwide over recent decades has accompanied substantial changes in the nature of FDI, mainly due to digitalization and corporate restructuring. Differentiated networks and ownership chains have replaced hierarchical structures. Services FDI has also become more important. The pursuit of tax efficiency has increased pass-through investment and corporate inversion, biasing the size of FDI and its geographical allocation. As a result, there is an increasing disconnect between the published FDI figures and the "real" economic impact of MNEs in host economies.

We review the FDI figures for three economies: one European (Ireland) and two Asian economies (Japan and Vietnam) to examine how these changes are revealed in the data. These countries display both similarities and differences in their

Chapter written by Clare O'MAHONY and Thi Ngoc DAO.

experiences with FDI. They vary in their stage of development, data availability and comprehensiveness, the nature of MNE activity and the relative importance of inward investment vis-à-vis outward investment. Ireland is a highly FDI-intensive economy where inward investment has been critical to economic prosperity. Japan, among the largest outward direct investors globally, has more recently actively sought to attract inward investment. For Vietnam, a developing country, inward FDI is an important force in the process of economic transformation.

3.1. Introduction

Many governments seek to attract FDI in order to boost economic growth and development. The expected economic benefits to the host economy are increased productive capacity, employment and exports, as well as various spill-over advantages such as productivity increases and technological transfer. FDI is also an important indicator of globalization.

Measured FDI has increased substantially in recent decades with worldwide FDI inward flows increasing six-fold from 1990, although there has been a sharp decline since 2020 due to the Covid-19 pandemic (UNCTAD 2019, 2021). However, the large increase in FDI observed worldwide over recent decades has accompanied substantial changes in the nature of FDI due to digitalization and corporate restructuring. Differentiated networks and ownership chains (the "global factory") have replaced hierarchical structures and there has been increased mobility of head offices (Buckley 2009; Desai 2009).

FDI is traditionally viewed as direct one-to-one investment from multinational parents to affiliates in the manufacturing industry. However, the nature of what constitutes FDI has evolved and shifted away from this common perception with reverse and indirect investment, increasing services FDI, and substantial levels of pass-through investment. The increased importance of intangible assets also makes it difficult to ascertain the ultimate sources and destinations of investment (Lipsey 2010). Lipsey (2007) points out that the use of intangible assets enables firms to shift the "nominal location" or reported location of production without moving real inputs such as labor. Tax planning is the main driver of many of these changes.

FDI is therefore increasingly disconnected from the "real" economic activity of multinational enterprises (MNEs). We cannot merely compare quantities of FDI in order to understand its potential impact on the host economy, as the headline figures measure financial flows of capital that may or may not be related to real economic activity. Various concerns, such as reverse investment and pass-through investment, will vary across countries depending on their institutional, legal and tax regimes, often affected by a country's stage of development. Our aim is to review the experiences of three economies, Ireland, Japan and Vietnam, in this evolving FDI global landscape to ascertain how these changes are revealed in their FDI statistics.

This chapter proceeds as follows: the next section explains the measurement of FDI by the main international agencies; we then briefly discuss the experience of the three economies in relation to FDI. Section 3.4 examines issues of data availability and comprehensiveness, important when making international comparisons. We then discuss two key issues affecting the relevance of FDI statistics: section 3.5 looks at the effects of reverse investment and section 3.6 examines the effects of pass-through investment and corporate inversion. Section 3.7 concludes.

3.2. Measuring FDI

The sixth edition of the IMF's Balance of Payments and International Investment Position Manual (BPM6) set out the international standards for recording FDI in the balance of payments (BOP). It defines FDI as "a category of cross-border investment associated with a resident in one economy having control or a significant degree of influence on the management of an enterprise that is resident in another economy" (IMF 2008). FDI has three components: equity, reinvested earnings (RIE) and other capital. RIE, in particular can be impacted by changes in taxation policies and are sometimes not measured. The measurement of FDI stocks has been slower to conform to international standards than the measurement of flow data and many countries have only begun to report them in recent years or still do not report them.

The main international agencies producing FDI data are the IMF, OECD and UNCTAD. MNE activity data is less available and lacks standardization. OECD has developed an activity (AMNE) database, but there are a host of missing values for many countries, and it only covers a limited range of countries members. The OECD produces the most detailed FDI data, with geographic and sectoral breakdowns. UNCTAD also produces disaggregated data. The IMF's focus is on the BOP itself, but it covers a wider range of countries.

FDI is essentially a financial flow, recorded in the BOP, but inward FDI is widely interpreted as a proxy for the activity of foreign-owned MNEs in the host economy with Clegg (1992), for example, describing the BOP data and MNE activity data as two sides of the same coin. However, there are key differences between the two concepts. First, for an investment to be classified as FDI, the investor is expected to hold at least a 10% equity in its affiliate (the "10% rule"), while MNE activity data looks at control, requiring majority ownership. Second, investment raised locally is not included in FDI, as it does not cross borders. Third, geographical sources and destinations of FDI data are commonly recorded on an immediate basis, whereas activity data report ultimate sources and destinations. Investment is not necessarily from parent to affiliate, but can also be from affiliate to parent (reverse investment), or between affiliates in the same or different countries (indirect investment).

There is increasing evidence of pass-through investment with no concomitant involvement in the real economic activity in the host economy. FDI tells us where the financial liabilities and assets are located, but this is increasingly disconnected from where production takes place and value is created. A number of authors point to the mismatch between FDI and MNE "real" economic activity with Blanchard and Acalin (2016), for example, stating that "measured FDI is not entirely true FDI" in the sense that it does not always imply investment in economic activity in the host economy. They suggest that a substantial share of inflows measured as FDI is actually pass-through investment, partially due to corporation tax considerations (Blanchard and Acalin 2016). Beugelsdijk *et al.* (2010) argue that FDI is not only an inaccurate measure of MNE activity, but is also a biased measure, also pointing out that taxation policies impact the levels of reverse investment and RIE.

Furthermore, data is also not always directly comparable due to different interpretation and implementation of the international standards. O'Mahony and Barry (2019) find differences in data collection methods, the measurement and treatment of the FDI components, especially RIE, the treatment of reverse and indirect investment, the treatment of the pass-through investment and geographical allocations. They find very substantial quantitative differences between six European countries, and suggest that differences are likely to be greater between countries which are more economically and institutionally diverse.

3.3. Country selection

We review three countries, Ireland, Japan and Vietnam, which vary in their stages of development, as well as in the nature of FDI activity that takes place in their economies. Figure 3.1 shows inward FDI flows as a share of GNI for the three economies. Ireland is by far the largest recipient of FDI, for its size.

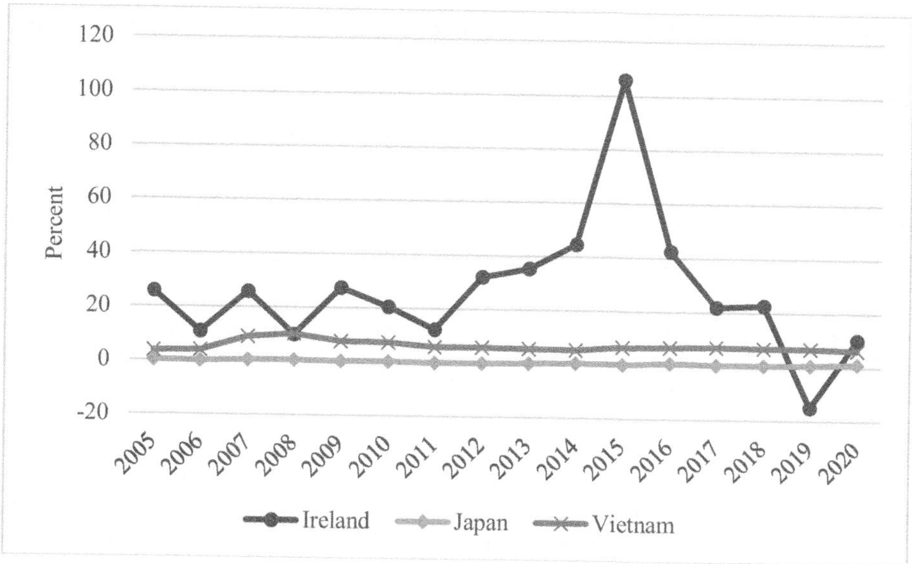

Figure 3.1. *Inward flows as share of GNI: 2005–2020 (source: World Development Indicators)*

All three countries have sought inward FDI to create jobs. Table 3.1 shows that Ireland has the greatest share of employment in the foreign-owned sector; it has also had the longest experience of substantial inward investment of the three countries.

Year	**2009**	**2010**	**2011**	**2012**	**2013**	**2014**	**2015**	**2016**	**2017**	**2018**	**2019**	**Mean**
Ireland	55.0	55.3	54.8	54.3	54.2	52.0	51.7	52.4	52.1	53.7	54.6	53.7
Japan	3.9	3.7	3.9	3.6	4.0	4.1	3.9	3.3	3.2	3.3	3.3	3.7
Vietnam	3.2	3.5	4.2	4.4	4.8	5.4	6.0	6.7	7.8	8.4	8.7	5.7

Table 3.1. *Foreign sector employment as share of total (percent) (source: Annual Business Survey of Economic Impact 2021; Ministry of Economy, Trade and Industry (METI) Survey of Trends in Business Activities of Foreign Affiliates; General Statistics Office (GSO) database)*

The importance of FDI for exports for Ireland and Vietnam, two countries that sought to attract FDI in order to increase exports, can be seen in Table 3.2.

Year	2009	2010	2011	2012	2013	2014	2015	2016	2017	2018	2019	Mean
Ireland	92.1	91.4	90.7	90.8	90.4	90.2	90.6	91.0	91.1	91.7	92.2	91.2
Japan	9.4	8.6	5.8	7.0	7.7	6.8	7.2	6.4	8.0	7.2	5.1	7.3
Vietnam	53.2	54.2	56.9	63.1	66.8	67.4	70.6	71.5	72.0	71.4	70.1	63.8

Table 3.2. *Foreign sector exports as share of total (percent) (source: Annual Business Survey of Economic Impact 2021; Ministry of Economy, Trade and Industry (METI) Survey of Trends in Business Activities of Foreign Affiliates; General Statistics Office (GSO) database)*

Ireland is one of the most globalized countries in the world (CSO 2020). Employment in foreign controlled affiliates averages around 54% over 2009–2019. This is the most reliable indicator of foreign MNE activity in the Irish economy. Foreign-owned firms account for a large share of exports but the importance of intra-group trade means that these figures may be inflated. We will see below that the Irish FDI figures may also be inflated, particularly due to pass-through investment and corporate inversion.

Both Ireland and Japan are developed economies but with different experiences with FDI. Vietnam is a developing country where FDI inflows have been a major force in the process of economic transformation. Ireland first sought inward FDI in the 1950s to boost jobs and exports. Japan, on the other hand, is among the largest outward direct investors globally, but has recently also begun to actively seek inward investment.

In 1986, Vietnam launched the Doi Moi (Renovation) reform process to transform the economy to a market-oriented model, following BOP crises. The reforms gradually aimed to reduce the dominance of the public sector in the economy and allow for private investment including foreign investment (OECD 2018). In 1987, *The Foreign Investment Law* intended to attract FDI primarily because of the need to expand exports, as Vietnam was experiencing trade deficits (Perkins and Vu 2008). Now known as *The Investment Law,* (which applies to both foreign and domestic investors), it has undergone several revisions since 1990. At the same time, Vietnam also actively engaged in global economic integration, participating in international agencies such as ASEAN, the World Trade

Organization and making bilateral free trade agreements with the US and other Asian countries such as Japan, Korea. Ireland's switch to outward-looking economic policies in the late 1950s, also followed BOP crises.

Japan is the largest economy of our group and a substantial outward direct investor. Dicken (1988) shows that a wide range of Japanese manufacturing firms relocated offshore after 1985 in response to higher costs in Japan and opportunities available in other markets. Hoshi and Kiyota (2019) show that in 2015 Japan had the lowest inward investment position in the OECD, at 4.2% of its GDP, compared to the OECD average of 50.4%. Historically, Japan discouraged inward FDI as part of its strategy for developing domestic industries (Mason 1992; Suginohara 2008). Although the restrictions were largely removed in the 1970s and 1980s, other structural impediments remained (Lawrence 1993). However, the attraction of inward FDI has been considered as a key pillar of the *Japan Revitalisation Strategy* published in 2013 (Prime Minister's Office 2013). Prior to the 1950s, Ireland pursued a policy of import-substitution and had the *Control of Manufactures Acts* in place, which required majority Irish ownership of industry. These were only repealed in 1964 (Barry and O'Mahony 2017).

Japan's *New Growth Strategy,* first published in 2013 and revised in 2016, aims to revitalize the economy to increase the growth rate using three action plans: industry revitalisation plan, strategic market creation plan, and strategy of global outreach (Prime Minister's Office 2013, 2016). Among them, the policy to promote inward FDI is the main policy of the third action plan. Similar to Ireland's decision to dramatically shift policy in the late 1950s, and Vietnam's in the 1980s, Japan's policymakers believe that only inward FDI can bring about the necessary economic restructuring required in the Japanese economy to revive growth. Hoshi and Kiyota (2019) find that the Abenomics policy has not been successful since the level of inward FDI still remained low, but their study ends in 2015. Unlike Ireland and Vietnam, Japan faces the challenge of rapid population aging and labor shortages. The share of the population over age 65 rose from 26% of the working-age population in 2000 to 50% in 2017 (OECD 2019). Japan remains among the largest outward direct investors globally, with outward investment dwarfing inward investment. As shown in Figure 3.2, outward stocks were seven times larger than inward stocks on average over the period 2014–2020.

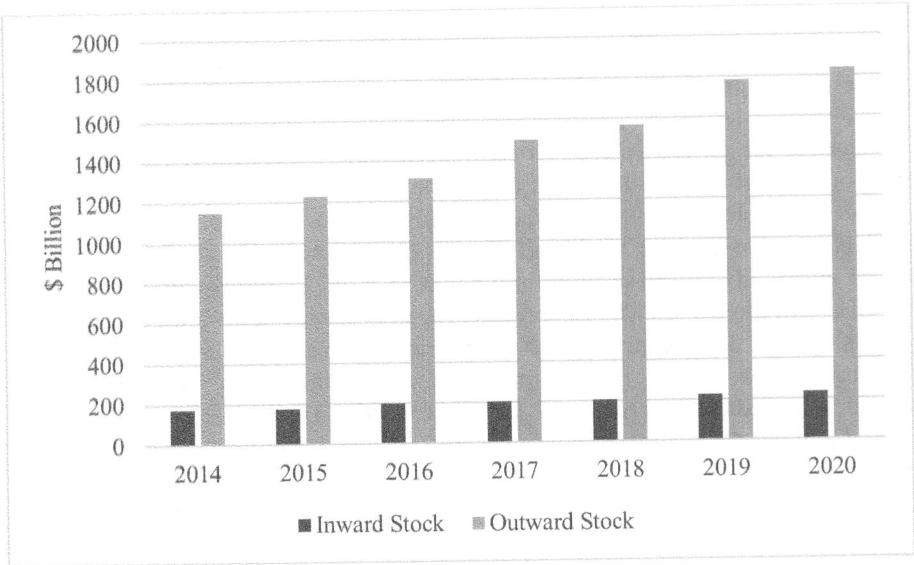

Figure 3.2. *Japan: stocks (directional principle) (source: author's own calculations based on data from the OECD International Direct Investment Database)*

According to UNCTAD (2021), in 2020, the world's largest recipient of FDI flows was the US, followed by China, Hong Kong, Singapore, India and Luxembourg. Ireland, Vietnam, and Japan were among the top 20 recipients. In the same year, the world's largest outward direct investor was China, followed by Luxembourg and Japan. In 2018 and 2019, Japan was the world's largest outward direct investor with outflows of $143 billion and $227 billion, respectively, falling to $116 billion in 2020 (UNCTAD 2019, 2021).

3.4. Data availability and comprehensiveness

Our two advanced economies, Ireland and Japan, have a greater level of availability of FDI data. Advanced economies also tend to produce more metadata to explain the methodologies employed. This is not the case for Vietnam, where the State Bank of Vietnam (SBV), responsible for the BOP, does not publish its methodology. The methodology for the BOP can be accessed from the General Statistics Office (GSO). However, MNE activity data is lacking for all three economies, particularly data that is internationally comparable.

In Vietnam, administrative data forms the backbone of the reported FDI data. This is common in developing countries where there is an underdeveloped statistical system (Fujita 2008). Both Barry and O'Mahony (2005) and Fujita (2008) show that administrative data, which tends to be based on planned investment, can differ substantially from the corresponding BOP data.

There are essentially two sets of FDI statistics compiled domestically in Vietnam. The first is the administrative data on FDI projects and the second is the BOP data. These two datasets differ in terms of coverage, definitions and classifications, and are not completely in line with international standards (OECD 2018). The Vietnamese administrative data, collected by the Ministry of Planning and Investment (MPI) and by GSO cover "registered capital" (effectively approvals or planned investment) and "implemented capital" (actual investment). *The Investment Law* in Vietnam does not distinguish FDI as such. Instead, there are two concepts related to foreign investment: foreign investors and foreign-invested economic organizations. The "registered capital" data includes breakdowns by partner country and by industry, but such breakdowns are not available for "implemented capital" and this disaggregated data is not reported by most international agencies, with the exception of the ASEAN Secretariat (IMF 2019a; UNCTAD 2019).

The second dataset is the BOP data produced by SBV and reported to IMF, UNCTAD and the ASEAN Secretariat. These generally follow the BPM6 framework, but the 10 percent rule is not always met and RIE data are not available (OECD 2018; IMF 2019a). In producing the FDI data for the BOP, SBV adjusts the MPI data to match the BPM6 concepts (OECD 2018). The SBV supplements with data from the banking system and the tax authorities.

The table below shows the difference between the MPI administrative data and the BOP data. The MPI data, which tends to be used in OECD reports, are the levels of investment by both foreign organisations and unaffiliated foreign investors.

Year	2009	2010	2011	2012	2013	2014	2015	2016	2017	2018	2019	2020
IMF	7.6	8.0	7.4	8.4	8.9	9.2	11.8	12.6	14.1	15.5	16.1	15.8
MPI	10.0	11.0	11.0	10.0	11.5	12.5	14.5	15.8	17.5	19.1	20.4	20.0

Table 3.3. *Vietnam: difference between FDI project data and balance of payments data (US $ Billion) (source: MPI, IMF databases)*

The FDI position statistics for Vietnam are underdeveloped. The stock data are available from national sources, but these refer to "registered" rather than "implemented" capital only and the periodicity is slightly different between the two sources. Vietnamese data is therefore not available in the *International Investment Position* statistics produced by the IMF (IMF 2019b). UNCTAD however produces stock data by accumulating flows. This estimation approach was more popular in the past when the collection of stock data was less comprehensive for many countries, but stock data produced in this way ignores valuation and depreciation changes. Furthermore, as Fujita (2008) points out, any deficiencies in earlier data are compounded later when flows are accumulated to calculate stocks.

Vietnamese data is expected to improve over time. OECD (2018) recommends that Vietnam should consider presenting statistics according to the directional principle, instead of using only an asset/liability presentation, and present detailed breakdowns by partner country and by industry, as well as providing stock data.

The Vietnamese BOP figures do not include RIE as these are not available (OECD 2018; IMF 2019a). Consequently, the OECD (2018) believe that the data for Vietnam are considerably understated. RIE can be impacted by changes in taxation policies. This has been important for US MNEs in Ireland, where they held substantial amounts of RIE, because of US tax policy, which were largely repatriated in 2018 due to US policy changes.

3.5. Effects of reverse investment

Although the common perception of FDI is a parent company investing in a subsidiary, affiliates also invest in the parent company (reverse investment). The precursor of BPM6 recommended the "directional principle" to record this as a disinvestment by the parent rather than as an outward investment from the affiliate to the parent, unless the affiliate owns more than 10% of its parent, in which case a separate direct investment (DI) relationship would exist (O'Mahony and Barry 2019). For example, if a Japanese parent invests $20 million in a Vietnamese subsidiary, an investment from the Vietnamese subsidiary to the Japanese parent of $4 million is deducted from the initial investment resulting in a "net inflow" from Japan to Vietnam of $16 million and not as an outward investment from Vietnam to Japan. BPM6 recommends using the asset/liability approach, which records whether the investment relates to an asset or a liability, although supplementary data are presented using the directional principle (IMF 2009). OECD also reports data using both approaches. As the directional method nets out reverse investment, it is more suited to situations where there is a large amount of pass-through investment, as is the case in the Irish economy (CSO 2017).

The asset/liability approach, measures assets (liabilities) as total assets (liabilities) held by home resident parent companies and affiliates. This approach is useful to see how DI affects holdings of assets and liabilities and allows an evaluation of an economy's exposure to crises. It aligns with other macroeconomic statistics but gives no indication of the direction of the DI relationship (CSO 2017). Both methods arrive at the same net figure (inflows minus outflows), but the data are presented differently and differences in measuring FDI by each approach is likely to be due to the extent of reverse investment (CSO 2017). Blanchard and Acalin (2016) argue that the directional approach is superior to the asset/liability approach, although they do not find large differences between the approaches for the countries in their study, which are all emerging economies. In Figure 3.3, we show the OECD inward flow data, recorded by both methods, for Ireland and Japan. For both countries, the asset/liability approach generally records higher values. We find some substantial differences for Japanese flows in some years, particularly in more recent years with an average difference of $17 billion annually for the 2012–2020, but lower for 2012–2018 at $10 billion. Given Japan's role as one of the major global outward investors, this may be due to reverse investment into Japanese parents by subsidiaries abroad. For Ireland, the asset/liability approach recorded inward flows an average of $10 billion higher, but again this is impacted by the most recent years with the average over 2012–2018 of $38 billion. This can be explained by large-scale reverse investment by Irish subsidiaries in their parent companies, for tax planning reasons (CSO 2017). This is clearly not so substantial in the Japanese case, where inward investment is not as significant in the economy. Furthermore, as reverse investment is often for tax planning reasons, it is likely to be smaller for Japanese MNEs, as they are less engaged in the use of FDI for tax avoidance compared with US MNEs (Ohno and Suzuki 2020).

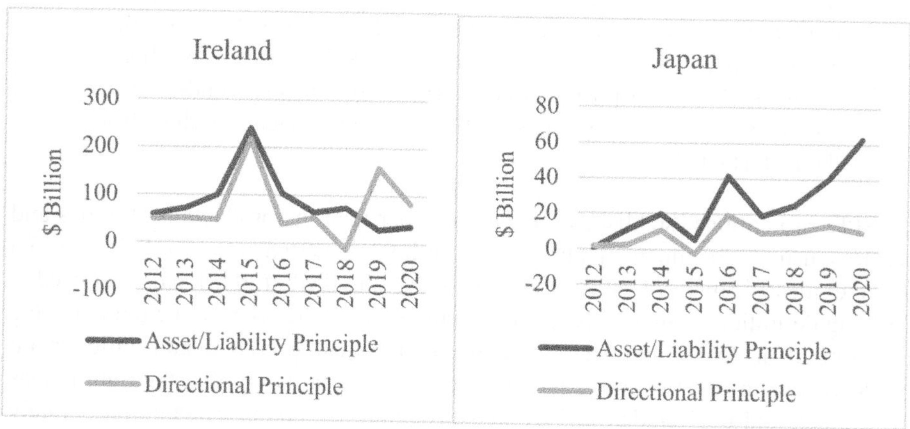

Figure 3.3. *Inward flows 2012–2020: comparison of different recording approaches (source: OECD International Direct Investment Statistics Database)*

3.6. Effects of pass-through investment and corporate inversion

Pass-through or transit investment, where DI from the parent in country X passes through country Y on its way to a third country Z (conduit investment), or DI flows from country X to an affiliate in country Y and back again (round-tripping), has increased in recent decades. In both cases, there are no "real" economy implications for country Y. Corporate inversion refers to the relocation of head offices abroad, with the original parent becoming a legal subsidiary. An US MNE, for example, may have its corporate headquarters in Bermuda or Ireland (for further discussion see Desai (2009)). Both phenomena result from the efficient operation of MNE overseas activities, often impacted by tax considerations.

As CSO (2020) argues, pass-through investment inflates both inward and outward FDI data in highly globalized economies. It overstates the amount of "real" investment in economies and distorts the geographical and sectoral sources and destinations of FDI, as "immediate" sources and destinations of investments are more commonly reported rather than the "ultimate" sources and destinations. Most conduit and round-tripped investment passes through special purpose entities (SPEs) in MNE ownership chains.

The IMF Task Force on SPEs states that

> In the upsurge of multifaceted and flexible multinational enterprise (MNE) structures, which have become increasingly global by seeking to obtain benefits from different legal and tax regimes, there has been a widespread use of SPEs. As a result, SPE-related cross-border financial flows and positions have grown significantly, underscoring the need for macroeconomic statistics to untangle their activities from the rest. (IMF 2018)

SPEs are entities established for reasons other than the production of goods and services, usually for financing purposes or for holding certain assets or liabilities. To aid the identification of SPEs internationally, the IMF (2018) has produced a working definition of an SPE based on a number of characteristics, including having no more than five employees, little or no physical presence and little or no production in the host country. The international standards say that the transactions of SPEs should be included in FDI statistics and most countries cannot separately identify them. However, some countries consider that due to its transit nature and lack of real economic effects this investment should not be included as FDI. The IMF (2018) lists Ireland among SPE hosting economies. Ireland separates out the transactions of SPEs from others, although the aggregates reported to international agencies do include them.[1] Using the IMF definition, SPE transactions accounted for just 6% of inward flows to Ireland in 2019. IMF (2018) also points out that a number of European countries state that pass-through FDI does not exclusively use SPEs, but also uses "regular enterprises". It is estimated that very little of Irish inward FDI goes through pure SPEs because as, CSO (2020) argue, larger MNEs in Ireland, which partially act as conduits, generally have large employment, so are outside the IMF's working definition of SPEs. Casella (2019) suggests that the share of pass-through investment in Ireland is 65%. However, as Table 3.4 shows, CSO (2020) estimates are substantially lower, at 31% in 2019, but much larger than the share of inward FDI passing through SPEs of 6% (CSO 2021).

Year	Ireland: Pass-Through as Share of Inward FDI (%)
2013	25
2014	19
2015	32
2016	33
2017	34
2018	35
2019	31

Table 3.4. *Pass-through as share of inward FDI (%) (source: CSO 2020)*

Many authors consider that countries having high levels of both inward and outward DI results from pass-through investment. Blanchard and Acalin (2016) calculate correlations between inflows and outflows for a range of emerging economies, including Vietnam. They find Vietnam's correlation to be approximately 0.4 over 1990–2015.

In Table 3.5, we take a selection of European and Asian economies to find the correlation between inflows and outflows for 2005–2020. These countries are a combination of those in Blanchard and Acalin (2016) and Mintz and Weichenrieder (2010), to which we add a selection of economies that account for large shares of global FDI, in part due to their size, France, Germany, United Kingdom, Japan and the United States. For brevity, Table 3.5 does not show our full set of correlations. As expected, conduit countries, such as Ireland, the Netherlands and Singapore, have high correlations, but so do many other advanced and emerging economies.

1 Dublin's International Financial Services Centre (IFSC) is home to many financial firms. The term IFSC is no longer lmited to companies physically located in the IFSC itself.

Country	2005–2020	Country	2005–2020
Europe: Advanced		**Asia: Emerging**	
France	0.50	China	0.89
Germany	0.67	Hong Kong, China	0.56
Ireland	0.69	Korea, Republic of (S Korea)	0.22
Netherlands	0.80	Indonesia	0.55
United Kingdom	0.52	Malaysia	0.52
Europe: Emerging		Singapore	0.60
Croatia	0.59	Vietnam	0.15
Hungary	0.97	India	0.27
Poland	0.47	**Other Advanced**	
Romania	0.49	Japan	0.38
		United States	0.19

Table 3.5. *The correlation between the size of inflows and outflows of a selection of European and Asian countries (source: author's own calculations based on data from UNCTAD World Investment Reports (2019, 2021))*

Although OECD (4th benchmark definition) recommended the production of data using ultimate sources and destinations, which show the Ultimate Controlling Parent (UCP) or beneficial owner, most countries only report immediate sources and destinations of investment. Increasingly, the immediate and ultimate geographical locations differ, due to pass-through investment and corporate inversion. From a BOP point of view, where capital flows are measured, this makes sense, but when we are interested in the "real" economic impact of the investment, we need to know the ultimate sources and destinations (i.e. where value is created).

In 2019 for Ireland, the top three immediate investor positions were held by the US, Bermuda and the Netherlands. The US was also by far the largest ultimate investor, but its position more than trebles as an ultimate investor (from \$248.6 billion to \$821.8 billion). Therefore, more than half of US investment into Ireland is through conduits located elsewhere – Bermuda and Netherlands being the more important locations in 2019, but Luxembourg has acted as an important conduit country in other years. Bermuda's ultimate investment was less than one-fifth of its immediate investment position (from \$197.2 billion to \$38.2 billion) and the investment from the Netherlands falls to less than one-tenth (from \$100.7 billion to

€6.6 billion) (CSO 2021). Ireland is the among the largest ultimate investors in itself – this may seem counter-intuitive but is due to corporate inversion, where MNEs have relocated their head offices to Ireland in response to tax changes in the US and the UK.

Figure 3.4 shows the more important immediate FDI sources and destinations for Japan (countries with $40 billion or more either inward or outward stock in at least one of the years over 2014–2020). Note the relative importance of small conduit countries, such as the Netherlands, the Cayman Islands and Singapore, despite tax planning being less important for Japanese MNEs compared with US MNEs (Ohno and Suzuki 2020).

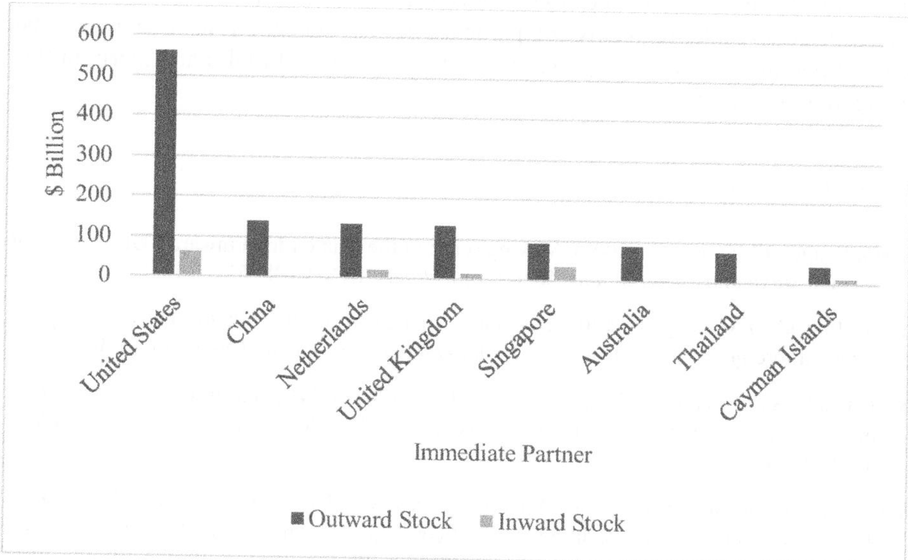

Figure 3.4. *Japan: main partners until the end of 2020 ($ Million) (source: OECD International Direct Investment Database)*

As already stated, Vietnam does not report stock data to the international agencies, but GSO data shows that its main immediate inward investors are South Korea, Japan and Singapore (with positions in 2020 of $70.6 billion, $60.3 billion and $56.6 billion, respectively). Data for ultimate sources is not available.

3.7. Concluding remarks

Our aim was to review the experiences of our three countries, Ireland, Japan and Vietnam, in the evolving FDI global landscape to ascertain how changes that impact

FDI and its relationship to the "real" economy are revealed in their FDI statistics. However, data was lacking in a number of areas, particularly for Vietnam. There was the greatest level of detail for Ireland, as the CSO has, in recent years, produced a number of studies on the effects of pass-through investment and corporate inversion on Irish macroeconomic statistics.

From our review, it is evident that the FDI data is not fully standardized and does not measure the same thing across different countries. RIE, for example, are not included in the Vietnamese data. Pass-through investment has important effects on the Irish data, but also impacts the Japanese data. We were not able to assess the impact for Vietnam. There are international efforts, most particularly by the IMF and OECD, to improve the FDI statistics, but the further development of standardized and internationally comparable activity data, still in its infancy, will be more important when assessing the real economy impact of FDI, particularly in this changing FDI landscape.

3.8. References

Barry, F. and O'Mahony, C. (2005). Making sense of the data on Irish inward FDI. *Journal of the Statistical and Social Inquiry Society of Ireland*, XXXIV, 28–57.

Barry, F. and O'Mahony, C. (2017). Regime change in 1950s Ireland: The new export-oriented foreign investment strategy. *Irish Economic and Social History*, 44(1), 46–65.

Beugelsdijk, S., Hennart, J., Slangen A., Smeets, R. (2010). Why and how FDI stocks are a biased measure of MNE affiliate activity. *Journal of International Business Studies*, 41(9), 1444–1459.

Blanchard, O. and Acalin, J. (2016). What does measured FDI actually measure? Policy brief 16–17, Peterson Institute for International Economics [Online]. Available at: https://piie.com/publications/pb/pb16-2.pdf [Accessed 27 May 2021].

Buckley, P.J. (2009). The impact of the global factory on economic development. *Journal of World Business*, 44(2), 131–143.

Casella, B. (2019). Looking through conduit FDI in search of ultimate investors – A probabilistic approach. *Transnational Corporations*, 26(1), 109–146.

CSO (2017). Two methods of measuring foreign direct investment [Online]. Available at: https://www.cso.ie/en/releasesandpublications/in/mfdi/twomethodsofmeasuringforeigndirectinvestment/ [Accessed 27 May 2021].

CSO (2020). Foreign direct investment in Ireland 2018 [Online]. Available at: https://www.cso.ie/en/releasesandpublications/ep/p-fdi/foreigndirectinvestmentinireland2018/ [Accessed 27 May 2021].

CSO (2021). Foreign direct investment in Ireland 2019 [Online]. Available at: https://www.cso.ie/en/releasesandpublications/ep/p-fdi/foreigndirectinvestmentinireland2019/ [Accessed 15 April 2022].

Desai, M. (2009). The decentering of the global firm. *World Economy*, 32(9), 1271–1290.

Dicken, P. (1988). The changing geography of Japanese foreign direct investment in manufacturing industry: A global perspective. *Environment and Planning A*, 20(5), 633–653.

Fujita, M. (2008). A critical assessment of FDI data and policy implications. *Transnational Corporations,* 17(2), 107–123.

General Statistics Office (GSO) (2019). Balance of payments methodology [Online]. Available at: https://www.gso.gov.vn/du-lieu-dac-ta/2019/12/htcttkqg-can-can-thanh-toan-quoc-te/ [Accessed 27 May 2021].

Hoshi, T. and Kiyota, K. (2019). Potential for inward foreign direct investment in Japan. *Journal of the Japanese and International Economies*, 52, 32–52.

IMF (2009). *Balance of Payments and International Direct Investment Position Manual*, 6th edition. IMF, Washington, DC

IMF (2018). Final report of the Task Force on Special Purpose Entities. IMF Committee on the Balance of Payments Statistics. IMF, Washington DC.

IMF (2019a). Balance of payments metadata responses by country – Vietnam [Online]. Available at: http://data.imf.org/regular.aspx?key=62755686 [Accessed 27 May 2021].

IMF (2019b). International investment position metadata responses by Vietnam [Online]. Available at: http://data.imf.org.elib.tcd.ie/regular.aspx?key=62805744 [Accessed 27 May 2021].

Lawrence, R.Z. (1993). Japan's different trade regime: An analysis with particular reference to Keiretsu. *Journal of Economic Perspectives*, 7(3), 3–19.

Lipsey, R. (2007). Defining and measuring the location of FDI output. NBER Working Paper 12996.

Lipsey, R. (2010). Measuring the location of production in a world of intangible productive assets, FDI, and intrafirm trade. *Review of Income and Wealth*, 56, S99–S110.

Mason, M. (1992). *American Multinationals and Japan: The Political Economy of Japanese Capital Controls, 1899–1980.* Harvard University Press, Cambridge, MA.

Mintz, J. and Weichenrieder, A.J. (2010). *The Indirect Side of Direct Investment.* MIT Press, Cambridge, MA.

OECD (2008). *Benchmark Definition of Foreign Direct Investment*, 4th edition. OECD Publishing, Paris.

OECD (2011). Japan's new growth strategy to create demand and jobs. Working paper [Online]. Available at: https://read.oecd-ilibrary.org/economics/japan-s-new-growth-strategy-to-create-demand-and-jobs_5kg58z5z007b-en#page2 [Accessed 27 May 2021].

OECD (2018). *OECD Investment Policy Reviews: Viet Nam 2018*. OECD Publishing, Paris.

OECD (2019). *Economic Surveys: Japan 2019.* OECD Publishing, Paris [Online]. Available at: https://www.oecd.org/economy/surveys/Japan-2019-OECD-economic-survey-overview.pdf [Accessed 27 May 2021].

Ohno, S. and Suzuki, Y. (2020). Deciding factors in the return on foreign direct investment: A comparison between Japan and the United States. *Policy Research Institute, Ministry of Finance, Japan, Public Policy Review,* 16(2).

O'Mahony, C. and Barry, F. (2019). Pitfalls in the use of foreign direct investment statistics. *World Economy*, 42(10), 2835–2853.

Perkins, D. and Vu, T.T.A. (2008). Vietnam's industrial policy: Designing policies for sustainable development. Policy Dialogue Paper Number 1, Harvard Kennedy School.

Prime Minister's Office (2013). Japan Revitalization Strategy – Japan is Back [Online]. Available at: https://www.kantei.go.jp/jp/singi/keizaisaisei/pdf/en-saikou-jpn-hon.pdf [Accessed 15 April 2022].

Prime Minister's Office (2016). Japan Revitalization Strategy [Online]. Available at: https://www.kantei.go.jp/jp/singi/keizaisaisei/pdf/hombun1_160602_en.pdf [Accessed 15 April 2022].

Suginohara, M. (2008). The politics of economic nationalism in Japan: Backlash against inward foreign direct investment? *Asian Survey*, 48(5), 839–859.

UNCTAD (2019). World Investment Report: Special economic zones. UNCTAD, New York.

UNCTAD (2021). World Investment Report: Investing in sustainable recovery. UNCTAD, New York.

4

Investigating the Influencing Factors Revealing a Trade Potential for EU–China Agricultural Products: A Trade Gravity Model Approach

This chapter has adopted the trade gravity model to investigate the impact of GDP, geographical distance, difference GDP per capita, institutional distance, WTO membership, and landlocking on EU–China agricultural trade flows. This is followed by a trade potential analysis at an EU member country's level. The study has found that instead of geographical distance, institutional distance has more influence on EU–China agricultural trade flows. Surprisingly, geographical distance can even have a positive impact on EU–China agricultural trade flows in the beverages and tobacco product group (SITC1). Moreover, many of the EU member countries had unexplored agricultural trade potential vis-à-vis China in 2016.

4.1. Introduction

The agricultural sector is considered as a strategic sector in both the EU and China. In the EU, the agricultural sector has been a key sector for its economic integration and represents 6% of GDP in 2016. It also provides about 44 million jobs and more than 500 million European consumers rely on this sector (EC 2017). In China, it matters not only for the well-being of the 1.4 billion Chinese people, but also for the Chinese Central Government's stability and legitimacy.

Since the 1960s, the agricultural sectors have undergone significant changes in both China and the EU. The Chinese reforms, the opening-up policy in 1979 and the

Chapter written by Junshi LI and Bernadette ANDREOSSO-O'CALLAGHAN.

accession of China to the World Trade Organisation (WTO) in late 2001 have made Chinese agricultural and trade policies go through dramatic changes. As a result, China's international agricultural trade has been decentralized and more market-oriented compared to the centrally-planned regime before and shortly after 1979. The Common Agricultural Policy (CAP) plays an important role in re-organising and administering the EU's agricultural sector and its trade in agricultural and food products. Since its commencement in 1962, a few significant reforms, especially in the 1990s, have been gradually changing CAP from a market-distorting policy with highly protective measures to a more market-orientated policy. These new policy frameworks in both China and the EU have provided a favourable platform for EU–China agricultural trade.

The extra-EU trade in agricultural products has increased both for exports and imports since 2008. In 2018, the EU exported agricultural products worth €172,656 million while it imported €194,402 million agricultural products (Eurostat 2019). After China's accession to the WTO in 2001, China's agricultural products trade has increased significantly. In 2017, the value of China's exports and imports of agricultural products was $75.1 billion and $124.68 billion respectively. The EU–China agricultural trade relations have developed very quickly and are still very promising, with China being the second top destination for EU's exports of agricultural products.

Given the fact that the EU–China agricultural trade relations have developed significantly and this agricultural trade relationship is still very promising, this study has adopted a trade gravity model to investigate the influence of a few important economic influencing factors on the EU–China agricultural trade flows of four different agricultural product groups by using STIC classification (see Appendix), and this is followed by a comparison of the actual trade value and predicted trade value, revealing the trade potential. The trade gravity model has borrowed the physics gravity equation of Isaac Newton. With the help econometrics, the trade gravity model allows the study to come up with empirical results in terms of the relationship between different economic factors (GDP, geographical distance, GDP per capita, institutional distance[1], WTO membership, landlocking). In a further step, this technique also enables trade potential to be made by comparing the actual value to the estimated value.

1 In this study, the institutional distance is represented by the business freedom index and trade freedom index (details can be seen in methodology section).

4.2. Literature review

The literature of this study has been reviewed from two perspectives: one is the theoretical foundation of the trade gravity model and the other is the empirical application of the trade gravity model. The trade gravity model is identified as one of the most widely used empirical research tools of international trade (CEPII 2013). This is mostly because of the theoretical constructions by estimating the trade gravity model with a diversity of explanatory variables and assumptions. Linnemann's (1966) work can be considered as one of the traditional applications of the gravity model. In this work, a partial equilibrium model is used and an additional variable is added in to the model to reflect the trade flow composition. The trade gravity model was customized by Leamer (1974), with income and population as additional independent variables. Anderson (1979) built up a theoretical foundation of the trade gravity model by applying utility functions and the assumption of product differentiation into the gravity model. Anderson (1979) and Anderson and Wincoop (2003) are the two most meaningful works. Anderson (1979) proposed different models based on Armington's assumption, which is that goods are differentiated by country of origin and consumers have different preferences on those differentiated products. In terms of trade costs, only a small amount of goods can arrive at the destination, the rest are damaged in transit. So transport costs do matter for trade flows when exports are measured at the trade term of Cost, Insurance, and Freight (CIF).

Besides the theoretical contribution mentioned above, Bergstrand (1989), Bergstrand (1990) and Deardorff (1998) used monopolistic competition and Constant Elasticity of Substitution (CES), as well as Hecksher-Ohlin's structure of world demand to explain specialization. Deardorff (1998) also proves that the trade gravity model is consistent with the Hechsher-Ohlin trade theory. They believe that identical countries trade in differentiated goods because of the variety of preferences of consumers. This has overcome the shortcomings of Armington's assumption which is that goods are differentiated by location of production. Krugman (1985) justified the gravity model with increasing returns to scale under the framework of product differentiation. The theoretical foundation of the trade gravity model provides the explanatory power of the results of the empirical application of the trade gravity model.

Besides the literature on the theoretical foundation of the gravity model in international trade, large amounts of empirical studies using the gravity model exist. A number of existing studies demonstrate clear and meaningful results in favour of their deployment with resulting important policy implications. The current literature demonstrates two general aspects: (i) using the trade gravity model to quantify the impact of economic factors on trade flows and (ii) applying the gravity model to predict the trade potential with trading partners. However, some of the following literature deals with both aspects at the same time in their studies. Therefore, the present study includes both aspects, which will be included in paragraph (i) below.

(i) Quantifying the impact of economic factors on trade flows. In the work of Khan *et al.* (2013), cultural similarities were added into the gravity model as a dummy variable, in line with the independent variables such as GDP, GDP per capita, and distance to detect the results that GDP and GDP per capita have positive relationships with Pakistan's bilateral trade, while distance and cultural similarities have negative relationships with Pakistan's bilateral trade. Rodriguez *et al.* (2017) estimated the determinants of intra-industry trade between Ecuador, the USA, Mexico, Panama, Venezuela, Peru, Brazil and Colombia from 2002 to 2014 using the trade gravity model: they found that economies of scale, the variety of differentiated products, and a larger market size have positive relationships with trade; in contrast, countries' income, transportation costs and different market sizes show negative relationships with intra-industry trade. Xie (2010) analysed the factors that affect China-Eastern Europe agricultural trade and concluded that scale economies and population size have positive effects on agricultural trade for both China and Eastern Europe, whereas the factors with negative effects were geographical distance and the EU enlargement. Moreover, this work brought Linder's demand similarity theory to agricultural trade between China and Eastern Europe. Wang (2016) also used the gravity model to analyse the influencing factors on China and the EU's bilateral trade with GDP, exchange rates, financial revenues and expenditure as independent variables. Tripathi and Leitao (2013) applied a static and dynamic panel data analysis by using the trade gravity model from 1998 to 2012, with 20 trading partners of India; they found that political globalization, cultural proximity, economic size, and having a common border have a positive impact on bilateral trade. Zhao and Lin (2008) undertook a quantitative analysis on the agricultural trade flows between China and ASEAN by using the trade gravity model to reveal the magnitude of effect factors on this trade, and then followed by assessing the trade potential. In the area of aquatic products, Shao and Hu (2013) used the trade gravity model and ascertained that economic size, differences of GDP per capita, and the FTA have positively affected aquatic products trade between China and ASEAN countries, while the geographical distance has a weak negative influence on this trade. Meanwhile, the size of the population and China's total production of aquatic products have no significant impact on the trade as expected. This study also looks at the revealed trade potential for policy implications.

(ii) Predicting the trade potential. By using the trade gravity model, Guo *et al.* (2017) found that China's oil import partner countries are changing under the background of China's "One Belt One Road" strategy. Khan *et al.* (2013) also compared the predicted value through the gravity model to the actual value of trade for the year of 2010; this work also found that Japan, Turkey, Malaysia, India and Iran have greater unseen trade potential with Pakistan. Shen (2016) used the trade

gravity model to assess the trade potential of three sets of trade relationships: China-Russia, China-Mongolia, and Russia-Mongolia. The results showed a different degree of trade potential between the three sets of trade relationships. Buongiorno (2016) used the trade gravity model through ordinary least squares, fixed-effects and random-effects, to predict the growth rate of trade flows of forest products from 2015 to 2020 based on exogenous GDP projections by the International Monetary Fund. Johnston *et al.* (2014) used a gravity model to explore the potential dynamics for the promotion of China's exports to Africa. Majali and Adayleh (2018) applied the gravity model into trade in the services sector in some Middle East and North African countries. The trade between Mercosur and EU has been assessed by Zarzoso and Lehmann (2003) by applying the trade gravity model; by using the fixed effect model they found a better estimation of the gravity model than by using the random effects model. What is worth noticing is that in this study, they added more independent variables, namely, infrastructure, income differences and exchange rates into the gravity model to forecast the trade potential between Mercosur and the EU. Renjini *et al.* (2017) assessed the agricultural trade potential between India and ASEAN countries and the results showed that the FTA has a significant positive influence on bilateral trade, while border trade has no significance on bilateral trade. More specifically, the results of the trade potential show that India has no more trade potential with Cambodia, Indonesia, Malaysia, Myanmar and Vietnam, while there is an opportunity to have more trade with Brunei, Lao, Philippines, Singapore and Thailand.

As can be seen from the literature reviewed above, empirical research using the trade gravity model is quite popular. However, a gap still emerges from the current literature, especially when considering the perspective of agricultural products bilateral trade between the EU and China. According to the reviewed literature, there are few studies on EU and China trade in terms of agricultural products. However, there are some out of date studies relating to agricultural trade between the EU and China, but they neither cover all of the EU member countries nor use agricultural products at a disaggregated level (see Guo *et al.* (2017), Xie (2010) and Renjini *et al.* (2017)). A notable exception is Buonogiorno's (2016) study, in which forest products are analysed at a disaggregate level with three different categories (HS44, HS47, and HS 48). Studies have mostly focused on China with ASEAN countries or Eastern European countries, rather than on China with the EU as a whole.

This paper will therefore be focused on finding out the degree of the relationship between different selected economic factors and the agricultural trade flows between the EU and China, given the clear research gap as highlighted above, as well as measuring the trade potential; it will also further develop Buongiorno's idea (2016) of using a more disaggregated level in line with the SITC classification to cover as many agricultural products as possible as a research objective.

4.3. Methodology

The trade gravity model used in this study has been established from the very basic gravity equation [4.1] to an augmented trade gravity equation with more independent variables in a form of an econometrics model. The equation [4.1] is as follows:

$$T_{ij} = \beta_0 \frac{GDP_i^{\beta_1} GDP_j^{\beta_2}}{D_{ij}^{\beta_3}} \varepsilon_{ij}. \qquad [4.1]$$

where,

T_{ij} = trade flow between the EU (i) and China (j);

GDP_i = Gross Domestic Production of the EU;

GDP_j = Gross Domestic Production of China;

D_{ij} = the geographical distance between the EU and China;

β_0 = intercept or constant;

$\beta_1, \beta_2, \beta_3$ = the estimated parameters to be estimated;

ε_{ij} = error terms.

The transformation of [4.1] to an econometrics model is as follows:

$$\log(Tradeflow_{ij}) = \beta_0 + \beta_1 \log(GDP_i) + \beta_2 \log(GDP_j) + \beta_3 \log(D_{ij}) + \varepsilon_{ij}. \qquad [4.2]$$

Equation [4.2] is the final basic econometric model for the regression analysis to estimate the parameters from both the sign (+ or -) and magnitude (the degree) perspectives. The reason for transforming [4.2] into a logarithm is because the log form can make nonlinear relationships for the purpose of regression econometric analysis. More explanatory variables (independent variables) are added into equation [4.2] and the justification of the selected independent variable for this study is as follows:

GDP of the EU and China (GDP_{EU}, GDP_{China}). The gross domestic production (GDP) is a proxy for economic size. A larger GDP implies a bigger economic size and vice versa. Countries that have a large GDP indicate that there is a big demand for importing goods and a high ability to produce goods for exporting. Countries with big economic sizes will increase bilateral trade flows between each other. As two big economies in the world with GDPs getting closer, more trade activities including agricultural products trade are bound to happen, which is reflected by the increasing trade flows between the two regions.

The expectation is that GDP_{EU} and GDP_{China} would both have a positive relationship with agricultural product trade. More specifically, agricultural product trade flows increase with the increase in the GDP of the EU and China.

The geographical distance between EU and China (Distance). The variable of geographical distance between two countries can be a proxy for trade costs and mostly the costs of transportation (Irshad *et al.* 2018). Longer distances between two trade partners means that there will be more spent on fuel for long-distance transportation, as well as the loss of goods or damaged goods during transportation. That is to say, the trade volume will decrease as the geographical distance gets longer between two trading partners. In this case the geographic distance is therefore expected to have a negative relationship with trade flows. However, with the development of technical innovation in international transportation systems following the trend of globalization, costs and risks due to geographical distance have been decreasing (Brei and Goetz 2017). Therefore, the influence of geographical distance is diminishing and may have an insignificant effect on trade flows.

Trade costs which are represented by geographical distance are commonly used in the trade gravity model. However, in this study the geographical distance can also be treated as a proxy for the different resource endowments, which is in line with the Hecscher-Ohlin trade theory. In this case, trade can be increased due to the unique products produced in the two different regions with a long geographical distance, especially in the background of the development of transportation and refrigeration technologies. In this case, the relationship between geographic distance and trade flows is not expected to be negative, which violates the traditional results of the trade gravity model.

The geographical distance in this study is measured as the distance between capital cities of EU member countries and the biggest international port city of China (Shanghai) in kilometres (km). Distance will have either a negative relationship or a positive relationship with trade flows depending on the conditions discussed above.

The absolute value of difference in GDP per capita (Diff). GDP per capita is an important indicator of macro-economic performance. It is useful to make cross-country comparisons in terms of average living standards and economic wellbeing. According to Linder's demand hypothesis, when the demand structures of two countries are similar, these two countries are more likely to trade with one another. Fortunately, GDP per capita can capture the demand structure of the given countries, for example, the EU and China. The smaller absolute value of the difference in GDP per capita indicates that there is a more similar demand structure. Therefore, the trade value increases as the absolute value of the difference in GDP per capita decreases. The expectation of the Diff is that it will have a negative relationship with agricultural products trade between the EU and China.

The business freedom index of both EU and China (BF_{EU}, BF_{China}). With the development of technology and the trend of globalization, there are new types of distance; for example, institutional and cultural distance is replacing the importance of the geographical distance, as mentioned in the "Distance" variable part earlier. It means that geographical distance is not playing an important role in international trade as before. Instead, other types of distance (cultural and institutional) have taken prominence. Some of the existing literature has looked at the notion of institutional distance; for example, the status of the trade agreement in Guo *et al.* (2017) and Renjini *et al.* (2017), trade openness in Majali and Adayleh (2018), and institutional arrangements in Shen (2016) etc.

The business freedom index is therefore chosen to be an independent variable proxied by the institutional distance between the EU and China. The idea of using the economic freedom index stems from Benáček *et al.* (2013). The business freedom index of a given country basically mirrors the efficient operation of businesses in terms of regulatory and infrastructural environments. Therefore, trade flows are expected to grow in line with the business freedom index.

Trade freedom index of EU and China (TF_{EU}, TF_{China}). The index of trade freedom is an opposite way to measure the tariffs and non-tariff barriers in trade activities. The higher the index, the lower the tariffs and the NTBs. Therefore, a high score in the trade freedom index should correspond to a large trade value. Agricultural products in international trade are always facing higher tariffs and non-tariffs barriers than other manufacturing goods. The trade tariffs and non-tariffs barriers can be considered as the biggest obstacle hindering the development of agricultural products trade between the EU and China. It is interesting to see to what extent the trade barriers in the form of tariffs and non-tariffs exactly affect EU–China agricultural products trade.

The equation to obtain the trade freedom index is shown as follows:

$$TF_i = [\left(\frac{Tariff_{max} - Tariff_i}{Tariff_{max} - Tariff_{min}}\right) * 100] - NTB_i. \quad [4.3]$$

where,

i = a specific country (in this study i represents EU or China);

$Tariff_{max}$ = upper bounds tariffs rate in %;

$Tariff_{min}$ = lower bounds tariff rates in %;

$Tariff_i$ = the weighted average tariff rate in % of country i;

NTB_i = the extent of NTBs in country i[2].

Equation [4.3] clearly states that the tariffs and non-tariffs factors are a constituent part of the trade freedom index.

The first intuition with respect to this variable is that the sign of the coefficient should be positive, since the higher the index, the greater the trade value. This is because a higher index implies lower tariffs and NTBs. However, note that equation [4.3] is composed of two parts; one is from the perspective of tariffs, the other is from the perspective of NTBs. When the first part is smaller than the second part and has more of an effect on the given product group, the sign of the estimator can be a negative sign, which implies that lower tariffs can create more trade. When the first part is bigger than the second part and has more effect on the given product group, then it can also be a negative relationship between trade value and trade freedom. Therefore, the hypothesis for the variables here can be either positive or negative depending on different scenarios.

Landlocked and WTO member. Two dummy variables are also used which are landlocked or not and WTO member respectively. The two dummy variables are given binary values (with a value "1" when the country is landlocked, and "0" otherwise); for the variable of WTO membership, "1" is the value when China and EU member countries are members of the WTO, "0" otherwise. The hypothesis of landlocked implies a negative relationship with trade flows, while the hypothesis of WTO membership implies a positive relationship to trade flows.

Consequently, the econometric model used in this study based on the basic equation [4.2] and adding more new explanatory variables is as follows:

$$\log(TradeFlow_{EU/China}) = \beta_0 + \beta_1\log(GDP_{EU}) + \beta_2\log(GDP_{China}) + \beta_3\log(Distance) + \beta_4\log(Diff) + \beta_5\log(BF_{EU}) + \beta_6\log(BF_{China}) + \beta_7\log(TF_{EU}) + \beta_8\log(TF_{China}) + \beta_9 Landlocked + \beta_{10} WTO. \quad [4.4]$$

2 NTBs here have four score categories: 20 (NTBs are used extensively across many goods and services and/or act to effectively impede a significant amount of international trade); 15 (NTBs are widespread across many goods and services and/or act to impede a majority of potential international trade); 10 (NTBs are used to protect certain goods and services and impede some international trade); 5 (NTBs are uncommon, protecting few goods and services, and/or have very limited impact on international trade); 0 (NTBs are not used to limit international trade).

where,

$TradeFlow_{EU/China}$ = Export or Import value between the EU and China from the EU standing point;

GDP_{EU} = gross domestic production of the EU;

GDP_{China} = gross domestic production of China;

Distance = geographical distance between the capital cities of the EU member countries and Shanghai (China's biggest port city);

Diff = square of the absolute value of the difference between GDP per capita of the EU and China;

BF_{EU} = business freedom index of the EU;

BF_{China} = business freedom index of China;

TF_{EU} = trade freedom index of the EU;

TF_{CN} = trade freedom index of China;

Landlocked = "1" when the country is landlocked, "0" otherwise;

WTO member = "1" when China and the EU member country are both in the WTO, "0" otherwise.

The existing literature has shown that the applications of the trade gravity model are mostly at an aggregate level, for example, overall bilateral trade or total agricultural products trade. However, studies are rare when it comes to a more detailed agricultural products trade. Therefore, with the intention of providing comprehensive empirical results on EU–China agricultural products trade relations, the application of the trade gravity model will be applied to trade flows of four different agricultural products groups by using the SITC classification at the 1-digit level after the application for total agricultural products (a sum of the trade flows of four STIC product groups). For each group of agricultural products, an econometric model is performed by using trade flows (the exports value plus the imports value) as the dependent variable. Using the SITC0 group as an example, the analysis proceeds as follows:

SITC0 (food and live animals)

$$\log(\text{Trade flows}) = \beta_0 + \beta_1\log(GDP_{EU}) + \beta_2\log(GDP_{China}) + \beta_3\log(\text{Distance}) + \beta_4\log(\text{Diff}) + \beta_5\log(BF_{EU}) + \beta_6\log(BF_{China}) + \beta_7\log(TF_{EU}) + \beta_8\log(TF_{China}) + \beta_9\text{Landlocked} + \beta_{10}\text{WTO}, \qquad [4.5]$$

where,

Trade flows = value of SITC0 products export to China from EU + value of SITC0 products import from China to the EU;

$TradeFlow_{EU/China}$ = Export or Import value between the EU and China from the EU standing point;

GDP_{EU} = gross domestic production of the EU;

GDP_{China} = gross domestic production of China;

Distance = geographical distance between the capital cities of the EU member countries and Shanghai (China's biggest port city);

Diff = absolute value of the difference between GDP per capita of the EU and China;

BF_{EU} = business freedom index of the EU;

BF_{China} = business freedom index of China;

TF_{EU} = trade freedom index of the EU;

TF_{CN} = trade freedom index of China;

Landlocked = "1" when the country is landlocked, "0" otherwise;

WTO = "1" when the EU member country and China are both the members of WTO, "0" otherwise.

Identical econometric models will be applied to both the total agricultural products trade and trade in product groups SITC1, SITC2 (excluding SITC27 and SITC28), and SITC4.

The pooled ordinary least square model (pooled OLS), least squares dummy variable (LSDV), and feasible generalized least squares (FGLS) are used as different estimators to estimate the coefficients of the independent variables. The LSDV estimator represents the fixed effect model, while the GLS estimator stands for the random effect model. Three tests are conducted after the regression estimation to identify the most appropriate estimation model. The F-test is used to distinguish between the pooled OLS and LSDV; Breusch and Pagan's (1980) Lagrange multiplier test (LM test) is used between pooled OLS and FGLS; and the Hausman test is applied to LSDV and FGLS. All of the results including the later trade potential are obtained by using the software Stata.

The agricultural products under this study are defined by the Standard International Trade Classification, Revision 3, whose short form is "SITC, Rev.3". The agricultural products include SITC0 (food and live animals), SITC1 (beverages and tobacco), SITC2 (crude materials, inedible, except fuels) excluding SITC27 (crude fertilizers, other than those of division 56, and crude minerals excluding coal, petroleum and precious stones) and SITC28 (metalliferous ores and metal scrap), and SITC4 (animal and vegetable oils, fats and waxes). More detailed information on the products can be seen in the Appendix (section 4.6).

The trade gravity model will firstly be applied at an aggregate level, which includes the total four groups of SITC classification mentioned above, and then the model will be applied to each SITC product group respectively. It allows the study to provide results not only at the aggregate level, but also at a disaggregate level. Note that the dependent variable in the model is the sum of exports value and imports value, which is defined as the trade flows. The dataset under analysis is panel data because it is composed of both cross-section data (EU member countries, trade flows, GDP, etc.) and time-series data (years from 1995 to 2016). Using panel data makes it possible to capture the relevant relationships among variables over time. The sources of the data and the unit have been organised in Table 4.1.

Data name and unit	Sources
Trade flow (export value and import value in US$)	UN Comtrade database: https://comtrade.un.org/db/
GDP of China and the EU in US$	World Bank, World Development Indicators, Data Bank: https://data.worldbank.org/indicator
Geographical Distance in km	World Distance Calculator https://distancecalculator.globefeed.com/World_Distance_Calculator.asp
GDP per capita of China and the EU in US$	World Bank, World Development Indicators, Data Bank: https://data.worldbank.org/indicator
Business Freedom Indicators of China and the EU	The Heritage Foundation Database: https://www.heritage.org/index/about
Trade Freedom of China and the EU	The Heritage Foundation Database: https://www.heritage.org/index/about

Table 4.1. *The sources of data used in the trade gravity model (source: author's own organization)*

In terms of the analysis of trade potential, the application of the trade gravity model also allows the prediction of the trade value so as to find out the difference between the actual trade value and the predicted trade value: such difference is therefore called trade potential. Trade potential is expressed by the ratio of actual value divided by predicted value. A ratio less than 1.0 (<1.0) indicates that the actual trade flows are less than the predicted value and therefore shows a trade potential; conversely a ratio greater than 1.0 (>1.0) indicates a bigger actual value than the predicted value and means that there is no trade potential; when the ratio equals 1.0, it means that the actual value is equal to the predicted value and indicates that the trade potential is perfectly used in practical trade activities. This study has used the latest actual trade value in 2016 as the benchmark and analysis of the agricultural trade potential for the EU member countries vis-à-vis China.

4.4. Empirical results

The estimated coefficient results from the three estimators for each independent variable with five different defined dependent variables presented in each of the following tables, respectively (see Table 4.2, Table 4.3, Table 4.4, Table 4.5, and Table 4.6). These results will be analysed at an aggregate level with the total agricultural trade flows as the dependent variable, and at a disaggregate level with the trade flows of SITC0, SITC1, SITC2, and SITC4 as the independent variables, respectively. In order to achieve a better understandable interpretation of the coefficient results, each independent variable corresponds to a sub-heading in this section.

The test results (see Table 4.7) for each of the estimation models suggest that the FGLS estimator is the most appropriate model and the estimated coefficients under this random effect model are therefore the most robust and unbiased results. However, some of the results obtained from the pooled OLS regression model and the results from FGLS are comparable. Therefore, in the following sections, results from the three estimation models will be analysed comprehensively.

4.4.1. *The effects of GDP on EU–China agricultural trade*

According to Table 4.2, the GDP of the EU and the GDP of China both show a positive relationship with the total agricultural products trade flows by using the three estimators. The results are all statistically significant at the 1% level. At a disaggregate level, the same relationships can be seen for food and live animals (SITC0 in Table 4.3), beverages and tobacco (SITC1 in Table 4.4), crude materials (SITC2 in Table 4.5) and animals and vegetable oils (SITC4 in Table 4.6). The only exception is that the coefficient of GDP (EU) with the trade flow of SITC1 as the dependent variable is statistically insignificant as it uses the LSDV estimator.

The results from using the pooled OLS estimator show that when the EU's GDP increases by 1%, the EU's total agricultural products trade flows will go up by 1.13%, holding all other independent variable constant,[3] while according to the LSDV and FGLS estimation, the trade flows will grow by 0.65% and 1.04%, respectively. However, the GDP of China has less influence on this trade flow compared to the effects of the EU's GDP in relation to the total agricultural products

3 Note that for the rest of the interpretation of the estimation, when explaining one variable, the other variables are all held constant.

trade. The results indicate that in response to a 1% growth in Chinese GDP, the total agricultural products trade flows are expected to increase by 0.42% (using the pooled OLS), 0.57% (using LSDV) and 0.48% (using FGLS), respectively.

At a disaggregate agricultural products level, the food and live animals (SITC0) trade flows between the EU and China are expected to increase by 1.06% (using pooled OLS), 0.77% (using LSDV) and 1.01% (using FGLS), respectively in response to a 1% increase of the GDP of the EU, while a 1% growth of China's GDP will lead to the trade flows of the SITC0 product group increasing by 0.30% (pooled OLS), 0.41% (LSDV) and 0.36% (FGLS). For this product group, Chinese economic growth has less effects compared to the EU on the trade flows.

In terms of the trade in the beverages and tobacco product group (SITC1), economic growth in the EU and China has similar degrees of effect on the trade flows. Specifically, a 1% increase in GDP (EU) can cause the trade flows to go up by 1.38% (pooled OLS) and 1.24% (FGLS), but is insignificant in the LSDV model. China's economy growing by 1% will cause the trade flows to increase by 1.21% (pooled OLS), 1.53% (LSDV) and 1.24% (FGLS), respectively.

The trade flows of the crude materials group (SITC2) are projected to grow by 1.23% (using pooled OLS), 0.68% (using LSDV) and 1.12% (using FGLS), respectively when the EU's economy grows by 1%. These trade flows will go up by 0.36%, 0.49% and 0.40% according to the three estimators. The effects of economic growth in China again show less influence on the trade flows of the crude materials product group.

For the last agricultural products group of animal and vegetable oils (SITC4), the trade flows could rise by 1.34%, 1.81% and 1.40%, respectively: this is shown by the three estimators, respectively, in line with a 1% escalation of the EU's GDP. A 1% growth in China's economy will bring up the trade flows by 1.51%, 0.92%, and 1.02% by using the pooled OLS model, LSDV model and FGLS model, respectively. The positive effect of Chinese economic growth is only a little weaker than in the case of the EU growth on the trade flows of the SITC4 product group.

Independent variables	Pooled OLS	LSDV (fixed effect)	FGLS (random effect)
GDP(EU)	1.127*** (0.020)	0.647*** (0.163)	1.038*** (0.071)
GDP(China)	0.424*** (0.064)	0.567*** (0.058)	0.480*** (0.048)
Distance	-0.850*** (0.290)	-	-0.845 (1.108)
Difference of GDP per capita	-0.248*** (0.037)	0.172 (0.113)	-0.075 (0.074)
Business freedom (EU)	1.519*** (0.239)	1.256*** (0.215)	1.265*** (0.211)

Business freedom (China)	1.187** (0.486)	1.236*** (0.357)	1.240*** (0.350)
Trade freedom (EU)	-0.710* (0.392)	-0.751** (0.311)	-0.983*** (0.298)
Trade freedom (China)	0.639*** (0.175)	0.544*** (0.122)	0.584*** (0.122)
WTO membership	-0.060 (0.108)	-0.076 (0.080)	-0.093 (0.078)
Landlocked	-0.484*** (0.068)	-	-0.610** (0.266)
Constant	-23.561*** (3.936)	-25.546*** (3.229)	-22.227** (9.856)
Observations	599	599	599
R-squared	0.907	0.815	-
Number of EU countries	28	28	28
*Standard errors in parentheses; *** $p<0.01$, ** $p<0.05$, * $p<0.1$*			

Table 4.2. *Results of trade gravity model (dependent variable: EU's total agricultural products trade flows with China)*

4.4.2. *The effects of geographical distance on EU–China agricultural trade*

The independent variable of the geographical distance between the EU and China is automatically dropped in the LSDV model, due to the fact that geographical distance is relatively fixed compared to other independent variables. In this case, the results of the geographical distance will only be interpreted under the pooled OLS model and the FGLS model. In general, geographical distance negatively affects the trade flows of total agricultural products between the EU and China. When using the pooled OLS estimator, the results indicate that with a geographical distance increase of 1%, the trade flows will decrease by 0.85%. However, the result from the FGLS model is insignificant.

At the disaggregate level, the results of geographical distance are insignificant in both the pooled OLS model and FGLS model in relation to the trade flows of the food and live animals product groups (SITC0). In terms of the trade flows of the beverages and tobacco products group (SITC1), surprisingly, geographical distance shows a positive relationship with the trade flows, and the pooled OLS and FGLS models both indicate a significant positive effect on trade flows. The result from the pooled OLS model shows that the trade flows will increase by 4.44%, with a 1% increase of the geographical distance, while the result from the FGLS model indicates that the trade flows will grow by 4.99%, which is very close to the results obtained by using the pooled OLS model when the geographical distance increases by 1%.

Geographical distance has a negative relationship with the trade flows of the crude materials product group (SITC2) under the pooled OLS estimator, while it has a positive relationship with the trade flows of the animal and vegetable oils product group (SITC4). However, the results for the two product groups in terms of geographical distance are statistically insignificant under the FGLS estimation model. For the trade flows of the crude materials product group, it will decline by 1.59% when the geographical distance increases by 1% (in pooled OLS model), while for the vegetable oils products group, the trade flows can surge by 2.44% in the pooled OLS model too.

Geographical distance is one of the classic variables used in the trade gravity model. The traditional version of the trade gravity model considered geographical distance as the proxy for trade costs (transportation costs or good damage) and it has a negative effect on trade volume. However, because of the development of technology, transportation costs have been reduced significantly and it is now possible to keep products safe and fresh during the course of transportation. The estimated results of geographical distance for some of the product groups therefore violate the traditional results by having a positive relationship with trade flows, and some of the results turn out to be insignificant. Product differentiation can also be used to explain this phenomenon. The products are produced in two different countries separated by a long geographical distance. Therefore, more trade will happen regardless of the long geographical distance.

Independent variables	Pooled OLS	LSDV (fixed effect)	FGLS (random effect)
GDP(EU)	1.062*** (0.023)	0.770*** (0.193)	1.009*** (0.083)
GDP(China)	0.297*** (0.075)	0.412*** (0.068)	0.357*** (0.056)
Distance	-0.204 (0.342)	-	-0.372 (1.288)
Difference of GDP per capita	-0.188*** (0.044)	0.138 (0.134)	-0.024 (0.087)
Business freedom (EU)	1.689*** (0.282)	1.033*** (0.255)	1.057*** (0.249)
Business freedom (China)	1.446** (0.573)	1.433*** (0.423)	1.425*** (0.413)
Trade freedom (EU)	-0.381 (0.463)	-0.522 (0.368)	-0.658* (0.351)
Trade freedom (China)	0.893*** (0.206)	0.805*** (0.145)	0.832*** (0.144)
WTO membership	-0.068 (0.128)	-0.097 (0.095)	-0.103 (0.092)
Landlocked	-0.297*** (0.080)	-	-0.399 (0.309)
Constant	-29.567*** (4.641)	-26.483*** (3.827)	-25.668** (11.466)

Observations	599	599	599
R-squared	0.867	0.753	-
Number of EU countries	28	28	28
*Standard errors in parentheses; *** $p<0.01$, ** $p<0.05$, * $p<0.1$*			

Table 4.3. *Results of trade gravity model (dependent variable: EU's trade flows with China in SITC0)*

4.4.3. The effect of GDP per capita on EU–China agricultural trade

The demand structures between the EU and China, which are measured by the difference in GDP per capita between the EU and China, are similar and this is proved by the negative relationship between the difference in GDP per capita and trade flows of total agricultural products, trade flows of the food and live animals product group (SITC0), trade flows of the beverages and tobacco product group (SITC1), and trade flows of the crude materials product group (SITC2). The result from the pooled OLS model shows that when the difference in GDP per capita increases by 1% (this means the demand structures are less similar), the total agricultural products trade flows will decrease by 0.25%. The results from the LSDV and FGLS models are not statistically significant.

More specifically, according to the pooled OLS model, when the difference in GDP per capita grows by 1%, the trade flows will decrease by 0.19%, 0.60% and 0.37% in terms of the food and live animals products group (SITC0), beverages and tobacco products group (SITC1), and crude materials products group (SITC2), respectively. However, the only result which is statistically significant in the FGLS model is in relation to the beverages and tobacco products group (SITC1), and the result explains that the trade flows will decline by 0.51% when the difference in GDP per capita increases by 1%. Therefore, these results have proved the accuracy of Linder's demand hypothesis, which is that when the demand structures of two countries are similar (small difference in GDP per capita), these two countries are more likely to trade with one another.

However, Linder's demand hypothesis is not consistent with the results in the case of the animal and vegetable oils products group (SITC4). Based on the performance of the pooled OLS model, the relationship between the difference in GDP per capita and the trade flows of this product group is positive with a coefficient of 0.239, but the sign is negative in the LSDV model at the 5% statistically significance level. Since the test has shown that the LSDV model is not the most appropriate model, the result here should not be a concern.

As Table 4.3, Table 4.4, Table 4.5, and Table 4.6 show, the results are contradictory with respect to the sign (positive or negative) within the three estimation models. This is mainly because the hypotheses of the three estimation models are different. However, according to the tests (see Table 4.7), the FGLS model is the most appropriate estimation model and therefore the interpretation of this independent variable should specifically be focused on the results from the FGLS model.

4.4.4. *The effect of institutional distance on EU–China agricultural trade*

Since the standard distance which is the geographical distance is not as important as before in relation to international trade, new types of distance, such as the so called institutional or cultural distance, are becoming more important to international trade instead. The independent variables of business freedom and trade freedom that are applied to the trade gravity model have proved that the institutional distance matters in international trade.

Business freedom represents the degree to which a country's regulations do not hinder business productivity and profitability. According to the performance of the three estimation models, both the business freedom of the EU and China have significant positive links with the total agricultural products trade flows. The degree of business freedom of the EU increasing by 1% can lead to trade flows growing by 1.52% (pooled OLS model), 1.26% (LSDV model) and 1.27% (FGLS model), while in the case of China, when Chinese business freedom goes up by 1%, the total agricultural product trade flows are expected to increase by 1.19% (pooled OLS model), 1.24% (LSDV model) and 1.24% (FGLS model).

At product level, the trade flows of the food and live animals products group (SITC0) will increase by 1.69% (pooled OLS model), 1.03% (LSDV model) and 1.06% (FGLS model) when the EU's business freedom goes up by 1%. However, the trade flows will be up by 1.45%, 1.43% and 1.43% in the three estimation models accordingly when Chinese business freedom grows by 1%.

The trade flows of the crude materials product group (SITC2) have a positive relationship with business freedom in both the EU and China. A 1% growth in the EU's business freedom can lead to the trade flows increasing by 1.44% (pooled OLS model), 1.75% (LSDV model) and 1.69% (FGLS model). While in China, a 1% increase in business freedom can increase the trade flows by 1.28% in the LSDV model and by 1.17% in FGLS model. However, the coefficient is not statistically significant under the pooled OLS model.

Unfortunately, the results for the beverages and tobacco products group (SITC1) and the animal and vegetables oils products group (SITC4) are statistically insignificant according to all three estimation models. This may be because the data on the business freedom of the EU and China has less of a link with the trade flows of SITC1 and SITC4 products.

Trade freedom is used to represent the market openness of the EU and China. The main features that are involved in trade freedom are the forms of tariffs, export taxes, trade quotas, and outright trade bans. In addition, the forms of regulatory barriers related to health and safety issues are included. In general, the trade freedom of China has a positive relationship with the total agricultural products trade flows. When Chinese trade freedom increases by 1% (= trade barriers decrease by 1%), the total agricultural trade flows should go up by 0.64% (pooled OLS model), 0.54% (LSDV model) and 0.58% (FGLS model).

Specifically, at product level, when China's trade freedom goes up by 1%, the trade flows in the food and live animals products group (SITC0) are expected to increase by 0.89%, 0.81% and 0.83% according to the three estimation models, respectively. The same positive relationship between Chinese trade freedom and the trade flows can be seen for the crude materials product group (SITC2). The trade flows of SITC2 will grow by 0.78% (pooled OLS), 0.70% (LSDV) and 0.75% (FGLS) when trade freedom in China goes up by 1%. The results for product groups SITC1 and SITC4 are either statistically insignificant or statistically significant at the 5% level or 10% level.

The coefficients of the trade freedom of the EU show a negative relationship with the trade flows in all cases, as expected earlier. In general, when the trade freedom of the EU increases by 1%, the total agricultural products trade flows will decrease by 0.75% (LSDV model) and 0.98% (FGLS model). More specifically, the results in relation to the food and live animals products group (SITC0) in terms of the trade freedom of the EU are all statistically insignificant. The coefficient (-2.024) of trade freedom (EU) in relation to the beverages and tobacco products group (SITC1) is only statistically significant at the 5% level in the pooled OLS model, while the results are both statistically insignificant in the other two models. For the crude materials product group (SITC2), the result is only statistically significant at the 1% level in the FGLS model with the coefficient of -1.085, while in terms of the animal and vegetable oils products group (SITC4), the result (coefficient: -2.518) is only statistically significant at the 1% level in the pooled OLS model.

The econometric results of the independent variable of trade freedom are expected to be positive. However, the results are contradictory, for example, the negative results of the trade freedom of the EU showed in Table 4.2, Table 4.3, Table 4.4, Table 4.5, and Table 4.6, as well as negative results of the trade freedom of China showed in Table 4.5 and 4.6. The study therefore explains these unexpected results from two perspectives: 1) Quality of data. The data of trade freedom is secondary data from the Heritage Foundation. The tariffs and non-tariffs used to calculate the score of trade freedom index (see equation [4.3]) are general tariffs, not the specific tariffs and NTBs on agricultural products that were selected in this study[4]. As a result, the dependent variable (trade flows of agricultural product groups) is not coordinated with the data of the trade freedom index. 2) Multicollinearity. If multicollinearity exists among the data of trade freedom index, the results can be opposite to the expectations. Fortunately, the good quality results of business freedom can show the significant influence of institutional distance on EU–China agricultural trade flows.

Independent variables	Pooled OLS	LSDV (fixed effect)	FGLS (random effect)
GDP(EU)	1.382*** (0.041)	-0.079 (0.375)	1.235*** (0.120)
GDP(China)	1.205*** (0.130)	1.533*** (0.133)	1.238*** (0.108)
Distance	4.439*** (0.585)	-	4.985*** (1.794)
Difference of GDP per capita	-0.604*** (0.075)	0.080 (0.260)	-0.514*** (0.146)
Business freedom (EU)	1.151** (0.482)	-0.275 (0.495)	0.021 (0.481)
Business freedom (China)	0.695 (0.976)	-0.025 (0.821)	0.416 (0.800)
Trade freedom (EU)	-2.024** (0.809)	-0.222 (0.732)	-1.075 (0.700)
Trade freedom (China)	-0.273 (0.358)	-0.570** (0.284)	-0.448 (0.286)
WTO membership	-0.179 (0.220)	-0.026 (0.187)	-0.177 (0.180)
Landlocked	-0.056 (0.136)	-	-0.165 (0.428)
Constant	-87.529*** (7.915)	-24.075*** (7.519)	-87.900*** (16.291)
Observations	587	587	587
R-squared	0.783	0.580	-
Number of EU countries	28	28	28
*Standard errors in parentheses; *** p<0.01, ** p<0.05, * p<0.1*			

Table 4.4. *Results of trade gravity model (dependent variable: EU's trade flows with China in SITC1)*

4 Due to the large amount of detailed agricultural products classification and the limitation of access to the national tariffs database, more specific tariffs and non-tariffs data has hardly been collected.

4.4.5. *The effects of two dummy variables on the agricultural trade between the EU and China: WTO membership and landlocked*

All of the results used by the three estimators in relation to the independent variable “WTO membership” are statistically insignificant. In practice, due to the endless Doha negotiations and unsettled agreements, more countries are seeking other solutions by concluding bilateral trade agreements rather than multilateral trade agreements. The influence of the WTO on international trade is therefore reducing. However, in its role of maintaining order in international trade, the WTO is still very important when it comes to the solution of trade disputes. The signs of the coefficient for the WTO membership variable are negative, except for animal and vegetable oils products (SITC4) under the LSDV estimator. These negative signs can be explained by the fact that the EU files cases against China to WTO because of its suspicion of dumping activities, and this indeed has negatively influenced EU–China’s agricultural products trade.

However, the landlocked factor still has a negative effect on the EU–China agricultural trade relationship. Landlocked countries refer to countries that are almost or entirely surrounded by land and have no navigable route to the sea. Among the 28 EU member countries, the Czech Republic, Hungary, Luxembourg and Slovakia are landlocked countries. In general, the pooled OLS model indicates that the total agricultural products trade between the EU and China will decrease by 0.48% when the EU member country is a landlocked country, while it is -0.61% in the FGLS estimation model. Product groups wise, trade flows of the food and live animals products group (SITC0) will be reduced by 0.30% when the country is landlocked, and this result is only statistically significant in the pooled OLS model. The trade flows of the crude materials products group (SITC2) will decline by 0.75% and 0.92% respectively in the pooled OLS model and FGLS model, while the trade flows of animal and vegetable oils products group (SITC4) are expected to decrease by 1.24% (pooled OLS) and 1.13% (FGLS model). However, the results for the beverages and tobacco products group (SITC1) are statistically insignificant.

Independent Variables	Pooled OLS	LSDV (fixed effect)	FGLS (random effect)
GDP(EU)	1.233*** (0.026)	0.681*** (0.221)	1.124*** (0.096)
GDP(China)	0.356*** (0.085)	0.494*** (0.078)	0.398*** (0.064)
Distance	-1.585*** (0.385)	-	-1.825 (1.505)
Difference of GDP per capita	-0.371*** (0.049)	0.254* (0.153)	-0.084 (0.101)
Business freedom (EU)	1.444*** (0.317)	1.751*** (0.291)	1.685*** (0.286)
Business freedom (China)	0.817 (0.645)	1.281*** (0.483)	1.174** (0.473)

Trade freedom (EU)	-0.804 (0.521)	-0.805* (0.421)	-1.085*** (0.403)
Trade freedom (China)	0.780*** (0.232)	0.702*** (0.165)	0.752*** (0.165)
WTO membership	-0.005 (0.144)	-0.089 (0.109)	-0.083 (0.106)
Landlocked	-0.748*** (0.090)		-0.919** (0.361)
Constant	-15.897*** (5.216)	-28.786*** (4.372)	-15.928 (13.387)
Observations	598	598	598
R-squared	0.863	0.723	-
Number of EU countries	28	28	28
*Standard errors in parentheses; *** p<0.01, ** p<0.05, * p<0.1*			

Table 4.5. *Results of trade gravity model (dependent variable: EU's trade flows with China in SITC2)*

Independent variables	Pooled OLS	LSDV (fixed effect)	FGLS (random effect)
GDP(EU)	1.341*** (0.050)	1.809*** (0.451)	1.399*** (0.144)
GDP(China)	1.151*** (0.154)	0.918*** (0.159)	1.015*** (0.130)
Distance	2.436*** (0.691)	-	3.356 (2.136)
Difference of GDP per capita	0.239*** (0.092)	-0.606** (0.305)	-0.120 (0.173)
Business freedom (EU)	0.101 (0.579)	0.098 (0.623)	0.266 (0.599)
Business freedom (China)	-1.101 (1.152)	-1.775* (0.984)	-1.376 (0.947)
Trade freedom (EU)	-2.518*** (0.957)	-1.051 (0.886)	-0.845 (0.829)
Trade freedom (China)	-0.677 (0.438)	-0.663* (0.353)	-0.718** (0.350)
WTO membership	-0.213 (0.267)	0.039 (0.231)	-0.045 (0.219)
Landlocked	-1.242*** (0.164)		-1.125** (0.511)
Constant	-61.092*** (9.276)	-40.858*** (9.037)	-70.364*** (19.382)
Observations	553	553	553
R-squared	0.765	0.503	
Number of EU countries	28	28	28
*Standard errors in parentheses; *** p<0.01, ** p<0.05, * p<0.1*			

Table 4.6. *Results of trade gravity model (dependent variable: EU's trade flows with China in SITC4)*

Three statistical tests are conducted in order to identify the most reliable and appropriate estimation model. The results for each test are displayed in Table 4.7. It turns out that the results from the FGLS model, which is the random effect model, are the most reliable and robust. By using the LSDV, which is the fixed effect model, two dependent variables are dropped (geographical distance and landlocked) by these two models, which are shown by blanks results in the result tables above). Therefore, it is difficult to compare the effects between geographical distance and institutional distance by using the fixed effect model. However, the results from the pooled OLS model and FGLS model are quite comparable for most independent variables.

Tests	Total agricultural products	SITC0	SITC1	SITC2	SITC4
F-test	30.11 Prob>F=0.000	25.95 Prob>F=0.000	17.87 Prob>F=0.000	30.08 Prob>F=0.000	17.04 Prob>F=0.000
LM test	1539.33 Prob>chibar 2= 0.0000	1568.49 Prob>chibar2= 0.0000	728.80 Prob>chibar2= 0.0000	1327.86 Prob>chibar2= 0.0000	711.06 Prob>chibar2= 0.0000
Hausman test	Chi2(8)=8.64 Prob>chi2= 0.3739	Chi2(8)=3.60 Prob>chi2= 0.8916	Chi2(8)=15.91 Prob>chi2= 0.0436	Chi2(8)=6.46 Prob>chi2= 0.5962	Chi2(8)=7.61 Prob>chi2= 0.4723
Appropri-ate model	FGLS	FGLS	FGLS	FGLS	FGLS
Source: Stata software					

Table 4.7. *Results of tests for the appropriate estimated model (with different dependent variables: trade flows of five defined groups)*

4.4.6. *The EU's trade potential vis-à-vis China in agricultural products*

At an aggregated product level (see Table 4.8), the EU member countries with an unexplored trade potential vis-à-vis China in 2016 are Austria, Croatia, Cyprus, Greece, Hungry, Lithuania, Luxembourg, Malta, Slovakia and Sweden, while the rest of the member countries have used all the trade potential in 2016.

Country	Trade potential	Country	Trade potential	Country	Trade potential	Country	Trade potential
Austria	0.33	Belgium	1.90	Bulgaria	1.03	Croatia	0.68
Cyprus	0.41	Czech	1.37	Denmark	3.34	Estonia	1.15
Finland	2.86	France	2.36	Germany	2.10	Greece	0.63
Hungry	0.85	Ireland	2.26	Italy	1.62	Latvia	1.29

Lithuania	0.75	Luxembourg	0.06	Malta	0.20	Netherlands	5.25
Poland	2.00	Portugal	1.19	Romania	1.88	Slovakia	0.33
Slovenia	1.78	Spain	3.16	Sweden	0.81	UK	1.42
Source: author's calculation							

Table 4.8. *EU member countries' trade potential vis-à-vis China in 2016 (total agricultural trade)*

At a disaggregated product level (see Table 4.9), the EU member countries with an unexplored trade potential vis-à-vis China in 2016 in relation to food and live animals agricultural products are Austria, Croatia, Finland, Greece, Italy, Latvia, Lithuania, Luxembourg, Malta, Portugal, Romania, Slovakia, Slovenia, Sweden and the UK, while the rest of the EU member countries have used all the trade potential with China in terms of food and live animals agricultural products (STIC 0).

Country	Trade potential	Country	Trade potential	Country	Trade potential	Country	Trade potential
Austria	0.46	Belgium	1.42	Bulgaria	1.04	Croatia	0.64
Cyprus	1.66	Czech	1.61	Denmark	5.02	Estonia	2.08
Finland	0.40	France	1.06	Germany	1.26	Greece	0.55
Hungry	1.85	Ireland	4.78	Italy	0.67	Latvia	0.88
Lithuania	0.77	Luxembourg	0.29	Malta	0.57	Netherlands	5.72
Poland	1.41	Portugal	0.91	Romania	0.45	Slovakia	0.83
Slovenia	0.76	Spain	2.37	Sweden	0.50	UK	0.78
Source: author's calculation							

Table 4.9. *EU member countries' trade potential vis-à-vis China in 2016 (SITC0: food and live animals)*

In terms of the beverages and tobacco (SITC1) product groups, the EU member countries with an unexplored trade potential in 2016 are Bulgaria, Croatia, Czech Republic, Finland, Greece, Ireland, Italy, Romania, Slovakia, Sweden and the UK (see Table 4.10). However, the rest of the member countries have no trade potential left in 2016.

Country	Trade potential	Country	Trade potential	Country	Trade potential	Country	Trade potential
Austria	1.05	Belgium	5.10	Bulgaria	0.75	Croatia	0.22
Cyprus	1.28	Czech	0.93	Denmark	1.12	Estonia	1.91
Finland	0.27	France	5.98	Germany	1.76	Greece	0.62
Hungry	1.05	Ireland	0.48	Italy	0.98	Latvia	6.60
Lithuania	3.55	Luxembourg	2.23	Malta	5.65	Netherlands	4.15
Poland	1.07	Portugal	2.15	Romania	0.40	Slovakia	0.32

Slovenia	1.63	Spain	1.21	Sweden	0.55	UK	0.65
Source: author's calculation							

Table 4.10. *EU member countries' trade potential vis-à-vis China in 2016 (SITC1: beverages and tobacco)*

Austria, Bulgaria, Cyprus, France, Germany, Greece, Hungry, Ireland, Italy, Luxembourg, Malta, Poland, Slovakia, Sweden and the UK are the member countries who had trade potential with China for crude materials (SITC 2) in 2016 (see Table 4.11).

Country	Trade potential	Country	Trade potential	Country	Trade potential	Country	Trade potential
Austria	0.47	Belgium	1.80	Bulgaria	0.64	Croatia	1.48
Cyprus	0.30	Czech	4.19	Denmark	2.31	Estonia	2.51
Finland	4.77	France	0.40	Germany	0.34	Greece	0.61
Hungry	0.75	Ireland	0.83	Italy	0.81	Latvia	3.44
Lithuania	1.36	Luxembourg	0.03	Malta	0.48	Netherlands	2.15
Poland	0.65	Portugal	1.65	Romania	1.79	Slovakia	0.65
Slovenia	18.82	Spain	1.02	Sweden	0.72	UK	0.50
Source: author's calculation							

Table 4.11. *EU member countries' trade potential vis-à-vis China in 2016 (SITC2: crude materials)*

In respect to animal and vegetable oils, fats, and waxes (see Table 4.12), Austria, Czech, Estonia, Finland, France, Ireland, Lithuania, Malta, Poland, Portugal, Slovakia and the UK had unexplored trade potential with China in 2016. While Belgium, Bulgaria, Croatia, Cyprus, Denmark, Germany, Greece, Hungry, Italy, Latvia, Luxembourg, Netherlands, Romania, Slovenia, Spain and Sweden had fully used the trade potential with China in 2016.

Country	Trade potential	Country	Trade potential	Country	Trade potential	Country	Trade potential
Austria	0.82	Belgium	4.73	Bulgaria	6.62	Croatia	1.46
Cyprus	3.35	Czech	0.61	Denmark	4.39	Estonia	0.96
Finland	0.19	France	0.48	Germany	1.06	Greece	5.06
Hungry	11.38	Ireland	0.68	Italy	1.20	Latvia	1.61
Lithuania	0.71	Luxembourg	1.47	Malta	0.23	Netherlands	3.80
Poland	0.89	Portugal	0.57	Romania	2.14	Slovakia	0.25
Slovenia	3.49	Spain	6.97	Sweden	3.48	UK	0.33
Source: author's calculation							

Table 4.12. *EU member countries' trade potential vis-à-vis China in 2016 (SITC4: animal and vegetable oils, fats, and waxes)*

4.5. Conclusion

This chapter has investigated the impact of selected economic influencing factors on EU–China agricultural trade flows. The identified economic influencing factors are GDP of the EU and China, geographical distance between the EU and China, GDP per capita, institutional distance (represented by business freedom index and trade freedom index), WTO membership, as well as whether the country is landlocked or not. The empirical results turned out broadly consistent with expectations.

The GDP of EU and China have a positive relationship with EU–China agricultural trade flows and this indicates that with the development of the economies in both the EU and China, more trade in agricultural products will happen accordingly. Apart from the trade flows of the animal and vegetable oils product group (SITC4), the rest of the product groups have proved Linder's demand hypothesis, which is that similar demand structure can lead to more trade between the EU and China. This is reflected by the empirical results of difference of GDP per capita between the EU and China. With the increasing income of Chinese people and the expanding number of middle class in China, the demand structure will become more similar and hence the agricultural trade is expected to further increase in the future. The traditional version of the trade gravity model believes that the geographical distance has a negative impact on trade flows because the high transportation costs will discourage international trade activities. However, this study has proved that due to the development of transportation (lowers trade costs), the impact of geographical distance on EU–China agricultural trade flows varies among different agricultural product groups. For food and live animals products (SITC0) the influence of geographical distance is insignificant; for beverage and tobacco products (SITC1) the geographical distance, surprisingly, enhanced trade flows and this can be explained by product differentiation and different resource endowments; for crude materials (SITC2) and animal and vegetable oils (SITC4) the impact of geographical distance is still negative. However, in modern international trade, the impact of institutional distance has surpassed the geographical distance. In order to improve trade relations between the EU and China, the EU and China should work on tariffs and non-tariffs reduction, as well as the simplification of business procedures etc. Moreover, the EU member countries which are landlocked still have a negative impact on EU–China agricultural trade flows.

In terms of trade potential, based on the potential analysis for 2016, there are still many EU member countries who have had unexplored trade potential with China. When looking at the trade potential, it is more practical to analyze the trade potential at the EU member states level instead of the EU level.

4.6. Appendix: Agricultural products defined by Standard International Trade Classification (SITC)

SITC 0: Food and live animals (including the following products from 00 to 09)

SITC 00: Live animals other than animals of division 03

SITC 01: Meat and meat preparations

SITC 02: Dairy products and birds' eggs

SITC 03: Fish (not marine mammals), crustaceans, molluscs and aquatic invertebrates and preparations thereof

SITC 04: Cereals and cereal preparations

SITC 05: Vegetables and fruit

SITC 06: Sugars, sugar preparations and honey

SITC 07: Coffee, tea, cocoa, spices, and manufactures thereof

SITC 08: Feeding stuff for animals (not including unmilled cereals)

STIC 09: Miscellaneous edible products and preparations

STIC 1: Beverages and tobacco (including the following products from 11 to 12)

SITC 11: Beverages

SITC 12: Tobacco and tobacco manufactures

STIC 2: Crude materials, inedible, except fuels (including the following products from 21 to 29, but excluding 27 and 28)

SITC 21: Hides, skins and furskins, raw

SITC 22: Oil-seeds and oleaginous fruits

SITC 23: Crude rubber (including synthetic and reclaimed)

SITC 24: Cork and wood

SITC 25: Pulp and waste paper

SITC 26: Textile fibres (other than wool tops and other combed wool) and their wastes (not manufactured into yarn or fabric)

SITC 27 (not included): Crude fertilizers, other than those of division 56, and crude minerals (excluding coal, petroleum and precious stones)

SITC 28 (not included): Metalliferous ores and metal scrap

SITC 29: Crude animal and vegetable materials, n.e.s.

SITC 4: Animal and vegetable oils, fats, and waxes (including the following products from 41 to 43)

SITC 41: Animal oils and fats

SITC 42: Fixed vegetable fats and oils, crude, refined or fractionated

SITC 43: Animal or vegetable fats and oils, processed; waxes of animal or vegetable origin; inedible mixtures or preparations of animal or vegetable fats or oils, n.e.s.

4.7. References

Anderson, J.E. (1979). A theoretical foundation for the gravity equation. *The American Economic Review*, 69(1), 106–116, March.

Anderson, J.E. and Wincoop, E.V. (2003). Gravity with gravitas: A solution to the border puzzle. *National Bureau of Economic Research*, Working Paper 8079 [Online]. Available at: http://www.nber.org/papers/w8079.

Benáček, V., Lenihan, H., Andreosso, B., Michalíková, E., Kan, D. (2013). Political risk, institutions and foreign direct investment: How do they relate in various European countries? *The World Economy*. DOI: 10.1111/twec.12112.

Bergstrand, J.H. (1989). The generalized gravity equation, monopolistic competition, and the factor proportions theory in international trade. *The Review of Economics and Statistics*, 71(1), 143–153.

Bergstrand, J.H. (1990). The Heckscher-Ohlin-Samuelson model, the Linder hypothesis and determinants of bilateral intra-industry trade. *Economic Journal*, 100(403), 1216–1229.

Brei, M. and Goetz, V.P. (2017). The distance effect in banking and trade. BIS Working Paper, No. 658.

Breusch, T.S. and Pagan, A.R. (1980). The Lagrange multiplier test and its applications to model specification in econometrics. *The Review of Economic Studies*, 47(1), 239–253.

Buongiorno, J. (2016). Gravity models of forest products trade: Applications to forecasting and policy analysis. *An International Journal of Forest Research*, (89), 117–126. DOI: 10.1093/forestry/cpw005.

CEPII (2013). Gravity equations: Workhorse, toolkit, and cookbook. CEPII Working Paper, No. 2013–27, September.

Deardorff, A. (1998). Determinants of bilateral trade: Does gravity work in a neoclassical world? *The Regionalization of the World Economy*, 7–32.

EC (2017). Agriculture: A partnership between Europe and farmers. The EU's common agricultural policy (CAP): For our food, for our countryside, for our environment. Publications Office of the European Union, Luxembourg. DOI 10.2775/64508.

Guo, X.P., Zhang, J.S., Xue, J., Yan, T.X. (2017). A research on the gravity model of China's oil trade in the strategic context of "One Belt One Road". *Journal of Economics and International Finance*, 9(10), 95–102 [Online]. Available at: http://www.academic journals.org/JEIF.

Irshad, M.S., Qi, X., Arshad, H. (2018). Competitiveness of Pakistani rice in international market and export potential with global world: A panel gravity approach. *Cogent Economics & Finance*, 6(1), 1–18.

Johnston, L.A., Morgan, S.L., Wang, Y.S. (2014). The gravity of China's African export promise. *World Economy*, 38(6), 913–934.

Khan, S., Haq, I.U., Khan, D. (2013). An empirical analysis of Pakistan's bilateral trade: A gravity model approach. *The Romanian Economic Journal*, 48, 103–120.

Krugman, P.R. (1985). Increasing returns and the theory of international trade. NBER Working Paper, No. 1752, October. DOI: 10.3386/w1752.

Leamer, E. (1974). The commodity composition of international trade in manufactures: An empirical analysis. *Oxford Economic Papers, New Series*, 26(3), 350–374.

Linnemann, H. (1966). *An Econometric Study of International Trade Flows*. Holland Publishing, Amsterdam.

Majali, A.A. and Adayleh, R.M. (2018). International competitiveness in services in some Middle East and North Africa countries using gravity model. *International Review of Management and Marketing*, 8(2), 53–62.

Renjini, V.R., Kar, A., Jha, G.K., Kumar, P., Burman, R.R., Praveen, K.V. (2017). Agricultural trade potential between India and ASEAN: An application of gravity model. *Agricultural Economics Research Review*, 30(1), 105–112. DOI: 10.5958/0974-0279.2017.00009.X.

Rodriguez, C.H., Gutierrez, J.P.L., Viloria, A., Salazar, J.A. (2017). Application of a gravity model in the evaluation of the determinants of intra-industrial trade in Colombia. *International Journal of Control Theory and Applications*, 9(44), 1–6.

Shao, G.L. and Hu, X. (2013). A study of trade flow and potential of Sino-ASEAN aquatic product trade based on a gravity model. *Journal of International Trade*, 5, 34–39.

Shen, Q. (2016). Analysis of Sino-Russia-Magnolia trade cooperation potential: Based on the perspective of trade gravity model. *Advances in Social Science, Education and Humanities Research*, 91.

Tinbergen, J. (1962). Shaping the world economy: An analysis of world trade flows. *New York Twentieth Century Fund*, 5(1), 27–30.

Tripathi, S. and Leitao, N.C. (2013). India's trade and gravity model: A static and dynamic panel data. Munich Personal RePEc Archive (MPRA), Paper No. 45502 [Online]. Available at: https://mpra.ub.uni-muenchen.de/45502/.

Wang, D.Q. (2016). China-EU trade influence factors analysis based on trade gravity model. *Exploration of Financial Theory*, 1, 34–40. DOI: 10.16620/j.cnki.jrjy.2016.01.007.

Xie, J. (2010). Empirical analysis of China – Eastern Europe agricultural trade: Gravity model approach. *International Conference on Network and Finance Development*, NFD.

Zarzoso, I.M. and Lehmann, F.N. (2003). Augmented gravity model: An empirical application to Mercosur-European Union trade flows. *Journal of Applied Economics*, 6(2), 291–316.

Zhao, Y.L. and Lin, G.H. (2008). A gravity model analysis of the bilateral agri-trade flows between China and the ten countries of ASEAN. *International Trade Issues (Chinese)*, 12, 69–77.

5

Understanding the US Restrictions on Huawei and their Impact on the Development of the EU Digital Single Market and on the Outlook of the 5G Market[1]

5.1. Introduction

The international trading system and the process of globalization have been changed since the administration of former US President Donald Trump triggered a series of trade wars with its major trading partners, including the PRC, the EU, and its neighbours, Mexico and Canada. At the frontier of all trading matters, the development of the international telecommunications industry has been challenged the most by the US backlash against the adaptation of 5G products provided by the Chinese tech company, Huawei. Since late 2018, along with Huawei being charged with a list of crimes, the United States have barred Huawei's equipment and services from American government contracts, blocked the company from contracting with American companies and announced the addition of Huawei to the Entity List, the list of individuals and entities prohibited from receiving certain items, except under US government license. This has resulted in giant American companies, such as Google,

Chapter written by Qin TANG.

For a color version of all the figures in this chapter, see www.iste.co.uk/morales/connectivity.zip

1 This article was originally drafted for the 25th Euro-Asia International Research Conference in Dublin (Ireland), June 14th–16th, 2020, and then revised with updates. If you have any suggestions and comments, please reach out to the author by email (qin.tang@rub.de).

Lumentum Holdings Inc., Intel, Qualcomm, AMD, and Xilinx etc. suspending their business services exchanges with Huawei. In addition, US officials also pressured their allies into banning Huawei products in their equivalent 5G networks, with the accusation that Huawei is able to spy on mobile data. While such technical flaws are known as a general issue among all major 5G technology providers, suspicions with respect to Huawei's information security are adding up (The Economic Times 2019; Niwa 2019). The global media had been flooded with arguments about the merits and potential security flaws of Huawei's 5G technology. As the Biden administration has no indication to revoke the sanctions, Huawei's situation may not be easier in the short run.

Is it that important for the United States to impede Huawei's 5G businesses, block its development through international pressure and force a particular tech company to step back from the 5G global market? What aspects of Huawei's new technology are subject to US national security concerns? If cross-border connectivity and multinational cooperation in the telecommunications industry are irreversible, where are these 5G confrontations leading to? If Huawei is withdrawing from the contest, who are the strongest remaining contestants to lead 5G in the global market? As Huawei had explored its business more in Europe, what changes from the continuity of confrontation will it bring to the EU and its efforts to advance the single digital market?

This chapter is a preliminary study that outlines the current phase of 5G development at the international level from two aspects. The first aspect of the study is to understand what the basics of the 5G industry are about. The other part outlines the different states' preparations for 5G deployment in light of the US/Huawei quarrel and other international players' relevant (policy) responses, such as the EU. By including all of this information, this study is expected to increase the understanding of the US, the PRC and the EU's perceptions of the 5G era and the values each side has behind the quarrel.

5.2. The epical US sanctions and EU undertakings

Huawei's CFO, Meng Wanzhou, was unexpectedly arrested in Canada in December 2018 at the behest of American officials (BBC 2019a). This evoked a shock internationally, but the arrest was merely the tipping point of a US universal attack on Huawei and other Chinese tech companies. From the beginning of 2018, Huawei lost AT&T support in January and retail business with Best Buy. After the banning of the sale of Huawei and ZTE phones on US military bases, major US companies such as Facebook, Google and Twitter were investigated by US lawmakers over their ties with Huawei (Keane 2020). Huawei had lost a considerable amount of business on the American mainland. In March, the United States Trade Representative (USTR) filed a report[2] to restrain American usage of telecom services from both Huawei and ZTE; then followed an executive order signed by the former US President Donald Trump (United States Department of Defense 2019). Both actions set in force the broadening of the ban on Huawei 5G business from North America to the international context.

As part of the Five Eyes group, Australia and New Zealand followed the American approach, announcing the exclusion of Huawei from their 5G network building. The largest telecom provider in New Zealand, Spark, was ordered to strip Huawei equipment from its 5G network amid government security concerns (Miao and Wen 2018; Al Jazeera News 2018). In the UK, Britain's largest carrier, BT, decided to strip Huawei equipment from its 4G network and rule it out of its 5G core, but to keep the smartphone business (Keane 2020). In April 2019, the US Federal Communications Commission (FCC) voted unanimously to ban Huawei and ZTE from the United States government contracts for the procurement of devices. Chinese officials were furious about the US "witch-hunt" with respect to Huawei so as to maintain its own technological monopoly (BBC 2019b). Local media in China compared the US campaign against Chinese companies, ZTE and Huawei, to campaigns against Japanese companies back in the 1970s-1980s, when the United States imposed import restrictions on some Japanese companies and prohibited Toshiba exports to the US in 1987 (Guo and Zhang 2019).

In countries that Huawei has long collaborated with, such as Japan and India, American pressure has been applied. Japan stopped buying equipment from Huawei and ZTE, and cut Huawei out of government procurement contracts (Guo and Zhang, 2019). The Indian government was at first indecisive: first banning the company from local 5G infrastructure purchases, but in early 2020 deciding to keep the company in its 5G trial phase (Keane 2020; Al Jazeera News 2018). However, due to the outbreak of border conflicts with the PRC in June 2020, the Indian government has now left out Huawei and ZTE from its 5G trails (BBC 2021).

In Europe, since February 2019, American officials have actively tried to persuade European states to rule Huawei out of their 5G rollouts, from both the edge and core of their wireless networks (Lewis 2019). Major European countries were preoccupied with dire warnings of a possible spying risk by Huawei smartphones (known as a "back door" dispute). Germany, as an affiliate of the Five Eyes group, was told to drop Huawei or it would face limitations on intelligence sharing (Whittaker 2019). This pressure however encountered push back. Former German chancellor Angela Merkel had pushed for a Huawei open-door policy, before German lawmakers passed

2 USTR findings of the investigation into China's Acts, Policies, and Practices Related to Technology Transfer, Intellectual Property, and Innovation under Section 301 of the Trade Act of 1974.

tougher 5G security legislation in April 2021 (Cerulus 2021). France has ruled Huawei out of its 5G core, but has kept the company's participation in its 5G network building as a supplier. Similar measures have been adopted in the Netherlands and Spain[3]. Austria, Portugal and Hungary chose to keep the markets open to all qualified investors, including Huawei, in their 5G plans (Reuters 2020a; Miao and Ye 2019).

The pressures are expanding. While US lobbying for total bans against Huawei does not appear to be convincing to all countries, it still deserves some attention. On the one hand, it may be that Huawei's technology capability as one of the leading vendors in the business field, because of the universal ban, has been better recognized. On the other hand, regardless of being recently described as outdated, the process of globalization still provides strong resistance to the geopolitical power play. Especially after the in-depth international economic integration of the last two decades, there are robust global supply chains in place among international corporations, and they have given rise to many Chinese corporations, like Alibaba, Tencent, ZTE and Huawei. By putting Huawei and other emerging Chinese companies on the Entity List (blacklist for businesses), American companies are also suffering from the disruption in trading in tech products with their Chinese partners. To avoid US companies' financial losses, the US Department of Commerce were obliged, time and time again, to issue a Temporary General Licence (TGL). This provides a 90-day wind-down period, allowing American companies to temporarily continue the usage of Huawei equipment or for other possible arrangements to be put in place. Up until May 2020, TGLs have been extended five times (Zhao 2020). Qualcomm received a license from its government to sell 4G mobile phone chips to Huawei as an exemption from US trade restrictions (Reuters 2020b). At that time, both Canada and the UK continued technical cooperation with Huawei with respect to certain areas, in a low-key manner, as this could help out the UK with a \$2 billion telecommunications operation issue and, as Canadian telecoms Telus and BEC indicated, provide savings of \$1 billion on the cost of 5G equipment if Huawei stayed in their 5G rollout (Guo and Zhang 2019).

Washington's political efforts to restrain Huawei from the global 5G development continue. So does Beijing's backlash. Even though the company continually posits itself as an international corporation, the American government has been firmly portraying it as a tech threat from the PRC, which is the biggest competitor of the US internationally, both economically and politically, as well as its major political rival in Asia. The deterrent approach to limit Chinese companies' share in the 5G markets goes observably deeper and beyond the 5G core. As the current Biden administration

3 In December 2021, Telefonica in Spain confirmed the purchase of 5G network equipment from Swedish manufacturer Ericsson, instead of the Huawei gear (Reuters 2021).

upholds the sanctions, Huawei continues to face severe challenges to its growth. While its market share of 5G base stations in mainland China reached up to 60%, by the end of 2021, the company revealed a 28.9% drop in revenues, from 891.4 billion RMB (136.7 billion USD) down to 634 billion RMB (99 billion USD), and it also lost its first-place perch for worldwide phone sales, dropping down the number six (Slotta 2022; Cheng 2021; Amadeo, 2021; Kharpal 2021). With this backdrop of severe confrontation, this chapter is going to outline the importance of 5G, its impact on economic growth, and its meanings particularly with respect to the United States, the PRC and the EU, trying to grasp what the impact of the US/Huawei confrontation on the deployment of the 5G layout would be on a global scale.

5.3. Basic ideas of 5G

5.3.1. *What is 5G?*

The term refers to the 5th generation mobile radio communication system (5G), or the fifth generation of cellular networking. Before 5G, there were four other development stages. Since the 1980s when 1G was introduced, every 10 years a new generation of cellular standards has arrived, defining an upgraded performance regarding mobile communications (ITU 2011). In the trajectory of wireless mobile telecommunications technology, 1G realized wireless connection via phones and calls, 2G was for the short message system (SMS), 3G for advanced image viewing and 4G for video surfing. From 3G to the current 4G system, there was not much of a technology breakthrough on setting standards; but the latter helps face-to-face communication and facilitates high resolution movies, which is largely responsible for the fast blooming of the visual industry and keeps the mobile communication industry growing vigorously (Zhao 2019; CCi 2020a).

The 5G generation, unlike 4G, is far more mature in terms of information transfer speed, large data capacity flow (upload and download), and in a considerably shorter time. It can be 10 times, 20 times, or even 100 times faster than 4G LTE transmission speed (Ai 2020; Jayadevan 2020; Li 2018). The high speed of data transfer from handphones and distant servers, significantly, makes massive machine type communication available. In other words, while the 1G-4G technology development realized people-to-people connection, the 5G system can extend that model of communication to a people-to-thing and thing-to-thing connectivity, as it is often called, the world of the Internet of Things (IoT) (XianZao 2019). The threefold connectivity, in theory, can enable automation to take place in certain industries: in retail, health, education, agriculture, remote manufacturing processes and car connected to the internet, etc. (Bloomberg 2019.12.2; Li 2018). This marks out the whole process differently. In short, 5G opens a door to all sorts of connectivity between people and things, everything and everywhere.

5.3.2. *Three use cases of the application of 5G*

Based on a rosy blueprint, the utility of 5G can broaden the nature of our living and business modes from this threefold connectivity. For people-to-people connectivity, the outstanding 5G high-speed information transfer rate categorizes a field featured by data-driven use cases, called enhanced Mobile Broadband (eMBB)[4]. By adding 5G New Radio carriers that supply eMBB, under the current 4G network, the speed of information transfer (or data transfer) can be significantly advanced (see Figure 5.1). This high-speed internet access can undertake real-time traffic alerts and stream real-time videos (Kavanagh 2020). With better connectivity, the already existing networking activities i.e., office work and medical activities in scans, computer games and virtual businesses (such as 4K movies and 3D printers) will be virtually improved at a brisk pace. A number of cases have shown enormous business potential already, such as Snapchat lenses and Pokémon Go in terms of Augmented Reality (AR), the requirement of Virtual Reality (VR) lenses advertized by Google and Meta, and the growing utility of short video communities, such as TikTok, Kuaishou and Watermelon Video, as well as the fast growth of YouTubers with 3D 4K videos (Gupton 2017).

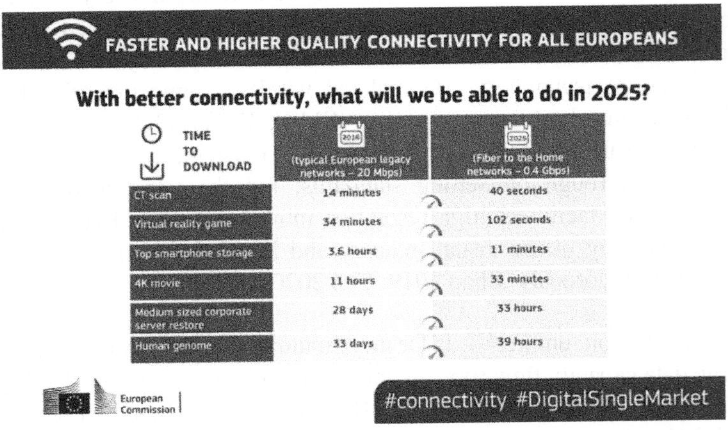

Figure 5.1. *5G quality connectivity (source: 5G PPP (2016)[5])*

---

4 Enhanced Mobile Broadband (eMBB) is one of three sets of use cases defined for 5G. As an extension to existing 4G broadband services, they are to be launched in the first commercial 5G services (Kavanagh n.d.).

5 The 5G Infrastructure Public Private Partnership (5G PPP) is a joint research initiative between the European Commission and European ICT industry to deliver 5G solutions, architectures, technologies and standards.

For the large data flows required by such scenarios, there is a requirement for wide area coverage of high data rate with low latency. The current availability of 5G technological support in this field is known as "multiple-in, multiple-out" (MIMO). With MIMO, different spectrums of radio frequency can exist without interruption within the same area of the 5G network. This new feature also creates a market for equipment support, generates businesses on base stations, set-top boxes, all-IP networks, etc. Each has its own 5G technical patent requirement. It further serves as a contributing factor to both research and businesses in the edge computing market. The current leading suppliers of 4G/5G networks are Samsung, Huawei, Ericsson and Nokia, etc. (Jayadevan 2020).

By realizing a far-speedier data transfer on a mass scale, another new industrial technology, machine connection, is emerging. The International Telecommunication Union (ITU), a UN agency that is responsible for issues regarding information and communication technologies, adds two use cases supported by the conduit of ultra-reliable low-latency communications (URLLC) for 5G business models: massive machine-type communication (mMTC) and critical machine-type communication (cMTC). Having URLLC support can help realize the controlling of autonomous cars and other vehicles (buses, trains, or planes) in the relevant infrastructure (Kavanagh 2020). Such a technical step-forward, therefore, boosts markets in both self-driving cars and industrial workflows in different fields, namely, industry 4.0 (also much discussed under the IoT theme) (Chandramouli 2020).

All of these above changes prompted different discussions. Take self-driving cars as an example. A survey by Adobe Analytics in October 2019 showed that about 40% of American adult drivers preferred self-driving cars (Hussain 2019). This instantly indicates high market expectations. In business fields, global carmakers such as General Motors Co, Hyundai Motor Group and BMW have actively invested in autonomous cars (Hussain 2019). Like the technology boost in autonomous vehicles, strong radio propagation and multi-track signal delivery can further facilitate many fields, upgrading manufacturing processes, removing the obstacle of distance for remote education and e-Health care, etc. Hence, market expectations for e-industrial development soar. Along with this comes a natural expansion of data usage in the relevant fields. Accordingly, major internet giants and tech companies, such as SoftBank Group, Lyft Inc., Tencent Holdings, Alibaba, etc. are also widely expanding their investment in cloud businesses (Hussain 2019; Xianzao 2019). By and large, a trillion-dollar investment can achieve a 10 trillion-dollar economic return in downstream industries via 5G technology (Deloitte 2018). State and regional actors are setting out their 5G development strategy, such as the PRC's Made-in-China 2025 (MIC 2025) in mid-2015, the EU's European Electronic Communications Code (EECC) in late-2016, and the US's 5G FAST plan in early-2019. As Qualcomm CEO Steve Mollenkopf stated, "The birth of 5G seems to be equally important as the birth of electricity and cars, which can bring long-term influence for the whole society and economic model" (Bloomberg 2019).

5.3.3. *5G: A new shuffle in the current global value chain?*

Adapting 5G technologies in support of time sensitive communications between people and machines requires corresponding infrastructure and specific technologies other than 4G networks (Jayadevan 2020). According to the 3rd Generation Partnership Project (3GPP), the widely accepted unity of telecommunications standards development organizations, 5G constitutes two different models: 5G NSA (Non-Standalone) and 5G SA (Standalone) (Xianzao 2020). The former represents a transitional framework that builds 5G networks on the skeleton of 4G network systems; hence, a hybrid system with a resource-saving and budget method for improving current networks performance. The latter is a brand-new network architecture that can fully support diversified industry breakthroughs into businesses and living. To complete the whole development of 5G rollout takes a few stages, from both the infrastructure and technology facets.

The current 5G rollout still stands at a very early phase, preparing 5G NSA for public access networks and 5G SA for specific industrial zones. Each category has specific facilitation and technologies that correspond to its own 5G network being deployed. Each 5G network constitutes three main areas: Access Network (AN), Bearer Network (BN) and Core Network (CN). Each area is subject to specific technologies and module parts, indicating a specific technology layout and the relevant industrial chain.

For instance, the technologies used in the AN include MIMO antenna, radio-frequency modules (RF devices), filter sets, cellular base stations, and chips that operate in the given equipment. Take base stations as an example, the architecture of the NR Radio Access Network (RAN) like base stations are different from LTE RAN ones, requiring a set of gNB[6] protocols that are implemented from two parts called the Central Unit (CU) and the Distributed Unit (DU). The core set for 5G Mobile Broadband (MBB) is activating the Antenna Unit (AAU), which fundamentally enables high spectrum bandwidth below 6GHz from sites and bands. Although after generating networks, adding additional bands and sites becomes increasingly difficult, each AAU that provides 5 bands and 3 modes can simultaneously define the network

6 The gNB (or gNodeB) is a new acronym to refer to the new base station in 5G. It is used to replace the eNB (or eNodeB or Evolved Node B) in 4G. See: http://www.5g-networks.net/5g-technology/5g-terminology-the-gnb/.

in more accurate and flexible ways (Huawei AAU paper 2015). In terms of these basic manufacturing infrastructures, Huawei, together with ZTE, Nokia and Ericsson, are the leading developers in site architecture (Lewis 2018).

In BN, data transfer is essential. The relevant core computing parts are fiber-optic cables, optical modules and optical communication equipment. The world's largest equipment provider of fiber-optic cable[7] is, according to the given report, a Chinese company, Yangtze Optical FC (YOFC) (Yezi Guping 2019). Given that the optical module is closely equipped with computing chips, the global market in this category is diversified mainly between American and Asian manufacturers. In 2018, American companies had a 36% global market share, including Finisar (14%), Lumemtum (7%), Oclaro (6%), II-IV (5%) and Acacia (4%), far ahead of their Chinese counterparts (16%) and those in Japan (8%) (OIDA 2018). Given its wide usage of cloud computing in all AN, BN and CN categories, American companies would benefit hugely from the vast potential in option market business during the global 5G rollout.

Similarly, in the CN category, the focus of 5G deployment is centralized on patent development of chip and cloud technologies. Over the years, the American companies, Qualcomm and Intel have been the leading baseband chip manufacturers and have obtained patent approvals with telecom giants like Apple, Huawei and Lenovo etc. Even earlier than the release of 3GPP's 5G R15 NSA (December, 2017) and the SA standard (June, 2018), Qualcomm released the world's first 5G modem in 2016 (the Snapdragon X50), and Intel followed with its own chip in November 2017. Half a year later, Huawei released its own 5G baseband chip. Even though the chip is too big to be widely adapted, the appearance of a Chinese company in chip computing is perceived as a crack in the American monopoly in the field (Chen 2019).

From the perspective of the industrial value chain, the deployment of 5G networks can bring increasing numbers of new businesses in sight for equipment manufacturers and carriers. The change in telecommunications technology that alters mandatory

7 The rank of the largest fiber optic companies was varied among different resources. According to Thomasnet, the top global fiber optic cable company is Corning, an American manufacturer of specialty glass, ceramics, and optics products. See "Top 10 US and International Fiber Optics Suppliers", Thomasnet., https://www.thomasnet.com/articles/top-suppliers/fiber-optics-manufacturers-suppliers/. In late 2020, however, the ranking was different. According to Insider Monkey, the largest fiber optic company in the world is the Japanese general trading company, Sumitomo Corp, after which is the Chinese company, Kaile Science and technology Co Ltd Hbe (Hubei). Nonetheless, China is the home of the largest fiber optic companies in the world like ZTE, HTGD, and YOFC. See: https://www.insidermonkey.com/blog/5-largest-fiber-optic-companies-in-the-world-895424/?singlepage=1.

standards can generate new market opportunities for large vendors of equipment and service providers, and lead to another new decade-long economic development. By 2025, the industrial internet is forecast to be a new economic opportunity estimated at $23 trillion. But the investment required at the early stages is large. The United States needs almost 800,000 base stations, and about $275 billion (appr. 234.16 billion Euros) to pave the way for the 5G network;[8] the PRC needs between 66 million to 164 million small transmitter sites by 2030. While the Chinese investment for the 5G rollout is estimated to 370 billion Euros, the European Commission has made a budget of 500 billion Euros available for its 5G deployment framework (Brake 2020; AG Barr Keynote Speech 2020; Blackman and Forge 2019). Changes ranging from telecommunication infrastructures, new standards settings in both patent registration and market access, etc. are expected. In short, the adoption of the 5G system is game-changing in many fields (see Figure 5.2).

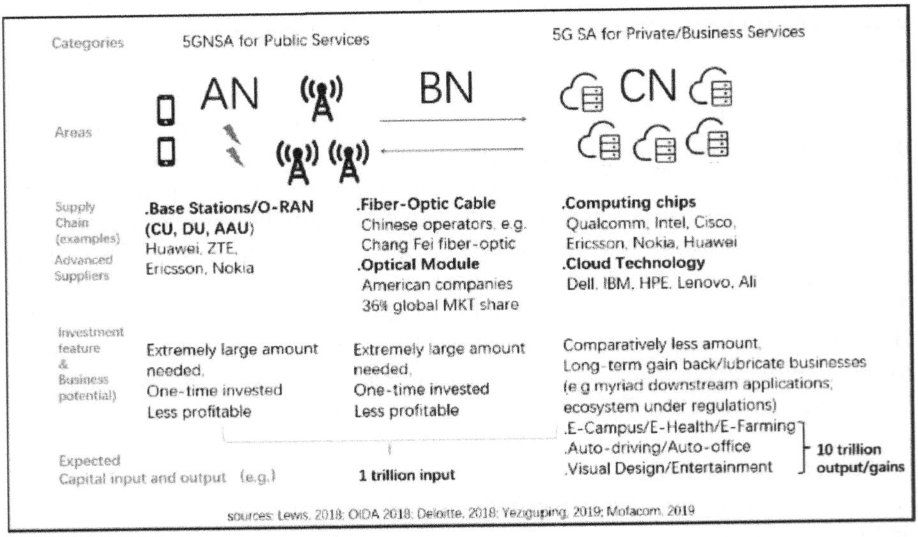

Figure 5.2. *Author's understanding of the 5G supply chain industry*

8 In June 2021 and February 2022, the United States enacted the US Innovation & Competition Act of 2021 (USICA) by the Senate and the America COMPETES Act of 2022 by the House of Representatives, respectively. Both bills included major federal funds to facilitate access to finance for start-ups and scale-ups, as well as for existing research and innovation related to increasing semiconductor manufacturing. While the former bill introduced $250 billion, the latter bill concludes $52 billion to chips manufacturing and $45 billion to advance supply chains in terms of critical items, outside $160 billion in R&D sectors (Walsh and Kim 2022).

5.4. Concerns and fallacies

According to the above, the 5G rollout appears to be much more advantage diversified. In other words, unlike the 4G technology monopoly, technical advantages in 5G are so far myriad. This can imply more industrial cooperation and infrastructure collaboration to accomplish the goal of 5G – an overall connectivity for a better life. With Asian technical advantages in infrastructure, particularly Chinese manufacturing capability, together with American-European innovative advantages, it seems that, ideally, an advance in globalization could bring more opportunities to companies and communities in the different regions, enhancing the already sophisticated interconnections.

However, the current confrontation seems destined to divert the future development of 5G in an unwanted direction. Most of the quarrel's focus is on two "threats": Huawei's technology advantages and a "backdoor threat" arising from its smartphone that the Chinese government could manipulate. Is this true? Firstly, the major economies have long been initiating their own proactive 5G deployments for a new economic boost. The United States was one of the very first countries to have an open high-frequency spectrum for 5G. Given its leading telecommunications heritage and 4G expertise, it appears as a strong performer in leading 5G deployment in the line of the User market-RAN-Core network. American companies, like Qualcomm, Cisco and Intel etc., are not only market leaders for standards-setting in 4G technologies, they continue to hold a leading market share for the most advanced and crucial components of 5G technologies, such as semiconductors (Lewis 2018). In short, the American technology giants remain the leading performers on a global scale.

While they were not among the actors initiating 5G technology R&D, Chinese companies have made a remarkably swift advance in 5G deployment. For instance, amongst manufacturers of core telecommunications network equipment in RAN, four companies that dominated in the field in 2018 were non-American companies. As shown in Figure 5.3, the Chinese-affiliated chip company, HiSilicon, stepped into the American-dominated fields of network processors and small cell chipset production (Lewis 2018). Albeit with no serious challenges remaining in the most important field of mobile equipment components and chip technology and no absence of US companies in any certain leading field, the multiplayer scenario can mean a comparatively weaker position of US companies in 5G infrastructure manufacturing, which appears to be alarming to the United States. One of the leading opinions is that whoever leads 5G technologies sets the standards and owns the intellectual property (IP), and that these are key indicators of technology security (Lewis 2018).

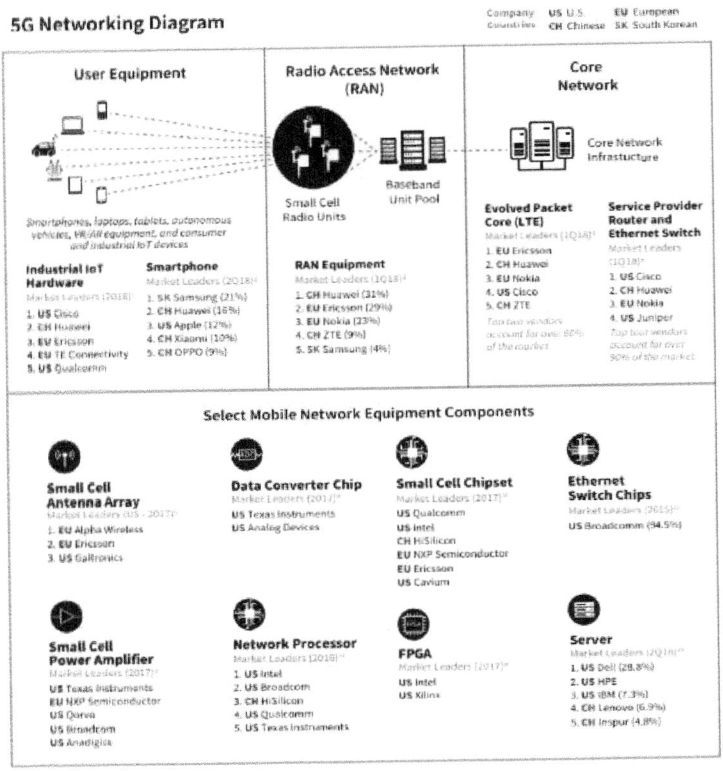

Figure 5.3. *World's leading companies for 5G networking (source: Lewis 2018)*

While US officials are deeply concerned by the idea that Huawei and other Chinese companies are leading in 5G patent approvals, other sources tell a different story. According to a recent report from the Japanese Cyber Creative Institute on the standardization contributions of candidates for 5G standard essential patents (SEPs), other companies, rather than Huawei, are leading the field in many aspects (CCi 2020a). Even though Huawei appears prominently in the list of 5G patent holders, NTT DoCoMo (Japan) is the world's No.1 owner of 5G essential patents (CCi 2020b). Samsung (South Korea) is in the first rank of the Top 5G-SEP corporate patent applicants (see Figure 5.4). These two companies compete for the 1st and 2nd places in terms of patent applications, with 65% and 53%, respectively, focusing on 5G standards; Huawei follows with a 33.9% share (see Figure 5.5). When counting the total number of technical items in the 5G technical area in first place, Samsung leads the group, followed by Huawei and Qualcomm (see Figure 5.6). Where Huawei truly outperforms others is, as the figures from March 2016 to June 2018 show, in its overall contribution to 5G infrastructure architecture (CCI 2020a).

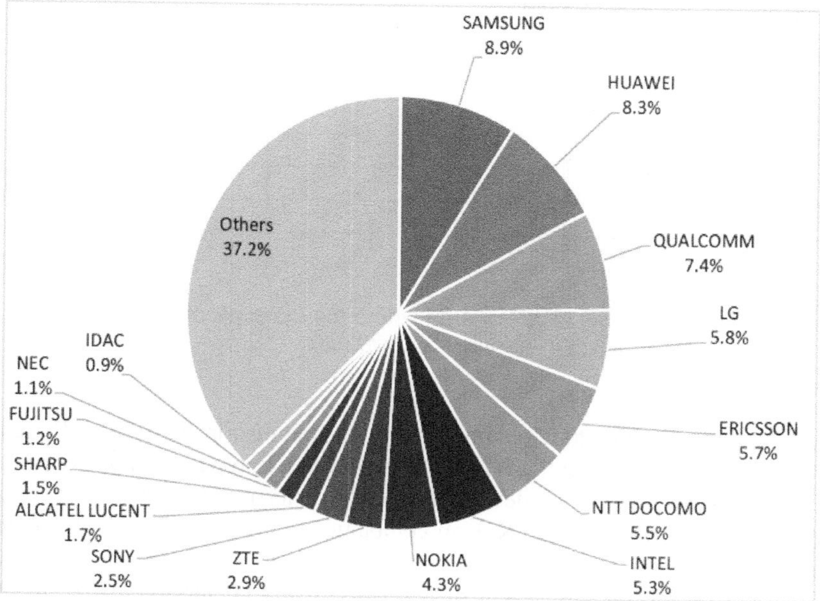

Figure 5.4. *The top 5G-SEP candidate application companies (source: CCi 2020a)*

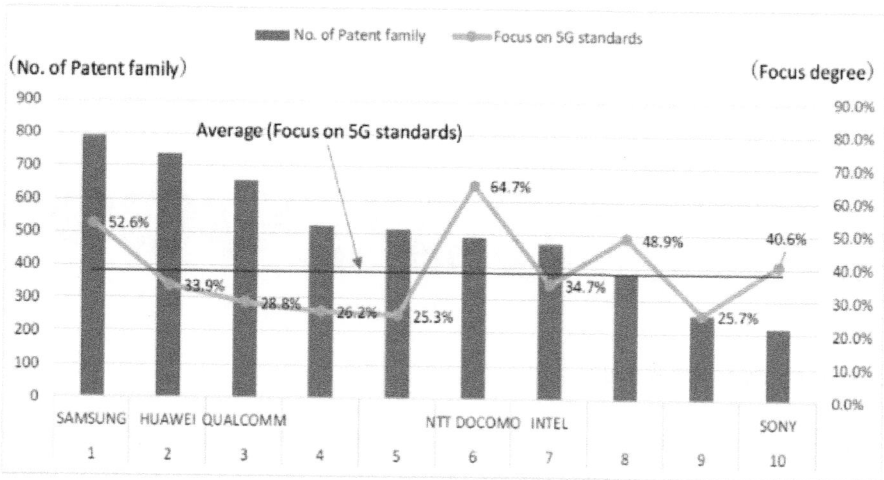

Figure 5.5. *Companies focusing on patent applications for 5G standards (source: CCi 2020a)*

Rank	Top six companies	No. of technical items within 10th place	No. of technical items in 1st place
1	SAMSUNG	40	12
2	HUAWEI	38	8
3	QUALCOMM	40	8
4	LG	36	3
5	ERICSSON	38	4
6	NTT DOCOMO	25	3

Figure 5.6. *5G technical area where the top applicants focus (source: CCi 2020a)*

Another independent study obtained the same findings: in Bird & Bird's report, when counting standard essential 5G patents (5G SEPs), European companies perform well in leading 5G technology development, with Ericsson at 15.8% at the top and Nokia at 10.9% in fourth place. Korean companies followed with a 22.9% share of overall 5G SEPs (Noble et al. 2019). Chinese and American companies jointly shared third place, with 19.5% and 19.4% shares, respectively (Petersson 2019). In other words, the EU is the true champion with respect to 5G SEPs at the given time (see Figure 5.7). This study does not perceive China's rise as a major power as a central problem (Ortega 2020).

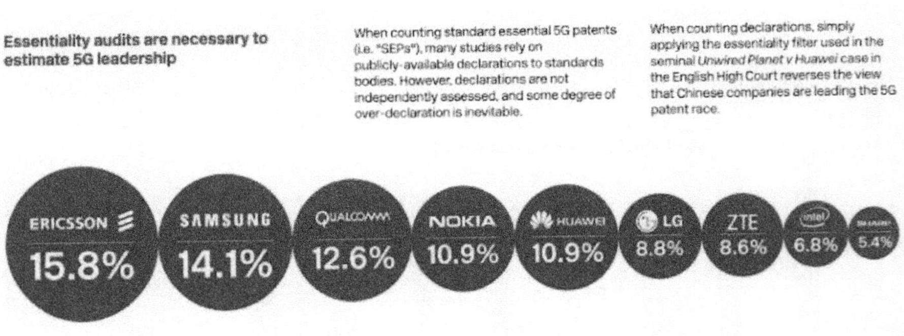

Image courtesy of Bird & Bird

Figure 5.7. *Why you shouldn't believe everything you read about 5G patents (source: Bird & Bird via Petersson 2019)*

The second heated issue is the "back door" concern over Huawei smartphones. While the allegations against Huawei by the US government led to considerable restrictions on hardware and software supplies to the company, there was no solid evidence supporting their claims (Hope 2020). The situation brought about extensive debates on the issue. For instance, experts from various nations often point out that "back door" vulnerability is much more of a technical matter. "Backdoors aren't just for bad guys; backdoors of the non-criminal variety are useful for helping customers who are hopelessly locked out of their devices" (Malwarebytes). There are reasons for such a technical existence.

However, the "back door" worries have been in existence for a long time. In the political field, the connection between technological capability and military superiority is a critical point. It is well known that defence technology capability is mainly backed up by technological advances. There is the possibility of the dual usage of 5G technologies, such as for/by robots, artificial intelligence, and advanced sensing devices, for military applications. It reveals a certain truth to the given concerns. In the meantime, there are also cases that have a negative impact on the public, for example, the 2013 US Massive Surveillance Scandal disclosed by Edward Snowden, the scandals between the Five-Eyes, Nine-Eyes and Fourteen-Eyes Alliances regarding wiretapping in 2015-2016, and the court cases with respect to the FBI vs. Apple Inc. in 2015-2016, etc. Because "modern age telecom equipment, irrespective of its source, may at times be susceptible to spyware or malware etc.", such potential threat can exist "in any telecom network elements by vendor or any other third-party source" (The Economic Times 2019). It is an objective fact that, if Huawei as the third largest provider carries that risk, then American companies as the world's largest suppliers have the same risk (Niwa 2019). Noteworthily, it was the "2013 Snowden leaks" which indicated Chinese technological vulnerability, and led Chinese companies to seek self-reliance and security in their network and information technologies (Lewis 2018).

Despite the above discussion, US officials show great concern at Chinese companies increasing the number of their patent applications and their share of 5G technologies. As James Lewis, the Senior vice President and Director at the CSIS, noted, "having two companies with close ties to a hostile power" is risky for the United States, and "espionage and the potential disruption to critical infrastructures" raises concerns for national security (Lewis 2018). In this way, the 5G rollout is overshadowed by political tensions and the nature of competition, rather than a willingness to cooperate with markets of a different nature. This can quickly generate protectionism.

As the World Economic Forum (2018) report indicated, increasing protectionism is one of the major factors in technology that is negatively impacting on business growth. Increasing the number and gravity of protectionist issues beyond a reasonable scale can be detrimental, as various technical issues will occur from time to time, or even emerge one after the other throughout the internet age. If the arrival of 5G is inevitable, associating technology issues with political ones is unwise (Der Standard 2019).

Instead, it seems necessary and more meaningful to seek a way of drawing up international regulations on security, for example, regulating government surveillance through certain universal agreements, rather than using concerns about it to crackdown on competitors. The ITU has openly stated that through building trust, cybersecurity can be converted into a public good (Taddeo 2019).

5.5. Focusing on policy regulation instead of geopolitical gameplaying?

Amidst warnings from the US about Huawei and growing concerns on the dual use of technology goods, the EU has undertaken its own assessment over the connections between the Chinese Communist government and the leading Chinese technology companies (BBC 2019b). Like the United States, both the EU and the PRC have had many disagreements in both political and social fields. Yet, the two sides manage to have a basic understanding of the need for mutually beneficial economic growth through the long years of EU-PRC interdependence in business and economics. The EU chooses to continue providing encouragement for good governance, but proceeds with caution (European Commission 2019).

The EU clearly understands the security risks involved in EU standards-setting and that the supply of critical equipment with full security features is needed. Combined with being a multi-member state institution, each with their own particular political features, the EU's 5G rollout appears to be further complicated, particularly with the necessity of integrating different national plans. On the one hand, the EU Commission has a goal of operating the roll-out of 5G across all urban areas and all major transport routes by 2025 and that of an EU-wide 5G coverage by 2030 (European Court of Auditors 2022). On the other hand, member states' approaches towards 5G security and the use of equipment provided by vendors vary. There is the burden of policy inconsistency and concerns about the uneven pace of 5G implementation among member states (Nicolás 2022). In addition, six of the eight largest vendors, including Huawei and Samsung, are non-EU companies. As their control centres are not located inside the EU, there is a potential security issue at the EU level (EAC Press 2022). With the mass usage of cloud technology involving personal information and data privacy in the upcoming advanced-communicative technology age, there is a basic question on how to assess different suppliers' trustworthiness and the security of their technologies in host countries.

To overturn the burden of policy inconsistency to the benefit of cross-border connectivity, to date, the European Commission has implemented the Network and Information Security Directive (2016), the Cybersecurity Act (2017) and the European Electronic Communications Code (2018), a proposed horizontal sanctions regime (2019) and the EU Chips Act (2022), from both legal and financial terms, to address collective conduct to counter cyber-attacks (European Commission, 2022).

To facilitate vendors in compliance with EU standards and legal requirements for private data protection, the commission has adopted the work of the Prague Proposal and the EU's 5G Toolbox, which is known as the US-EU approach, a mechanism involving criteria for public carriers and network owners to seek trustworthy 5G partners (CSIS 2020). Regarding the issues of surveillance technology, the EU issues an export control regulation (2016) to monitor exports in key technologies and those with dual use. Regarding critical assets and technology infrastructure, it implements a screening framework as an instrument to monitor foreign direct investment in these key areas (European Commission 2019).

By inventing a set of legal instruments, the EU has been prudently encouraging 5G development, while offering strong legal protections for privacy, (personal) data security and free and secure data flows. For the given infrastructure building phase where the expenditure matters, the EU's decision to not exclude Chinese companies in its 5G rollout, with the proviso of the rollout being accommodated with the Toolkit for risk management before their services can be approved, appears to be tactful and discerning. In this sense, with legal preparation and education, after having the infrastructure equipment set in place, the European companies are expected to boost their own market presence with service upgrading through its long-term comparative advantages (see Figure 5.8).

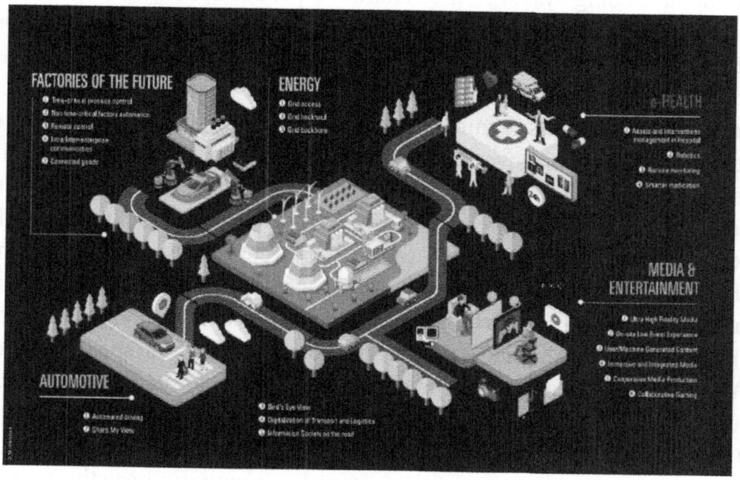

Figure 5.8. *EU vision for 5G (source: 5GPPP 2016)*

5.6. Conclusion: 5G future in juncture

The development of 5G technologies has brought about a mixture of opportunities and challenges. The hope is that a thoroughly connected and convenient lifestyle can be attained by this technology boost. The challenges, apart from those of a technical nature, arise out of distrust and power plays, which apparently seem to be associated with US insecurity towards its technological monopoly. Besides, there are more aspects to consider.

First, the fast growing presence of Chinese technology companies indeed appears concerning. Stimulated by the "going-out" policy that the Chinese government initiated against domestic overcapacity in 2009, there has been a sudden boost in the internationalization of Chinese companies. Such a policy-oriented development mode, occasionally accompanied by substantial investment, is often portrayed as aggressive and unstable. It is true that such a pattern of growth can and has already caused concerns from international economies, mixed with scepticism over its non-democratic policy-decision mechanism. It is also true that Chinese companies have learned about and grown significantly from the international supply chain. In the construction phase of 5G rollouts, they are capable of providing goods and advanced services. In this sense, Chinese companies which are prone to further internationalization need to be more accommodating with respect to cross-border cooperation.

Secondly, US perceptions of 5G seemingly play a rather critical role in reshaping the international trading system. Since Huawei's products, as well as those of Alpha and Ericsson, appear to be alternative options for many to American suppliers, there are indeed mounting American fears of losing absolute dominance and being replaced by, in this 5G case, the Chinese in all three 5G-related industrial areas. By endeavouring to maintain its dominant status via embargoes, U.S. trade restrictions in turn accelerate the Chinese government's efforts to bolster Huawei's development. It is understandable from a strategic perspective, but what is really worrying is that the worldwide trade bans on Huawei will unfortunately derogate Huawei from being a solid international hardware provider, simply (or forcefully) turning it into a national player. The phenomenon risks diminishing (or ceasing) Huawei being a channel for more Chinese and foreign expertise forging together new common codes of conduct that can benefit the whole human society. This not only delays the speed of 5G rollouts for the American market and other regions, but also fosters severe animosity that can last for decades. All of this does not appear to be proportionate for the purpose of achieving safeguard security, or to more comprehensive and broader connectivity. Like trade wars, restricting competition depresses economic growth for all of the countries involved (Amadeo 2019).

Of all these matters, a re-examination of the current competition-focus conduct is necessary. In the context of where the premium is on Chinese hardware and American software, European legal regulations are specifically featured. It seems more promising for cross-border collaboration to polish security measures. Changing mindsets into paving a fair, safe, and convenient 5G ecosystem can be more meaningful and sustainable than another Cold War Space Race. As a prominent Chinese scholar in Sino-American relations, Zi Zhongjun, back in 2012, indicated that "Technology is supposed to bring Human beings' welfare, not disasters. Considering that we have hardly contributed anything beneficial to human society in modern times, except for the previous four innovations that we as Chinese contributed to the world a thousand year ago [...] our entrepreneurs can do differently in this new era" (China Entrepreneur Club 2012). As a scholar, she urged the decision-makers and leading scientists to focus on working to deliver a fair, sustainable and prosperous living environment for both the Chinese and the entire international society. Similarly, Huawei CEO Mr Ren Zhengfei has many times, openly, outlined the great contributions made by Google, Apple and Microsoft to society. Inspired by how technologies change the world, by breaking geographic barriers and assembling intellectuals from all over the world, he advocated, "Huawei is determined to work through international cooperation for an open and secure 5G environment for all" and "contribute to working on a unilateral global cloud standard" (Tech. 163 2019).

Those statements can be perceived as part of Chinese propaganda. However, if they are the genuine sentiments of the speakers, are there not substantial gains for the international community to be made by allowing them to play their part in these programs? In addition, the Chinese mainland is the world's largest domestic market; it consumes over 50% of the world's semiconductors and has captured up to 40% of the global 5G infrastructure market (C-Span 2020). Would it not be better to have a group of capable and responsible Chinese counterparts (considering the population compacity) working together with other such groups across the world to boost connectivity with trust and cooperation? After all, raising walls is perceived in the wrong way (Knolle 2019). If we cannot find ways to solve the deliberate decoupling issues, they can continue into the future, into the 6G era and beyond.

As the Chief Security Officer of the KPN Group, Jaya Baloo, once answered to the question as to what real, good security in the information age (cyber security) should be: "my long term hope for cyber security is that the telecommunications company and cyber security becomes like the electrical company and electricity that is just something you have already, [...] that it's just something that is there that you can trust, that we've imbedded into our security processes, our architecture by design, our products and our services, that it is just something we have by default without having to think too much about" (Huawei Archive 2013). In general, it may be difficult to predict what kind of 5G future will eventually emerge after the current chaotic phase. But one thing is for sure; there is still some space for people in action, including decision-makers, across the regions to adjust the choices they make based on one concern: what kind of 5G future shall we shape?

5.7. References

5G PPP (2016). 5G empowering vertical industries. 5G PPP brochure, February [Online]. Available at: http://5g-ppp.eu/wp-content/uploads/2016/02/BROCHURE_5PPP_BAT2_PL.pdf [Accessed 6 April 2020].

Ai, S. (2020). Singapore's 5G licenses have been issued and the goal is to build a nationwide network by 2025. *C114 News*, April 30 [Online]. Available at: http://m.c114.com.cn/w116-1123887.html [Accessed 30 May 2020].

Al Jazeera News (2018). Why are countries banning Huawei? December 7 [Online]. Available at: https://www.aljazeera.com/news/2018/12/countries-banning-huawei-181206130850129.html [Accessed 29 May 2020].

Amadeo, K. (2019). Trade wars and their effect on the economy and you. Why trade wars are bad and nobody wins. *The Balance*, December 7 [Online]. Available at: https://www.thebalance.com/trade-wars-definition-how-it-affects-you-4159973 [Accessed 14 February 2020].

Amadeo, R. (2021). From first to sixth: Huawei's phone business tanks thanks to US sanctions. *Ars Technica*, January 28 [Online]. Available at: https://arstechnica.com/gadgets/2021/01/huaweis-phone-sales-plummet-42-percent-in-q4-2020-its-now-in-sixth-place/ [Accessed 14 March 2022].

BBC (2019a). US files charges against China's Huawei and CFO Meng Wanzhou. January 29 [Online]. Available at: https://www.bbc.com/news/world-us-canada-47036515 [Accessed 3 April 2020].

BBC (2019b). Huawei faces US charges: The short, medium and long story. May 7 [Online]. Available at: https://www.bbc.com/news/world-us-canada-47046264 [Accessed 3 April 2020].

BBC (2021). Huawei and ZTE left out of India's 5G trials. May 5 [Online]. Available at: https://www.bbc.com/news/business-56990236 [Accessed 14 March 2022].

Blackman, C. and Forge, S. (2019). 5G deployment. State of play in Europe, USA and Asia. PE 631.060 [Online]. Available at: https://www.europarl.europa.eu/RegData/etudes/IDAN/2019/631060/IPOL_IDA(2019)631060_EN.pdf [Accessed 31 May 2020].

Bloomberg (2019). Qualcomm CEO Steve Mollenkopf on 5G technology (audio). December 2 [Online]. Available at: https://www.bloomberg.com/news/audio/2019-12-02/qualcomm-ceo-steve-mollenkopf-on-5g-technology-audio [Accessed 6 April 2020].

Brake, D. (2020). A U.S. national strategy for 5G and future wireless innovation. Information Technology & Innovation Foundation [Online]. Available at: https://itif.org/publications/2020/04/27/us-national-strategy-5g-and-future-wireless innovation [Accessed 12 August 2020].

CCi (2020a) Investigation report on candidates for 5G standard essential patents (5G-SEP) and standardization contributions [Online]. Available at: https://www.cybersoken.com/file/5G-SEP-ENG.pdf [Accessed 9 April 2020].

CCi (2020b) Docomo is the world's No. 1 carrier in 5G essential patents [Online]. Available at: https://www.cybersoken.com/en/trend/2020/02/05/223/ [Accessed 9 April 2020].

Cerulus, L. (2021). Germany falls in line with EU on Huawei. *Politico* [Online]. Available at: https://www.politico.eu/article/germany-europe-huawei-5g-data-privacy-cybersecurity/ [Accessed 14 March 2022].

Chandramouli, D. (2020). 5G for Industry 4.0. *3GPP* [Online]. Available at: https://www.3gpp.org/news-events/2122-tsn_v_lan [Accessed 8 June 2020].

Chen, X. (2019). The battle of 5G baseband chips: The beginning of the top five pattern (part 1). *Guancha*, December 26 [Online]. Available at: https://www.guancha.cn/kegongliliang/2019_12_26_529530.shtml [Accessed 13 June 2020].

Cheng, E. (2021) Huawei expects 2021 revenue to drop by 28.9% as sanctions drag on. *CNBC*, December 30 [Online]. Available at: https://www.cnbc.com/2021/12/31/huawei-expects-2021-revenue-to-drop-by-28point9percent-as-sanctionsdragon.html#:~:text=The%20company%20reported%20891.4%20billion,revenue%20of%20858.8%20billion%20yuan [Accessed 14 March 2022].

China Entrepreneur Club (2012). Zi Zhongjun's keynote speech. China Green Companies Summit (Wuhan), April 21 [Online]. Available at: http://www.daonong.com/green/2012nianhui/baodao/hui2/2012/0421/33788.html [Accessed 30 May 2020].

C-Span (2020). Attorney General Bill Barr Keynote Speech [Online]. Available at: https://www.c-span.org/video/?469051-1/fbi-director-wray-attorney-general-barr-deliver-remarks-chinese-threats [Accessed 22 June 2020].

CSIS (2020). Criteria for security and trust in telecommunications networks and services. CSIS Working Group on Trust and Security in 5G Networks [Online]. Available at: https://csis-website-prod.s3.amazonaws.com/s3fs-public/publication/200511_Lewis_5G_v3.pdf [Accessed 23 May 2020].

Davis Polk and Wardwell LLP (2020). China Anti-Trust Law Review of 2019 [Online]. Available at: https://www.davispolk.com/files/2019_china_antitrust_review_chinese.pdf [Accessed 24 May 2020].

Deloitte (2018). 5G: The chance to lead for a decade [Online]. Available at: https://www2.deloitte.com/content/dam/Deloitte/us/Documents/technology-media-telecommunications/us-tmt-5g-deployment-imperative.pdf [Accessed 14 August 2020].

Der Standard (2019). Telekom-Austria-Chef: "Schließen Huawei nicht aus" [Online]. Available at: https://www.derstandard.at/story/2000097962193/verkehrsministerium-huawei-ausschluss-koennte-innovationen-bremsen [Accessed 28 May 2020].

European Commission (2019). EU-China – A strategic outlook. JOIN (2019) 5 final, Strasbourg [Online]. Available at: https://ec.europa.eu/commission/sites/beta-political/files/communication-eu-china-a-strategic-outlook.pdf [Accessed 22 May 2020].

European Commission (2020). Telecoms factsheet [Online]. Available at: https://ec.europa.eu/digital-single-market/sites/digital-agenda/files/telecoms_package2.png [Accessed 6 April 2020].

European Commission (2022). European Chips Act – Questions and Answers. February 8 [Online]. Available at: https://ec.europa.eu/commission/presscorner/detail/en/qanda_22_730 [Accessed 15 March 2022].

European Court of Auditors (2022). 5G in the EU needs a booster [Online]. Available at: https://www.eca.europa.eu/Lists/News/NEWS2201_24/INSR_Security-5G-networks_EN.pdf [Accessed 18 April 2022].

Guo, X.J. and Zhang, R. (2019). The anxious United States behind the Huawei incident *Duoweicn* [Online]. Available at: https://duoweicn.dwnews.com/zh/CN-2019 年 041 期/10007379.html [Accessed 14 February 2020].

Gupton, N. (2017). What's the difference between AR, VR, and MR? *The Franklin Institute* [Online]. Available at: https://www.fi.edu/difference-between-ar-vr-and-mr [Accessed 26 May 2020].

Hope, A. (2020). US shares evidence of Huawei backdoor access to mobile phone networks with UK and Germany. *CPOMagazine*, February 27 [Online]. Available at: https://www.cpomagazine.com/tech/u-s-shares-evidence-of-huawei-backdoor-access-to-mobile-phone-networks-with-uk-and-germany/ [Accessed 10 August 2020].

Huawei Archive (2013). Huawei calls for an integral global cybersecurity standard [Online]. Available at: https://www.huawei.com/cn/about-huawei/cyber-security/related-content/hw_310625 [Accessed 11 April 2020].

Hussain, N.Z. (2019). American drivers warming to self-driving cars – Survey. *Reuters*, October 23 [Online]. Available at: https://www.reuters.com/article/us-usa-autos-selfdriving-cars/american-drivers-warming-to-self-driving-cars-surveyidUSKBN1X22CX [Accessed 28 May 2020].

ITU (2011). All about the technology [Online]. Available at: https://www.itu.int/osg/spu/ni/3G/technology/index.html [Accessed 28 May 2020].

Jayadevan, P. (2020).When will 5G be available in India? *Computerworld*, April 29 [Online]. Available at: https://www.computerworld.com/article/3540254/when-will-5g-be-available-in-india.html [Accessed 25 May 2020].

Kavanagh, S. (n.d.). What is enhanced Mobile Broadband (eMBB). *5G* [Online]. Available at: https://5g.co.uk/guides/what-is-enhanced-mobile-broadband-embb/ [Accessed 26 May 2020].

Keane, S. (2020). Huawei ban timeline: Chinese company's CFO loses case to dismiss extradition to US. *CNet* [Online]. Available at: https://www.cnet.com/news/huawei-ban-full-timeline-us-restrictions-china-trump-executive-order-india/ [Accessed 14 February 2020].

Kharpal, A. (2021). Huawei's growth slowed dramatically in 2020 as U.S. sanctions take their toll. *CNBC*, March 31 [Online]. Available at: https://www.cnbc.com/2021/03/31/huawei-2020-revenue-growth-slows-dramatically-as-us-sanctions-hit.html [Accessed 15 April 2022].

Knolle, K. (2019). Austria calls for European stance on Huawei to ensure competition. *Reuters*, February 13 [Online]. Available at: https://de.reuters.com/article/us-huawei-europeaustria/austria-calls-for-european-stance-on-huawei-to-ensure-competition-idUSKCN1Q22BO [Accessed 28 May 2020].

Lewis, J. (2018). How 5G will shape innovation and security. *CSIS* [Online]. Available at: https://csis-website-prod.s3.amazonaws.com/s3fspublic/publication/181206_Lewis_5G Primer_WEB.pdf [Accessed 23 May 2020].

Lewis, J. (2019). 5G: To ban or not to ban? It's not black or white. *CSIS* [Online]. Available at: https://www.csis.org/analysis/5g-ban-or-not-ban-its-not-black-or-white [Accessed 24 May 2020].

Li, Y. (2018). Israel plans the release of 5G network audition in 2019. *State Radio Regulation of China* [Online]. Available at: http://www.srrc.org.cn/article22408.aspx [Accessed 25 May 2020].

Li, H. (2019). Optical communications market: The turning point and market resonance value enhancement investment opportunity. *CAITONG SECURITIES* [Online]. Available at: http://stock.tianyancha.com/ResearchReport/eastmoney/bf055f02119ceefd5c4c1d6774d88092.pdf [Accessed 26 May 2020].

Malwarebytes (n.d.). Backdoor. Security basics [Online]. Available at: https://www.malwarebytes.com/backdoor/ [Accessed 10 August 2020].

Miao, Z. and Wen, S. (n.d.). Huawei cited controversy overseas repeatedly hit a wall. *Deutsche Welle* [Online]. Available at: https://p.dw.com/p/39ZBF [Accessed 14 February 2020].

Miao, Z. and Ye, X. (2019). Portugal does not rule out Huawei bid for first Dutch auction of 5G spectrum. *Deutsche Welle* [Online]. Available at: https://p.dw.com/p/3UHmQ [Accessed 20 May 2020].

MOFACOM (2019). The in-depth analysis on global and Chinese cloud security services market of 2018 [Online]. Available at: http://coi.mofcom.gov.cn/article/y/wbxt/201906/20190602870799.shtml [Accessed 14 August 2020].

Nicolás, E.A. (2022). EU auditors slam fragmented, sluggish 5G rollout. *Euobserver*, January 25 [Online]. Available at: https://euobserver.com/rule-of-law/154179 [Accessed 18 April 2022].

Niwa, U. (2019). A former Chinese ambassador makes a bold prediction! The future of the U.S.-China trade war. *Toyokeizai*, January 11 [Online]. Available at: https://toyokeizai.net/articles/-/258925 [Accessed 3 April 2020].

Noble, M., Mutimear, J., Vary, R. (2019). Determining which companies are leading the 5G race. *Wireless technology, Bird&Bird LLP* [Online]. Available at: https://www.twobirds.com/-/media/pdfs/news/articles/2019/determining-which-companies-areleading-the-5grace.pdf?la=en&hash=8ABA5A7173EEE8FFA612E070C0EA4B4F53CC50DE [Accessed 7 April 2020].

Ortega, A. (2020). The U.S.-China race and the fate of transatlantic relations. Part II: Bridging differing geopolitical views. *CSIS* [Online]. Available at: https://www.csis.org/analysis/us-china-race-and-fate-transatlantic-relations-0 [Accessed 24 May 2020].

OSA Publishing (2018). OIDA market update: Optical communications market – Internet content providers and 5G [Online]. Available at: https://www.osapublishing.org/abstract.cfm?uri=OIDA-2018-4 [Accessed 26 May 2020].

Petersson, C. (2019). Why you shouldn't believe everything you read about 5G patents. *Ericsson* [Online]. Available at: https://www.ericsson.com/en/blog/2019/10/5G-patent-leadership [Accessed 20 May 2020].

Reuters (2020a). Austria to collaborate with EU partners on Huawei 5G decision. January 20 [Online]. Available at: https://www.reuters.com/article/us-austria-5g-huawei-tech/austria-to-collaborate-with-eu-partners-on-huawei-5g-decision-idUSKBN1ZJ10R [Accessed 14 March 2022].

Reuters (2020b). Qualcomm receives U.S. permission to sell 4G chips to Huawei in exception to ban. November 14 [Online]. Available at: https://www.reuters.com/article/qualcomm-huawei-tech-idINKBN27U0MW [Accessed 14 March 2022].

Reuters (2021). Telefonica buys Ericsson 5G equipment to replace some Huawei gear. December 27 [Online]. Available at: https://www.reuters.com/markets/deals/telefonica-buys-ericsson-5g-equipment-replace-some-huawei-gear-2021-12-27/ [Accessed 14 March 2022].

Slotta, D. (2022). Market share of 5G base station manufacturers in China in 2021. *Statista*, March 14 [Online]. Available at: https://www.statista.com/statistics/1194757/china-market-share-of-5g-base-stations-by-manufacturer/ [Accessed 14 March 2022].

Taddeo, M. (2019). To build trust, we could treat cybersecurity as a public good: Opinion. *ITU News* [Online]. Available at: https://news.itu.int/15753-2/ [Accessed 10 August 2020]

Tech 163 (2019). CCTV interview of Ren Zhengfei. May 26 [Online]. Available at: http://tech.163.com/19/0526/22/EG4U284I00097U7S.html [Accessed 24 May 2020].

The Economic Times (2019). Manoj Sinha says no plan yet to ban Huawei telecom equipment. January 5 [Online]. Available at: https://economictimes.indiatimes.com/industry/telecom/telecom-news/manoj-sinha-says-no-plan-yet-to-ban-huawei-telecom-equipment/articleshow/67391143.cms?from=mdr [Accessed 14 May 2020].

Trend Watch (2020). Docomo is the world's No. 1 carrier in 5G essential patents [Online]. Available at: https://www.cybersoken.com/en/trend/2020/02/05/223/ [Accessed 9 April 2020].

United States Department of Defense (2019). Agency Financial Report (AFR). Fiscal Year 2019 [Online]. Available at: https://comptroller.defense.gov/Portals/45/Documents/afr/fy2019/DoD_FY19_Agency_Financial_Report.pdf [Accessed 23 May 2020].

Walsh, D. and Kim, C. (2022). The House passed a bill aimed at boosting U.S. competitiveness with China. *NPR.org*, February 4 [Online]. Available at: https://www.npr.org/2022/02/04/1078226282/u-s-house-passes-china-competition-bill?t=1647330981764 [Accessed 15 March 2022].

Whittaker, Z. (2019). US threatens to reduce intelligence sharing if Germany doesn't ban Huawei. *Techcrunch*, March 11 [Online]. Available at: https://techcrunch.com/2019/03/11/germany-intelligence-sharing/?guccounter=1&guce_referrer=aHR0cHM6Ly93d3cuZ29vZ2xlLmNvbS8&guce_referrer_sig=AQAAADam5wbsPRJzuxP5r9CRzFzYZ9exnXaPBW9gFlnmSciuXQt_t1oC9cTcIsZSnL80MXsSDXziQkiDrJNTrD3ffOug-mooPZ1DfycLiX56K_1nwlQ4yWH4hn7xv6zfgida_z68iY63xJCiub48hBGWt8F5lkKJidXJhcfl0wAjNA6i[Accessed 2 June 2020].

World Economic Forum (2018). The Future of Jobs Report 2018 [Online]. Available at: http://www3.weforum.org/docs/WEF_Future_of_Jobs_2018.pdf [Accessed 30 May 2020].

XianZao (2019). About 5G true value. Blog series [Online]. Available at: https://zhuanlan.zhihu.com/p/56574728 [Accessed 26 May 2020].

XianZao (2020). 5G SA core network, fantastic. Individual analysis [Online]. Available at: https://zhuanlan.zhihu.com/p/141977586 [Accessed 28 May 2020].

Yezi Guping (2019). The most comprehensive list of the 2019 leading stocks in 5G supply chain. Individual analysis [Online]. Available at: https://zhuanlan.zhihu.com/p/57540681 [Accessed 7 April 2020].

Zhao, Q. (2019) The 5G competition. What for *Duoweicn*? [Online]. Available at: https://duoweicn.dwnews.com/zh/CN-2019%E5%B9%B4041%E6%9C%9F/10007380.html [Accessed 22 May 2020].

Zhao, H. (2020). US govt extends comment period for Huawei. *China Daily*, March 26 [Online]. Available at: https://www.chinadaily.com.cn/a/202003/26/WS5e7c226ba31012821728232e.html [Accessed 14 February 2020].

6

Analyzing the Quality of Online Product Reviews and their Antecedents

Consumers rely heavily on online product reviews to make their purchase decisions, yet online reviews are often brief and empty and not very helpful. This chapter puts forward the key concept of online product review quality by operationalizing their two dimensions: length and concreteness. We then go on to investigate two antecedents, product type and monetary incentives, and examine their effects on online review quality by empirical research. We collected 850 real online product reviews from the biggest Chinese e-commerce website TAOBAO.COM and present our hypothesis. We find that compared to utilitarian products, consumers create longer and more concrete online reviews for hedonic products. Monetary incentives have a positive effect on the length of online reviews but no effect on the concreteness of reviews. Moreover, product type moderates the relationship between monetary incentives and online review quality.

6.1. Introduction

With the rapid development of online shopping, consumers' decision making processes have been changed. Online shoppers can search for and obtain enormous amounts of information on the Internet to facilitate their decisions. One of the most important sources of information are online consumer product reviews ("online reviews") created by users and based on personal usage experience (Chen and Xie 2008). A survey by Jupiter Research finds that 75% of consumers search for relevant online reviews before online shopping, and more than 90% of large companies believe that online reviews are important to consumers' purchase decisions (Yin 2012).

Chapter written by Yin XU and Sam DZEVER

Why do consumers rely so heavily on online reviews? For consumers, online reviews are generally considered to be more credible when published by third parties than information published by manufacturers (Senecal and Nantel 2004; Ye *et al.* 2009) and they have a greater impact on consumers (Racherla *et al.* 2012). Moreover, with the development of professional online product review sites (such as the Public Remark Web, ComScore) and online review platforms of e-commerce giants (such as Taobao and Amazon), it becomes cheaper and more convenient for consumers to search for reviews online than offline word-of-mouth information (Moe and Schweidel 2012).

However, not all online reviews can provide valuable information and effective guidance for consumers. Online reviews are often brief and empty, mixed with meaningless sentences, inaccurate descriptions, useless remarks, careless conclusions, and even spurious opinions. With the increase of online reviews, consumers have to spend more time on filtering and extracting valuable information. Moreover, low-quality online review may reduce consumers' trust in sellers and negatively affect product sales (Burtch *et al.* 2018).

To solve this problem, companies increasingly employ monetary rewards to stimulate more high-quality online reviews. The common practice is to provide rewards simply based on the number of reviews written. This strategy does not seem completely successful and often leads to more reviews but with little increase in review quality. Due to operational difficulties, rewards are seldom based on review quality (Khern-am-nuai *et al.* 2018).

To help consumers better screen online reviews and help companies better stimulate more valuable online reviews we suggest the concept of online review quality in this chapter and raise two specific research questions: (1) what kind of online review can be considered as high quality? We seek to identify two direct and easy-to-measure dimensions of high-quality review, considering review length and concreteness. In particular, the introduction of the novel dimension "concreteness" can enable companies to design their reward mechanism and boost more valuable reviews; (2) what kind of factors influence the quality of online review? We investigate the roles of two factors, i.e., product type and monetary rewards. We then examine their dependent and interactive influences on the quality of online reviews.

6.2. Literature review

6.2.1. *Definition and measurement of online review quality*

Previous research has defined online review quality from different perspectives. Bickart and Schindler (2001) use "relevance" to measure review quality. Rieh (2002) defines information quality as the usefulness, correctness and promptness for its users. Liu (2006) uses the word "helpfulness" to describe quality and argues that online consumer reviews can be helpful only when they contain concrete details and credible evidence. Park and Lee (2007) find that consumers are more likely to use relevant, easy-to-understand, and adequate information considered as high-quality reviews to guide their choices. Forman *et al.* (2008) suggest the use of "readability" while Pentina *et al.* (2018) use "persuasiveness" to reflect the quality of online reviews. It is important to note, however, that the above definitions and measurements of the quality of online reviews are mainly based on the evaluations of review readers. As a result the measurement of review quality depends on whether the review platform offers the function of reader evaluation.

Recent research has increasingly utilized this concept from its textual features by text mining techniques (Archak *et al.*, 2011; Ludwig *et al.*, 2013; Khern-am-nuai *et al.* 2018). Because of the unstructured nature of online reviews, operational measurement of review content quality has always been the key challenge. Studies in the fields of linguistic research and computer systems explore this problem by analyzing the linguistic features of sentences such as average sentence length, word length, expression extremeness, degree of specialization, etc. (Cao *et al.* 2011, Humphreys and Wang 2017), while most of the studies in marketing use the number of reviews, review ratings and variance to measure the quantitative aspects of online reviews. Ludwig *et al.* (2013), for example, argue that these methods cannot sufficiently capture real content and delicate differences between online reviews. The authors employ a text mining method to analyze the semantic content and style properties of online reviews and find that affective contents play an important role in increasing the conversion rate of online reviews. Büschken and Allenby (2016) use sentence structure contained in reviews for further text analysis. Humphreys and Wang (2017) integrate linguistic theory and consumer research and present an automated text analysis technique.

6.2.2. *Antecedents of online review quality*

Research of antecedents of online review quality is far more limited than that of their consequences (Berger and Schwartz 2011). Prior studies examine four kinds of antecedents which include consumer-related, interaction-related, product-related and firm-related variables. With the motivation of entertainment and socialization, consumers are more likely to submit long and objective reviews (Tang *et al.* 2016). According to Moe and Schweidel (2012) the rating, number, and controversy of existing online reviews will induce new high-quality reviews. Consumers have more desire to publish online reviews when the product is interesting and used in public (Berger and Schwartz 2011). Mudambi and Schuff (2010) find that consumers publish more specialized reviews for search products than experiential products. Li and Zhang (2013) find that consumers publish more personalized reviews for hedonic products than utilitarian products. Li and Ruan (2016) focus on the marketing input of companies and find that companies can improve consumer initiatives to write reviews with monetary incentives. Through a detailed empirical study Khern-am-nuai *et al.* (2018) find that monetary rewards effectively increase the number of reviews but decrease the quality of reviews thereby making reviews more positive and skewed. In contrast Burtch *et al.* (2018) come to an adverse conclusion in their experiment and argue that monetary rewards improve online review quality and make them lengthier. The mix and controversial results are partly due to the difference in measurement of online review quality and research methodology.

6.3. Theoretical model and hypothesis development

In this paper we focus on two specific dimensions of online review quality: length and concreteness. Online review length refers to the number of words contained in a review: put simply, more words there are in a review the longer it is. This measurement has been used in prior studies (Cao *et al.* 2011; Büschken and Allenby 2016; Burtch *et al.* 2018).

Concreteness of online reviews is a novel dimension in the domain of online reviews. In linguistics literature, sentence concreteness has been defined as the association between language and sensory experience reflecting the degree to which language can use non-character spatial imagination (Gorman 1961). The more concrete the language is the faster it can stimulate people's imagination to form non-linguistic image codes and store them in the brain spatially parallel rather than in sequential character code (Begg and Pavio 1969, 821). A concrete language expression (1) contains more temporal and spatial information; (2) contains details of sensory experience; (3) contains more categories of word attributes (nouns, verbs, adjectives, adverbs, quantifiers, etc.); (4) makes more use of the first person, less use of the passive voice; (5) makes more use of emotion-related words; (6) has longer sentences (Paivio *et al.* 1968; Pavioo 1990). In this chapter we measure concreteness by the number of categories of word attributes (noun, verb, etc.). When an online review contains more categories of word attributes it is considered to be more concrete.

6.3.1. *The effect of product type on the quality of online reviews*

Hedonism is dominated by the emotions of consumers (Wertenbroch and Dhar 2000), whereas utilitarianism is mainly guided by knowledge and often for the purpose of fulfilling functional or practical tasks (Strahilevitzhe and Myers 1998). According to the above description, products can be divided into hedonic products and utilitarian products. Utilitarian product mainly refers to a product that meets the consumer's basic daily needs and functions which can help them accomplish their own goals and basic tasks. These include clothes and air conditioning. Consumers buy utilitarian products with little emotional involvement, low quality uncertainty, and low purchase risk. In contrast, hedonic product refers to a product which can make the consumer feel sensually happy or satisfy their curiosity and enjoyment of desire such as games consoles, jewelry, etc. Consumers buy hedonic products with more emotional involvement, high quality uncertainty, and high purchase risk (Clement *et al.* 2006).

To start with, for all hedonic products whose quality cannot fully be perceived before purchase, online reviews can help potential customers to effectively reduce the risk of purchase (Zhu and Zhang 2010). Bei *et al.* (2004) find that customers who purchase hedonic products spend more time reading online reviews and are more inclined to use online reviews than those who purchase utilitarian products. With the motivation of reciprocation, consumers are more likely to post more information after purchasing and consuming hedonic products.

Second, it is relatively easy for companies to provide detailed information such as technical specifications and features for utilitarian products. As a result, information from consumers has less marginal value and consumers are less motivated to post repeat information online. For hedonic products, however, consumers place more value on experiential sensory details and matching information between usage conditions and product attributes based on personal experiences which can only be provided by consumers (Chen and Xie 2008). Posting these kinds of information is of great value and can satisfy consumers' altruistic motivations.

Third, information in hedonic product reviews is mainly related to the consuming process and personal experience which by nature contains more details whereas information of utilitarian product review is related to the consuming function, which as a result tends to be abstract and conclusive.

Based on the above analysis we suggest the following hypotheses for our work:

H1a: Online reviews are longer for hedonic products than for utilitarian products.

H1b: Online reviews are more concrete for hedonic products than for utilitarian products.

6.3.2. *The effect of monetary incentive on the quality of online reviews*

Sellers are increasingly adopting monetary incentives such as coupons, gifts, etc. in order to stimulate online reviews and, in turn, improve sales. The common incentive system designed by sellers is to provide a monetary reward according to the number of reviews written or the number of words in a review. As this is not based on the content of reviews, it is hard to evaluate (Khern-am-nuai *et al.* 2018). As a result this is more likely to increase review length. Hsieh *et al.* (2010) find that monetary incentive induce higher volume and longer answers but have no effect on the quality of the answers in a knowledge sharing platform. Burtch *et al.* (2018) on the other hand find that monetary rewards effectively increase review length when combined with social norms.

Online reviewers can be categorized into voluntary reviewers and incentivized reviewers. According to Marinescu *et al.* (2018) voluntary reviewers are those who have the intrinsic desire to post their opinions online; incentivized reviewers are those who will not post anything without monetary incentive. Providing incentive for reviews has the potential to attract incentivized reviewers to write which, in turn, encourages voluntary reviewers to write more as a reward. But as Khern-am-nuai *et al.* (2018) have observed that monetary incentive is unable to trigger emotions and experiences nor change the writing ability and styles of writers and thus improve deliberation and engagement. As a result, monetary incentives are not likely to improve the concreteness of online reviews.

Based on the above analysis we suggest the following additional hypotheses for our work:

H2a: Monetary incentive has a positive effect on the length of online reviews.

H2b: Monetary incentive has no effect on the concreteness of online reviews.

6.3.3. *Interactions between monetary incentives and product type*

We argue that the effects of monetary incentives on online review length could be moderated by product type. Monetary incentive stimulates reviewers to write longer reviews. However, it is easy to add new words and sentences for the review of utilitarian products which are mainly technical specifications, features and functions. In fact, sellers provide sufficient information and details which a reviewer can easily copy and paste. On the other hand reviews related to hedonic products are mainly personal experiences with particular usage conditions. It is hard to add new words and sentences of personal emotion and feeling with general usage conditions as a result of monetary incentive. Thus, the effect of monetary incentive on review length is greater for utilitarian products than for hedonic products.

Based on the preceding argument we suggest the following further hypotheses to guide our work:

H3a: Compared with hedonic products, monetary incentive has a greater effect on the length of online reviews for utilitarian products.

H3b: Product type has no moderating effect on the relationship between monetary rewards and review concreteness.

In summary the theoretical framework of this chapter is depicted in Figure 6.1 below.

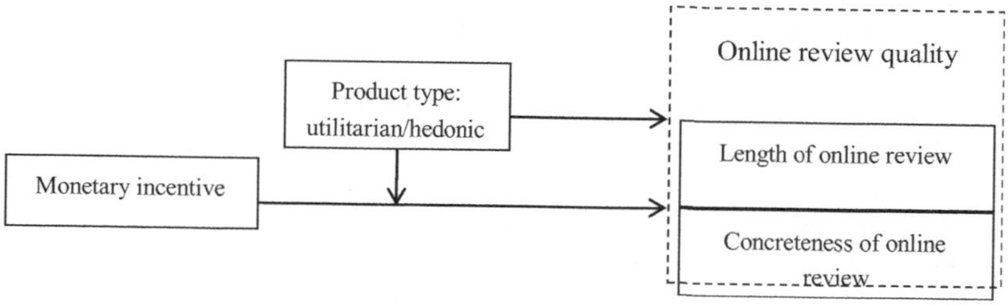

Figure 6.1: *Theoretical framework*

6.4. Data collection

To test the research hypotheses outlined above, we collected data from www.taobao.com which is the largest e-retailer in China and globally and has the largest number of reviews in the Chinese market. Taobao reviews are widely used by consumers as a valuable and reputable source of information. Taobao offers two types of distribution channels for companies to sell their products. One is to open an e-direct-store on the Tmall platform which is a subsidiary of Taobao and sell products to consumers directly; the other is to distribute the product through Taobao Supermarket or other e-agents in which companies sell products to e-agents and e-agents, in turn, sell the products to consumers. Consumers can search for reviews and buy products through either type of channel which operates independently and adopts different promotion strategies to encourage reviews and sales. This provides the researchers with the opportunity naturally experiment by matching product reviews in two different channels and thus exploring the effects of different strategies.

As for the product type, we chose the milk and yogurt category for the following reasons. Firstly, although milk and yogurt both belong to the dairy category and are similar in many marketing elements, the former, according to previous studies,

(Zhang and Huang 2014; Tian *et al.* 2011) is considered to be utilitarian product while yogurt is considered to be a hedonic product. Secondly, food quality and safety is a critical question in China and reviews have great impact on consumers in that market.

During our empirical data collection period from November 1, 2017 to January 31, 2018, "New Hope", a reputable national dairy brand, offered coupons to encourage online reviews on their e-direct-store (RMB 10 off for every 50 spent if submitting a review). At the same time no monetary reward for leaving a review was available in the e-agent-store of New Hope. Note that there were no differences in price and postal fee of the products with respect to the two channels of distribution. We obtained 1,162 online reviews through the GooSeeker web crawler software. By eliminating invalid reviews with less than 10 words we had 850 reviews for New Hope products which included 223 for milk in the e-agent-store; 221 for milk in the e-direct store; 205 for yogurt in the e-agent-store; and 201 for yogurt in the e-direct-store.

To measure the length of reviews we calculated the number of words in each review. To measure the concreteness of each review we marked each word with their word attribute according to Modern Chinese Word Classification Norm GB/T 20532-2006 and calculated the number of word attribute categories in each review. From this we found that the top 10 most frequently written words were: delicious (adj.), good (adj.), taste (n.), yogurt (n.), milk (n.), like (v.), package (n.), wonderful (adj.) promotion (n.), and Tmall (n.). The summary statistics of the review elements and characteristics are presented in Table 6.1. The statistics are calculated separately for the four groups divided by product type (utilitarian-milk vs. hedonic-yogurt) and monetary reward (yes-direct store vs. no-agent store).

	Review length (number of words)				Review concreteness (number of word attribute categories)			
	Milk e-agent-store	Milk e-direct-store	Yogurt e-agent-store	Yogurt e-direct-store	Milk e-agent-store	Milk e-direct-store	Yogurt e-agent-store	Yogurt e-direct-store
Mean	15.53	20.86	22.01	23.69	5.54	5.76	6.55	6.67
S.D.	12.508	12.059	19.570	14.408	1.871	1.531	1.888	1.477
N.	223	221	205	201	223	221	205	201

Table 6.1. *Summary statistics of the review elements*

6.5. Analysis and results

6.5.1. *Research model and analysis method*

Based on the hypotheses outlined above, this study involves two independent variables: product type (utilitarian vs. hedonic products) and monetary rewards (yes vs. no); and two dependent variables: review length and review concreteness reflecting review quality. The descriptive statistics and correlation coefficients for all variables involved are presented in Table 6.2. There is a significant correlation between product type and monetary incentives and the length of online reviews; furthermore there is a significant correlation between product type and the concreteness of online reviews. The correlation between monetary incentives and the concreteness of online reviews is not strong. However, the correlation coefficient cannot reveal the independent and interactive effect of multiple variables on the length and concreteness of online reviews.

	Product type	Monetary incentive	Review length	Review concreteness
Product type	1.000			
Monetary incentive	-0.003	1.000		
Review length	0.154**	0.118**	1.000	
Review concreteness	0.270**	0.050	0.639**	1.000
Maximum	1.000	1.000	90.000	11.000
Min	0.000	0.000	4.000	2.000
Mean	0.478	0.496	20.408	6.109
Standard deviation	0.500	0.500	15.133	1.769

** Represents statistically significant when P<0.01 (two-tails).

* Represents statistically significant when P<0.05 (two-tails).

Table 6.2. *Variable description statistics and correlation analysis*

Next, we establish moderating regression models to further examine the impact of product type (*Protype*), monetary incentive (*Monreward*), and their interaction with the length and concreteness of online reviews. The models are presented in equations [6.1] and [6.2.]

$$Length = \beta_0 + \beta_1 \times Protype + \beta_2 \times Monreward + \beta_3 \times Protype \times Monreward + \varepsilon \quad [6.1]$$

$$Concreteness = \beta_0 + \beta_1 \times Protype + \beta_2 \times Monreward + \beta_3 \times Protype \times Monreward + \varepsilon \quad [6.2]$$

In the above equations, product type (*Protype*) and monetary incentive (*Monreward*) are dummy variables. Product type equals 1 for hedonic products and 0 for utilitarian products, while monetary incentive equals 1 for reviews in the e-direct-store which offered coupon for reviews and equals 0 for reviews in the e-agent-store which offered no monetary reward for reviews.

By hierarchical regression, Model 1 examines the effect of product type and monetary incentives on review length, while Model 2 introduces the interaction between product type and monetary incentives. Similarly, Model 3 examines the effect of product type and monetary incentives on review concreteness, while Model 4 introduces the interaction between product type and monetary incentives. In order to reduce the adverse effects of multicollinearity on regression we conduct a collinearity test on the independent variables. The results show that the variance inflation factor (VIF) of all the models is less than 3 which indicates that there is no serious multicollinearity problem in the regression equations.

The results of the hierarchical regression of this study are shown in Tables 6.3 and 6.4.

Independent variable	Model 1			Model 2		
	Coefficient	Standard error	Significant	Coefficient	Standard error	Significant
Product type	4.670 (4.576)	1.021	***	6.485 (4.516)	1.436	***
Monetary incentive	3.583 (3.514)	1.020	***	5.331 (3.784)	1.409	***
Product Type* Monetary incentive				-3.659 (-1.795)	2.039	•
N	850			850		
Correct R^2	0.035			0.038		

F-stat	16.600***	12.170***
ΔR^2		0.003

Note: *** indicates P<0.001, ** indicates P<0.01, * indicates P<0.05, • indicates P<0.1, and dependent variable is length of online comment; () is the t value corresponding to the regression coefficient.

Table 6.3. *Analysis of the impact of product types and monetary incentives on online review length*

Independent variable	Model 3			Model 4		
	Coefficient	Standard error	Significant	Coefficient	Standard error	Significant
Product type	0.958 (8.191)	0.117	***	1.008 (6.115)	0.165	***
Monetary incentive	0.178 (1.525)	0.117		0.227 (1.401)	0.162	
Product Type* Monetary incentive				-0.101 (-0.433)	0.234	
N	850			850		
Correct R^2	0.074			0.073		
F-stat	34.676***			23.158***		
ΔR^2				0.001		

Note: *** indicates P<0.001, ** indicates P<0.01, * indicates P<0.05; dependent variable is online commentary; () is regression coefficient corresponding to the value of t.

Table 6.4. *Analysis of the impact of product types and monetary incentives on online review concreteness*

6.5.2. *Findings*

Models 1 and 2 are regression analyses of the influence of product type, monetary incentives, and their interaction on the length of online reviews. Model 1 validates the direct effect of product type and monetary incentives on the length of online reviews. The coefficients of product type and monetary incentives are 4.670 and 3.583, and the standard errors are 1.021 and 1.020 respectively. Both are statistically significant and the revised R^2 is 0.035. This demonstrates that product type and monetary incentives have significant impacts on the length of online reviews.

Model 2 is based on Model 1 and introduces the interaction between product type and monetary incentives. The results show that the regression coefficient of product type is 6.485 and the standard error is 1.436 which is statistically significant. The regression coefficient of monetary incentives is 5.331 and the standard error is 1.409 which is also statistically significant. These results provide strong support for our hypotheses 1a and 2a – i.e. that product type and monetary rewards have positive effects on review length. In addition, in model 2 the regression coefficient for the interaction of product type and monetary incentive interaction on review length is -3.659, and the standard error is 2.039. This coefficient is slightly statistically significant if relaxing to $p< 0.1$ level. The corrected R^2 for Model 2 is 0.038, and the R^2 difference between the two models is 0.003 indicating that product type weakly moderates the effect of monetary rewards on review length. Thus our hypothesis H3a is supported.

Through the analysis of Models 1 and 2 we can conclude that the length of online reviews varies according to product type. Specifically, reviewers tend to write longer reviews for hedonic products than utilitarian products. Also, monetary rewards induce reviewers to spend more time and energy to write long reviews. Moreover, monetary rewards have greater effect for utilitarian products than hedonic products. The interaction between product type and monetary reward implies that there is an interaction between intrinsic and extrinsic rewards. When consumers purchase utilitarian products, the intrinsic motivation for making comments is weak, leading to a stronger effect of external monetary incentives. As a result the review length gap between utilitarian products and hedonic products is narrowed.

Models 3 and Model 4 investigate the effects of product type and monetary incentives and their interaction with the concreteness of online reviews. Model 3 validates the direct impact of product type on review concreteness. In Model 3 the coefficient of product type is 0.958 with a standard error of 0.117. This coefficient is statistically significant. The coefficient of monetary incentive is 0.178 with a standard error of 0.117 which is not statistically significant. When introducing the interaction between product type and monetary rewards, as shown in Model 4, the coefficient of product type is 1.008 with a standard error of 0.165 which is still statistically significant. The coefficient of monetary incentive is 0.227 with a standard error of 1.401 which is not statistically significant. These results provide strong empirical support for our hypotheses H1b and H2b: reviewers write more concrete reviews for hedonic products than they do for utilitarian products, and that monetary rewards have no influence on review concreteness.

In addition, in Model 4, the regression coefficient of interaction between product type and monetary incentives is -0.101 with a standard error 0.234, showing no statistical significance. Therefore, product type has no moderating effect on the relationship between monetary rewards and review concreteness. Unsurprisingly, our hypothesis H3b is empirically supported. Concrete reviews are mainly based on consumers' real personal experiences, limited to their personal writing skills and habits, both of which cannot be changed easily by monetary rewards. As a result, triggered by monetary rewards, it is easy for reviewers to write longer reviews, but not more concrete reviews. These results are consistent with the study of Khern-am-nuai *et al.* (2018) which finds that monetary rewards do not improve review quality. In their research the authors measure review quality with review readability and a helpfulness score. Note that these results are based on the common practice of review platforms which provide rewards based simply on the number of reviews written.

6.6. Conclusion and implications

This research focuses on two important factors of online review quality (i.e. review length and concreteness) and investigates their antecedents. One antecedent is product type which has its influence through a likely intrinsic motivation, and the other is monetary reward which has its effect through extrinsic motivation. Compared with utilitarian products, reviewers tend to write longer and more concrete reviews. Yet, monetary rewards tend to only increase the length of reviews but not the concreteness whereas their ability to increase review length is more profound for utilitarian products.

Previous literature has defined the concept of online review quality as usefulness, helpfulness, length, persuasiveness, popularity, readability, etc. The present research contributes to the existing literature by adding a novel dimension of "concreteness" and operationalizing it by the number of word attribute categories. Moreover, we investigate the driving factors for online review quality through intrinsic and extrinsic mechanisms. From intrinsic mechanisms, we differentiate products with utilitarian and hedonic classifications which has rarely been explored in prior studies. In addition, we study the interaction between product type and monetary rewards. Using and comparing review data from two e-channels of the same brand by text mining techniques, our hypotheses obtain strong empirical support.

These conclusions have important managerial implications. The objective of online review platforms is to get paying consumers to write reviews, to get more reviews and to improve review quality. Using traditional monetary rewards based on the number of reviews, the platforms enjoy the benefit of longer reviews especially for utilitarian products and yet without significant improvement on review concreteness. The present research opens a new avenue for companies to design their monetary reward system based on review concreteness.

The contributions outlined above notwithstanding, it is clear that this study is not without limitations. Although collecting and comparing review data from two e-channels of the same brand contributes to external validity, other factors influencing online reviews cannot be perfectly controlled. Web design and attractiveness, promotion strategies and customer heterogeneity might affect our results. Secondly, in our study, the e-direct-store pays reviewers based on the number of reviews which is a common practice. If the monetary rewards mechanism were different, for example, introducing a reward based on review quality, the results might be different.

6.7. References

Anderson, E. (1998). Customer satisfaction and word of mouth. *Journal of Service Research*, 1(1), 5–17.

Arcgajm N., Ghose, A., Ipirotis, P.G. (2011). Driving the pricing power of product features by mining consumer reviews. *Management Science*, 57(8), 1485–1509.

Arndt, J. (1967). Word of mouth advertising and informal communication. In *Risk Taking and Information Handling in Consumer Behavior*, Cox, D (ed.). Division of Research, Graduate School of Business Administration, Harvard University, Boston, MA.

Bae, S. and Lee, T. (2011). Product type and consumers' perception of online consumer reviews. *Electronic Markets*, 21(4), 255–266.

Begg, I. and Paivio, A. (1969). Concreteness and imagery in sentence meaning 1. *Journal of Verbal Learning & Verbal Behavior*, 8(6), 821–827.

Bei, L.T., Chen, E.Y.I., Widdows, R. (2004). Consumers' online information search behavior and the phenomenon of search vs. experience products. *Journal of Family & Economic Issues*, 25(4), 449–467.

Berger, J. and Schwartz, E.M. (2011). What drives immediate and ongoing word of mouth? *Journal of Marketing Research*, 48(5), 869–880.

Bi, D.Y., Zhang, M.M., Xiong, Q. (2017). The dynamic mechanism of user online review information generation from the perspective of attachment theory. *Library and Information Service*, 61(18), 5–11.

Cao, Q., Duan, W., Gan, Q. (2011). Exploring determinants of voting for the "helpfulness" of online user reviews: A text mining approach. *Decision Support Systems*, 50(2), 511–521.

Chen, Y. and Xie, J. (2008). Online consumer review: Word-of-mouth as a new element of marketing communication mix. *Management Science*, 54(3), 477–491.

Chen, X., Sheng, J., Wang, X. (2016). Exploring determinants of attraction and helpfulness of online product review: A consumer behaviour perspective. *Discrete Dynamics in Nature and Society*, (1), 1–19.

Chevalier, J.A. and Mayzlin, D. (2006). The effect of word of mouth on sales: Online book reviews. *Social Science Electronic Publishing*, 43(3), 345–354.

Chitturi, R., Raghunathan, R., Mahajan, V. (2008). Delight by design: The role of hedonic versus utilitarian benefits. *Journal of Marketing*, 72(3), 48–63.

Clement, M., Fabel, S., Schmidt-Stolting, C. (2006). Diffusion of hedonic goods: A literature review. *International Journal on Media Management*, 8(4), 155–163.

Dellarocas, C. and Narayan, R. (2006). A statistical measure of a population's propensity to engage in post-purchase online word-of-mouth. *Statistical Science*, 21(2), 277–285.

Dhar, R. and Kim, E.Y. (2007). Seeing the forest or the trees: Implications of construal level theory for consumer choice. *Journal of Consumer Psychology*, 17(2), 96–100.

Doll, W.J. and Torkzadeh, G. (1988). The measurement of end-user computing satisfaction. *MIS Quarterly*, 12(2), 259–274.

Duan, W., Gu, B., Whinston, A.B. (2008). Do online reviews matter? An empirical investigation of panel data. *Decision Support Systems*, 45(4), 1007–1016.

Floyd, K., Freling, R., Alhoqail, S. (2014). How online product reviews affect retail sales: A meta-analysis. *Journal of Retailing*, 90(2), 217–232.

Forman, C., Ghose, A., Wiesenfeld B. (2008). Examining the relationship between reviews and sales: The role of reviewer identity disclosure in electronic markets. *Information Systems Research*, 19(3), 291–313.

Ghose, A. and Ipeirotis, P.G. (2007). Designing novel review ranking systems: Predicting the usefulness and impact of reviews. *International Conference on Electronic Commerce*, August 19–22, Minneapolis, MN.

Godes, D. and Mayzlin, D. (2004). Using online conversations to study word-of-mouth communication. *Marketing Science*, 23(4), 545–560.

Gong, Y.P. and Liang, S.L. (2014). Research on the impact of online reviews on consumers' willingness for new technology products based on ELM perspective. *Soft Science*, 28(2), 96–99.

Gorman, A.M. (1961). Recognition memory for nouns as a function of abstractness and frequency. *J. Exp. Psychol.*, 61(1), 23–29.

Guo, G.Q. and Yang, X.C. (2006). Word of mouth marketing and application strategies in the internet era. *Finance and Trade Economics*, (9), 56–59.

Hennig-Thurau, T., Gwinner, K.P., Walsh, G. (2004). Electronic word-of-mouth via consumer-opinion platforms: What motivates consumers to articulate themselves on the Internet? *Journal of Interactive Marketing*, 18(1), 38–52.

Hsieh, G., Kraut, R.E., Hudson, S.E. (2010). Why pay? Exploring how financial incentives are used for question and answer. *Conference on Human Factors in Computer Systems*, April 10–15, Atlanta, GA.

Huang, W.Y. and Lao, C.F. (2013). Research on the impact of internet word-of-mouth on customer perceived value and purchase intention. *Consumer Economy*, (5), 48–53.

Huang, Y. and Zhu, J.R. (2012). An empirical study on the effect of internet word-of-mouth quality on apparel consumers' purchase intention. *Jiangsu Business Theory*, (14), 22–24.

Jiang, X.D. (2015). What kind of product reviews are the most useful? The study of the influence of the quantity features and text features of online reviews on their usefulness. *Foreign Economy and Management*, (4), 41–55.

Jiang, Z. and Benbasat, I. (2007). Investigating the influence of the functional mechanisms of online product presentations. *Social Science Electronic Publishing*, 18(4), 454–470.

Khern-am-nuai, W., Kannan, K., Ghasemkhani, H. (2018). Extrinsic versus intrinsic rewards for contributing reviews in an online platform. *Information Systems Research*, 29(4).

Kim, S.M., Pantel, P., Chklovski, T. (2006). Automatically assessing review helpfulness. *Conference on Empirical Methods in Natural Language Processing*, July, Sydney.

Klein, L.R. (1998). Evaluating the potential of interactive media through a new lens: Search versus experience goods. *Journal of Business Research*, 41(3), 195–203.

Lei, L.F. (2013), Study on the impact of online reviews on consumers' purchase intention. *Management Review*, 28(3), 11–15.

Leskovec, J., Adamic, L.A., Huberman, B.A. (2007). The dynamics of viral marketing. *ACM Transaction on the Web*, 1(1), 1–15.

Li, Z.Y. (2013). Research on utility ranking models of online product reviews. *Modern Library Information Technology*, (4), 62–68.

Li, Q. and Yan, Y.Y. (2016). Incentive mechanism for online writing: Taking a coupon as an example. *Journal of Systems Management*, 25(3), 477–483.

Li, Z.W. and Zhang, Y.H. (2013). Disparity analysis of online reviews of hedonistic and utilitarian products. *Modern Management Science*, (8), 42–45.

Li, H., Yu, K., Xia, J.B. (2011). The impact of negative online reviews on consumer internet purchase decisions: An experimental study. *Journal of Information*, 30(5), 202–206.

Liu, Y. (2006). Word of mouth for movies: Its dynamics and impact on box office revenue. *Journal of Marketing*, 70(3), 74–89.

Liu, J., Cao, Y., Lin, C.Y., *et al.* (2007). Low-quality product review detection in opinion summarization. *EMNLP-CoNLL 2007, Proceedings of the 2007 Joint Conference on Empirical Methods in Natural Language Processing and Computational Natural Language Learning*, June 28–30, Prague.

Liu, J., Fu, X.D., Liu, W., *et al.* (2017). Analysis and research on the influencing factors of popular B2C shopping portal user reviews. *Computer Applications and Software*, 97(3), 71–75.

Ludwig, S., de Ruyter, K., Friedman, M., *et al.* (2013). More than words: The influence of affective content and linguistic style matches in online reviews on conversion rates. *Journal of Marketing*, 77(1), 87–103.

Ma, J.J., Ma, X.Y., Zhang, L. (2008). Different preference for product applicability and hedonism in choosing and abandoning: Taking computer discs and music CDs as examples. *Journal of Marketing Science*, (1), 107–119.

McKinney, V., Yoon, K., Zahedi, F.M. (2002). The measurement of web-customer satisfaction: An expectation and disconfirmation approach. *Information Systems Research*, 13(3), 296–315.

Mela, C.F., Gupta, S., Lehmann, D.R. (1997). The long-term impact of promotion and advertising on consumer brand choice. *Journal of Marketing Research*, 34(2), 248–261.

Moe, W.W. and Schweidel, D.A. (2009). Online product opinions: Incidence, evaluation, and evolution. *Marketing Science*, 31(3), 372–386.

Mudambi, S.M. and Schuff, D. (2010). What makes a helpful online review? A study of customer reviews on amazon.com. *Social Science Electronic Publishing*, 34(1), 185–200.

Niu, Y.F., Li, G.Q., Qi, X.X. (2016). The influence of the quantity and quality of online reviews on online shopping willingness: The regulatory role of cognitive needs. *Psychological Science*, (6), 1454–1459.

Paivio, A., Yuille, J.C., Madigan, S.A. (1968). Concreteness, imagery, and meaningfulness values for 925 nouns. *Journal of Experimental Psychology*, 76(1), 1–25.

Park, D.H., Lee, J., Han, I. (2007). The effect of online consumer reviews on consumer purchasing intention: The moderating role of involvement. *International Journal of Electronic Commerce*, 11(4), 125–148.

Pentina, I., Ainsworth, A.B., Lixuan, Z. (2018). Exploring effects of source similarity, message valence, and receiver regulatory focus on Yelp review persuasiveness and purchase intentions. *Journal of Marketing Communications*, 2(24), 125–145.

Qu, Z., Zhang, H., Li, H. (2009). Determinants of online merchant rating: Content analysis of consumer comments about Yahoo merchants. *Decision Support Systems*, 46(1), 440–449.

Racherla, P. and Friske, W. (2015). Perceived credibility of online consumer reviews: An investigation across three service categories. *Proceedings of the 2010 Academy of Marketing Science (AMS) Annual Conference*, May 26–29, Portland, OR.

Racherla, P., Mandviwalla, M., Connolly, D.J. (2012). Factors affecting consumers' trust in online product reviews. *Journal of Consumer Behaviour*, 11(2), 94–104.

Rieh, S.Y. (2002). Judgment of information quality and cognitive authority in the web. *Journal of the Association for Information Science & Technology*, 53(2), 145–161.

Senecal, S. and Nantel, J. (2004). The influence of online product recommendations on consumers' online choices. *Journal of Retailing*, 80(2), 159–169.

Snelders, D. and Schoormans, J.P.L. (2004). An exploratory study of the relation between concrete and abstract product attributes. *Journal of Economic Psychology*, 25(6), 803–820.

Strahilevitz, M. and Myers, J.G. (1998). Donations to charity as purchase incentives: How well they work may depend on what you are trying to sell. *Journal of Consumer Research*, 24(4), 434–446.

Sundaram, D.S., Mitra, K., Webster, C. (1998). Word-of-mouth communications: A motivational analysis. *Advances in Consumer Research*, (25), 527–531.

Tang, J.S., Wang, Y.Y., Wang, C.Y. (2016). Research on the impact of commentary motivation on online commentary features and moral perception. *Soft Science*, 30(7), 109–112.

Tian, Z.L., Wang, R., Fan, J.F., *et al.* (2011). Product category differences and population characteristics of consumer CSR responses. *Nankai Management Review*, 14(1), 107–118.

Trusov, M., Bucklin, R.E., Pauwels, K. (2009). Effects of word-of-mouth versus traditional marketing: Findings from an internet social networking site. *Journal of Marketing*, 73(5), 90–102.

Wang, Z.Z. and Chen, Z.Q. (2016). The dimensions and research methods of e-commerce online review quality. *Journal of Academic Library & Information Literature*, 122(04), 99–103.

Wang, Y., Goes, P., Wei, Z. *et al.* (2019). Production of online word-of-mouth: Peer effects and the moderation of user characteristics. *Production and Operations Management*, 28(7), 1621–1240.

Wertenbroch, K. and Dhar, R. (2000). Consumer choice between hedonic and utilitarian goods. *Journal of Marketing Research*, 37(1), 60–71.

Wu, F. and Huberman, B.A. (2008). How public opinion forms. *Internet & Network Economics*, 1(1), 334–341.

Wu, Q.Q., Xu, Y.K., Liang, J.J., *et al.* (2012). Research on the quality of online review and the influence of website image in the context of the internet. *Scientific Management Research*, 30(1), 81–83.

Yan, J., Jiang, Y.B., Chang, Y.P. (2011). Relationship between motivation of internet word-of-mouth and word-of-mouth behavior. *Management Review*, 23(12), 84–91.

Ye, Q., Zhang, Z., Law, R. (2009). Sentiment classification of online reviews to travel destinations by supervised machine learning approaches. *Expert Systems with Applications*, 36(3), 6527–6535.

Yin, G.P. (2012). What kind of online reviews do consumers think is more useful? The influence of social factors. *The World of Management*, (12), 115–124.

Yu, M.N., Wu, F., Zhang, M.M. (2014). Research on the influence of online reviews on customers' purchase intention. *Market Journal of Theory Research*, (4), 58–60.

Yu, W., Zu, X., Sun, Y.B. (2016). The influence of online reviews of different product categories on the purchase intention of heterogeneous consumers. *Journal of Dalian University of Technology (Social Sciences Edition)*, 37(1), 1–5.

Yuan, X.N., Zhang, H.L., Jiang, X.P., *et al.* (2009). Internet word of mouth marketing analysis: An empirical study based on Korean online film critics and box office income. *2009 JMS China Marketing Science Academic Annual Meeting and Doctoral Forum*.

Zhang, Y.Y. (2015). An empirical study on the impact of online reviews on consumer purchase decisions. Zhejiang University of Finance and Economics, Hangzhou.

Zhang, S.T. and Huang, R.H. (2014). Influence of product type, advocacy and consumer gender on advertising effectiveness. Department of Management Sciences, Jiaotong University, Taiwan.

Zhang, X. and Jing, F.J. (2012). The impact of types of online shopping on online impulse purchase behavior. *Management Sciences*, 25(3), 69–77.

Zhang, R. and Yu, T.J. (2016). The impact of online comment features on consumers' purchase decisions. *Science & Technology and Management*, 18(6), 93–98.

Zhang, Z., Ye, Q., Law, R., *et al.* (2010). The impact of e-word-of-mouth on the online popularity of restaurants: A comparison of consumer reviews and editor reviews. *International Journal of Hospitality Management*, 29(4), 694–700.

Zhang, Y.H., Li, Z.W., Zhao, Y.C. (2017). The effect of information quality based on Taobao review data on the usefulness of online reviews. *Chinese Journal of Management*, (01), 77–85.

Zhao, Y.X., Fan, Z., Zhu, Q.H. (2012). The concept analysis and research progress of user-generated content (UGC). *Journal of the China Society for Libraries*, 38(5), 68–81.

Zheng, X.P. (2008). Empirical research on the influence of online reviews on online consumer purchasing decisions. Renmin University of China, Beijing.

Zhou, J.J. (2010). Research on influence of online customer reviews on consumer purchasing decisions. Zhejiang University, Hangzhou.

Zhu, Y.M. (2014). Enjoyment or utility: Effects of product types and reward types on consumers' referral will. *Journal of Marketing Science*, 10(2), 15–28.

Zhu, F. and Zhang, X. (2010). Impact of online consumer reviews on sales: The moderating role of product and consumer characteristics. *Journal of Marketing*, 74(2), 133–148.

Zhu, L.Y., Yuan, D.H., Zhang J.Y. (2017). The impact of online user review quality and reviewer rating on consumers' purchase intention: The regulation of product involvement. *Management Review*, (2), 87–96.

7

Climate Policy Challenges in China: Spatial and Econometric Analysis

Environmental issues are becoming an important area of concern to the sustainability of existing economic models and business activities. The scientific evidence has offered significant proof of the negative impact of human activities on the ecosystem and their potential implications for a deteriorating environment and rising temperatures associated with climate change. Economic growth and development are significant drivers of worsening environmental problems due to higher energy needs and pressures on business activities, enhanced by growing consumption and production patterns. Within the outlined context, the case of China requires insights as the country is considered the world's leading polluter with higher levels of CO_2 emissions. This chapter examines China's climate policy challenges with the support of econometric analysis and spatial techniques to contribute to the debate on China's contribution to pollution and environmental degradation. To examine the relationship between China's carbon emissions levels, economic growth, and the Shanghai Stock Exchange 180, Pesaran's ARDL model was applied to quarterly data ranging from 1992 to 2020. The spatial analysis added significant value to the research as it helped to enrich the study and brought new insights. The variables under investigation include carbon emissions, carbon intensity, coal consumption, and expenditure on healthcare per capita. The econometric findings offered evidence of carbon emissions having a significant impact on China's economic growth. Similarly, the Shanghai Stock Exchange 180 affects China's economic growth; however, it has a lower impact than the carbon emissions levels. The province-based spatial analysis explored China's climate challenges between 2014 and 2016 in its 31 provinces. The core findings revealed that the most extensive carbon emissions and coal consumption concentrations are

Chapter written by Miroslava ZAVADSKA, Lucía MORALES, Jarmila ZIMMERMANNOVÁ and Vít PÁSZTO.

focused mainly on the northeast regions. It also showed significant evidence of an increasing trend in healthcare expenditure per capita in most provinces, flagging the connection between pollution and the deterioration of human health and the importance of active climate policies that offer guidelines on required changes in alignment with environmental needs.

7.1. Introduction

The rapid economic growth experienced by the Chinese economy over the past three decades has led to severe environmental problems, including air pollution, water pollution, and rapidly growing carbon emissions. These environmental and ecological problems are associated with severe health problems and economic losses (Shilei *et al.* 2020). As a result of fast-developing economic activity and in close association with human activities, the global ecosystem is facing an acceleration of growing temperatures and the deterioration and destruction of natural habitats. China has been identified as the world's biggest carbon emitter and polluter, accounting for approximately 27% of global GHGs (greenhouse gases) emissions – excluding land use, land-use change, and forestry (Climate Action Tracker 2019). Overall, China's 2030 Paris Agreement[1] Nationally Determined Contribution (NDC) has been rated as being *"highly insufficient"*; however, the country has made significant efforts to tackle the problem. But, the environment remains subject to substantial worsening, and Chinese authorities face growing pressures to ensure that the economy keeps developing and growing. On a more positive note, existing research studies suggest that current domestic policies are heading in a slightly better direction, rated as *"insufficient,"* which is an improvement from the initial *"highly insufficient"* rating, indicating that the country is moving in the right direction, but at a slow pace (Lomborg 2016; Chen *et al.* 2018; Chen *et al.* 2019). On the other hand, and quite worryingly, the country has experienced a rise in the exploitation of coal resources and its dependency on fossil fuels. This is mainly due to increased levels of coal consumption, which remain the primary energy resource to fuel the country's economic model, and that has aggravated as a result of the Global Health Crisis and the ongoing war between Russia and Ukraine (Madi *et al.* 2022; Mastoi *et al.* 2022; Reuters 2021).

Given the increasing difficulties associated with the country's environmental situation, the government gradually issued several laws and regulations to create the foundations of a multi-governance system. The core idea is to develop the guidelines that enable alignment between the ecological environment, with governmental organisations having the leading role, enterprises being the main body, and citizens

1 The Paris Agreement is an agreement within the United Nations Framework Convention on Climate Change, which is dealing with GHG emissions mitigation.

and social organizations becoming the core participants (Song *et al.* 2020). As such, it is of significant importance to make efforts that aim to coordinate the relationship between economic development and environmental quality in parallel with the achievement of greener developmental goals (Chang 2014). While there have been hopeful signs that China's policies regarding CO_2 emissions will contribute to lowering its GHGs mark, the increasing use of fossil fuels registered over the past few years, particularly due to the ongoing energy crisis, is quite discouraging. The central fact is that China's power sector is dominated by fossil fuels and the increasing consumption of non-renewable energy powered primarily by coal, which produces up to twice the amount of CO_2 compared to other fossil fuels (ChinaPower 2020). In 2018 an estimated 2.3%, and a 4% increase in CO_2 emissions in the first half of 2019, showed the consolidation of a deteriorating picture. This is mainly due to increased coal power generation, which would need to be reduced by 63% by 2030 to get below 2010 levels, where coal power generation accounted for 655GW (IEA 2019). For China's energy mix to be compatible with the Paris Agreement, there is a need for a more active approach towards developing energy alternatives that enable the transition from a coal-dependent economy to a more diversified energy model (Climate Action Tracker 2019). This is worrying as the increasing trend in China's CO_2 emissions goes in hand with its economic growth, where coal plays a prime role. Coal remains the most affordable and available resource at the global level, and currently, there is no substitute for it. Within the outlined context, this chapter contributes to the debate by applying econometric and spatial analysis to understand the potential connection between carbon emissions levels, China's economic growth, coal as the primary energy source, and patterns in healthcare expenditure. The econometric analysis examines the relationship between carbon emissions, China's economic growth, and China's stock exchange through the Shanghai SE 180 Index to add evidence of potential associated between the outlined variables in the long- and short-term. The main goal of the spatial analysis is to visually identify the highest concentrations of CO_2 emissions, carbon intensity, and healthcare levels based on China's provinces' data. The rich methodological framework offers essential insights to better understand the degree of carbon emissions and their interwoven connection between China's GDP and its future policies regarding climate policy for economic sustainability. The remainder of the chapter is structured as follows: sections 7.2 and 7.3 discuss the background of China's economic growth, carbon emissions, and environmental challenges. Section 7.4 outlines the data and methodologies for econometric and spatial analysis. Section 7.5 presents the econometric results, and section 7.6 highlights the spatial findings. The chapter conclusions are presented in section 7.7.

7.2. China's carbon emissions and economic growth

Between 2002 and 2012, Chinese carbon emissions increased by 158% (Chen *et al.* 2018), making China the world's most significant contributor to CO_2

emissions. Gong *et al.* (2019) looked at this matter by engaging in the analysis of environmental policies between 1995 and 2019. The authors' supported their study with clustering methods that considered the country's Five-Year-Plan of decarbonisation. The core research findings suggested the existence of different patterns among the identified clusters that integrated China's provinces, which are trying to use cleaner energy to reduce CO_2 emissions. Figure 7.1 offers some interesting insights, as the comparison between actual CO_2 emissions and forecasting patterns suggests that the country will manage to stabilize emission levels, and it is predicted that the emissions will decline in the future. The forecast presents an optimistic view of future trends if we consider that the country has increased the exploitation and usage of coal to counteract the effects of the 2022 energy crisis (Madi *et al.* 2022). China's quarterly growth rate fluctuates between 5 and 15%. This trend includes jumps around the Global Economic and Financial Crisis (GEFC) of 2008 and, more recently, during the 2020 Global Health Crisis. Ongoing effects are causing severe concerns in China as the authorities are pursuing a zero-Covid-19 strategy that has demonstrated to be quite challenging (BBC 2022). The Covid-19 pandemic led to a Global Health Crisis that has had a significant impact on the economy, where the decline in growth rates fell below 6%. Another element to be considered as part of the analysis relates to the SSE 180 Index. The index could offer insights into the historical development of blue-chip companies within the Chinese economy. It is of interest to understand to which extent China's top businesses impact its growth rate. This is a significant indicator of business activity that could help in understanding the importance of policies to guide environmentally friendly growth.

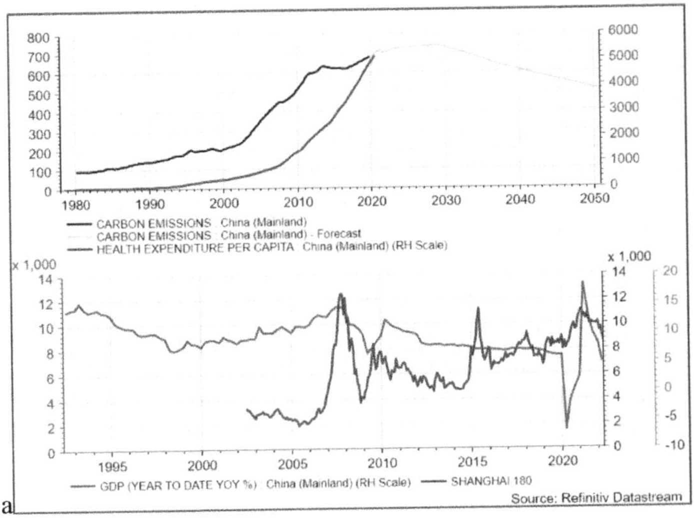

Figure 7.1. *China's carbon emissions, health expenditure, GDP growth and the Shanghai 180 Price Index. For a color version of this figure, see www.iste.co.uk/morales/connectivity.zip*

An early research study by Zhang and Xu (2012) examined the causal relationship between energy consumption and GDP in China from a sectoral and regional perspective. The research findings suggest that energy consumption is associated with CO_2 levels, so its behaviour directly affects China's GDP and economic growth. Furthermore, the study suggests that economic growth causes more energy consumption at national, regional, and sectoral levels. The authors noted that energy prices had only a limited effect on energy consumption; however, the opposite trend was registered regarding economic growth, where energy prices were linked with government-orientated mechanisms.

The implications for the environment of growing coal consumption due to increasing levels of carbon emissions in China are significant from the global perspective. Coal is the primary energy source in China, producing twice the amount of CO_2 emissions than other fossil fuels. Thus, it is vital to monitor the situation in China and its regions to have explicit knowledge of its development and its potential sustainability. Xian *et al.* (2018) focused on achieving the proposed target emissions reduction during 2016–2020 for China's power industry. Their findings suggest that the reduction target of 18% nationwide is just not feasible through upgrading technology or technical improvements. That means that technical efficiency or upgrading technology on electricity generation and carbon reduction is not achievable in the short or medium term. However, there are ways to get on target through national policies, where the Chinese government made three key commitments. Firstly, it announced that the CO_2 emissions will peak no later than in 2030. Secondly, they stated that they would reduce the CO_2 emissions intensity of GDP by 60–65% by 2030 relative to its 2005 level. And thirdly, they committed to increasing the non-fossil fuel energy share in the total primary energy supply to 20% by 2030 (Lomborg 2016). The Five-Year-Plan for 2016 to 2020 clearly shows that the policies and regulations aim to adjust its future energy structure to comply with reducing carbon emissions (NDRC 2016). Furthermore, in June 2018, the State Council of China issued a three-year action plan called the "blue sky defensive war." The plan seeks to promote energy conservation and emission reduction in critical sectors such as coal burning and industrial pollution through regional joint prevention and control. Overall, environmental regulation represents governments' direct or indirect control and intervention of enterprises' resource utilization for environmental protection and resource conservation (Song *et al.* 2020). Decarbonization of the power sector is one of the most critical efforts to meet the climate mitigation targets under the Paris Agreement. The carbon intensity of China's electricity is still much higher than the global average, but the country has made important strides toward a low-carbon transition based on two main pillars: improvement of energy efficiency and decreasing the share of fossil fuels. An updated study from Peng *et al.* (2020) focused on decoupling indicators in 30 provinces in China between 2005 and 2015. Their decomposition analysis shows that improvement of energy efficiency was the dominant driver for decarbonization of 16 provincial power sectors, while the access to low-carbon electricity and substitution of natural gas for coal and oil further accelerated their decarbonisation.

The reviewed literature shows evidence of the type of recommendations that have been offered concerning China's approach to carbon dioxide reductions. The Chinese government has issued a series of policies and regulations, such as the environmental tax, the carbon trading system, and the deforestation ban (Shilei *et al.* 2020). Carbon policies can be expected to increase fossil fuel prices directly through the carbon trading system or carbon tax, or indirectly by regulations that place an implicit tax on fossil fuels (Zhang and Cross 2020). One way the government can improve China's power industry's ecological and economic efficiency is by effectively implementing their policies in the context of carbon/pollution taxes. Wang *et al.* (2019a) looked at the economic cost and ecological impact of energy input reallocation strategies to improve efficiency. They assessed the possible effects of pollution taxes depending on sulphur dioxide levels. Their findings suggest that energy input costs and sulphur dioxide levels could be reduced by increasing technical efficiency. Moreover, they indicate that it is possible to adjust the energy mix to achieve ecological improvement. Besides pollution taxes, the Chinese government uses various "green" tax incentives. For example, by June 2019, China introduced 89 tax incentives and critical entrepreneurship and employment regions. Notably, 78 new tax incentives have been issued since 2013, covering the entire life cycle of enterprises to comprehensively promote R&D and innovation activities (Song *et al.* 2020). Pan *et al.* (2019) also have positive views on reducing carbon emissions as per China's commitment to the Paris Agreement. They analysed carbon emission data for 30 Chinese provinces from 2006 to 2016, showing an improving situation. However, the situation is not the same for all provinces. A disaggregated analysis is needed to identify which areas are associated with heavy pollution levels so that policies are developed more effectively. Nonetheless, their findings confirm that China has been able to decrease carbon intensity by 46.1% between 2005 and 2017 and carbon emissions per unit of GDP. In addition, it is expected that CO_2 emissions will decrease by more than 65% by 2030. This contradicts the skeptical views of Xian *et al.* (2018) within the power industry, which are not certain regarding carbon emissions reduction goals and their achievement through technical and technological improvements. Also, such a reduction could have a considerably negative impact on China's GDP growth due to the country's historical connection to coal.

7.3. Environmental issues and greenhouse gases

The effect of environmental regulation and R&D tax incentives on green product innovation from a disciplinary and incentive perspective has been examined by Song *et al.* (2020). The authors used inter-provincial panel data to conduct an empirical analysis of 30 inter-provincial panel datasets in China from 2009 to 2017. Due to the regional differences in industrial structure and economic development levels in the various regions of China, the inflection point of environmental regulations across provinces was subject to a study. The research findings showed a U-shaped relationship between environmental regulation and green product innovation; given the increasing intensity of environmental regulation, its effect will gradually change from inhibition to promotion. Based on the findings, the authors underline that most provinces in China are close to the inflection point of environmental regulation, meaning that regulation levels need to be further improved. As such, the Chinese government should consider the characteristics of different provinces and the heterogeneity of environmental regulation to formulate differentiated environmental regulation policies. A regional approach is also essential in the cap-and-trade system – emission allowances and trading. China is facing a severe situation requiring energy conservation and emission reduction, especially in some metropolitan areas such as Beijing, Shanghai, and Guangzhou, where environmental deterioration has gradually become a threat to the public health of urban residents (Zhang *et al.* 2017).

As the world's largest developing country and carbon dioxide emitter, China hoped to achieve emission reduction targets that helped to ameliorate global greenhouse effects at the lowest possible economic cost through the carbon market. Therefore, eight pilot carbon markets have been approved and established successively since 2012. In 2017, China announced the establishment of a unified national carbon market, launching the world's largest carbon market late in 2017 (Lyu *et al.* 2020). China's carbon market is nationwide, but it applies only to the power generation sector during its early phase. It was expected that by 2020, China would reduce average thermal coal consumption by thermal power units to 310 grams of standard coal per kWh and decrease emissions intensity of thermal power units to 865 grams of carbon dioxide per kWh (Zhang and Cross 2020). Initial insights suggest that the performance rate of each pilot market is continually increasing, and the quantity and price rise during the trading period are evident. However, it is still accompanied by an immature market environment, inadequate infrastructure, limited emissions trading volume, and low market liquidity. In parallel, the price of carbon emissions fluctuated sharply in the early stage of market establishment. The unsafe and unstable operation of the carbon market will affect the regulative efficiency of the market and thus, affect the final carbon emission reduction results (Lyu *et al.* 2020). So far, only a few studies have considered the impact assessments of pilot markets, and most of them draw qualitative conclusions (Jiang *et al.* 2016). In this context, making a more comprehensive and quantitative ex-post impact assessment study is of great value in guiding the design and operation of China's regional and national ETS.

The total amount of greenhouse gases in the atmosphere results from several synergistic effects (Hajek *et al.* 2019). On the one hand, it is the consequence of the behaviour of economic entities, mainly households and companies (Kolstad 2010;

Büchs and Snepf 2013). General indicators can measure GDP, or specific indicators, such as the household final consumption expenditure, companies' investments, or consumption of fuels, including solid fuels. On the other hand, it is the effect of national environmental regulations enacted and economic instruments adopted for the environment and climate protection purposes (Samuelson and Nordhaus 2010). For instance, the EU countries use various economic instruments of environmental policy, such as environmental taxes, fees, charges, tradable permits, deposit-refund systems, or subsidies (Eurostat 2013; European Commission 2016). Another aspect to consider relates to the impact of economic growth. Some researchers underline that economic growth is connected with rapid urbanization, an increase in production levels, and growing transport demand (Kolstad 2010; Lee at al. 2018). Therefore, a positive impact on GDP regarding the expansion of GHG emissions can be expected. Concerning the consumption of fuels, there is a theoretical assumption that solid fuel consumption and the combustion of fossil fuels are drivers of the upward trend in atmospheric CO_2 levels (Kolstad 2010). Overall, there seems to be widespread scientific agreement that pollution taxation can effectively lower atmospheric CO_2 levels; however, optimal emission pricing poses a key challenge (Kickhöfer *et al.* 2018). Given that both scientists and institutions (Eurostat 2016; Goulder 2013) include the carbon tax along with the cap and trade (ETS) system under the one category, "green tax," we can discuss the effects of these instruments together. The reason is that they have some common characteristics, especially in the case of the EU ETS, with respect to the EU ETS revenues if the emission allowances are traded in auctions. Various countries have increasingly favoured such instruments because they provide a flexible and cost-effective means for reinforcing the polluter-pays principle and reaching environmental policy objectives (Hájek *et al.* 2019). On the other hand, relatively few research papers have addressed the impact and eco-efficiency of the already established carbon taxes and/or emission trading systems.

For example, Nordhaus (2005, 2011, 2017) compared the efficiency of environmental taxes and tradable emission allowances. He studied the EU ETS, focusing on EUA market price fluctuations and volatility within one EU ETS trading period. He argued that emission trading is not suitable for planning long-term investments. As a recommendation to policymakers and regulators, he proposes a pure carbon tax as the most appropriate economic tool for reducing GHGs emissions. A uniform carbon tax proposed by the Nordhaus studies is also supported by Tol (2018), who advocates a more constructive climate policy, given the currently expanding state bureaucracies, economic inefficiencies, and a diffuse political debate on global climate change issues. The theoretical assumption is that the rising price of allowances would reduce GHG (Kolstad 2010). However, carbon tax supporters criticize emission trading, primarily due to a significant fluctuation of emission allowance prices. For instance, Andersen and Greaker (2017) prove that the initial allocation of pollution permits between countries/regions affects the price of emission allowances, "the global distribution of abatement effort," and total GHG mitigation costs. Moreover, there are not many studies that focus on the spatial aspect of emission pricing in the existing literature. For example, Xiangmei and Yang (2018) analyzed the spatial issues in China, observing temporal and spatial distribution characteristics of the air pollution index (API) and its correlation with the improvement of environmental tax law. Their paper discussed the general trend of the China air pollution index and studied the daily air pollution index of important cities focusing on the three dimensions of time, space, and associated trends. To analyse API's relationship with environmental tax laws, the authors studied regional differences in the economic discipline, especially the Searl index. The discussion underlines the importance of how to allocate the resources in the redistribution of tax rationally. Another study carried out by Skovgaard *et al.* (2019) explored adoption patterns (both implemented policies and those scheduled to be) through cluster analysis to investigate factors that could explain policies' decisions to adopt carbon pricing. The study contributed empirically by studying carbon taxes and emissions trading together and by clustering the polities adopting carbon pricing. Zeng (2017) deals with both direct and indirect double environmental regulations (i.e. the emission trading system and a carbon tax) in the EU and China. However, China's national emission trading system was introduced in the last years. Therefore, we should still consider it a new project with negligible impact. We can expect significant environmental influence only in selected regions that introduced ETS separately as a pilot project.

Despite the expected positive impact, the influence of environmental regulation can be overestimated, as pointed out by Shilei *et al.* (2020). Considering the environmental improvement, China has experienced an economic slowdown since 2013. The slowing growth with a more inclusive and sustainable economic structure is considered as *"the new normal"* status of China's economy (Andreosso-O'Callaghan and Morales 2022). This *"new normal"* plays an essential role in pollution reduction through economic restructuring and slowing growth. Shilei *et al.* (2020) estimated the effect of the economic slowdown using a dynamic Computable General Equilibrium model (CHINAGEM). They found that the contribution of the economic slowdown to pollution reduction ranged from 10% to 30%. This indicates the importance of considering the economic slowdown when evaluating the effects of other factors related to the environmental improvement in China. In the context of the reviewed literature, this research study aims to develop an analysis aligning with Pászto and Zimmermannová (2019), whose work portrays and examines carbon emissions levels and their implications for policymaking. An important addition to the work is that the spatial analysis would be supported by an econometric framework that offers further insights regarding the economic implications of carbon dioxide emissions and plans to target them. Furthermore, the research study seeks to provide graphical insights into carbon emissions development on a regional basis in China, highlighting the current trend in CO_2 emissions and coal consumption, as discussed in the sections that follow.

7.4. Data and methodological framework

7.4.1. *Data*

The dataset applied to support the econometric analysis to examine the impact of CO_2 on China's GDP includes quarterly records from Q1 1992 to Q2 2020; changes in China's growth rates and CO_2 emissions, and the Shanghai Stock Exchange 180 Index (SSE 180) from Q2 2002 to Q2 2020 (based on data availability). The short-run relationship examination between selected variables offers perceptions of the importance of CO_2 levels on the Chinese economy. The SSE 180 Index was integrated into the analysis to highlight the dynamics of the top 180 indexed companies on China's economic growth with connection to CO_2 emissions. The spatial dataset examines Coal Consumption measured in tens of thousands ton; Consumption Expenditure per capita on Health Care for urban areas, rural areas, resident areas, and Total Health Care Consumption Expenditure in RMB currency for 2014 and 2016. The data set includes further carbon emissions in ton per capita and carbon intensity in ton per ten thousand RMB obtained from research conducted by Wang *et al.* (2019b) (China Energy Statistic Yearbook). The data were attained for 30 Chinese provinces (Anhui, Beijing, Fujian, Gansu, Guangdong, Guangxi, Guizhou, Hainan, Hebei, Heilongjiang, Henan, Hubei, Hunan, Chongqing, Jiangsu, Jiangxi, Jilin, Liaoning, Nei Mongol, Ningxia Hui, Qinghai, Shaanxi, Shandong, Shanghai, Shanxi, Sichuan, Tianjin, Xinjiang, Xizang, Uygur, Yunnan, and Zhejiang). Both econometric and spatial datasets were obtained from Thomson Reuters DataStream.

7.4.2. *Econometric models*

The econometric methodological strategy divides the macroeconomic relationship between China's growth rates, CO_2 emissions, and Shanghai Stock Exchange 180 Index into four main steps. These steps were conducted with the help of Eviews software. The first step covers unit root testing for stationarity. The stationarity tests include the augmented Dickey-Fuller (ADF) and Phillips-Perron (PP) tests for robustness. The second step examines the optimal lag length selection using the Vector Autoregressive (VAR) framework, as the cointegration and causality tests are sensitive to the selected number of lags. The third step consists of time series cointegration-long-run-analysis using the Autoregressive Distributed Lag (ARDL) model for different order variables (I(0) and I(1)). The fourth step is applying the causality-short-run-Error Correction Model (ECM) in cases where the cointegration was established. The stationarity methodology is not discussed in detail as it is based on the standard approach to examine time series. Details can be found in Dickey and Fuller's (1979) and Phillips and Perron's (1988) research papers. Similarly, the Vector Autoregression (VAR) is commonly used to forecast lag lengths of time series.

To test for causality, there is a need to examine if there is a cointegrating relationship between variables. For a combination of I(0) and I(1) variables, the ARDL (p,q_1, q_2) model by Pesaran *et al.* (2001) is applied, and the theoretical equation is specified as follows:

$$\Delta y_t = \alpha_{01} + \sum_{i=1}^{p} \alpha_{1i}\Delta y_{t-i} + \sum_{i=1}^{p} \alpha_{2i}\Delta x_{j,t-1} + \sum_{i=1}^{p} \alpha_{3i}\Delta x_{j,t-i} + \varepsilon_t \quad [7.1]$$

The unrestricted constant and restricted linear trend can be written as follows:

$$\Delta y_t = \alpha_0 + \alpha_1 t + \beta_0 y_{t-1} + \sum_{j=1}^{k} \beta_j X_{j,t-1} + \sum_{i=1}^{p-1} c_{0,i}\Delta y_{t-i} + \sum_{j=1}^{k} \sum_{lj=1}^{pj-1} c_{j,l}\Delta x_{,j,t-l} + \sum_{j=1}^{k} d_j \Delta x_{j,t} + \varepsilon_t \quad [7.2]$$

$$EC_t = y_t - \sum_{j-1}^{k} \frac{b_j}{b_0} x_{j,t} - \frac{a_1}{b_0} t \quad [7.3]$$

$$H_0: a_1 = b_0 = b_j = 0, \forall_j$$

where y_t is a dependent variable, x_t is an independent variable, $\alpha_0$is a constant term, α_1 is the trend, EC_t is the appropriate cointegrating relationship and H_0 is the bounds test null-hypothesis.

If there is cointegration, the Error Correction model (ECM) is applied and specified as follows:

$$\Delta y_t = \alpha_{01} + \sum_{i=1}^{p} \alpha_{1i}\Delta y_{t-i} + \sum_{i=1}^{p} \alpha_{2i}\Delta x_{t-1} + \sum_{i=1}^{p} \alpha_{3i}\Delta x + \lambda ECM_{t-1} + \varepsilon_t \quad [7.4]$$

where λ = (1-$\sum_{i=1}^{p} \delta_i$) is the speed of adjustment parameter with a negative sign; ECM = (y_{t-i} - θX_t) is the error correction term, which is the extracted residuals from the regression of the long-run equation; $\theta = \frac{\sum_{i=0}^{p} \beta_i}{\alpha}$ is the long-run parameter; $\alpha_{1i}, \alpha_{2i}, \alpha_{3i}$ are the short-run dynamic coefficients of the model's adjustment long-run equilibrium. In case of no cointegration, the ARDL model is followed by short-run OLS estimation.

7.4.3. *Spatial methods*

The spatial analysis was supported by a methodology framework that has been applied to previously published research studies (e.g. Pászto and Zimmermannová

2019; Pászto *et al.* 2019; Marek *et al.* 2015a, 2015b). More specifically, geovisual analytics is based on cartographical displays of data and spatial statistics (clustering) to define similar types of regions. The methodological approach for the spatial part was divided into three steps: 1) tabular data linkage with its spatial component, 2) map-making for geovisual analysis, and 3) multivariate clustering to identify typologically similar regions. In the first step, it was important to unify Chinese regions' geographical names (geonyms). Due to the diverse sources of tabular economic data, the geonyms were transcripted into English equivalents in order to link indicators with spatial data (administrative regions of China) within the Geographical Information System (GIS) using the "Join" function. The second step was followed by the implementation of geovisual analytics. According to Andrienko *et al.* (2007) it represents a scientific process of analytical reasoning in the decision-making process concerning geographic information displayed in the form of a visual interface (map). Moreover, as Pászto *et al.* (2020) explained, starting the (geographical) analysis by displaying and searching for a primary geographical context is advised. With this in mind, and following fundamental cartographic rules (e.g. Kraak and Ormeling 2011), the data was visualized in the form of a pseudo-choropleth map (for relative values) or with the use of proportional symbols (in the case of absolute values). The Jenks method was used to set the intervals for individual categories; this method minimizes differences within the interval and maximizes differences between them (Jenks 1967). It has to be noted that these intervals were also manually adjusted to meet cartographic rules. The World Geodetic System (WGS 1984) was utilized for all map visualizations.

Lastly, in the third step, multivariate clustering was applied, which allowed the analysis of multiple variables simultaneously to obtain types of regions with common properties. In general, such clustering is based on the regions based on their similarities and differences (Tryon 1939), and clustering of geographical data has been well described in other research papers (e.g. Shaffer and Zolnik 2014; Netrdová and Nosek 2016). For this research study and based on geographical data, the Multivariate Clustering tool in ArcGIS Pro with K-means algorithm was used. The K-means algorithm was chosen as it is popular among scientists for its ease of implementation, simplicity, efficiency, and empirical success (Jain 2010). According to Jain (2010), the K-means algorithm finds a partition such that the squared error between the empirical mean of a cluster and the point in the cluster is minimized. For more details about the algorithm, see also Kaufman and Rousseeuw (2005). An additional strength of the ArcGIS Pro K-means is that it works sequentially, as it groups the data from two to thirty clusters and evaluates the best-fitted result based on pseudo-F-statistic values, which describes the ratio of between-cluster variance to intra-cluster variance (Caliński and Harabasz 1974), and thus measures cluster quality for a different numbers of clusters. Based on that, the target number of clusters (types) could be selected. In the case of this research study, expert-based and empirical knowledge was followed, and the target number of clusters was set to four. This decision was made regarding the number of input data ("only" 31 administrative units to be grouped) and cartographic rules for map visualisation, leading to further ease of interpretation.

7.5. Econometric findings

The results of unit root testing showed that China's economic growth is an I(1), and natural logarithms of CO_2 together with Shanghai Stock Market 180 are an I(0). The Akaike information criterion (AIC) and the Schwarz criterion (SC) showed the same results for the lag length selection. Table 7.1 offers descriptive statistics of selected variables.

	Growth rate	**CO_2 emissions**	**Shanghai SE 180**	**ΔGrowth rate**	**ΔCO_2 emissions**	**ΔShanghai SE 180**
Mean	9.45	1613.687	5885.363	-2.007768	1.241945	1.33457
Median	9.3	1566.8	6020.5	-1.134468	1.244329	2.083357
Maximum	15.3	2654.76	12416.01	26.07263	7.998823	38.43798
Minimum	-6.8	623.799	2124.87	-144.6919	-11.24522	-33.2416
Std. Dev.	3.053773	760.6812	2389.21	15.59076	2.008566	15.31803
Skewness	-1.355593	0.099938	0.188473	-6.992824	-1.66563	0.305205
Kurtosis	9.670578	1.322866	2.653747	64.39298	15.32195	3.362075
Jarque-Bera	246.2739	13.66932	0.796853	18501.92	773.907	1.511094
Probability	0	0.001076	0.671376	0	0	0.469753
Sum	1077.3	185574	429631.5	-224.87	141.5817	96.08906
Sum Sq. Dev.	1053.785	65964496	4.11E+08	26980.96	455.8802	16659.58
Observations	114	115	73	112	114	72

Table 7.1. *Descriptive statistics*

The growth rates between Q1 1992 and Q2 2020 exhibit a maximum value of 15.3% in Q1 1993 and a minimum value of negative 6.8%, which is the recent Q1 in 2020 due to the Covid-19 pandemic and derived from the Chinese government imposing a series of restrictions and actions seeking to slow down the spread of the virus, which resulted in a significant impact on economic performance. Concerning Covid-19 and economic constraints in China, the CO_2 emissions declined in the first quarter of 2020, despite the upward sloping long-term trend. The data for the Shanghai Stock Exchange 180 are available in quarterly data from Q2 2002 and show frequent jumps over the whole period. Once the basic properties and series specifics were obtained, the analysis continued with the cointegration and causality examination aligning with standard techniques associated with time series analysis. Table 7.2 highlights the results for the ARDL bounds test, which is applied to capture any long-run relationship between variables. Table 7.3 presents the bounds for the F-statistics of I(0) and I(1) processes. If the F-statistic is below I(0) in absolute values, then there is no evidence of a cointegrated relationship. On the other hand, if the F-statistic is above I(1) in absolute values, then there is the presence of cointegration, and the ECM model should be applied. If the F-statistic is between I(0) and I(1) in absolute values, the long-run relationship is inconclusive.

Dependent variable	F-statistics	Cointegration	Selected model
Growth rate	F = 31.72	Yes	ECM model
CO_2 emissions	F = 4.30	No	ARDL model
Shanghai SE 180	F = 8.58	Yes	ECM model

Table 7.2. *Bounds test for cointegration*

F-statistics	I(0)	I(1)
10%	3.38	4.02
5%	3.88	4.61
1%	4.99	5.85

Table 7.3. *Bounds test F-statistics*

The F-statistics show that a long-run relationship is present when the growth rate is selected as a dependent variable. The same applies when the Shanghai Stock Exchange 180 is designated as a dependent variable. On the other hand, there was no evidence of a long-run relationship in the case of CO_2 emissions being the dependent variable and the growth rate and Shanghai Stock Exchange 180 being the explanators. The findings from the bounds test helped to proceed further with the analysis. In cases of no cointegration, the ARDL model is a final step in causality testing. The tests show that the dependent CO_2 emissions variable model is the ARDL (1,1,0). The OLS model outcomes are presented in Table 7.4 and clearly show that there is no evidence of a short-run relationship between the growth rate and the Shanghai Stock Exchange running to CO_2 emissions.

ΔCO_2 emissions (dependent variable)	Coefficient	Probability
ΔGrowth rate	-0.0131	(0.5678)
ΔShanghai SE 180	0.0135	(0.2996)

Table 7.4. *ARDL causality model*

Following the bounds test outcomes, two ECM regressions were implemented, one for the growth rate and the second for the Shanghai Stock Exchange as the dependent variable. The results for the ECM model show that when the growth rate is selected as a dependent variable (see Table 7.5), then the adjustment speed from the previous period is -91.27%, which is given by the ECM term. The ECM term must be negative between 0 and negative 1 and significant, and both conditions are met in the implemented model. The significant positive 2.51 coefficient of the CO_2 emissions on China's growth rate demonstrates a short-run relationship running from CO_2 emissions affecting the growth rate. The Shanghai Stock Exchange is also significant at 0.14, which suggests that the behaviour of stock exchange prices has a smaller, nevertheless, short-run impact on the growth rate.

ΔGrowth rate (dependent variable)	**Coefficient**	**Probability**
ΔCO_2 emissions	2.5126	(0.0118)
ΔShanghai SE 180	0.1436	(0.0181)
ECM (long run coefficient)	-0.9127	(0.0111)

Table 7.5. *ARDL causality model with long run error correction model: Model 1*

The second ECM model presented in Table 7.6, shows that the adjustment speed of the ECM coefficient from the previous period is -52%. However, the growth rate and CO_2 emissions do not significantly impact the Shanghai Stock Exchange in the short-run. When we looked at the R-squared and adjusted R-squared it is very low at 27% and 23%, respectively, meaning that other factors than the growth rate and CO_2 emissions affect the stock market behaviour in the short run. This was predictable and confirmed that the Shanghai Stock Exchange impacts China's growth rate, but not the other way around.

ΔShanghai SE 180 (dependent variable)	**Coefficient**	**Probability**
ΔCO_2 emissions	0.685	(0.7447)
ΔGrowth rate	-0.1646	(0.3585)
ECM (long run coefficient)	-0.5284	(0.002)

Table 7.6. *ARDL causality model with long run error correction model: Model 2*

The econometric results are followed by the spatial analysis, where visual maps and cluster analysis are used to display results based on obtained data for 2014 and 2016.

7.6. Spatial findings

From the geographical point of view, the geovisual analysis and multivariate clustering results will be described for input indicators for both observed years, i.e., 2014 and 2016. This allows immediate comparison of economic and environmental performance changes between these two years. The interpretation is based on visual analytics of resulting maps using interval classifications, which may cause some generalization of data. Therefore, we provide exact input values in Table 7.7 to complement the map information hereafter.

Indicator	Coal consumption [ten of thousands ton]		Consumption Expenditure per Capita (Urban areas): Health Care [RMB]		Consumption Expenditure per Capita (Residential areas): Health Care [RMB]		Consumption Expenditure per Capita (Rural areas): Health Care [RMB]		Consumption Expenditure per Capita (Total): Health Care [RMB]		Carbon Emissions [t/per capita]		Carbon Intensity [t/10,000 RMB]	
Province // year	2014	2016	2014	2016	2014	2016	2014	2016	2014	2016	2014	2016	2014	2016
Anhui	15786,98	15728,68	976,54	1269,26	869,98	1092,06	778,84	931,89	2625,35	3293,20	1,69	1,77	0,91	0,77
Beijing	1736,54	847,62	2044,44	2629,82	1914,16	2455,73	1088,64	1346,96	5047,24	6432,51	1,65	1,54	0,42	0,38
Fujian	8198,30	6826,50	1058,97	1178,47	926,85	1053,86	735,94	866,95	2721,75	3099,28	2,00	2,01	0,54	0,46
Gansu	6715,87	6377,52	1048,23	1583,36	737,22	1122,73	546,20	821,29	2331,65	3527,38	2,25	2,29	1,78	1,57
Guangdong	NA	NA	988,32	1304,48	890,45	1144,87	686,95	803,88	2565,72	3253,23	1,69	1,72	0,52	0,42
Guangxi	6796,51	6517,77	845,95	1065,92	679,26	907,44	553,51	781,76	2078,72	2755,12	1,34	1,33	0,83	0,80
Guizhou	13117,60	13642,75	927,39	1050,11	572,01	724,70	372,98	527,83	1872,39	2302,63	2,34	2,33	2,43	2,14
Hainan	1018,30	1015,31	960,30	1399,85	926,85	1053,86	454,12	593,00	2341,26	3046,70	1,77	1,79	0,89	0,85
Hebei	29635,54	28105,65	1304,50	1549,85	1027,52	1225,37	788,71	928,22	3120,73	3703,44	3,74	3,81	1,64	1,50
Heilongjiang	13595,53	14034,39	1457,62	2007,54	1258,29	1694,66	992,06	1269,91	3707,98	4972,11	2,79	3,01	1,04	0,97
Henan	24249,88	23226,52	1204,14	1524,52	928,99	1113,36	731,38	797,80	2864,51	3435,68	2,11	2,01	1,12	0,91
Hubei	11887,83	11685,88	1187,81	1792,04	1056,23	1528,15	907,33	1213,47	3151,37	4533,66	2,10	2,11	0,81	0,71
Hunan	10899,51	11443,53	1209,76	1362,56	972,17	1164,96	771,41	986,49	2953,34	3514,01	1,47	1,41	0,75	0,61
Chongqing	NA	NA	NA	NA	NA	NA	NA	NA	NA	NA	1,72	1,77	0,80	0,61
Jiangsu	26912,61	28048,13	1616,71	1624,50	1331,30	1453,71	845,33	1148,02	3793,33	4226,22	2,84	2,91	0,69	0,60
Jiangxi	7477,31	7617,59	760,70	887,45	635,01	764,47	525,21	649,99	1920,92	2301,90	1,26	1,22	0,78	0,68
Jilin	10379,34	9416,84	1838,38	2059,25	1458,02	1681,70	1008,05	1230,49	4304,45	4971,44	3,07	3,04	1,23	1,05
Liaoning	18002,27	16943,70	1630,76	2313,64	1419,23	1912,10	1026,38	1139,21	4076,37	5364,95	4,74	4,89	1,25	1,02
Nei Mongol	36465,97	36675,32	1470,81	1840,17	1319,69	1569,95	1114,39	1187,67	3904,90	4597,79	9,06	9,41	2,86	2,66
Ningxia Hui	8857,00	8665,09	1616,88	1874,00	1239,95	1473,18	856,93	1040,56	3713,76	4387,74	7,99	8,32	5,44	5,14
Qinghai	1816,51	1962,43	1212,97	1750,38	1071,20	1503,91	944,46	1278,77	3228,63	4533,05	2,22	2,57	1,31	1,32
Shaanxi	18375,34	19670,75	1495,88	2016,74	1178,16	1528,17	883,70	1044,13	3557,73	4589,04	2,90	3,21	1,70	1,73
Shandong	39561,73	40939,20	1188,00	1610,01	989,62	1339,03	776,42	1027,26	2954,04	3976,29	3,48	3,71	1,04	0,98
Shanghai	4895,78	4625,62	2327,62	2839,93	2223,90	2720,69	1330,33	1707,12	5881,85	7267,73	3,30	3,20	0,54	0,48
Shanxi	37587,43	35621,03	1240,86	1651,55	1008,59	1227,50	770,21	769,58	3019,66	3648,63	6,14	6,40	3,81	3,55
Sichuan	11045,39	8869,49	1283,60	1423,36	964,48	1172,64	723,74	972,51	2971,82	3568,51	1,18	1,28	0,63	0,55
Tianjin	5027,28	4230,16	1721,30	2172,16	1584,47	2022,90	979,68	1334,50	4285,46	5529,56	4,25	4,11	0,76	0,65
Xinjiang Uygur	16088,03	18985,00	1310,93	1934,80	978,31	1333,17	717,18	846,84	3006,42	4114,81	4,10	4,68	2,36	2,44
Xizang	NA	NA	552,52	585,28	197,65	257,69	91,65	152,56	841,81	995,53	NA	NA	NA	NA
Yunnan	8674,67	7461,18	1115,16	1526,73	739,41	976,43	513,95	620,07	2368,52	3123,22	1,59	1,71	1,22	1,07
Zhejiang	13824,37	13948,49	1526,95	1691,87	1358,18	1506,54	1068,33	1173,20	3953,45	4371,60	2,41	2,35	0,63	0,52

Table 7.7. *Input indicators for the analysis*

7.6.1. *Coal consumption*

When comparing 2014 and 2016 regarding coal consumption, there were visually no significant changes (see Figures 7.2 and 7.3). Only three provinces (Jilin, Tianjin, and Sichuan) registered a decrease in this indicator, which resulted in a change of interval for these provinces. As of 2016, Tianjin belongs to the group of provinces with coal consumption levels lower than 5,000 ten of thousand tons (together with Qinghai, Hainan, Shanghai, Beijing). However, except for Qinghai and Hainan, these provinces represent big agglomerations with the highest population density. On the contrary, very high coal consumption is evident in provinces spanning northwest from Shanghai in the central-east part of China, with the highest consumption in Shandong, Shanxi, and Inner Mongolia (Nei Mongol) provinces.

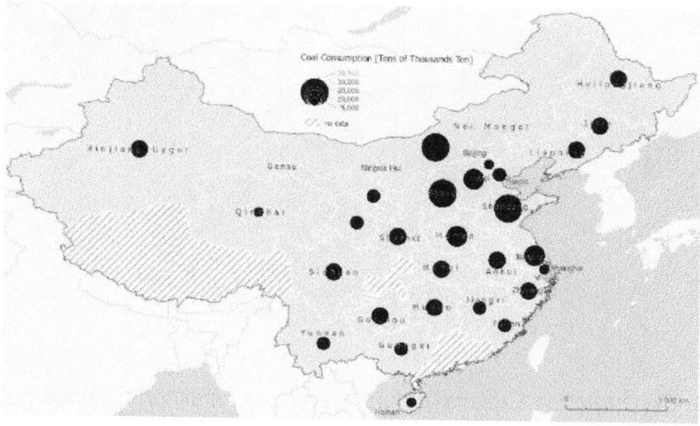

Figure 7.2. *Coal consumption in Chinese provinces in 2014*

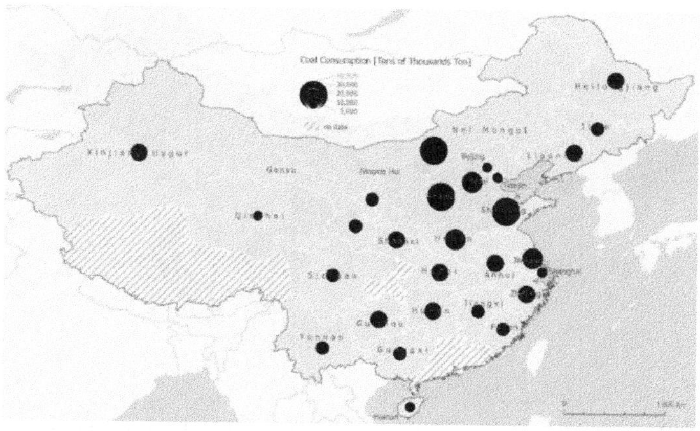

Figure 7.3. *Coal consumption in Chinese provinces in 2016*

7.6.2. *Consumption expenditure per capita on health care*

For the geovisual analysis of health care spending, the total consumption expenditures per capita on health care were calculated as a sum from the sub-indicators initially divided by the settlement characteristics, i.e., urban, residential, and rural areas. When looking at both years' visualisation (see Figure 7.4 and Figure 7.5), it is clear that the overall expenditures on health care grew from 2014 in most provinces throughout the country. The only exceptions are Beijing and

Shangai (staying in the highest interval). Xizang remained in the lowest; Giuzhou, Jiangxi, Henan, Anhui, and Ningxia Hui provinces stayed in their middle categories.

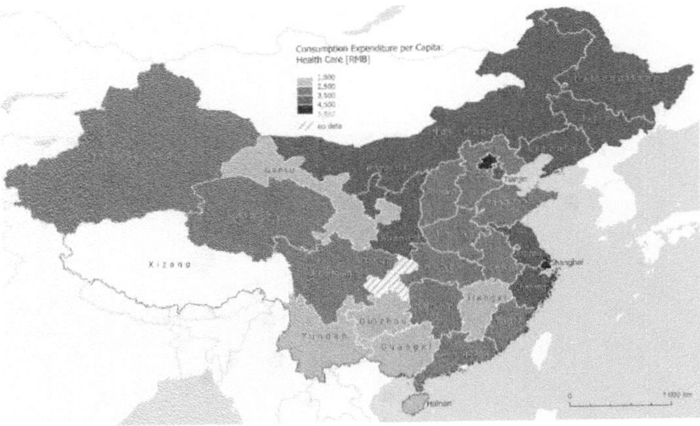

Figure 7.4. *Consumption Expenditure per Capita on Health in Chinese provinces in 2014. For a color version of this figure, see www.iste.co.uk/morales/connectivity.zip*

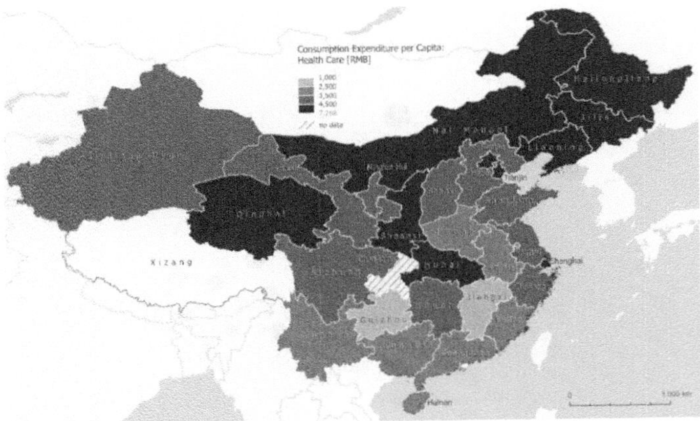

Figure 7.5. *Consumption Expenditure per Capita on Health in Chinese provinces in 2016. For a color version of this figure, see www.iste.co.uk/morales/connectivity.zip*

7.6.3. *Carbon emissions*

Carbon emissions in both years are the highest in the case of Nei Mongol and Ningxia Hui provinces (see Figure 7.6 and Figure 7.7), which may relate to the highest levels of coal consumption (it is visible in the case of Nei Mongol province), and to the relative nature of this indicator – per capita (in the case of Ningxia Hui province, with relative low population density). Similarly, relatively high carbon emissions can be seen in provinces around the biggest agglomerations of Beijing and Tianjin in northeast China. There are no moves between intervals except in Qinghai and Shandong provinces; both of them raised their carbon emissions per capita, resulting in promotion to the upper interval. In both years, the lowest carbon emissions are identified in the central provinces of south-east China (i.e. Sichuan, Hunan, Jiangxi, and Guangxi) and Beijing.

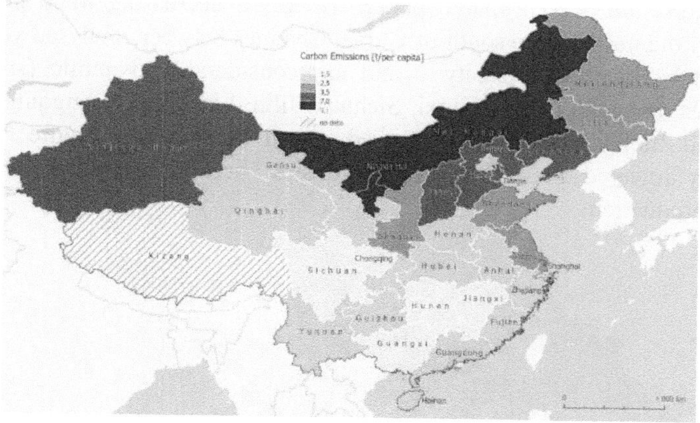

Figure 7.6. *Carbon emissions in Chinese provinces in 2014. For a color version of this figure, see www.iste.co.uk/morales/connectivity.zip*

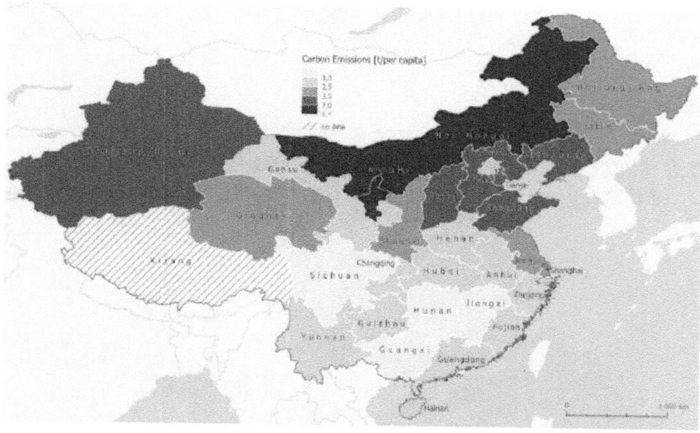

Figure 7.7. *Carbon emissions in Chinese provinces in 2016. For a color version of this figure, see www.iste.co.uk/morales/connectivity.zip*

7.6.4. *Carbon intensity*

Carbon intensity takes the Chinese currency into account (instead of "per capita" denominator), which indirectly reduces the effect of population. This indicator may be interpreted as a value of carbon emissions. A higher number indicates that the carbon emissions are more intensive than the intensity of one-unit output in a region. The highest values of carbon intensity can be observed in two provinces in 2014 (see

Figure 7.8) – Ningxia Hui and Shanxi. From the other end of the ranking, the lowest values are visible in the case of Bejing, Shanghai, Fujian, and Guangdong. Again, considering the indicators, these regions produce 10,000 RMB (one-unit output) with a less polluted environment than the rest of China. Overall, as in other years and indicators, the overall spatial pattern reveals a decreasing trend in indicator values from the north to the south of China. Changes between analysed years are in this indicator – carbon intensity – and are considerably dynamic (similarly to expenditures on health care). Shanxi, Sichuan, Jilin, Liaoning, Chongqing, Yunnan, Jiangsu, and Zhejiang provinces decreased carbon intensity (see Figure 7.9), which means they lowered their carbon emissions or became wealthier in terms of economic production.

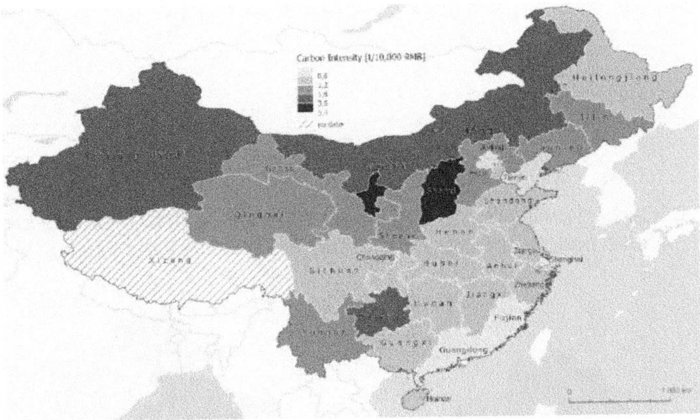

Figure 7.8. *Carbon intensity in Chinese provinces in 2014. For a color version of this figure, see www.iste.co.uk/morales/connectivity.zip*

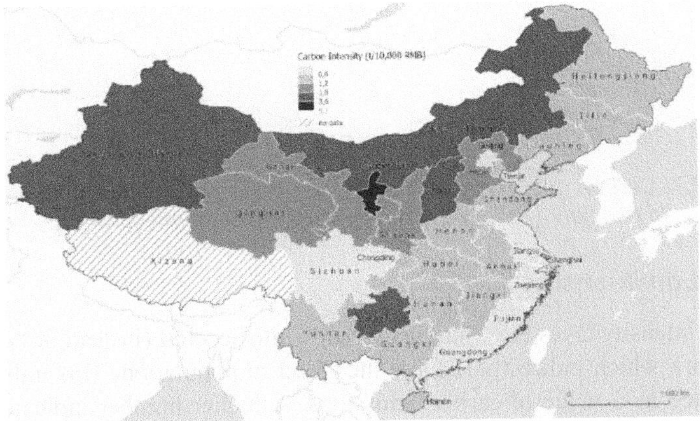

Figure 7.9. *Carbon intensity in Chinese provinces in 2016. For a color version of this figure, see www.iste.co.uk/morales/connectivity.zip*

7.6.5. *Typology of Chinese provinces based on cluster analysis*

Firstly, it is essential to mention that for the indicator of consumption expenditure on health care, the former division based on the settlement was used for the cluster analysis. This step allowed the different types of provinces to be found and grouped with respect to their rural/urban differentiation. For both years, there has been a stable type of region (group one, red color) in the north of China consisting of Ningxia Hui, Nei Mongol, and Shanxi provinces (see Figure 7.10 and Figure 7.11). When looking at the median of standardized values of this type (see Figure 7.12 and Figure 7.13), their carbon emissions and intensities are incredibly high (relative to the other types), and coal consumption reaches a considerably high value. The rest of their indicators (health care indicators in general) are in the IQR (interquartile range, also called midspread), but still above the median values. Almost an opposite behaviour could be seen in the case of type four (yellow color), especially in 2016, in which only the three biggest agglomerations form the group (Beijing, Tianjin, and Shanghai). In short, the fourth type is typical of its high expenditures on health care, while having a low impact on carbon emissions and coal production at the same time. The most “average” and the biggest type (in terms of the number of provinces) is the first one (blue color). All of the indicators of this type remain in the IQR. Interestingly, in 2014, the values were almost at the median (except for coal consumption), while in 2016, they are close to the third (upper) quartile. Lastly, the fourth type (green color) does not deviate from the IQR in the case of coal consumption and carbon emissions and intensity. On the other hand, regions included in this type significantly “suffer” in health care expenditures with values out of IQR beyond the first lower quartile. There is one interesting shift between 2014 and 2016 in this type, namely in the indicator of carbon intensity. In 2014, the carbon intensity was the second highest (after type one – red color); however, in 2016, the carbon intensity values were right at the median (and type one showed a slight increase). As noted previously, this may indicate either a decrease in carbon emission or an increase in overall wealth in these regions.

7.6.6. *Cluster analysis types*

There were four types of clusters that were considered as follows:

– Type 1: average type;

– Type 2: the most environmentally affected type – significant emissions and intensity and extraction, as well as relatively large spending on health care;

– Type 3: relatively healthy regions – the least spending on health care and fairly low emissions, intensity, and extraction;

– Type 4: developed type of regions – they have minor emissions and intensity, but at the same time, they spend a lot on health care.

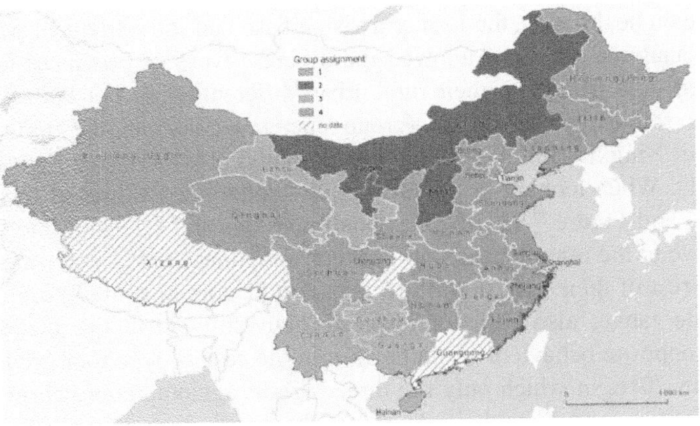

Figure 7.10. *Four main types of Chinese provinces in 2014 based on cluster analysis. For a color version of this figure, see www.iste.co.uk/morales/connectivity.zip*

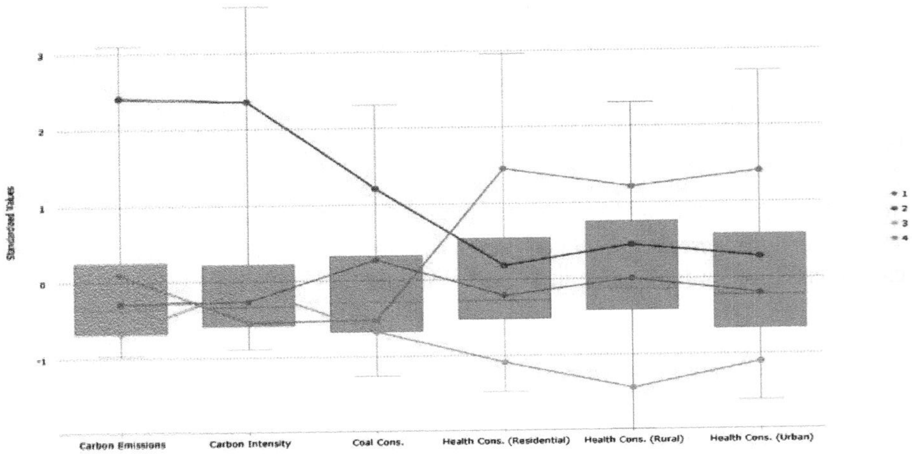

Figure 7.11. *Median of standardized values of input data for individual types of regions in 2014 (parallel boxplots). For a color version of this figure, see www.iste.co.uk/morales/connectivity.zip*

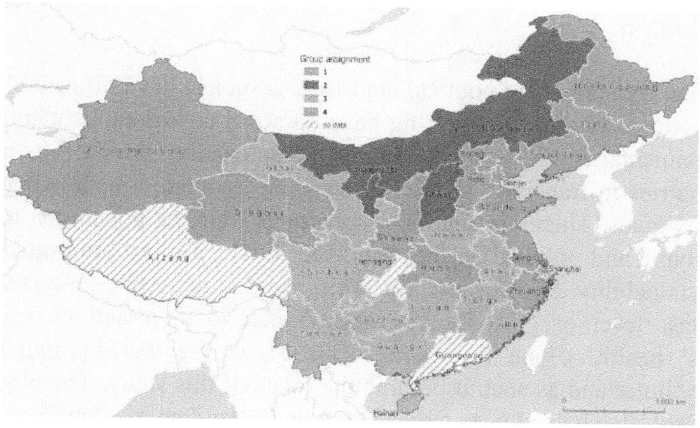

Figure 7.12. *Four main types of Chinese provinces in 2016 based on cluster analysis. For a color version of this figure, see www.iste.co.uk/morales/connectivity.zip*

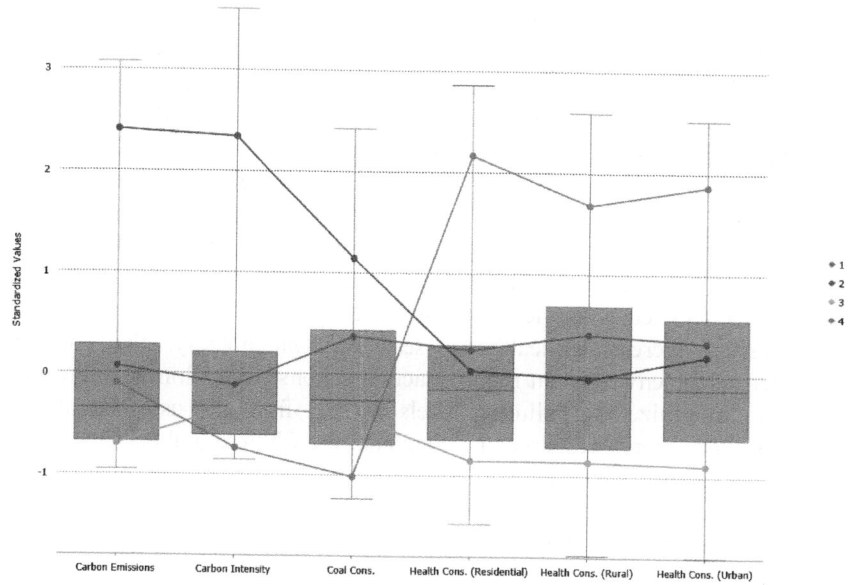

Figure 7.13. *Median of standardized values of input data for individual types of regions in 2016 (parallel boxplots). For a color version of this figure, see www.iste.co.uk/morales/connectivity.zip*

7.7. Conclusion

The global economic and political landscape is subject to significant change, and carbon emissions and their monitoring have attracted considerable attention due to their environmental and health implications. Undoubtedly, more efforts are needed to help countries to transition to more sustainable economic models that integrate sustainability goals. There are significant pressures from the population towards the world economic and political leaders that need to take a more committed approach towards sustainability. Social pressures are rising due to severe concerns emerging from the fast level of global environmental deterioration and their impact on populations' health. China has been identified as the world's biggest carbon emissions polluter and as such it became the focus of this study. The objective was to offer insights that helped us to gain a better understanding of China's performance with regard to GHGs emissions, to which extent emissions are linked to economic activity and their implications for health expenditure, the Chinese government policy on sustainability, and the way forward as the country seeks to move towards a more environmentally friendly energy model. But is this feasible for an economy that needs fast economic growth and with a historical dependence on coal? The econometric findings offered evidence of carbon emissions having a significant impact on China's economic growth. Similarly, the Shanghai Stock Exchange 180 affects China's economic growth; however, it has a lower impact than the carbon emissions levels. The province-based spatial analysis revealed that the most extensive carbon emissions and coal consumption concentrations are focused mainly on the northeast regions. It also showed an increasing trend in healthcare expenditure per capita in most provinces, flagging the connection between pollution and the deterioration of population health. Furthermore, the chapter offered insights into how the dynamics between carbon emissions and China's economic growth are significantly associated with the intensified use and exploitation of coal and the rising costs of increasing healthcare services. Undoubtedly, the continuous deterioration of the environment requires active actions from Chinese authorities if they seek to minimize the pollution levels derived from the use of coal as the country's primary energy resource. To conclude, the Chinese authorities are facing significant challenges as they try to identify alternatives that are compliant with the needed economic growth and the protection of the environment, while simultaneously enabling high levels of growth and development.

7.8. References

Andreosso-O'Callaghan B and Morales L. (2022). China's economic connectivity to the world economy [version 1; peer review: awaiting peer review]. F1000Research, 11:317 [Online]. Available at: https://doi.org/10.12688/f1000research.109984.1.

Chen, X., Huang, J., Yang, Q., Nielsen, C.P., Shi, D., Michael, B. (2018). Changing carbon content of Chinese coal and implications for emissions of CO_2. *Journal of Cleaner Production*, 194, 150–157 [Online]. Available at: https://doi.org/10.1016/j.jclepro.2018.05.128.

Chen, Y., Wang, Z., Zhong, Z. (2019). CO_2 emissions, economic growth, renewable and non-renewable energy production and foreign trade in China. *Renewable Energy*, 131, 208–216 [Online]. Available at: https://doi.org/10.1016/j.renene.2018.07.047.

ChinaPower (2020). How is China managing its greenhouse gas emissions? *ChinaPower Project* [Online]. Available at: https://chinapower.csis.org/china-greenhouse-gas-emissions/.

Climate Action Tracker (2019). China [Online]. Available at: https://climateactiontracker.org/countries/china/.

Dickey, D. and Fuller, W. (1979). Distribution of the estimators for autoregressive time series with a unit root. *J. Am. Stat. Assoc*, 74, 427–431.

Gong, B., Zheng, X., Guo, Q., Ordieres-Meré, J. (2019). Discovering the patterns of energy consumption, GDP, and CO_2 emissions in China using the cluster method. *Energy*, 166, 1149–1167.

IEA (2019). World Energy Outlook 2017: China – Analysis [Online]. Available at: https://www.iea.org/reports/world-energy-outlook-2017-china.

Jain, A.K. (2010). Data clustering: 50 years beyond K-means. *Pattern Recognition Letters*, 31(8), 651–666.

Jiang, J., Xie, D., Ye, B., Shen, B., Chen, Z. (2016). Research on China's cap-and-trade carbon emission trading scheme: Overview and outlook. *Applied Energy*, 178, 902–917. DOI: 10.1016/j.apenergy.2016.06.100.

Kaufman, L. and Rousseeuw, P.J. (2005). *Finding Groups in Data: An Introduction to Cluster Analysis*. Wiley-Interscience, John Wiley & Sons Inc, Hoboken, NJ.

Kraak, M.J. and Ormeling, F. (2011). *Cartography: Visualization of Spatial Data*. Guilford Press, New York.

Levin, A., Lin, C.F., Chu, C.S.J. (2002). Unit root tests in panel data: Asymptotic and finite-sample properties. *Journal of Econometrics*, 108(1), 1–24.

Lomborg, B. (2016). Impact of current climate proposals. *Global Policy*, 7(1), 109–118 [Online]. Available at: https://doi.org/10.1111/1758-5899.12295.

Lyu, J., Cao, M., Wu, K., Li, H. (2020). Price volatility in the carbon market in China. *Journal of Cleaner Production*, 255, 120171. DOI: 10.1016/j.jclepro.2020.120171.

Madi, I., Morales, L., Andreosso-O'Callaghan, B. (2022). China rise in the Middle East: Fuelling a tired dragon? In *Sustainable Development in Asia. Contributions to Economics*, Andreosso-O'Callaghan, B., Rey, S., Taylor, R. (eds). Springer, Cham [Online]. Available at: https://doi.org/10.1007/978-3-030-94679-1_5.

Marek, L., Pászto, V., Tuček, P. (2015a). Using clustering in geosciences: Examples and case studies. *15th International Multidisciplinary Scientific Geoconference, Informatics, Geoinformatics and Remote Sensing*, 2, 1207–1214.

Marek, L., Tuček, P., Pászto, V. (2015b). Using geovisual analytics in Google Earth to understand disease distribution: A case study of campylobacteriosis in the Czech Republic (2008–2012). *International Journal of Health Geographics*, 14(1), 7.

Mastoi, MS., Munir, HM., Zhuang, S., Hassan, M., Usman, M., Alahmadi, A., Alamri, B. (2022). A critical analysis of the impact of pandemic on China's electricity usage patterns and the global development of renewable energy. *Int. J. Environ. Res. Public Health*, 19(8), 4608. DOI: 10.3390/ijerph19084608. PMID: 35457478; PMCID: PMC9031183.

NDRC (2016). The 13th five-year-plan for national economic and social development [Online]. Available at: http://en.ndrc.gov.cn/newsrelease/201612/P020161207645765233498.pdf.

Pan, W., Pan, W., Liu, S., Tsai, S., Hu, C., Tu, H. (2019). China's provincial energy-related carbon emissions-economy nexus: A two-stage framework based on decoupling analysis and panel vector autoregression. *Energy Science & Engineering*, ese3.340 [Online]. Available at: https://doi.org/10.1002/ese3.340.

Pászto, V. and Zimmermannová, J. (2019). Relation of economic and environmental indicators to the European Union Emission Trading System: A spatial analysis. *GeoScape*, 13(1), 1–15 [Online]. Available at: https://doi.org/10.2478/geosc-2019-0001.

Pászto, V., Macků, K., Burian, J., Pánek, J., Tuček, P. (2019). Capturing cross-border continuity: The case of the Czech-Polish borderland. *Moravian Geographical Reports*, 27(2), 122–138.

Peng, X., Tao, X., Feng, K., Hubacek, K. (2020). Drivers toward a low-carbon electricity system in China's provinces. *Environmental Science & Technology*, 54(9), 5774–5782. DOI: 10.1021/acs.est.0c00536.

Pesaran, M.H., Shin, Y., Smith, R.J. (2001). Bounds testing approaches to the analysis of level relationships. *Journal of Applied Econometrics*, 16(3), 289–326.

Phillips, P.C.B. and Perron, P. (1988). Testing for unit root in time series regression. *Biometrica*, 75, 335–346.

Reuters (2021). China coal surge puts supply record, power jump within reach [Online]. Available at: https://www.reuters.com/business/energy/china-coal-surge-puts-supply-record-power-jump-within-reach-2021-10-22/.

Shilei, L., Yu, L., Lunyu, X., Jintao, X. (2020). The environmental improvement under China's "New Normal". *China Economic Journal*. DOI: 10.1080/17538963.2020.1755097.

Song, M., Xie, Q., Wang, S., Zhang, H. (2020). Could environmental regulation and R&D tax incentives affect green product innovation? *Journal of Cleaner Production*, 120849 [Online]. Available at: https://doi.org/10.1016/j.jclepro.2020.120849.

Wang, K., Mi, Z., Wei, Y.M. (2019a). Will pollution taxes improve joint ecological and economic efficiency of thermal power industry in China?: A DEA-based materials balance approach. *Journal of Industrial Ecology*, 23(2), 389–401. DOI: 10.1111/jiec.12740.

Wang, S., Wang, H., Zhang, L., Dang, J. (2019b). Provincial carbon emissions efficiency and its influencing factors in China. *Sustainability*, 11(8), 2355.

Xian, Y., Wang, K., Shi, X., Zhang, C., Wei, Y.M., Huang, Z. (2018). Carbon emissions intensity reduction target for China's power industry: An efficiency and productivity perspective. *Journal of Cleaner Production*, 197, 1022–1034 [Online]. Available at: https://doi.org/10.1016/j.jclepro.2018.06.272.

Zhang, J. and Cross, M.L. (2020). Carbon policies, fossil fuel price, and the impact on employment. *Clean Technologies and Environmental Policy*, 1–11. DOI: 10.1007/s10098-020-01850-x.

Zhang, C. and Xu, J. (2012). Retesting the causality between energy consumption and GDP in China: Evidence from sectoral and regional analyses using dynamic panel data. *Energy Economics*, 34(6), 1782–1789.

Zhang, Y.J., Peng, Y.L., Ma, C.Q., Shen, B. (2017). Can environmental innovation facilitate carbon emissions reduction? Evidence from China. *Energy Policy*, 100, 18–28.

8

The Connecting Role of Home Country Institutions on SME Internationalization: China's OFDI Support in Germany

8.1. Introduction

In recent years, growing numbers of international business (IB) scholars have investigated the role that home country institutional environments play in the international expansion of emerging-market and small- and medium-sized enterprises (SMEs) (Deng and Zhang 2018; Li *et al.* 2018; Aguilera and Grøgaard 2019; Cuervo-Cazurra *et al.* 2019; Wu and Deng 2020; Hernández *et al.* 2021; Hänle *et al.* 2022). Institutional theory (North 1990; Powell and DiMaggio 1991; Scott 2013) suggests that institutional contexts play a vital role in shaping firms' strategic choices. However, the role of institutions in IB requires a nuanced perspective that takes institutional diversity and its effects into account (Aguilera and Grøgaard 2019). This is particularly the case in China, where the options of SMEs are conditioned by the environment and state policies they operate in and under (Cardoza *et al.* 2014). In this growing research domain, two contrasting streams have emerged – the "escape" and the "fostering" view. An integral part of institutional theory, the escape perspective suggests that the internationalization of emerging market firms is partially a response to home country institutional constraints (Pinkham and Peng 2017; Deng and Zhang 2018; Wu and Deng, 2020). On the other hand, the fostering view proposes a facilitating role for advanced domestic Chinese institutions that support China's SMEs in their expansion abroad (Luo *et al.* 2010; Sun *et al.* 2015; Deng and Zhang 2018; Wu and Deng 2020; Yan *et al.* 2020).

Chapter written by Fabian HÄNLE, Stefanie WEIL and Bart CAMBRÉ.

However, scholarly research has mainly focused on the escape view (e.g., Witt and Lewin 2007; Boisot and Meyer 2008; Deng and Zhang 2018; Wu and Deng 2020). This has led to an unbalanced perspective. In line with Deng and Zhang (2018), we argue that both sides are interconnected and equally important to gaining a comprehensive picture of Chinese outward foreign direct investment (OFDI). A recent study in China (Hänle *et al.* 2022) shed light on the internationalization motives of SMEs and the role China's institutional environment plays in leading to escapism. Extending this research, we address the "fostering" side in this chapter.

In the fostering domain, previous research mainly examined how Chinese governmental and state institutions facilitate OFDI of its SMEs at the domestic level. Drawing on the political economy perspective (Breslin 2007; Huang 2008; Zeng 2019), existing IB studies, for example, analyzed how major Chinese governmental institutions, such as the State Council, the State Administration of Foreign Exchange (SAFE), or the Ministry of Commerce of China (MOFCOM), promote firms' outward FDI via different domestic levels, policy instruments, and support processes and how this contributes to China's economic development (Buckley *et al.* 2008; Li 2009; Luo *et al.* 2010; Bernasconi-Osterwalder *et al.* 2012; Wang *et al.* 2012a; Wang *et al.* 2012b Caseiro and Masiero 2014). In another study, Sun *et al.* (2015) investigated domestic Chinese institutions, and the role home country institutional open access plays on firms' outward internationalization within different Chinese regions, confirming the "fostering" view (Wan and Hoskisson 2003).

While we see great value in these studies to better understand the OFDI institutions in the home country, there is a gap in IB research regarding how the Chinese Government transnationalizes and implements its OFDI-support policies to the investment host countries. Specifically, through which Chinese governmental organizations and intermediaries abroad does Beijing implement OFDI-support for SMEs in the developed economy (DE) of Germany, and what are their mechanisms to support SMEs abroad effectively?

Addressing this research question is crucial because institutional factors play an important part in shaping the trajectory and international expansion of Chinese SMEs (Cardoza *et al.* 2014). In China, SMEs account for more than 60% of the GDP and substantially contribute to economic growth and social development (Deng and Zhang 2018). The majority is privately-owned and differs fundamentally from large and state-owned firms in ownership structures, strategies, and the smaller number of resources (Zhang *et al.* 2016; Yan *et al.* 2018). In many cases, these firms also have limited experience, managerial skills, and knowledge when entering international markets (Fornes and Cardoza 2018), which imposes constraints for growth (Ahlstrom *et al.* 2004). Pursuing strategic-asset-, resource-, market-, and efficiency-seeking goals (Hänle *et al.* 2022), the "going-out" (走出去) of China's

SMEs to developed economies (DE) is vital for stimulating the economy's innovativeness in line with the ambitious "Made in China 2025" (中国制造 2025) initiative. This is one reason China's Ministry of Industry and Information Technology (MIIT 2016, 2017, 2018) recently instituted a series of new policies specifically tailored to promote the OFDI of China's SMEs. Thus, understanding how this overarching direction of China's Government translates into actual support mechanisms and institutions in a developed investment country is a compelling question for IB scholars and an essential issue for China's economic development (avoiding a potential "middle-income" trap, Liu *et al.* 2017; Ahlstrom *et al.* 2018).

Using Germany as a case study, we conduct qualitative research to analyze Chinese OFDI promotion institutions and mechanisms for SMEs in a large developed economy abroad. We employ the empirical setting of Germany because large parts of China's OFDI soon found their way into DE (Athreye and Kapur 2009). In 2020, China was Germany's most important trading partner for the fifth consecutive year (Statistisches Bundesamt 2021). Despite the Covid-19 crisis, foreign trade turnover with China increased by 3% compared to 2019, with goods worth 212.1 billion euros traded between China and Germany (Statistisches Bundesamt 2021). Over the last 20 years, Germany has received the second-most Chinese investments in Europe (UNCTAD 2020). China's Ministry of Commerce explicitly mentions Germany as a politically desired investment destination (MOFCOM 2004). Germany's large market and central location in Europe, high innovativeness, strong brand reputation, and technological knowledge (Venohr and Meyer 2007; De Massis *et al.* 2018) offers an attractive environment for Chinese firms to invest and cooperate. Therefore, this chapter will close the gap in research and provide empirical evidence by examining which organizations and fostering mechanisms the Chinese Government uses to institutionalize OFDI-support for its SMEs in the DE of Germany.

We derive our findings from elite interviews (Aberbach and Rockman 2002; Harvey 2011) with senior representatives of Chinese governmental institutions, intermediary parties, and specialized Chinese lawyers and consultants that frequently accompany Chinese OFDI to Germany. Additionally, we analyze secondary data such as presentations, governmental documents, websites, brochures, social media (WeChat), and recent Chinese OFDI policies for SMEs (MIIT 2016, 2017, 2018). For triangulation, we hold interviews with senior executives and business owners of Chinese SMEs that plan to or already have invested in Germany.

This study delivers the following key contributions: First, it enhances our understanding of how overarching Chinese Government OFDI promotion policies transnationalize into institutional mechanisms in a DE abroad. This contributes and adds to the recent discussion on the role home country institutional environments play in the international expansion of small- and medium-sized firms (Deng and

Zhang 2018; Li *et al.* 2018; Aguilera and Grøgaard 2019; Cuervo-Cazurra *et al.* 2019; Wu and Deng 2020; Hernández *et al.* 2021). Second, by contrasting and discussing the findings in light of previous research on institutional escapism, we contribute to connecting the previously diverging and separate research streams of the escape and fostering sides. Viewing these contributions together stakes out promising territory for future research (Deng and Zhang 2018), which we lay out in our discussion.

Third, the study also offers practical contributions. Understanding better how governments can support internationalization is vital as it determines the effectiveness of policymaking and fosters international mutual understanding, cultural exchange, firm growth and innovation (Ahlstrom 2010), and hence ultimately contributes positively to society. Moreover, knowing the specific OFDI-support institutions and measures China is currently adopting can serve as a helpful orientation for Chinese business-owners who plan to invest in the German market.

The chapter is structured as follows: Drawing on an institutional theory, we first review literature on the role of home country institutions in OFDI promotion in the specific context of China. Subsequently, we outline our research methods, followed by a presentation and discussion of the findings. We then illustrate the chapter's theoretical contributions and address limitations, suggestions for future research, and practical implications.

8.2. Literature review

In IB literature, institutional theory (North 1990, Powell and DiMaggio 1991; Scott 2013) suggests that institutional environments play a vital role in shaping a firm's strategic choices (Lin *et al.* 2020). North (1990) described institutions as formal and informal "rules of the game", which at the most fundamental level consist of three dimensions (Peng 2003; Yamakawa *et al.* 2008; Lin *et al.* 2020): the regulative, the normative and the cultural-cognitive (Scott 2013). These pillars explain how individuals and organizations are influenced. The regulative dimension comprises governmental legislation and industrial standards and agreements with which organizations should comply (Bruton *et al.* 2010; Lin *et al.* 2020). "In this conception, regulatory processes involve the capacity to establish rules, inspect other's conformity to them, and, as necessary, manipulate sanctions – rewards or punishments – in an attempt to influence future behavior" (Scott 2013). The basis of order is grounded on regulative rules with coercive mechanisms and rules, sanctions, and laws as indicators. Hence, in the broadest sense, this dimension encompasses governmental policies and regulatory frameworks that derive from distinct political systems and institutions. The normative dimension consists of norms (specifying how things should be done, consistent with values and professional standards) and values (what is considered proper) that require little codification in local commercial or social situations (Scott 2013; Lin *et al.* 2020). The cultural-cognitive dimension consists of subjective cultural and linguistic rules that follow conceptions of what other reasonable people would do in a certain situation (Scott 2013).

Together, the three dimensions serve as an analytical-conceptual tool enabling investigators to identify the elements at work, and they can change over time (Scott 2014). This study focuses on the regulative pillar in the form of home government support, as this aspect has been revealed as an outstanding feature of China's Go Global policy (Amann *et al.* 2018). State support is frequently reported as a main determinant of China's OFDI (McNally 2012; Freeman 2013, 2017; Ten Brink 2013). In China, institutional frameworks are constantly changing, economic activities are under the control of the state, and the strategic options of SMEs are conditioned by the government policies and regulatory frameworks they operate in (Cardoza *et al.* 2014). However, the role of institutions in IB requires a nuanced perspective that takes the effects of institutional diversity on domestic and foreign levels into account (Bruton *et al.* 2010; Aguilera and Grøgaard 2018). As illustrated in the introduction, previous studies that explore the role of home country OFDI-support institutions on SME internationalization either focus on the domestic level in China or are situated in different emerging market contexts (e.g., Wan and Hoskisson 2003; Luo *et al.* 2010; Young *et al.* 2014; Sun *et al.* 2015; Yan *et al.* 2020). However, these lenses might not be able to fully explain the phenomenon in the particular context of China:

– First, in IB studies, most authors still define China as an emerging market (EM) or emerging economy (EE), but as Peng *et al.* (2018) noted, they use these terms loosely without addressing which underlying definition they follow. From existing definitions, "mid-range EE" by Hoskisson *et al.* (2013), characterized by lower institutional development and high infrastructure and factor development, probably comes closest to contemporary China, as it considers its strong economic growth. However, there are still distinctive features that make China an outstanding example. First, building on Athreye and Kapur (2009), Yang (2018) argues that comparing Chinese multinationals to peers from other EM, OFDI flows took place much faster, and large parts found their way into DE sooner. Referring to Deng and Yang (2015), Yang (2018) further concludes: "Due to distinct features of Chinese multinationals, one should take caution in generalizing Chinese firms to represent all other emerging economy firms."

– Second, China's political system is unique and cannot be compared to other EM, exemplified by the extent to which communist-socialist politics interfere in China's economic system (Andreosso-O'Callaghan and Gottwald 2013; Weil 2017). Therefore, we also draw on the political economy perspective, which offers rich streams of up-to-date research that shed light on China's unique state capitalism. This interdisciplinary approach can enrich the growing debate in IB studies and contribute to answering the research question.

Perceived from a political economy perspective, Beijing's state-driven capitalist model is the key to China's economic success. Although the Chinese economy has liberalized since its WTO membership, it cannot be ignored that the Chinese Communist Party (CCP) retains control over its economy. China's economic development is distinct from those of other emerging economies such as Brazil or India. In contrast to other EE, China successfully balances the role of the Communist Party as both a capitalist and socialist actor (Nolan 2001; Harvey 2005; Pearson 2005; Heberer 2014; Li 2014; Brown, 2019).

China's unique capitalist system cannot be captured with mainstream business- or political economy theories. Communist-socialist politics interfere in China's economic system (Andreosso-O'Callaghan and Gottwald 2013). To describe China's economic system as "Capitalism with Chinese Characteristics" (Huang 2008), "Guanxi Capitalism" (McNally 2011), "Red capitalism" (Dickson 2003), or "New capitalism" (Ten Brink 2013) shows the attempts to capture the socialist-capitalist paradox of Chinese capitalist institutions. It underpins the difficulty of embracing the contradictions in a state-permeated capitalist system that simultaneously fosters a competition-minded corporate spirit from the top down. As such, China's capitalism is very distinct from Germany's "sozialer Marktwirtschaft" (social market economy). In China's regulatory system, political institutions hold a powerful position to drive investment policies (Beeson and Li 2015; Economy 2018).

State support is frequently reported as a main determinant of China's OFDI (McNally 2012; Freeman 2013, 2017; Ten Brink, 2013). As illustrated above, the fostering perspective suggests a facilitating role of advanced domestic Chinese institutions that support China's firms to go abroad and expand worldwide (Luo *et al.* 2010; Sun *et al.* 2015; Deng and Zhang 2018; Yan *et al.* 2020). However, previous research has mainly focused on larger Chinese multinationals or state-owned firms (Buckley *et al.* 2008; Li 2009; Wang *et al.* 2009; Luo *et al.* 2010; Klossek *et al.* 2012; Wang *et al.* 2012; Bruton *et al.* 2015; Sun *et al.* 2015), which underpins the need for firm-level studies on China's SMEs.

8.3. Methodology

We apply an inductive research method (Yin 2018) to answer the research question because in addition to identifying Chinese OFDI organizations in the German market, we aim to better understand the underlying mechanisms of how these organizations support Chinese SMEs' OFDI. We thereby aim to gain a rich, in-depth understanding through the multiple-case study method, which allows theorizing from cases and can identify new variables and causal explanations (Eisenhardt 1989; George and Bennett, 2005; Welch *et al.* 2011).

Cases are Chinese governmental organizations and possible intermediary parties in the German market that support OFDI of China's SMEs. As such, we adopt a purposive sampling strategy (Morse 1994; Patton 2015; Fletcher *et al.* 2018) that aims to spot and conduct interviews with Chinese OFDI-supporting organizations in the German economy. Originally, we identified cases by consulting with China's International Investment Promotion Agency (CIIPA) in Frankfurt, Germany, and the local Chinese government in Taicang (Suzhou), Jiangsu province, China. Out of the two cases initially identified, we continued by snow-balling (Patton 2015; Fletcher *et al.* 2018), i.e., we either enquired with the interviewees for further contacts at other Chinese governmental organizations or intermediary parties that support Chinese SMEs in the German market, or we analyzed related secondary data such as websites. This resulted in the identification of seven total cases and 19 additional organizations that are linked to the cases via close cooperation and partnerships.

For data collection (Table 8.1), we employed elite interview techniques from political science (Aberbach and Rockman 2002; Harvey 2011) to conduct semi-structured interviews prepared with a guideline of open-ended and specific follow-up questions around the areas of query (Clifford *et al.* 2016). In total, we carried out 21 interviews that lasted 67 minutes on average and 1,408 minutes in total. We held 10 interviews with senior representatives of Chinese governmental organizations, intermediary parties, industry experts, and specialized Chinese lawyers and consultants that frequently accompany Chinese OFDI to the German market. In addition, we collected and carefully analyzed 167 items of secondary data, such as websites, governmental documents, presentations, brochures, leading social media in China (WeChat), and the most recent official Chinese OFDI policies for SMEs (MIIT 2016, 2017, 2018). All interviews, as well as the analyzed documents, were either related to our cases or to their surrounding environment, for instance, through linked partner organizations or intermediary parties. To triangulate, we further conducted and analyzed 11 interviews with nine executives and business owners of Chinese SMEs that plan to or already have invested in the German economy. These interviews further improved our data quality and hence the reliability of our findings because these SMEs have close contacts ("guanxi") and insights into numerous additional Chinese firms and their experiences regarding OFDI-support and investing in Germany. To facilitate unbiased, open discussions, interviewees were guaranteed anonymity.

We collected the data between April 2019 and May 2021, both in Germany and China. The interviews were held in the respondent's preferred language (Chinese,

English or German) by a trilingual researcher, taped, and subsequently transcribed to allow for the free and more accurate expression of ideas. The interviews resulted in 428 pages of transcripts in total. Towards the end of the interviews, we repeatedly encountered the same topics, and no significant new insights were emerging. Following the recommendations of Strauss and Corbin (1998), we stopped the data collection process at this point of theoretical saturation. For the analysis of our interview notes, we used NVivo by QSR International. In this process, we continuously reviewed interview transcripts as our data collection advanced. This helped in identifying emerging ideas and specific topics that guided our subsequent data collection. We adopted the open, axial, and selective coding schemes of Strauss and Corbin (1998). During the open coding, we identified essential concepts by applying in-vivo codes, i.e., codes which emerged from the text based on keywords and short phrases used by the respondents. In the following step, of axial coding, we repeated the process in second and third cycles to further increase the accuracy and merge and relabel codes that share the same meaning. Subsequently, we grouped the remaining in-vivo codes into higher-level concepts (first-order categories) based on their underlying similarities. We then used selective coding to find relations among the first-order categories and assigned them into overarching second-order themes. We carried this process on until no new relations in data were found. In line with Gioia *et al.* (2013), our coding was not linear, but recursive, analytic, and process-oriented.

Type of data	**Data collection**
Documents studied	167
websites	119
presentations	7
catalogs and brochures	20
social media	15
laws or policies	6
Semi-structured interviews	10
Interviews for triangulation	11
Time period of data collection	April 2019–May 2021
Total	**188**

Table 8.1. *Overview of data collection*

8.4. Findings and discussion

8.4.1. *Overview of findings*

The findings indicate that following the overarching "Go Global" strategy and with the help of Germany's Government, Beijing has implemented a multi-facetted institutional OFDI-support set-up in Germany. Figure 8.1 illustrates the Chinese governmental OFDI-support institutions in Germany. The main actors include: *(1) official Chinese governmental institutions* such as the China International Investment Promotion Agency (CIIPA) headquartered in Frankfurt, the Chinese Chamber of Commerce Germany (CHKD) in the capital Berlin, and the Departments of Economy and Trade of the Chinese Embassy in Berlin and the Chinese General Consulates in Frankfurt, Düsseldorf, Munich, and Hamburg; *(2) selected national champions* such as the Zhongde Metal Group which established the Zhongde China SME Center in Berlin; and *(3) German-Chinese business associations, think tanks, and cooperation centers* that serve as an intermediary party, for example the German-Chinese business association (DCW) or the China Center Bavaria (CZB).

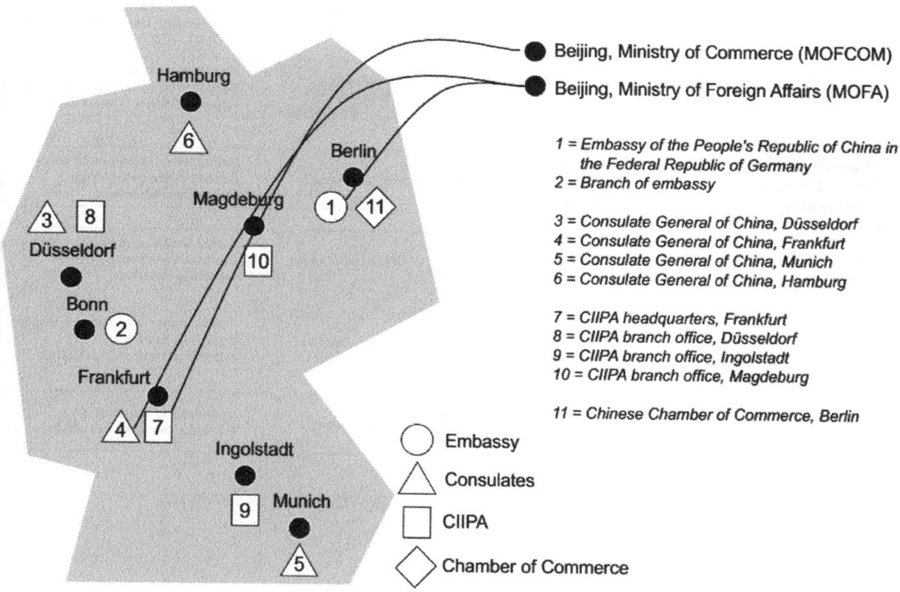

Figure 8.1. *The Chinese governmental OFDI-support institutions in Germany*

Summarizing our findings and in line with prominent approaches for conducting analyses through cases study research (Eisenhardt 1989; Yin 2018), our additional results are structured according to sets of support mechanisms (second-order themes) that emerged during the analysis process. The identified organizations support the OFDI of China's SMEs in Germany mainly through four distinct mechanisms (Figure 8.2): *(1) facilitating networking and information* in Germany through match-making events, specialized industrial clusters, and publications on investment news; *(2) mutual knowledge transfer* via a supported integration of Chinese SMEs in local business associations and the establishment of German-Chinese research projects and institutes; *(3) lobbying* to foster an objective, correct picture of the existent cooperation possibilities with Chinese firms in Germany and reduce liability of foreignness; as well as *(4) facilitating investment services* that encompass comprehensive consulting services and support for delegation visits and international trade fairs.

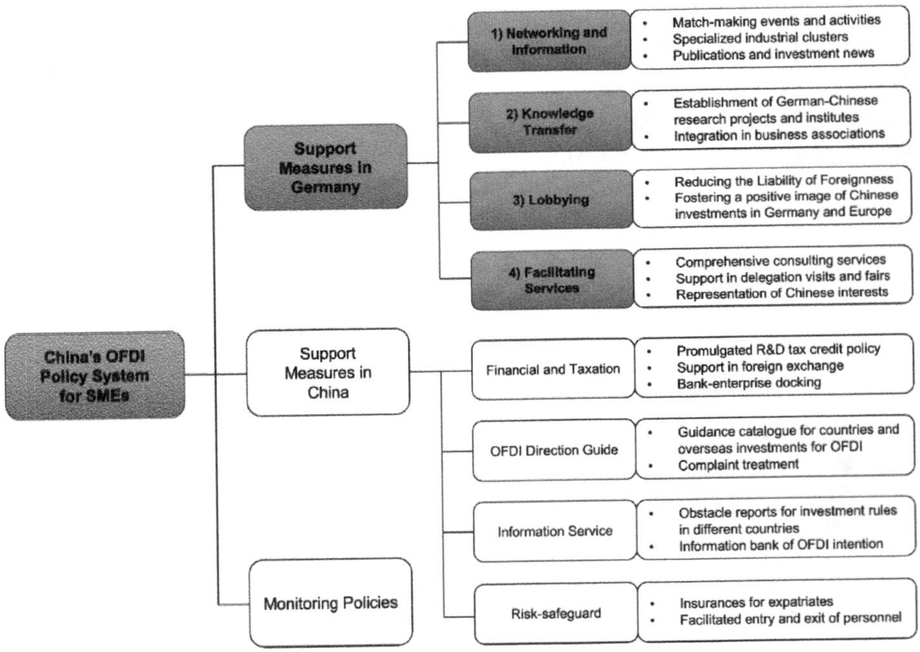

Figure 8.2. *China's OFDI-support measures in Germany*

8.4.1.1. *Specialized OFDI policies for Chinese SMEs*

Our analysis also contained an examination of Beijing's overarching OFDI strategy for its SMEs to better understand the background of the institutional setup and support mechanisms. Recently, China's Ministry of Industry and Information Technology (MIIT 2016, 2017, 2018) entered a series of new policies specifically tailored to promote the OFDI of China's SMEs into force. For example, an updated

"SME promotion law" assures support in foreign exchange and entry and exit of personnel (MIIT 2017, Article 42). Beijing plans to create 1,000 Chinese Hidden Champion firms with a budget of $1.3 billion on this project (China Quality Supervision 2020). Hidden Champions are highly specialized small- to medium-sized businesses that are global leaders in their niche markets. They show very high degrees of internationalization and are extremely important for the innovativeness and export performance of countries (Simon 1996, 2009, 2022). In addition, a "five-year action plan for SME promotion", jointly launched with the Bank of China, and an "SME development plan 2016–2020" specify further actions to promote OFDI of China's small and medium-sized businesses (MIIT 2016, Chapter 4, Article 6):

> We will speed up the "going out" and bringing in of SMEs, encourage qualified SMEs to set up raw material bases, R&D and design bases and marketing networks abroad, support SMEs to acquire advanced technology and latest scientific research achievements abroad, merge and acquire foreign innovative SMEs, and support SMEs to "go global" in technology, brand, marketing, and service.
>
> We will deepen the cooperation mechanism between government, banks, and enterprises, encourage various forms of bank-enterprise docking and cross-border matchmaking activities, provide a platform for financial institutions and SMEs to communicate and exchange, and support the internationalization of small and medium-sized enterprises.

Following this overarching grand strategy, China's Ministries of Commerce (MOFCOM) and Industry and Information Technology (MIIT) implemented and established a versatile supportive network at home and abroad in Germany. As one respondent explained:

> The Chinese Government actively promotes (OFDI) by investment bureaus, for example in Changzhou, Nanjing, Taicang [...]. These offices facilitate information flow, introduce parties by match-making activities and organize events, such as the Taicang day in Frankfurt, Germany (Interview 10).

8.4.1.2. *The central Chinese OFDI-support institutions in Germany*

8.4.1.2.1. China International Investment Promotion Agency (CIIPA)

Investigating the main Chinese OFDI-support institutions in Germany and their activities on a deeper level reveals that CIIPA plays a vital and active role in connecting the German and Chinese economy. Headed by China's Ministry of

Commerce in Beijing, CIIPA itself has set up an extensive network in Germany (Figure 8.3) (for a detailed illustration of OFDI institutions in China, see Luo *et al.* 2010). This includes good relations and contacts with German innovation and technology centers (e.g., "Innovation center Niedersachsen" or "Bavaria innovative"), German governmental agencies that foster foreign investments in Germany ("Germany Trade and Invest" and "Hesse Trade and Invest"), business associations ("Association of German Hidden Champions e.V."), as well as local city governments (state capital Marburg), business magazines ("Global Business Magazine in Stuttgart"), and industry associations ("medways e.V. medical and biotechnology association", "Life Science Nord – German network for innovative medicine", or "Mahreg – Automotive network"). Through CIIPA, this network is made available to China's SMEs that are planning to invest in the German market. CIIPA (2020) promotes the cooperation between SMEs in China and Europe, publicizes the two countries' investment policies, and establishes specialized industrial clusters that concentrate on key industries of China's "Made in China 2025" (MOFCOM 2021) initiative, such as automotive, biotechnology, industry 4.0, and automation. At the same time, China's governmental institutions are also very active in attracting foreign investments to their home market in China. CIIPA in Germany organized as many activities promoting German investors to China as those introducing Chinese businesses to the German market.

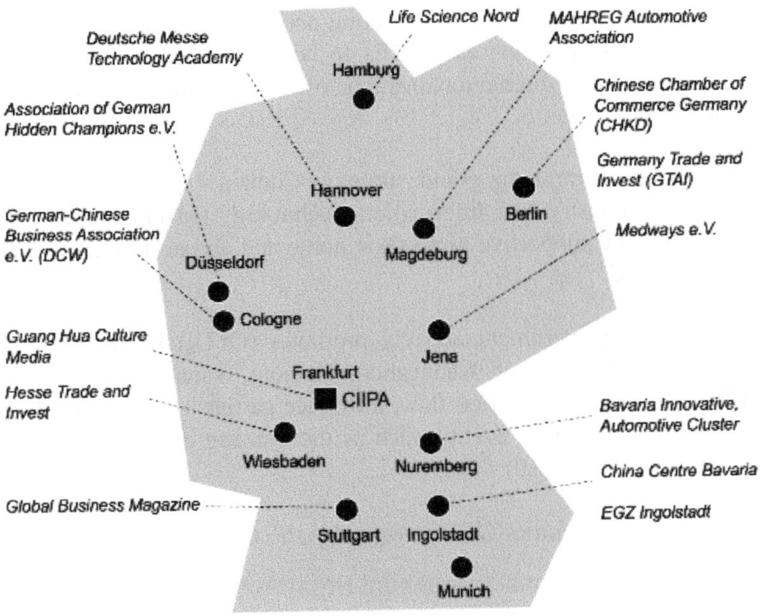

Figure 8.3. *CIIPA's cooperation network in Germany*

8.4.1.2.2. Chinesische Handelskammer in Deutschland (CHKD)

CHKD is the first Chinese Foreign Chamber of Commerce in Europe and the official representative of the Chinese economy in Germany (CHKD 2021a). It has 350 member companies, half of which belong to the 500 economically strongest firms in China. CHKD represents the Chinese interests towards the German economy and society. Like CIIPA, CHKD organizes events to foster cooperation and networking among Chinese firms in Germany and German institutions and partners. Additionally, CHKD provides comprehensive consulting services for Chinese firms to enter the German market, operate sustainably in Germany, and find partners. The services cover legal consulting, event planning, PR consulting, group visits, talent recruitment, and two-way visas for China and Germany (CHKD 2021a). As its elected President, Mr. Zheng Donglin serves as the Managing Director of the Industrial and Commercial Bank of China (ICBC) Frankfurt branch, and since the China Construction Bank (CCB) Frankfurt branch has been elected to the executive board as well, the network of CHKD also encompasses China's financial sector (CHKD 2021b).

8.4.1.2.3. Embassy and General Consulates

On the website of MOFCOM, the Economic and Commercial Department of the Embassy of the People's Republic of China in the Federal Republic of Germany in Berlin is described as the general consulting agency for investment in Germany (MOFCOM 2021). It belongs to the Ministry of Foreign Affairs (MOFA 2021). Together, the Chinese General Consulates in Frankfurt, Düsseldorf, Munich, and Hamburg, along with China's embassy publicize investment news for Chinese OFDI in Germany and serve as contact points for Chinese firms. Furthermore, these institutions actively shape the public image of China in Germany through corresponding news sections on their website or interviews with leading German newspapers and media (MOFA 2021).

8.4.1.2.4. German-Chinese Business Association e.V. (DCW)

The German-Chinese Business Association (DCW) in Cologne, established in 1987, describes itself as an impartial and non-profit organization that aims to promote economic relationships between China and Germany (DCW 2021). An analysis of its inter-organizational relationships reveals that DCW is closely interlinked with CIIPA Germany, CHKD, and China's Embassy in Germany. For example, one former president of DCW also served as Head of the CIPA branch in Düsseldorf simultaneously. In the introduction section of the yearly report of DCW (2021), Wu Ken, the Chinese Ambassador to Germany, argues:

> China and Germany, in their respective regions, are the most important cooperation partners for each other. [...] For more than two

> years, a representative group of German enterprises such as BMW, AXA, and BASF enjoys the further opening of the Chinese market. More than 200 German firms enthusiastically participated in the 2nd China International Import Exhibition (CIIE). [...]
>
> However, it must be emphasized that while the Chinese side is very concerned to establish a fair business environment for foreign firms, Chinese businesses in Germany are partly treated repellently. Chinese investors in Germany repeatedly face resistance when it comes to mergers or take-overs. When bewildering gossip of a sellout of the German economy arises, and some politicians and media negate the reached high level of bilateral relationships, these allegations diametrically oppose Germany's constitutional principles and the spirit of free trade. [...]
>
> Hopefully, the German side is able to establish a fair, just, transparent, and predictable business environment for Chinese investments in Germany. [...] I sincerely hope that the German-Chinese Business Association continues its intermediary role in shaping the bilateral cooperation in economy and trade and the future of the bilateral economic cooperation!

On DCW's advisory board, one finds prominent names of the German and Chinese political and economic realm involved, such as Dr. Michael Schäfer (Chairman of the Board, BMW Foundation Herbert Quandt, and former Ambassador of the Federal Republic of Germany in the People's Republic of China), Dr. Shaojun Sun (Executive President, Weichai Power Co., Ltd.), Dr. Marc Wucherer (Member of the Executive Board of Bosch Rexroth AG), and Prof. Dr. Ulrich Lehner (Chairman of the Supervisory Board of Deutsche Telekom AG). In 2013, DCW established its own think tank – the German-Chinese Bureau of Economic Research (GCB 2021) – to "promote the understanding of the economic relations between China and Germany in an international context. Our research aims to provide insights on the development of the Chinese economy and, in particular, on the trajectory of Chinese outbound and inbound investment. [...] Our research is rooted in the principles of independent, impartial and open-minded inquiry. [...] As a non-profit institute, we aim to disseminate research to a wide audience."

8.4.1.2.5. Zhongde Metal Group

Another significant player supporting Chinese OFDI in Germany is the company Zhongde Metal Group GmbH. It was established in Stuttgart in 2015 as a daughter subsidiary of the Chinese Zhongde Metal Group Co., Ltd., which is privately owned and headquartered in Jieyang City of Guangdong Province. In China, Zhongde develops, constructs, and runs several industrial parks, such as the Sino-German

Metal Eco-City. The former Guangdong Party chief and today's Vice Premier of China's State Council, Hu Chunhua, visited the Metal Eco-City several times, expressing the government's support (Zhongde 2021a). In Germany, its subsidiary helps Chinese firms to open up the German and European market. China's Ministry for Industry and Information Technology (MIIT 2020; Jieyang Government 2021) actively supports Zhongde Germany and in 2018 and 2021 officially awarded them the title "China SME Center Germany". Their mission is to develop into the "central platform for the Chinese and German Mittelstand, a center of competence that encompasses a comprehensive network of experts, business associations, and political institutions and companies in Europe and China. To achieve this goal, the Zhongde Metal Group GmbH draws on a comprehensive network from politics, science, and economy..." (Zhongde, 2021b). In line with this strategy, Zhongde consolidated and streamlined its former six branch offices (Berlin, Dresden, Frankfurt, Munich, Stuttgart, and Düsseldorf) in 2020 in its new headquarters in the German capital, Berlin:

> In Berlin, we are integrated into a comprehensive network of economy, politics, and science. From here, we can operate all over Germany and support our cooperation partners effectively (Zhongde Germany 2020b).

In this way, Zhongde is actively cooperating with influential German personalities from the political and economic spheres. Prominent examples are cooperation agreements with the RSBK GmbH, a German consulting firm led and inspired by the former Minister-President of Rhineland-Palatinate and former Federal Minister of Defence of Germany, Rudolf Scharping (Zhongde 2021a). Moreover, Prof. Dr. Dieter Hundt, Honorary President of the Confederation of German Employers' Associations (Bundesvereinigung der Deutschen Arbeitgeberverbände BDA), is integrated and serves as the Chairman of the Supervisory Board of Zhongde Germany (Zhongde Germany 2020b). Such relationships are significant because BDA is the leading association for labor and social policy in the German economy (BDA 2021).

8.4.2. *Discussion of theoretical contributions*

The findings provide several key contributions to this research. First, they advance OFDI theory and extend the growing discussion on home country institutions and the internationalization of emerging market SMEs (Deng and Zhang 2018; Li *et al.* 2018; Aguilera and Grøgaard 2019; Cuervo-Cazurra *et al.* 2019; Wu and Deng 2020; Hernández *et al.* 2021; Hänle *et al.* 2022) by illustrating how governmental directions on outward FDI translate into actual support institutions and mechanisms in a DE abroad. Central Chinese governmental institutions that have been identified in previous research on Chinese OFDI policy (Luo *et al.* 2010), such as China's Ministry of Commerce or the State Council, also manifested as influential players in our case study of Chinese OFDI in Germany, as they are directing overseas agencies such as CIIPA. In contrast to the OFDI set up in China and the study of Luo *et al.* (2010), we also found privately owned Chinese enterprises, such as the national champion Zhongde, Chinese-German business associations, think tanks, and linked intermediary parties as supporting institutions for Chinese SMEs' investments in the German market. This comprehensive network offers wide-ranging support mechanisms that cause different effects. In the area of networking and information, institutions such as CIIPA (2020, 2021) and its partners are very active in orchestrating the establishment of specialized industrial clusters that are mutually beneficial for both Germany and China, for example, in environmental, automotive (e-mobility), digital, or medical technology. Thereby, delegations from both countries are invited, and the participants encompass leading and rising enterprises from both China and Germany with the aim of match-making and networking. This offers access to the German and Chinese market and can help to reduce psychic distance (PD) and its impact on firms. Psychic distance is defined as "the distance perceived by managers between the characteristics of the home country and the foreign country" (Vaccarini *et al.* 2018). Such perceived differences generate distance and unfamiliarity among managers (Marini Thomé *et al.* 2017), leading to obstacles in possible OFDI endeavors. Previous research in IB investigated the impact of PD on OFDI (e.g., Child *et al.* 2002; Brewer 2007; Child *et al.* 2009; Puthusserry *et al.* 2014) and demonstrated that the perceptions of managers significantly differ before and after entering foreign markets due to the gathering of experience (Vaccarini *et al.* 2017). As such, the possibility of accessing information networks provides a valuable and facilitating "soft factor" for Chinese SMEs' OFDI in the far-distant German market and contributes to the advancement of this debate by illustrating through which mechanisms home country governments can reduce psychic distance and hence spur the "going out" of its SMEs.

Second, as Ahlstrom (2010) points out: "Through innovation and growth firms can do untold good for society [...] particularly to those at the base of the pyramid". Via the networks of governmental institutions such as CIIPA or CHKD, Beijing is supporting the integration of Chinese SMEs in German business associations. Such integrations foster mutual understanding, cultural exchange between Germany and China, firm growth and innovation (Ahlstrom 2010). Memberships or close contacts to, for example, the Association of German Hidden Champions e.V., the German-Chinese Business Association (DCW), or the medical associations medways e.V. and Life Science Nord, in turn, enable a facilitated knowledge transfer and exchange between German and Chinese businesses (Easterby-Smith *et al.* 2008; Argote and Fahrenkopf 2016). Knowledge can be of a technological (environmental, product, or manufacturing knowledge, R&D capabilities) and managerial nature (strategic capabilities, sales and marketing, management skills) (Wang *et al.* 2004). Knowledge transfer is "the transfer of either skills or capabilities (that is, expertise) or external information of strategic value – such as globally relevant information about key customers, competitors or suppliers, from the foreign subsidiary to its parent company" (Rabbiosi 2008). The integration in local associations or the foundation of joint research projects provides a valuable channel to mutually exchange knowledge that is embedded in the local environment of the Chinese subsidiaries in Germany and, vice versa, German subsidiaries in China (e.g., suppliers, customers, R&D partners and projects, business associations). This is very important for both countries, because as Simon illustrates (2022): "No country has more Hidden Champions than Germany. After a phase of hyper globalization the Hidden Champions are facing new challenges [...]. They have to increase their R&D activities once again and include unfamiliar areas of knowledge in the process. They need to relocate their centers of excellence to the best place, which is often China. New drivers such as digitalization, business ecosystems and sustainability require them to adapt and open up their traditionally closed corporate cultures. This applies equally to cooperation partners and foreign environments".

In this context, Germany's state agency for international trade, Baden-Württemberg International (bw-i 2022), for example, arranges networking and match-making events with firms from Southwest Germany and innovative companies from their Chinese partner province Jiangsu in regard to environmental protection and green technology. As today China is one of the largest and fastest growing markets for environmental technologies (bw-i 2022), such connecting and integrating events offer new possibilities in international cooperation between China and Germany, which are beneficial for both countries' sustainability and future.

This cooperation and exchange, fostered by internationalization, benefits the realization of the ambitious "Made in China 2025" initiative and adds to the on-going debate on how China's SMEs can further shift up the "smile-curve" of value added (Ahlstrom *et al.* 2018, Meng *et al.* 2020; Hänle *et al.* 2022). At the same time, it can contribute to extending the innovativeness of German firms into areas where China is leading the field, for example when it comes to digitalization in consumer markets or e-mobility. As Simon (2022) points out: "In 2005, China entered the top 10 in the number of international patents for the first time and overtook Germany in 2012. Today, China is number one, even ahead of the United Stated. Adjusted for size, Chinese Hidden Champions employ about three times as many people in research and development as their German counterparts."

However, as Holtbrügge (2018) pointed out, China's OFDI partially cause unfounded negative public responses in the investment host countries (Zhang and Ebbers 2010; Meunier 2014), especially in Western DE (Luo *et al.* 2010; Wang *et al.* 2012; Deng 2013; Clegg and Voss, 2018). Holtbrügge (2018) summarized these concerns, that often derive from prejudices and stereotypes: Chinese investors could gain access to managerial and technological expertise, which might reduce the competitive advantages of domestic companies (Meyer *et al.* 2014); trade unions are afraid of possible job transfers from Germany to the Chinese headquarters (Burgoon and Raess 2014; Meunier 2014); environmental organizations fear a decrease of ecological standards (Gugler and Shi 2008; Holtbrügge and Kreppel 2015); and Chinese MNEs with a state background are perceived to carry out political interests and are, therefore, viewed as non-beneficial or even harmful for the host country (Child and Rodrigues 2005; Buckley *et al.* 2007; Globerman and Shapiro 2009). In response, and to establish an objective picture of Chinese OFDI, Chinese governmental institutions and firms have increased communication and lobbying efforts to correct the often-misleading media image by fostering mutual understanding and cooperation possibilities. This also helps to reduce the liability of foreignness of Chinese firms in the German market.

Lobbying can be "broadly defined as the attempt to actively influence policy-making and refers to collective bargaining of interest groups" (Weil 2018). This is actively employed by official Chinese institutions such as CHKD or the Chinese Embassy, and also via intermediary parties such as the German-Chinese Business Association (DCW) or the Frankfurt Chinese Enterprise Association e.V., which is supported by the Chinese Consulate in Frankfurt and states as one of the aims of their association the "fostering of a positive image of the Chinese firms in the Rhine-Main region" (FCEA 2021). While the political systems of the European Union not only enable but actively foster lobbying (Bennedsen and Feldmann 2002), Weil (2018) has drawn a different picture for China. In Western political systems, political contest within society is an accepted assumption that underpins the right to shape public policy. Hence, conflict is seen as a needed instrument of policy-making (Schattschneider 1975). In contrast, China does not regard conflict as an inherent part of society and policy-making, but rather as a threat to societal harmony (Weil 2018). As a consequence, political bargaining in China is not conducted in the open, and methods of influence are different to those in Western systems. Chinese actors try to influence policy through direct ties and mutual agreement rather than via direct opposition (Kennedy 2003). For example, Chinese associations prefer to contact and discuss with local governments in private meetings (Deng and Kennedy 2010) and empower each other in dialectic relationships (Shue 1994) between the entrepreneurs and the policy-maker (Weil 2018).

While in China lobbying is thus performed differently than in Western pluralist systems and one does not openly confront the Government, the findings indicate a different picture when it comes to Chinese lobbying in Germany. The Chinese Ambassador to Germany, Ken Wu, openly points out: "When bewildering gossip of a sellout of the German economy arises, and some politicians and media negate the reached high level of bilateral relationships, these allegations diametrically oppose Germany's constitutional principles and the spirit of free trade" (DCW 2020). The findings indicate that in Germany, China is adopting and combining a Western approach of shaping policy where interest-groups are able to openly debate and engage with their environment (Weil 2018), while simultaneously employing typical Chinese inter-personal and inter-organizational "guanxi" relationships (Meng *et al.* 2016; Yan *et al.* 2020) with German business associations, research institutes, as well as influential figures of the German political and economic realm. Guanxi can be understood as an "informal, particularistic personal connection between two individuals" (Chen and Chen 2004), including key characteristics such as "favour exchange, reciprocity, long-term orientation, loyalty and obligation" (Yan *et al.* 2020). It can also be employed to benefit an organization (Park and Luo 2001).

This is not to say that, vice versa, Western actors in China do not aim to shape their business environment. Previous research has shown that Western companies in China prefer collective bargaining to individual lobbying (Weil 2018). Here, firms are concerned that individual company lobbying can lead to direct confrontations and subsequent negative governmental consequences (Mahoney 2008). To avoid this outcome, many European firms in China joined EU interest groups (Weil 2018). For example, the European Chamber of Commerce in China (EUCCC) counts more than 1,700 member firms. In 2020, their Shanghai Chapter has held 87 events with 4,296 attendees, 89 media reports "to enlarge the chapter's influence in the region" and five vice minister-level meetings with the Shanghai vice mayor, Shanghai CPPCC vice chairman, and Hubei vice governor (EUCCC 2021).

Third, by contrasting and discussing the findings in light of earlier research on institutional escapism, our study connects the previously diverging and separate research streams of the escape and fostering perspectives. Viewing these two contributions together stakes out promising territory for future research (Deng and Zhang 2018). Here, Deng and Zhang (2018) recently argued: "Despite being the backbone of the Chinese economic growth, relatively little work has been done on how the domestic institutions influence Chinese private SMEs in their international venturing, and the findings are mixed." Indeed, on the one hand, the fostering view (Wan and Hoskisson, 2003) argues that policies such as the establishment of financial funds and a credit guarantee system at Chinese central and local government levels have facilitated SME competition in the global market (Luo *et al.* 2010; Sun *et al.* 2015). On the other hand, the escape view postulates that the internationalization of EE firms and Chinese SMEs is partially due to home country institutional constraints (Witt and Lewin 2007; Boisot and Meyer 2008; Wu and Deng 2020). For instance, the favorable governmental policies that promote the OFDI of large Chinese state-owned firms (Bruton *et al.* 2015; Sun *et al.* 2015) at the same time limit the chances of SMEs, who escape and invest abroad for institutional alternatives (Huang 2008; Morck *et al.* 2008; Child and Marinova 2014; Deng and Zhang 2018). It appears that the scholarly debate has focused on "confirming" the one or "rejecting" the other view. This has led to diverging research streams.

Summarizing the findings of these streams, we believe that the question of which view is right does not hit the mark, but rather explains and derives from which aspect of the complex overall picture of Chinese OFDI each study looks at. In line with Deng and Zhang (2018), we make a point that both the escape and fostering views exist as interconnected "two sides of one coin" – China's unique institutional environment. There is profound evidence of quantitative (Deng and Zhang 2018; Wu and Deng 2020) and qualitative studies (Hänle *et al.* 2022) on institutional escapism of Chinese SMEs. These studies shed light on institutional quality and hardships in the domestic context of China. Hence, looking through such lenses, institutional escapism can partially explain the internationalization of SMEs from China. At the same time, this research has shown that the Chinese Government is actively helping and supporting its SMEs to go abroad, as seen in the example of the developed economy of Germany. In our sample we found SMEs who invested abroad to escape from institutional hardships in China while benefitting from the illustrated Chinese OFDI-support network in Germany at the same time. This extends the recent findings of Deng and Zhang (2018). In their study, they empirically proved that Chinese SMEs invest overseas as they are pushed out by domestic institutional handicaps and bolstered by domestic quality institutions. Our study contributed by shedding light on which overseas quality institutions Beijing is drawing from when implementing OFDI-support abroad, and through which mechanism these organizations support China's SMEs exactly.

8.5. Limitations and future research

Several limitations can be discussed. First, at the fundamental level institutions consist of three dimensions: the regulative, the normative, and the cultural-cognitive (Scott 2013). Our study focused on the regulative aspect of China's complex institutional environment, as this aspect reveals an outstanding feature of China's Go Global Policy (Amann *et al.* 2018) and is "key to the internationalization of SMEs" (Deng and Zhang 2018). Future research could therefore provide additional insights based on fine-toothed measures for normative and cultural-cognitive factors in the context of Chinese SMEs' outward FDI and home government support. Thereby, this research could consider and integrate the distinct characteristics of China's SMEs and their owners. Especially in small firms, key decision-makers directly shape the agenda and determine firm outcomes such as OFDI (Hermans *et al.* 2017; Vanderstraeten *et al.* 2020). This control contrasts with large firms, where decision-making power is more structurally determined (Yu *et al.* 2020) and is particularly relevant for China. Here, most private SMEs are highly centralized, and the owning entrepreneurs are making the major decisions (Tsai and Eisingerich 2010; Yan *et al.* 2020). A large number of entrepreneurial owner-managers have evolved during the rapid growth of China's private economic sector (Atherton and Newman 2017; Lin *et al.* 2020). Recently, Yan *et al.* (2018) summarized "considering that SMEs are at a resource disadvantage compared to large multinational enterprises (MNEs), it is likely that their strategic orientation, particularly with respect to international involvement, is a person-driven phenomenon (Martineau and Pastoriza 2016) and susceptible to managers'/founders' cognitive characteristics". Hence, possible further normative and cultural-cognitive factors can provide a promising ground for future research.

Second, our assessed OFDI set-up mainly takes the Chinese institutional side into account. When SMEs invest abroad, they inevitably face institutional environments in the investment host countries that can be demanding (Deng and Zhang 2018) or supportive (Yamakawa *et al.* 2008). The interaction with these foreign institutional environments presents another challenge and fertile ground for future research, for example when it comes to strategies to reduce "liability of foreignness" in DE (Edman 2016; Holtbrügge 2018).

Another limitation results from our chosen methodology. As we adopted an inductive posture and qualitative research method, our findings naturally cannot be generalized for all Chinese overseas institutions and business associations. The inherent differences between China and EE (Deng and Yang 2015; Deng and Zhang 2018) also prevent us from generalizing our findings to small- and medium-sized firms in other EE.

8.6. Implications and conclusion

Our study has important practical implications. First, we believe that understanding better how governments can spur OFDI is vital as it determines both the effectiveness of policymaking and fosters mutual understanding, cultural exchange, firm growth and innovation (Ahlstrom 2010), and hence connects and contributes positively to international peace and society. This is important for both the EU and China, where policymakers assert that their bilateral economic relationships are very important to each other (Freeman 2021).

For example, the German Chamber of Commerce in China (GCCC) reports that in China there are around 5,000 German foreign invested enterprises operating, employing a large labor force (GCCC 2020). Equally, while Chinese OFDI to Western countries is sometimes criticized, it also brings significant positive aspects and opportunities to investment host countries such as Germany. For example, as a global high-tech company and spin-off of the Chinese automobile manufacturer Great Wall Motors, SVOLT develops and produces lithium-ion batteries and innovative cobalt-free battery systems for electric vehicles as well as energy storage (SVOLT 2021). In Germany, SVOLT initiated the largest investment of any Chinese battery maker in Europe. Over the next five years their investment comprises more than 2 billion euros (CIIPA 2021) and will create more than 2,000 new jobs in the federal state of Saarland. Currently, SVOLT employs around 5,500 people worldwide, with more than 1,500 experts in research and development (R&D) and production technology. In 2019, SVOLT registered over 550 patents. Another example is NIO. The innovative Chinese electrical-vehicle company established an advanced engineering center in Oxford (UK) and its global design and brand center in Munich. Such investments not only create jobs and contribute to German society but can also inspire and positively challenge the German economy in those areas where China is at the global forefront (e.g., digitalization or e-mobility). This can contribute to learning from each other, which strengthens both countries' competitiveness on the world stage. Therefore, while our aim is not to ignore the concerns Chinese OFDI to Western DE is causing, we advocate overcoming prejudices and instead drawing a finer-grained and more balanced picture taking both the concerns but also the opportunities associated with Chinese OFDI for Western DE into account.

Second, to avoid a middle-income trap in China (Liu et al. 2017; Ahlstrom *et al.* 2018), SMEs are an important factor for Beijing. They are the backbone of China's economy and hence its future (Deng and Zhang, 2018). SMEs contribute more than 50% of China's tax revenue, more than 60% of its GDP, and more than 70% of its technological innovation achievements (National Bureau of Statistics of China 2017). Previous research (Hänle *et al.* 2022) has shown that establishing a subsidiary in a DE like Germany can help Chinese SMEs to link, leverage, and learn, and stimulate a company's innovative capabilities and creativeness. In this way, firms can move up the "smile curve" of value added (Meng *et al.* 2016; Ahlstrom *et al.* 2018) by internalizing higher value activities such as research, design, and branding (Woetzel *et al.* 2015). Thus, fostering their OFDI both at home and through quality institutions abroad appears essential for strengthening China's national innovation system (Jia *et al.* 2020).

At the same time, Germany's economy and society can also significantly benefit from cooperating with Chinese partners and investors, as the example of Dürkopp Adler shows (Bertelsmann Stiftung 2009). Since the 1980s many working places in Europe's and Germany's textile industry have shifted to Eastern Europe and Asia, leaving local manufacturers such as German industrial sewing machine manufacturer Dürkopp Adler with existence-threating challenges. In 2005, the Chinese group ShangGong took over Dürkopp Adler and further invested in the company's innovativeness. Due to a successful integration phase and the resulting synergy effects, ShangGong managed to turn the company around and continuously increased sales and profits. Today, the company still produces in Germany and the Chairman of Dürkopp Adler's working committee Mr Stark states: "We are successful because of the support from China" (SRF 2017).

Moreover, knowing the specific OFDI-support institutions and measures China is currently adopting can serve as a helpful orientation to and complementary resource for Chinese business-owners who increasingly invest in the German economy (Holtbrügge and Berning 2018). This is particularly valuable for China's SMEs, which face several constraints for international growth: highly centralized organizations with desires for owner control (Weidenbaum 1996; Carney 1998; Ahlstrom *et al.* 2002; Tsang 2002), unfamiliarity with foreign markets and business practices and limited contacts (Poutziouris *et al.* 2002; Fornes and Cardoza 2018), high degrees of family control and involvement (Ahlstrom *et al.* 2004; Liang *et al.* 2014) and an underlying mistrust of managers that are outsiders to the family (Weidenbaum 1996; Tsang 2002), intuitive strategic decision making and informal FDI approaches (Tsang 2001, 2002), limited governmental and political ties (Huang 2008; Deng and Zhang 2018), and a lack of marketing, little R&D, and difficulties in access to financing (Ahlstrom *et al.* 2004). Therefore, the identified OFDI-support mechanisms complement the illustrated internal capabilities and resources of China's SMEs and foster their OFDI endeavors.

To summarize, our central aim was to investigate through which organizations and fostering mechanisms the Chinese Government institutionalizes OFDI-support for its SMEs in the developed economy of Germany. To answer this question, we interviewed representatives of Chinese governmental institutions, intermediary parties, Chinese lawyers and consultants specializing in OFDI, and analyzed secondary data such as governmental documents, websites, presentations, brochures, social media (WeChat), and recent Chinese OFDI policies for SMEs (MIIT 2016, 2017, 2018). For triangulation, we held interviews with senior executives and business owners of Chinese SMEs that plan to or already have invested in Germany. We could illustrate that following the overarching "Go Global" strategy, China's ministries have implemented a complex institutional OFDI-support network in Germany as the investment host country. This includes overseas Chinese governmental institutions, selected national champions, German-Chinese business associations, and multiple linked intermediary parties. The findings also showed that these organizations support Chinese SMEs through four key mechanisms, namely networking and information, knowledge transfer, lobbying, and facilitating investment services. The study extended the growing scholarly debate on the effects of home country institutional environments (Boisot and Meyer 2008; Luo *et al.* 2010; Sun *et al.* 2015; Shi *et al.* 2017; Deng and Zhang 2018; Aguilera and Grøgaard 2019; Wu and Deng 2020) by illustrating how China's governmental OFDI policy for SMEs translates into actual support organizations and mechanisms in Europe's largest economy and how this connects and mutually benefits both China and Germany.

8.7. References

Aberbach, J. and Rockman, B. (2002). Conducting and coding elite interviews. *Political Science and Politics*, 35(4), 673–676.

Ahlstrom, D. (2010). Innovation and growth: How business contributes to society. *Academy of Management Perspectives*, 24(3), 11–24.

Ahlstrom, D., Chan, E., Bruton, G. (2004). Facing constraints to growth? Overseas Chinese entrepreneurs and traditional business practices in East Asia. *Asia Pacific Journal of Management*, 21, 263–285.

Ahlstrom, D., Yang, X., Wang, L., Wu, C. (2018). A global perspective of entrepreneurship and innovation in China. *Multinational Business Review*, 26(4), 302–318.

Amann, B., Jaussaud, J., Zhang, B. (2018). Chinese outward foreign direct investment: Strategies for international development. In *China's Global Political Economy*, 1st edition, Taylor, R. and Jaussaud, J. (eds). Routledge, London.

Andreosso-O'Callaghan, B. and Gottwald, J.-C. (2013). How red is China's red capitalism? Continuity and change in China's financial services sector during the global crisis. *Asia Pacific Business Review*, 19(4), 444–460.

Argote, L. and Fahrenkopf, E. (2016). Knowledge transfer in organizations: The roles of members, tasks, tools, and networks. *Organizational Behavior and Human Decision Processes*, 136, 146–159.

Atherton, A. and Newman, A. (2017). *Entrepreneurship in China: The Emergence of the Private Sector*. Routledge, London.

Athreye, S. and Kapur, S. (2009). Introduction: The internationalization of Chinese and Indian firms – Trends, motivations and strategy. *Industrial and Corporate Change*, 18(2), 209–221.

Audretsch, D.B., Lehmann, E.E., Schenkenhofer, J. (2018). Internationalization strategies of hidden champions: Lessons from Germany. *Multinational Business Review*, 26(1), 2–24.

BDA (2021). Information about BDA [Online]. Available at: https://arbeitgeber.de [Accessed 5 May 2021].

Beeson, M. (2018). Geoeconomics with Chinese characteristics: The BRI and China's evolving grand strategy. *Economic and Political Studies*, 6(3), 240–256.

Beeson, M. and Li, F. (2015). What consensus? Geopolitics and policy paradigms in China and the United States. *International Affairs*, 91(1), 93–109.

Bennedsen, M. and Feldmann, S.E. (2002). Lobbying and legislative organization: The effect of the vote of confidence procedure. *Business and Politics*, 4(2), 187–203.

Bernasconi-Osterwalder, N., Johnson, L., Zhang, J. (2012). Chinese outward investment: An emerging policy framework. Compilation, International Institute for Sustainable Development, Winnipeg.

Bertelsmann Stiftung (2009). *Chinesische Unternehmen in Deutschland: Chancen und Herausforderungen*. Bertelsmann Stiftung, Gütersloh.

Boisot, M. and Meyer, M. (2008). Which way through the open door? Reflections on the internationalization of Chinese firms. *Management and Organization Review*, 4(3), 349–365.

Bräutigam, D. and Tang, X. (2012). Economic statecraft in China's new overseas special economic zones: Soft power, business or resource security? *International Affairs*, 88(4), 799–816.

Bremmer, I. (2010). Article commentary: The End of the Free Market: Who wins the war between States and Corporations? *European View*, 9(2), 249–252.

Breslin, S. (2007). *China and the Global Political Economy*. Palgrave Macmillan, Hampshire.

Breslin, S. (2020). China's global cultural interactions. In *China and the World*, Shambaugh, D. (ed). Oxford University Press, Oxford.

Brewer, P. (2007). Psychic distance and Australian export market selection. *Australian Journal of Management*, 32(1), 73–94.

Brown, K. (2019). *The World According to Xi*. I.B. Tauris, London and New York.

Bruton, G.D., Ahlstrom, D., Li, H.-L. (2010). Institutional theory and entrepreneurship: Where are we now and where do we need to move in the future? *Entrepreneurship Theory and Practice*, 34(3), 421–440.

Bruton, G.D., Peng, M.W., Ahlstrom, D., Stan, C., Xu, K. (2015). State-owned enterprises around the world as hybrid organizations. *Academy of Management Perspectives*, 29(1), 92–114.

Buckley, P.J., Clegg, L.J., Cross, A.R., Lin, X., Voss, H., Zheng, P. (2007). The determinants of Chinese outward FDI. *Journal of International Business Studies*, 38(4), 499–518.

Buckley, P.J., Cross, A.R., Tan, H., Xin, L., Voss, H. (2008). Historic and emergent trends in Chinese outward direct investment. *Management International Review*, 48(6), 715–748.

Burgoon, B. and Raess, D. (2014). Chinese investment and European labor: Should and do workers fear Chinese FDI? *Asia Europe Journal*, 12(1/2), 179–197.

bw-i (2022). Südwest-Unternehmen vernetzen sich mit der chinesischen Partnerprovinz Jiangsu zum Thema Umwelttechnik [Online]. Available at: https://www.bw-i.de/newsroom/news/nachricht/suedwest-unternehmen-vernetzensich-mit-der-chinesischen-partnerprovinz-jiangsu-zum-thema-umwelttechnik. [Accessed 26 March 2022).

Cardoza, G., Fornes, G., Li, P., Xu, N., Xu, S. (2014). China goes global: Public policies' influence on small- and medium-sized enterprises' international expansion. *Asia Pacific Business Review*, 21(2), 188–210.

Carney, M. (1998). A management capacity constraint? Obstacles to the development of the overseas Chinese family business. *Asia Pacific Journal of Management*, 15, 137–162.

Caseiro, C.Z. and Masiero, L. (2014). OFDI promotion policies in emerging economies: The Brazilian and Chinese strategies. *Critical Perspectives on International Business*, 10(4), 237–255.

Chen, X.P. and Chen, C.C. (2004). On the intricacies of the Chinese guanxi: A process model of guanxi development. *Asia Pacific Journal of Management*, 21, 305–324.

Child, J. and Marinova, S. (2014). The role of contextual combinations in the globalization of Chinese firms. *Management and Organization Review*, 10(3), 347–371.

Child, J. and Rodrigues, S.B. (2005). The internationalization of Chinese firms: A case for theoretical extension? *Management and Organization Review*, 1(3), 381–410.

Child, J., Ng, S.H., Wong, C. (2002). Psychic distance and internationalization: Evidence from Hong Kong firms. *International Studies of Management and Organization*, 32(1), 36–56.

Child, J., Rodrigues, S.B., Frynas, J.G. (2009). Psychic distance, its impact and coping modes: Interpretations of SMEs decision-makers. *Management International Review*, 49(2), 199–224.

China Quality Supervision (2020). A comparative study of special and special new small giants, manufacturing single champion and invisible champion [Online]. Available at: https://www.imsilkroad.com/news/p/423266.html [Acessed 7 April 2021].

CHKD (2021a). Current affairs [Online]. Available at: https://chk-de.org/de/ [Accessed 7 April 2021].

CHKD (2021b). The executive board [Online]. Available at: https://chk-de.org/de/praesidium/ [Accessed 7 April 2021].

CIIPA (2020). Our service [Online]. Available at: https://www.ciipa.de/unser-service [Accessed 7 January 2020].

CIIPA (2021). Jahresbericht 2020–2021. Annual report, CIIPA, Frankfurt.

Clegg, J. and Voss, H. (2018). Chinese outward FDI as a stimulus to research in international business. *Management International Review*, 58(1), 1–8.

Clifford, N.J., Cope, M., Gillespie, T.W., French, S. (2016). *Key Methods in Geography*, 3rd edition. Sage, Los Angeles, CA.

Cuervo-Cazurra, A., Mudambi, R., Pedersen, T. (2019). Clarifying the relationship between institutions and global strategy. *Global Strategy Journal*, 9(2), 151–175.

DCW (2021). Jahrbuch 2020. Yearbook, Deutsch-Chinesische Wirtschaftsvereinigung e.V., Cologne.

De Massis, A., Audretsch, D., Uhlaner, L., Kammerlander, N. (2018). Innovation with limited resources: Management lessons from the German Mittelstand. *Journal of Product Innovation Management*, 35(1), 125–146.

Deng, P. (2013). Chinese outward direct investment research: Theoretical integration and recommendations. *Management and Organization Review*, 9(3), 513–539.

Deng, G. and Kennedy, S. (2010). Big business and industry association lobbying in China: The paradox of contrasting styles. *The China Journal*, 63, 101–125.

Deng, P. and Yang, M. (2015). Cross-border M&A by emerging market firms: A comparative investigation. *International Business Review*, 24, 157–172.

Deng, P. and Zhang, S. (2018). Institutional quality and internationalization of emerging market firms: Focusing on Chinese SMEs. *Journal of Business Research*, 92, 279–289.

Dickson, B.J. (2003). *Red Capitalists in China: The Party, Private Entrepreneurs, and Prospects for Political Change*. Cambridge University Press, Cambridge and New York.

Easterby-Smith, M., Lyles, M.A., Tsang, E.W.K. (2008). Inter-organizational knowledge transfer: Current themes and future prospects. *Journal of Management Studies*, 45(4), 677–690.

Edman, J. (2016). Reconciling the advantages and liabilities of foreignness: Towards an identity-based framework. *Journal of International Business Studies*, 47(6), 674–694.

Eisenhardt, K.M. (1989). Building theories from case study research. *Academy of Management Review*, 14(4), 532–550.

EUCCC (2021). Annual report 2020. European Chamber of Commerce in China, Shanghai and Beijing.

FCEA (2021). Association website [Online]. Available at: https://www.ceafrankfurt.org/index.php?lang=DE [Accessed 7 April 2021].

Fletcher, M., Zhao, Y., Plakoyiannaki, E., Buck, T. (2018). Three pathways to case selection in international business: A twenty-year review, analysis and synthesis. *International Business Review*, 27(4), 755–766.

Fornes, G. and Cardoza, G. (2018). Internationalization of Chinese SMEs: The perception of disadvantages of foreignness. *Emerging Markets Finance and Trade*, 55(9), 2086–2105.

Freeman, D. (2013). China's outward investment: Institutions, constraints and challenges. *Brussels Institute of Contemporary China Studies. Asia Paper*, 7(4), May.

Freeman, D. (2017). Redistributing the EU-China economic relationship: The role of domestic change in China. *Asia Europe Journal*, 15, 187–198.

Freeman, D. (2021). The EU and China: Policy perceptions of economic cooperation and competition. *Asia Europe Journal* [Online]. Available at: https://doi.org/10.1007/s10308-021-00609-3.

GCB (2021). Main page [Online]. Available at: https://www.gcber.org [Accessed 17 April 2021].

GCCC (2020). Annual report 2019. German Chamber of Commerce in China, Shanghai.

George, A.L. and Bennett, A. (2005). *Case Studies and Theory Development in the Social Sciences*. MIT Press, Cambridge, MA.

Gioia, D.A., Corley, K.G., Hamilton, A.L. (2013). Seeking qualitative rigor in inductive research: Notes on the Gioia methodology. *Organizational Research Methods*, 16(1), 15–31.

Globerman, S. and Shapiro, D. (2009). Economic and strategic considerations surrounding Chinese FDI in the United States. *Asia Pacific Journal of Management*, 26(1), 163–183.

Gugler, P. and Shi, J.Y.J. (2008). Corporate social responsibility for developing country multinational corporations: Lost war in pertaining global competitiveness? *Journal of Business Ethics*, 87(1), 3–24.

Hänle, F., Cambré, B., Weil, S. (2021). A systematic review on the internationalization of Chinese SMEs: Thematic expansion, new impulses and potential avenues for future research. *Journal of Entrepreneurship in Emerging Economies* [Online]. Available at: https://doi.org/10.1108/JEEE-05-2021-0197.

Hänle, F., Weil, S., Cambré, B. (2022). Chinese SMEs in Germany: An exploratory study on OFDI motives and the role of China's institutional environment. *Multinational Business Review*, 30(1), 103–126.

Harvey, D. (2005). *A Brief History of Neoliberalism*. Oxford University Press, Oxford.

Harvey, W.S. (2011). Strategies for conducting elite interviews. *Qualitative Research*, 11(4), 431–441.

Heberer, T. (2014). China in 2013: The Chinese dream's domestic and foreign policy shifts. *Asian Survey*, 54(1), 113–128.

Heilmann, S. (2017). *China's Political System*. Rowman & Littlefield, London.

Heilmann, S. and Dirk, S. (2014). *China's Foreign Political and Economic Relations: An Unconventional Global Power*. Rowman & Littlefield, London.

Hermans, J., Slabbinck, H., Vanderstraeten, J., Brassey, J., Dejardin, M., Ramdani, D., van Witteloostuijn, A. (2017). The power paradox: Implicit and explicit power motives, and the importance attached to prosocial organizational goals in SMEs. *Sustainability*, 9(11), 2001.

Hernández, V., Nieto, M.J., Rodríguez, A. (2021). Home country institutions and exports of firms in transition economies: Does innovation matter? *Long Range Planning*. doi: 10.1016/j.lrp.2021.102087.

Holtbrügge, D. (2018). Political strategies of Chinese firms in Germany: An institutionalist perspective. *International Journal of Emerging Markets*, 13(6), 1438–1456.

Holtbrügge, D. and Berning, S.C. (2018). Market entry strategies and performance of Chinese firms in Germany: The moderating effect of home government support. *Management International Review*, 58(1), 147–170.

Holtbrügge, D. and Kreppel, H. (2015). Employer attractiveness of Chinese, Indian and Russian firms in Germany: Signaling effects of HR practices. *Corporate Reputation Review*, 18(3), 223–242.

Hoskisson, R.E., Wright, M., Filatotchev, I., Peng, M.W. (2013). Emerging multinationals from mid-range economies: The influence of institutions and factor markets. *Journal of Management Studies*, 50, 1295–1321.

Huang, Y. (2008). *Capitalism with Chinese Characteristics, Entrepreneurship and the State.* Cambridge University Press, Cambridge and New York.

Jia, C., Tang, X., Kan, Z. (2020). Does the nation innovation system in China support the sustainability of small and medium enterprise (SME) innovation? *Sustainability*, 12(6), 2562.

Jieyang Government (2021). Zhongde awarded China SME Center Germany, news of 09.03.2021 [Online]. Available at: http://www.jieyang.gov.cn/jygxj/gkmlpt/content/0/522/post_522323.html#279 [Accessed 18 March 2021].

Kennedy, S. (2003). The price of competition: Pricing policies and the struggle to define China's economic system. *The China Journal*, 49, 1–30.

Kennedy, S. (2008). The price of competition: The failed government effort to use associations to organize China's market economy. In *Associations and the Chinese State*, Unger, J. (ed). M.E. Sharpe, New York and London.

Kroeber, A.R. (2011). Developmental dreams, policy and reality in China's economic reforms. In *Beyond the Middle Kingdom, Comparative Perspectives on China's Capitalist Transformation*, Kennedy, S. (ed). Stanford University Press, Stanford, CA.

Li, C. (2014). China's communist party-state: The structure and dynamics of power. In *Politics in China*, Joseph, W.A. (ed). Oxford University Press, Oxford and New York.

Liang, X., Wang, L., Cui, Z. (2014). Chinese private firms and internationalization. *Family Business Review*, 27(2), 126–141.

Lieberthal, K. and Oksenberg, M. (1988). *Policy Making in China: Leaders, Structures, and Processes*. Princeton University Press, Princeton, NJ.

Liefner, I., Si, Y.-F., Schäfer, K. (2019). A latecomer firm's R&D collaboration with advanced country universities and research institutes: The case of Huawei in Germany. *Technovation*, 86–87, 3–14.

Lin, W.-T., Chen, Y.-Y., Ahlstrom, D., Wang, L.C. (2020). Does international expansion constrain growth? Business groups, internationalization, institutional distance, and the Penrose effect. *Multinational Business Review*, 29(1), 70–95

Liu, X., Schwaag Serger, S., Tagscherer, U., Chang, A.Y. (2017). Beyond catch-up – Can a new innovation policy help China overcome the middle income trap? *Science and Public Policy*, 44(5), 656–669.

Luo, Y., Xue, C., Han, B. (2010). How emerging market governments promote outward FDI: Experience from China. *Journal of World Business*, (45)1, 68–79.

Mahoney, C. (2008). *Brussels versus the Beltway: Advocacy in the United States and the European Union (American Governance and Public Policy)*. Georgetown University Press, Washington, D.C.

Marini Thomé, K., Joslin Medeiros, J., Hearn, B.A. (2017). Institutional distance and the performance of foreign subsidiaries in Brazilian host market. *International Journal of Emerging Markets*, 12(2), 279–295.

McNally, C.A. (2011). China's changing Guanxi capitalism: Private entrepreneurs between Leninist control and relentless accumulation. *Business and Politics*, 13(2), Article 5.

McNally, C.A. (2012). Sino-capitalism: China's reemergence and the international political economy. *World Politics*, 64, 741–776.

Menegazzi, S. (2018). *Rethinking Think Tanks in Contemporary China*. Palgrave Macmillan, Cham.

Meng, F., Rieckmann, J.M., Li, C. (2016). Empirical evidence how social capital effects the internationalisation process of SME in Zhejiang. *Transnational Corporations Review*, 8(3), 196–206.

Meng, B., Ye, M., Wei, S.-J. (2020). Measuring smile curves in global value chains. *Oxford Bulletin of Economics and Statistics*, 82(5), 988–1016.

Meunier, S. (2014). A Faustian bargain or just a good bargain? Chinese foreign direct investment and politics in Europe. *Asia Europe Journal*, 12(1/2), 143–158.

Meyer, K.E., Ding, Y., Li, Y., Zhang, H. (2014). Overcoming distrust: How state-owned enterprises adapt their foreign entries to institutional pressures abroad. *Journal of International Business Studies*, 45(8), 1005–1028.

MIIT (2016). Five-year Development Plan (2016–2020) [Online]. Available at: http://www.miit.gov.cn/n1146285/n1146352/n3054355/n3057527/n3057529/c5180549/content.html [Accessed 10 October 2019].

MIIT (2017). SME promotion law [Online]. Available at: http://www.miit.gov.cn/n1146285/n1146352/n3054355/n3057254/n3057259/c5780661/content.html [Accessed 18 December 2019].

MIIT (2018). Zhongde China SME Center Germany, news of 01.06.2018 [Online]. Available at: https://www.miit.gov.cn/jgsj/qyj/gjhz/art/2020/art_f63c6636858e4bea8416f3d1052df1f0.html [Accessed 19 November 2020].

MOFA (2021). Chinese embassy in Germany [Online]. Available at: https://www.fmprc.gov.cn/mfa_eng/wjb_663304/zwjg_665342/2490_665344/2495_665354/t14486.shtml [Accessed 8 April 2021].

MOFCOM (2004). Catalogue for the guidance of foreign investment industries [Online]. Available at: http://english.mofcom.gov.cn/aarticle/policyrelease/gazette/200505/20050500093692.html [Accessed 23 September 2019].

MOFCOM (2021). Germany status information [Online]. Available at: http://fec.mofcom.gov.cn [Accessed 21 March 2021].

Morck, R., Yeung, B., Zhao, M. (2008). Perspectives on China's outward foreign direct investment. *Journal of International Business Studies*, 39(3), 337–350.

Morse, J.M. (1994). Designing funded qualitative research. In *Handbook of Qualitative Research*, Denzin, N.K. and Lincoln, Y.S. (eds). Sage, Thousand Oaks, CA.

National Bureau of Statistics of China (2017). *2017 China Statistical Yearbook*. China Statistics Press, Beijing.

Naughton, B. (2020). China's global economic interaction. In *China and the World*, Shambaugh, D. (ed). Oxford University Press, Oxford.

Nee, V. and Opper, S. (2012). *Capitalism from Below, Markets and Institutional Change in China*. Harvard University Press, Cambridge, MA.

Nolan, P. (2001). *China and the Global Economy, National Champions, Industrial Policy and the Big Business Revolution*. Palgrave, New York.

North, D.C. (1990). *Institutions, Institutional Change and Economic Performance*. Cambridge University Press, Cambridge.

Oksenberg, M. (2001). China's political system: Challenges of the twenty-first century. *The China Journal*, 45, 21–35.

Park, S.H. and Luo. Y. (2001). Guanxi and organizational dynamics: Organizational networking in Chinese firms. *Strategic Management Journal*, 22(5), 455–477.

Patton, M.Q. (2015). *Qualitative Research & Evaluation Methods*. Sage, Thousand Oaks, CA.

Pearson, M. (2005). The business of governing business in China: Institutions and norms of the emerging regulatory state. *World Politics*, 57(2), 296–322.

Pearson, M. (2011). Variety within and without. In *Beyond the Middle Kingdom: Comparative Perspectives on China's Capitalist Transformation*, Scott, K. (ed). Stanford University Press, Stanford, CA.

Peng, M.W., Lebedev, S., Vlas, C.O., Wang, J.C., Shay, J.S. (2018). The growth of the firm in (and out of) emerging economies. *Asia Pacific Journal of Management*, 35, 829–857.

Pinkham, B.C. and Peng, M.W. (2017). Overcoming institutional voids via arbitration. *Journal of International Business Studies*, 48(3), 344–359.

Poutziouris, P., Wang, Y., Chan, S. (2002). Chinese entrepreneurship: The development of small family firms in China. *Journal of Small Business and Enterprise Development*, 9(4), 383–399.

Powell, W.W. and DiMaggio, P.J. (1991). *The New Institutionalism in Organizational Analysis*. University of Chicago Press, Chicago, IL.

Puthusserry, P.N., Child, J., Rodrigues, S.B. (2014). Psychic distance, its business impact and modes of coping: A study of British and Indian partner SMEs. *Management International Review*, 54(1), 1–29.

Rabbiosi, L. (2008). The impact of subsidiary autonomy on MNE knowledge transfer: Resolving the debate. SMG Working Paper 16/2008 [Online]. Available at: http://dx.doi.org/10.2139/ssrn.1121291.

Schattschneider, E.E. (1975). *The Semi-Sovereign People: A Realist's View of Democracy in America*. Wadsworth Publishing, London.

Scott, W.R. (2013). *Institutions and Organizations*. Sage, Thousand Oaks, CA.

Scott, W.R. (2014). Institutions and Organizations. Ideas, Interests and Identities. Reviewed. *M@n@agement*, 2(17), 136–140.

Shi, W., Sun, S., Yan, D., Zhu, Z. (2017). Institutional fragility and outward foreign direct investment from China. *Journal of International Business Studies*, 48(4), 452–476.

Shue, V. (1994). State power and social organization in China. In *State Power and Social Forces: Domination and Transformation in the Third World*, Migdal, J.S., Kohli, A., Shue, V. (eds). Cambridge University Press, Cambridge.

Simon, H. (1996). You don't have to be German to be a hidden champion. *Business Strategy Review*, 7(2), 1–13.

Simon, H. (2009). *Hidden Champions of the Twenty-First Century: Success Strategies of Unknown World Market Leaders*. Springer, New York.

Simon, H. (2022). Hidden champions in the Chinese century: Ascent and transformation. *International Business & Economics Studies*, 4(1), 2022.

SRF (2017). Chinesische Investoren [Online]. Available at: https://www.srf.ch/news/wirtschaft/natuerlich-war-skepsis-vorhanden [Accessed 19 March 2022].

Statistisches Bundesamt (2021). Press release nr. 77 from 22.02.2021 [Online]. Available at: https://www.destatis.de/EN/Press/2021/02/PE21_077_51.html [Accessed 25 March 2021].

Strauss, A.L. and Corbin, J. (1998). *Basics of Qualitative Research*. Sage, Thousand Oaks, CA.

Sun, S.L., Peng, M.W., Lee, R.P., Tan, W. (2015). Institutional open access at home and outward internationalization. *Journal of World Business*, 50(1), 234–246.

SVOLT (2021). Svolt in Saarland [Online]. Available at: https://svolt-eu.com/en/home-en/ [Accessed 20 May 2021].

Ten Brink, T. (2013). *Chinas Kapitalismus: Entstehung, Verlauf, Paradoxien*. Campus Verlag GmbH, Frankfurt am Main and New York.

Ten Brink, T. (2014). Strained dependencies. How the rise of China's new elites is changing global economic power constellations. *International Studies Association Annual Convention*, Toronto.

Tsai, K. (2007). *Capitalism Without Democracy: The Private Sector in Contemporary China*. Cornell University Press, Ithica, NY.

Tsai, H.T. and Eisingerich, A.B. (2010). Internationalization strategies of emerging markets firms. *California Management Review*, 53(1), 114–135.

Tsang, E.W.K. (2001). Internationalizing the family firm: A case study of a Chinese family business. *Journal of Small Business Management*, 39(1), 88–94.

Tsang, E.W.K. (2002). Learning from overseas venturing experience: The case of Chinese family businesses. *Journal of Business Venturing*, 17, 21–40.

UNCTAD (2020). *World Investment Report 2020*. United Nations, New York.

Vaccarini, K., Lattemann, C., Spigarelli, F., Tavoletti, E. (2017). Chinese FDI and psychic distance perceptions on regulations in the German renewable energy sector. *Energy Policy*, 101, 723–732.

Vaccarini, K., Lattemann, C., Spigarelli, F., Tavoletti, E. (2018). Managers' psychic distance and its impact on Chinese FDI to Germany in the environmental industry. *International Journal of Emerging Markets*, 14(1), 155–170

Vanderstraeten, J., Loots, E., Hamelin, A., van Witteloostuijn, A. (2020). Micro-foundations of small business internationalization: Introduction to the special section. *Cross Cultural and Strategic Management*, 27(3), 265–283.

VDHC (2021). Our mission [Online]. Available at: https://verband-deutscher-hidden-champions.de/en/vdhc-2-2/ [Accessed 20 March 2021].

Venohr, B. and Meyer, E. (2007). The German miracle keeps running: How Germany's Hidden Champions stay ahead in the global economy. Working papers, Institute of Management Berlin at the Berlin School of Economics (FHW Berlin).

Wan, W.P. and Hoskisson, R.E. (2003). Home country environments, corporate diversification strategies, and firm performance. *Academy of Management Journal*, 46(1), 27–45.

Wang, P., Tong, T.W., Koh, C.P. (2004). An integrated model of knowledge transfer from MNC parent to China subsidiary. *Journal of World Business*, 39(2), 168–182.

Wang, C., Hong, J., Kafouros, M., Wright, M. (2012a). Exploring the role of government involvement in outward FDI from emerging economies. *Journal of International Business Studies*, 43, 655–676.

Wang, C., Hong, J., Kafouros, M., Boateng, A. (2012b). What drives outward FDI of Chinese firms? Testing the explanatory power of three theoretical frameworks. *International Business Review*, 21(3), 425–438.

Weidenbaum, M. (1996). The Chinese family business enterprise. *California Management Review*, 38(4), 141–156.

Weil, S. (2017). *Lobbying and Foreign Interests in China: Politics and Development of Contemporary China*. Palgrave Macmillan, New York.

Weil, S. (2018). The strange case of pluralist lobbying in a corporatist setting: Defending Western business interests in China. *Business and Politics*, 20(1), 70–97.

Welch, C., Piekkari, R., Plakoyiannaki, E., Paavilainen-Mäntymäki, E. (2011). Theorising from case studies: Towards a pluralist future for international business research. *Journal of International Business Studies*, 42(5), 740–762.

Witt, M.A. and Lewin, A.Y. (2007). Outward foreign direct investment as escape response to home country institutional constraints. *Journal of International Business Studies*, 38(4), 579–594.

Wu, B. and Deng, P. (2020). Internationalization of SMEs from emerging markets: An institutional escape perspective. *Journal of Business Research*, 108, 337–350.

Yamakawa, Y., Peng, M.W., Deeds, D.L. (2008). What drives new ventures to internationalize from emerging to developed economies? *Entrepreneurship Theory and Practice*, 32(1), 59–82.

Yamakawa, Y., Khavul, S., Peng, M.W., Deeds, D.L. (2013). Venturing from emerging economies. *Strategic Entrepreneurship Journal*, 7(3), 181–196.

Yan, H., Wickramasekera, R., Tan, A. (2018). Exploration of Chinese SME's export development: The role of managerial determinants based on an adapted innovation-related internationalization model. *Thunderbird International Business Review*, 60(4), 633–646.

Yan, H., Hu, X., Liu, Y. (2020). The international market selection of Chinese SMEs: How institutional influence overrides psychic distance. *International Business Review*, 29(4), 101703.

Yang, J.Y. (2018). How does Chinese M&A investment in Germany create value? PhD dissertation, WHU Otto Beisheim School of Management, Vallendar.

Yin, R.K. (2018). *Case Study Research and Applications: Design and Methods*. Sage, Beverly Hills, CA.

Yu, Y., Hu, X., Wang, Y., Ward, P. (2020). A patulous progress: International entrepreneurship effects on Chinese born-global firm performance. *Sustainability*, 12(14), 1–19.

Zeng, K. (2019). *Handbook on the International Political Economy in China*. Edward Elgar Publishing, Cheltenham [Online]. Available at: https://doi.org/10.4337/9781786435064.

Zhang, J. and Ebbers, H. (2010). Why half of China's overseas acquisitions could not be completed. *Journal of Current Chinese Affairs*, 39(2), 101–131.

Zheng, N., Wei, Y., Zhang, Y., Yang, J. (2016). In search of strategic assets through cross-border merger and acquisitions: Evidence from Chinese multinational enterprises in developed economies. *International Business Review*, 1(25), 177–186.

Zhongde (2021a). News [Online]. Available at: http://www.zhongdemetal.com/en/ [Accessed 1 May 2021].

Zhongde (2021b). About us [Online]. Available at: http://www.zhongdemetal.com/de/about.asp?id=3&classid=10 [Accessed 1 May 2021].

Zhongde Germany (2020a). Network for medium-sized firms [Online]. Available at: https://zhongdemetal.de [Accessed 27 April 2020].

Zhongde Germany (2020b). Statement of Prof. Dr. Dieter Hundt on the German-Chinese cooperation [Online]. Available at: https://zhongdemetal.de/blog/blogdetailallgemein/detail/News/deutsche-wirtschaft-begruesst-oeffnung-chinas-fuer-auslaendische-investoren.html [Accessed 27 April 2020].

Zhu, X. (2009). The influence of think tanks in the Chinese policy process: Different ways and mechanisms. *Asian Survey*, 49(2), 333–357.

Zhu, Z. (2010). *China's New Diplomacy: Rationale, Strategies and Significance*. Ashgate, Farnham.

9

Stock Markets and Cultural Dimensions: A Comparison Between Japan, South Korea and China

The cultural context has many consequences on the behavior of individuals, as well as on organizations. Considering the transactions on the stocks markets, the cultural differences between countries have not been investigated. This is why we analyzed the relationship between cultural dimensions and the stock market patterns in Japan, China and South Korea. Our results show that the tendency towards autocorrelation of daily returns, and thus to some extent to mimicry, is weaker in China than in Japan and South Korea. Meanwhile, as we could anticipate, the results for South Korea are between those of Japan and China for most of its patterns, i.e. risk taking, return and mimicry. Considering the various cultural dimensions we used, Hofstede's model undoubtedly provides the most accurate understanding of the relationship between cultural dimensions and financial behavior. We can notice a stronger acceptance of risk in China and a more pronounced search for profitability, while the propension to take risk and require high returns is smaller in Japan, and the figures are intermediate for South Korea.

The cultural specificities of Japan in relation to its main neighbors have been studied in many disciplinary fields, along with the great events that have built their political and military relations over the centuries. Likewise, the history of the Japanese economic rise since the 1950s, the South Korean boom since the 1980s and the Chinese huge development since the 1990s have led to many analyses. However, little has been done to investigate the relationships between the cultural

Chapter written by Sophie NIVOIX and Serge REY.

characteristics and the financial market situation of these three countries. The objective of this research is therefore to examine the extent to which common or divergent cultural factors have contributed to financial trajectories and help their understanding. Our approach includes both qualitative variables, related to the measures of cultural aspects and the diversity of methods that underlie them, and quantitative variables, representative of risk and return, which represent the two main indicators of financial markets.

The aim of this research is not only to detect whether an association exists between some cultural dimensions and the stock market characteristics, but also to examine whether such an association appears to be similar from one country to another. The purpose is therefore to better understand the potential expectations of investors in each country, and to see the investment possibilities given by each market. According to investors, asset allocations may then vary within the East Asian area.

The first section of this paper presents the theoretical relationships between cultural values and financial decisions. The second section details the measures of cultural dimensions and values for the three countries. The third section compares the cultural orientations of each country with the empirical characteristics of their financial markets, and is followed by the conclusion.

9.1. The relationships between cultural values and financial decisions

Culture encompasses various factors, such as values, beliefs, norms, behaviors and common benchmarks that are shared by individuals among a group or a country. As a result, there are some attitudes and ways of acting that enable us to distinguish one country from another (Hofstede 1980). Several authors investigated the implications of the cultural context on economic decision taking. Dang *et al.* (2019) noticed that firms located in a country with an individualistic culture run a higher risk of stock price collapse than the other firms. Kwok and Tadesse (2006) showed that in countries with high uncertainty avoidance, the financial system is based more on banks than on markets. Lavezzolo *et al.* (2017) also concluded that the social preferences related to the acceptance of uncertainty help to explain the differences between financial systems from one country to another. Eun *et al.* (2015) mention that the economic and financial opening of a country reduces the effects of the cultural variables. This last result does not raise any problem for our study as on the stock market viewpoint the three countries analyzed here have an open financial system, including liquid markets and various transactions (individuals, institutional investors, firms).

9.1.1. *The cultural dimensions of Hofstede*

Without being exhaustive, we rely on the most recognized international academic works on cultural dimensions in this research.

First of all, we can consider the five cultural dimensions defined by Hofstede. Even if they were not defined for this purpose, we can highlight the implications they are likely to have in terms of financial behavior. In this way, Griffin *et al.* (2017) indicate that the dimensions of individualism and aversion to uncertainty explain 90% of national cultural variations related to corporate governance.

The first dimension of Hofstede, i.e. the power distance, indicates the degree of acceptance of hierarchical decisions, or the credit given to the decisions of people or organizations located at a higher level of competence or power. In financial terms, respect to a higher level of expertise can lead to adopting the same decisions as the economic agents seen as experts. This reasoning, which is rational for an individual, can however lead to mimetic behavior in the financial markets, when all investors take the same decisions up to a bubble market. A large power distance therefore tends to favor the momentum effect in stock market trends, possibly along with a higher risk. The next dimension is individualism and it underlines the personal responsibility of individuals towards the collective context. This variable is associated with higher risk taking according to the international study of Li *et al.* (2013) in 35 countries, as well as according to the results of Shao *et al.* (2013) on business investment. For a sample of several tens of thousands of firms located in 41 countries, Chen *et al.* (2015) concluded that the tendency to invest, and therefore to seek profitability and accept risk, is more present in countries with a high level of individualism. At the opposite of power distance, this dimension favors investors' autonomy and reduces the risks of mimetic behaviors, as mentioned by Eun *et al.* (2015) on the stock markets. The risk takings, potentially higher on an individual level, lead to a lower volatility through an average effect of heterogeneous anticipations of the investors, and thus to a lower risk level of the whole market.

Another dimension is masculinity and it underlines success and material goals. From an investor's viewpoint, this means financial achievement with high profits. As a consequence, the return requirement comes first. Considering the uncertainty avoidance dimension, it implies cautiousness in every field. Thus, an investor wanting to avoid the market randomness will choose low risk financial assets, i.e. the lowest possible volatility, in accordance with the results of Li *et al.* (2013) at the macro-economic level, and with the conclusions from Li and Zahra (2012) for top executives at the micro-economic level. Chen *et al.* (2015) indicated that the propensity to invest, and thus the desire for profitability and risk tolerance, is higher in countries with low uncertainty avoidance. Finally, the long term orientation dimension leads to the short term results of the decisions being neglected, in favor of objectives set over a longer horizon. For an investor, this means that low profitability or high risk can be accepted in the short term, if in the longer term the profitability is sufficient while the volatility remains moderate.

9.1.2. *The Schwartz dimensions*

Another major author in the study of international cultural characteristics is Schwartz (1992) who based his analysis on data collection in 73 countries and identified seven groups of transnational cultures. For this purpose, he highlighted seven cultural dimensions, divided into three axes allowing oppositions between the items. The first opposes autonomy to embeddedness (or social incorporation). Autonomy can be broken down into an intellectual sub-dimension and an affective sub-dimension. Autonomy implies an expression of individual wishes and aspirations, as well as the search for satisfaction, freedom and creativity. In financial terms, it therefore implies the search for profits, or the best possible outcomes, while accepting the taking of risks in order to achieve this goal. This would also be consistent with the results of Li *et al.* (2013), who showed a positive association between individualism and risk-taking. Conversely, embeddedness tends to favor security, obedience, discipline, moderation, conservatism and maintaining a good image in society, which implies conformism to some extent. Such a psychological viewpoint leads to the avoidance of risk, as in Chui *et al.* (2016). In a study including 33 countries, they show that there is a negative relationship between embeddedness and the cost of debt, and that profitability is not necessarily sought in a financial decision. Chui *et al.* (2002) found that firms exhibit higher risk avoidance and lower debt levels when there is stronger social incorporation. Social conformism can then create momentum or even mimetic behaviors in the markets.

The second axis developed by Schwartz opposes egalitarianism and hierarchy. Egalitarianism leads to each person being responsible for their own actions, which should contribute to the collective goal of social justice. The consequences in terms of financial choices are then to moderate or even forget individual profit demands, while accepting personal risk taking, which is considered as less dangerous thanks to the support of the society. At the same time, the integration of a collective objective can lead some investors to have mimetic behavior, out of concern for the homogeneity of the group they belong to. Conversely, the "hierarchy" pole is synonymous with the search for social power, the enhancement of authority and wealth. The result is a greater attraction for profitability, but less acceptance of risk, which is borne individually and therefore perceived as more threatening.

Finally, the third axis opposes harmony to mastery. Harmony means a good relationship with the natural environment, preserved rather than used, and protection of the natural environment in a long term perspective. As Li *et al.* (2013) have pointed out, the issue here is for an investor to avoid risk taking and to not focus on profits, in order to promote sustainable and peaceful development. On the other hand, mastery means control over the environment and the material realm, and values success in all its forms, courage and ambition. With such a perspective, an investor will naturally tend to set high objectives in terms of profitability, while accepting the associated risks. For example, Chui *et al.* (2016) observed that control is associated with higher corporate debt. Depending on the market situation, mimetic behavior induced by overconfidence is then quite possible.

A more sociological study was conducted by Ingelhart (1997) and is beyond the scope of this research. However, Schwartz (2006) pointed out that a comparative analysis of Hofstede's, Schwartz's and Ingelhart's dimensions makes it possible to identify cultural groups corresponding to similar regions around the world. Thus, Japan, Korea and China (as well as Taiwan) systematically belong to the "Confucian" or North-East Asian group. However, within their extensive data collections, the approaches of the three authors were different: IBM employees for Hofstede, teacher and student groups for Schwartz, and representative samples of the population for Ingelhart. Moreover, the periods of study spanned from the 1970s to the first decade of this century, and the methods of data processing are not identical. These findings reinforce the conclusions of these authors and help to make the present study relevant.

9.1.3. *The approach of Trompenaars*

The work of Trompenaars (1994) identified seven cultural dimensions, each established with two polarities. The first one is universalism (as opposed to particularism), which reflects adherence to cultural norms and laws that are considered fair to all, and avoids personal adaptations to situations. It includes the notion of loyalty to the community and conformity, which reduces individual initiatives, leading to risk-taking and seeking abnormal profitability. The tendency to mimic is therefore quite possible in such a cultural configuration.

Secondly, the dimension of individualism (as opposed to collectivism) is close to the Hofstede dimension of the same name. As indicated previously, this dimension encourages the autonomy of investors in their search for high return and reduces mimetic behavior. The risk acceptance then potentially generates more volatility for the investors themselves, but not for the market as a whole. Secondly, a particular dimension of Trompenaars' work, neutrality (as opposed to affectivity) is characterized by a control of the feelings and emotions of the individuals in their professional relationships. For the investor, such control means a cool head towards risk-taking, possible without excessive stress, within the framework of an objective of high profitability, and without allowing ourselves to be carried away by a movement of mimicry, sometimes leading to irrational behavior.

Another dimension pointed out by Tompenaars is the specific aspect (as opposed to diffuse), which leads the individual to set precise limits between the areas of their life, namely family, professional, friendly or others. Such a separation makes it possible to focus on each area separately, without interfering with parameters affecting another area. For the investor, this leads to a better concentration on the goals of profitability, acceptance of risk, and avoidance of investment mimicry due to a lack of information.

The next dimension is that of ascription or attributed social status (as opposed to achievement), which is therefore inherited, according to the social category or to the age, for example. The individual's social position then depends little on actions and decisions, successes or failures. This does not encourage the investor to take risks or seek high returns, which have little effect on their status. Mimicry towards our social or professional category then tends to increase.

As for the temporal dimension, contrary to Hofstede's, it is centred here on the sequential aspect (as opposed to the synchronic approach), which leads to perceiving time and acting chronologically, tackling one objective after another. In this mindset, risk-taking is reduced because attention is focused on one task at a time, thus it avoids dispersion. Similarly, the objective of profitability is possible without the risk of mimicry, since the investor is focused on one type of financial decision at a time.

Finally, the locus of control dimension is either internal or external and it governs the individual's relationship with their natural environment. Internal control implies that everyone can control nature and transform it according to their needs, i.e. use it to serve our own goals. Such a mindset encourages risk-taking by investors, who do not consider themselves threatened by external factors (such as the consequences of the earthquake in Fukushima in 2011 and on the Japanese economy) in setting their profitability benchmarks. They are also less prone to mimicry, since they believe that markets can be influenced and controlled from within by the economic agents.

9.1.4. *The GLOBE project*

The GLOBE (Global Leardership and Organizational Behavior Effectiveness) project is focused on leadership with an enterprise viewpoint, seeing that – as in Hofstede studies – its cultural data have been collected in the firms of more than 60 countries. As the results of the GLOBE survey for 2020 were not yet available, we used those of 2014. To our knowledge, up until now, the results of GLOBE have not been analyzed in relation with stock market patterns, and there are no financial comparisons between East Asian countries. Most analyses tackled leadership more specifically, as in Chai *et al.* (2016) for South Korea, for instance.

In this study we intend to investigate the financial implications of the nine dimensions of GLOBE for individual investors, as well as for institutional ones. The performance orientation is a first dimension we can consider, and it leads directly to seeking a high return on the financial markets, whether they include stocks or other financial assets. Then, the assertiveness dimension helps to express our opinions and ideas, which means autonomy in decision making and risk acceptance. As for the future orientation dimension, it is close to Hofstede's one, i.e. it is an incentive to accept a low return and a high risk in the short run if they are compensated by the reverse situation in the long run (high return and lower risk). Then, the humane orientation stresses the decision criteria related to altruistic, generous behavior instead of strictly financial and economic ones. This helps to accept low returns as profitability is not the main assessment criterion. As for the institutional collectivism, it is focused on the group interest towards the individual one, and it reduces the risk taking of individual investors in order to moderate the risks of high volatility of the markets for the whole "group" (firm, industry or country). The in-group collectivism (or indulgence dimension) means that individuals are loyal and attached to their reference group, considering values and behavior. This implies that in this dimension there is a risk of mimicry of decisions inside the group, and this may create momentum effects in the financial markets. The gender equality dimension can be seen as mind openness and the absence of fear of diversity. As a consequence, it can be seen as a synonymous of some risk acceptance when we deal with financial decisions. Considering the power distance dimension, it is similar to the one of Hofstede. The larger this distance, the higher the obedience to hierarchy, and thus the more frequent the mimicking behaviors. Finally, the uncertainty avoidance dimension is close to the same dimension of Hofstede. The financial consequences are similar, which means that investors are looking for low risk and low volatility investments.

9.2. The measures of the cultural dimensions and their financial implications

The values associated with each dimension of the main academic cultural models give a set of benchmarks that we can compare to financial data. The possible mismatches between the different models give opportunities to qualify these comparisons.

9.2.1. *The Hofstede dimensions for Japan, South Korea and China*

As the analyses of Hofstede are available on the website of this author, the comparative data collection is shown in Table 9.1. The values of each dimension, except the last one, are normalized between 0 and 100.

	Japan	South Korea	China
Power distance	54	60	80
Individualism	46	18	20
Masculinity	95	39	66
Uncertainty avoidance	92	85	30
Long term orientation	80	75	118
Consequence: risk acceptance	Moderate	Moderate	High
Consequence: return requirement	Moderate	High	High
Consequence: tendency to mimic decisions	Low	Moderate	High

Table 9.1. *Values of the cultural dimensions of Hofstede for Japan, South Korea and China and their financial consequences (source: https://www.hofstede-insights.com/country-comparison/ and authors for the financial consequences)*

The figures of these five dimensions reveal the diversity of cultural characteristics among the three countries. According to the analysis of the dimensions proposed in section 9.1, the financial implications in terms of risk and profitability are as follows. The Japanese market is expected to show a low propensity for momentum, an attraction for long-term profitability, and an acceptance of possibly low profits and high volatility in the short term, due to relatively low hierarchical distance, greater individualism and masculinity than its neighboring countries. As for the Korean market, it is likely to record more mimicry or momentum effects and a better risk tolerance than the Japanese market, due to a slightly greater hierarchical distance and less individualism, but also a slightly lower aversion to uncertainty. As for the Chinese market, it should tend to show even more momentum and a higher level of risk than its neighbors, especially in the long run, due to a strong hierarchical distance, low individualism, less aversion to uncertainty and an extreme long-term orientation.

When these values are compared with the average for the ASEAN countries, there is no specific difference, other than a stronger long-term orientation for these three countries.

9.2.2. *The results of Schwartz for Japan, South Korea and China*

Schwartz's (1992) work has also shown that Japan, South Korea and China, distinct from South Asian countries, are part of the same grouping, referred to as "Confucian". This relatively small group is highly culturally homogeneous, although Japan occupies a slightly lagging position. Thus, based on the results of Schwartz (2006) and following the developments outlined in section 9.1, we can propose the following characteristics for each country (see Table 9.2). As we did not have access to the exact values for each cultural dimension, we set a low/high score for each financial dimension, and established a score ranging from 0 (low dimension for all three cultural axes) to 3 (high dimension for all three axes).

	Japan	South Korea	China
Autonomy (affective and intellectual)	High	Low	Low
Embeddedness	Low	High	High
Egalitarianism	Low	Low	Low
Hierarchy	Low	High	High
Harmony	High	Low	Low
Mastery	Low	High	High
Risk acceptance score	1	2	2
Return requirement score	2	1	1
Mimicry tendency score	2	2	2

Table 9.2. *Cultural dimensions of Schwartz for Japan, South Korea and China, and risk acceptance, return requirement and mimicry scores (source: Schwartz (2006) for the dimensions and authors' estimates for the scores)*

An analysis of the correlations between the Hofstede and Schwartz dimensions over all available countries enables us to observe similarities, which are statistically perceivable through the existence of three clusters. Indeed, a typology analysis brings out a first cluster, which explains 25.1% of the variance of the cultural dimensions, and is characterized by the avoidance of uncertainty, the search for harmony and egalitarianism. A second group, which explains 21.7% of the variance, highlights aspects related to individualism and long-term orientation. Finally, the third group, which explains 16.7% of the variance, clearly displays a dimension of risk attractiveness.

9.2.3. *The Trompenaars dimensions for Japan, South Korea and China*

The analyses of Trompenaars (1994) and Trompenaars and Hampden-Turner (2000) have been displayed through a score that we built. Indeed, as we did not have access to the exact values for each dimension, we used a low/high score for each financial dimension, and established a score ranging from 0 (low dimension for the three cultural axes) to 7 (high dimension for the three axes), detailed in Table 9.3.

	Japan	South Korea	China
Universalism (vs. particularism)	Moderate	Low	Low
Individualism (vs. collectivism)	Moderate	Low	Low
Neutral (vs. affective)	High	High	High
Specific (vs. diffuse)	Low	Moderate	Low
Ascription (vs. achievement)	Low	Low	Low
Sequential (vs. synchronous)	Moderate	Moderate	Moderate
Internal orientation (vs. external)	Moderate	Low	Low
Risk acceptance score	3	3	2
Return requirement score	4	4	3
Mimicry tendency score	2	4	3

Table 9.3. *Cultural dimensions of Trompenaars for Japan, South Korea and China and their financial consequences (source: Trompenaars (1994) and Trompenaars and Hampden-Turner (2000) for the dimensions and author's calculations for the consequences)*

9.2.4. *Scores of the GLOBE project for the three countries*

We can now consider the scores of practices noticed by the GLOBE project (see Table 9.4), in order to see their financial implications. The results are normalized on a scale ranging from 1 to 7, which leads to fairly small differences between countries.

	Japan	South Korea	China
Performance orientation	4.3	4.7	4.5
Assertiveness	3.6	4.5	3.8
Future orientation	4.2	4	3.8
Humane orientation	4.2	3.8	4.3

Institutional collectivism	5.2	5.2	4.8
In-group collectivism	4.7	5.5	5.9
Gender equality	3.1	2.5	3
Power distance	5.1	5.5	5
Uncertainty avoidance	4	3.5	4.9
Risk acceptance score	Low	Moderate	Low
Return requirement score	Moderate	High	Moderate
Mimicry tendency score	Moderate	Moderate	High

Table 9.4. *Results of "practice" scores of GLOBE 2014 for Japan, South Korea and China (source: https://globeproject.com/results/countries/)*

With a moderate orientation towards performance, relatively low assertiveness and a rather high degree of institutional collectivism, the Japanese market would tend to not give too much priority to the objective of financial profitability, but rather focus on reducing risk-taking. With less orientation towards human values than its neighbors, two fairly high dimensions of collectivism, low gender equality and a fairly high distance to power, the South Korean equity market should show some tendency towards mimicry and moderate risk taking. Finally, in China, with low assertiveness, strong in-group collectivism and high risk aversion, investors should favor mimicking behavior and low volatility assets.

Despite its less solid academic status, another approach can be used to address cultures. The World Value Survey association, which has brought together researchers from many countries since 1981, studies changes in values and beliefs and their cultural and political impact. Its work is supervised by the Institute for Future Studies in Stockholm. The results of the 2010–2014 survey wave are available on the association's website and provide the following conclusions (see Table 9.5).

	Japan	South Korea	China
From survival values (<0) to self-expression values (>0) for the risk taking propensity	0.20	-1.3	-1.2
From traditional values (<0) to secular-rational values (>0) for the return seeking	2	0.6	0.8

Table 9.5. *Results of the World Values Survey for Japan, South Korea and China (source: http://worldvaluessurvey.org/wvs.jsp)*

Considering the proximity between the propensity for risk taking and the opposition between survival and expression values, we observe that Japan is the country most likely to accept risk. This trend is moderate, however, compared to the very strong risk aversion in China and Korea. In terms of return seeking, all countries tend to look for profitability, but Japan is more inclined to do so.

9.2.5. *Summary of risk and return assumptions for the three countries*

In order to synthesize all of the results related to the dimensions of the different analysis frames presented previously, we have opted for a rating of each element, without weighting. A "-" was assigned when the cultural parameter had a low value, a "0" when its value was moderate and a "+" when it was high. Table 9.6 provides details following the chronology of the models discussed in section 9.1. Even when there were small differences between the three countries, we have chosen to highlight these spreads, in order to compare them with the financial characteristics detailed in section 9.3. Such methodology is obviously a tricky one, since the three countries belong on the worldwide level to the same cultural group, which is fairly small (East Asia).

- (low); 0 (moderate); + (high)	Japan	South Korea	China
Risk acceptance	0-0-0 thus --	0+00- thus 0	++--- thus -
Return requirement	0++0+ thus +++	+-++0 thus ++	+-000 thus 0
Mimicry tendency	-+-0 thus -	0++0 thus ++	++0+ thus +++

Table 9.6. *Scoring of the different cultural models and summary for the three countries (source: analysis of authors)*

Despite the divergence of some results, Japan seems to accept a lower risk level than China, and both countries are less prone to risk taking than South Korea. Meanwhile, Japan is the main return seeker, followed by South Korea and China. Considering mimicry behavior among investors, this phenomenon seems to be more probable in China than South Korea, and should be fairly weak in Japan.

9.3. Main financial patterns among the three stock markets

As the three countries did not experience the same economic growth level in recent decades, this can influence the attitude of the investors about risk taking and return requirement. Figure 9.1 presents the GDP growth rate since 1962 for the three countries and shows that in the long run this rate progressively decreased for Japan and South Korea. As the economic rise of China is more recent, the growth rate was high since the 1990s and just began to slow down after 2012. This indicates that Chinese investors were used to high economic forecasts in the last three decades.

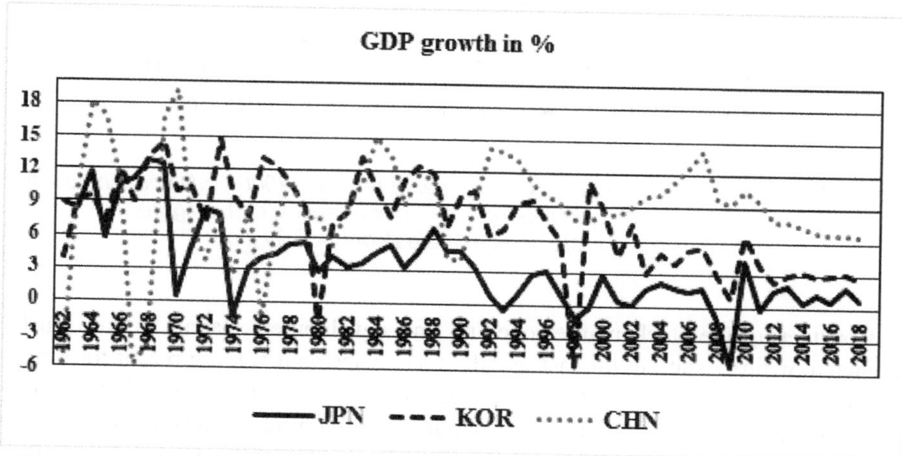

Figure 9.1. *GDP growth in % since 1962 for the three countries (source: World Bank). For a color version of this figure, see www.iste.co.uk/morales/connectivity.zip*

As for the per capita GDP, the comparison between the three countries during the same time period is not the most relevant as their economic phase of development is not the same. This is why Figure 9.2 displays the GDP per capita with a common starting point, i.e. the year when this value reached 2000 USD. This was in 1970 for Japan, in 1982 for South Korea and in 2006 for China. The x-axis values indicate the values of GDP per capita during the 15 years following this basis as a common benchmark. Very interestingly we can see that the growth pace is very similar from one country to the other, and after 13 years of GDP above 2000 USD the value of this indicator was close to 10000 USD for the three countries. As a consequence, we can consider that these countries followed about the same development path, but at a different time. This may indicate that the mindset of investors is comparable between these countries, but with a time lag.

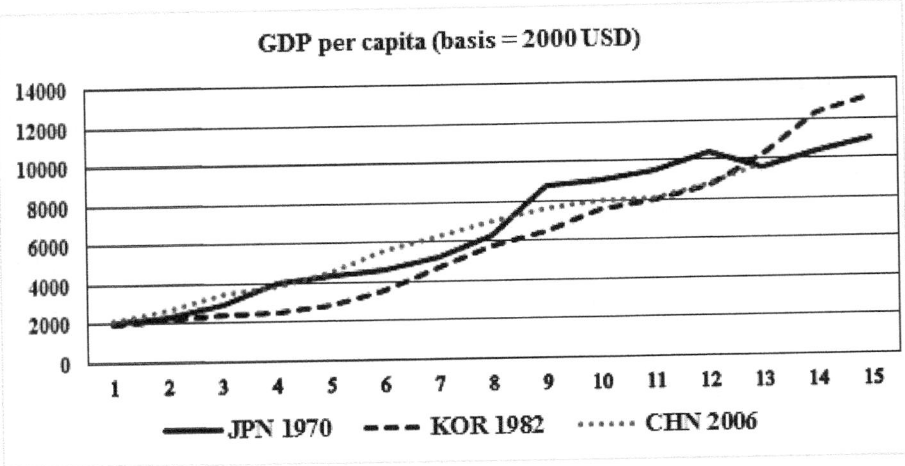

Figure 9.2. *Yearly GDP per capita since its value reached 2000 USD in each country (source: authors' calculation). For a color version of this figure, see www.iste.co.uk/morales/connectivity.zip*

Considering the stock market opening and development, Japan has obviously reached a maturity state in the last few decades, whereas it is more recent for South Korea and China has not yet experienced this situation. Table 9.7 shows some indicators about the stock markets. Despite its 1.4 billion inhabitants, in 2019 China had about the same number of listed shares as Japan (115 million inhabitants). But of course there are more state-owned companies in China than in Japan. Comparatively, South Korea (45 million inhabitants) has a fairly high number of listed shares.

	Japan	South Korea	China
Number of listed shares (end 2019)	3668	2186	3615
Stock market capitalisation (end 2019 in billion USD)	6 122	1413	6325
GDP growth rate in 2019	0.7%	2.1%	6.1%
GDP in 2017 (in billion USD)	4872	1531	12240

Table 9.7. *Main financial indicators for the three countries (source: World Bank and websites of stock markets)*

In order to summarize the changes of each stock market, we used an internationally used index: TOPIX 100 for Japan, KOSPI 200 for South Korea and

SSE Composite for China. The data comes from the Factset international database. It is worth mentioning that the use of various indexes (TOPIX 100 or NIKKEI 225 for Japan, KOSPI 100 or KOSPI 200 or KOSPI Composite for South Korea and SSE 180 or SSE Composite or SZSE Component for China) did not modify the results much (see Table 9.8).

	Japan (TOPIX100) over 1985–2019	South Korea (KOSPI 200) over 1990–2019	China (SSE Composite) over 1992–2019
Average daily returns R (in %)	0.006619	0.01309	0.02708
Standard-error of R	0.0128	0.0172	0.0232
Skewness of R	-0.3855	-0.1254	5.5875
Kurtosis of R	9.0546	6.4238	24.0192

Table 9.8. *Descriptive statistics for each stock market (source: authors' calculations)*

We can see that for all three markets the long term trend exhibits an average positive daily profitability, with a higher value for the Chinese market, which also appears riskier with a higher average standard deviation. The skewness is slightly negative for Japan and Korea, but it is clearly positive for China, indicating a high number of abnormally high profitability levels in this market. Finally, the kurtosis has a value in China and indicates that extreme returns (low or high) are clearly more frequent than in a Gaussian distribution. The Chinese market therefore experiences more shocks on returns (which are reflected in its volatility) than the other two markets. These results based on daily data differ from those of Dan *et al.* (2019), who observe higher volatility and skewness of returns in Japan than in China over the period 1990–2015. It therefore appears that since 2015 the Chinese market has proved to be more profitable and more volatile than the other two, with, in particular, more highly positive variations. This does not converge with the trends pointed out in Table 9.6, except maybe the mimicry tendency of China, which could be perceived through a high kurtosis. This could indicate possible large market momentums and stock price changes, with a small mean reverting effect. This point is clarified below with the results about the autocorrelations of returns. Meanwhile, as we could anticipate, South Korea lies in an intermediate position between Japan and China for most of its patterns (risk taking, return requirement and return asymmetry).

The differences between what investors are culturally prone to and the situation observed on the equity markets can be explained in several ways. First, measures of cultural dimensions are several years old and are not always updated as countries develop economically. This also explains their limited explanatory scope. Second, a country experiencing major financial and social changes can also see its culture change in the medium or long term. This is the case for Japan, which has faced both the crucial problem of a declining population since the beginning of this century, and a rapidly ageing population. Cultural changes also happened in South Korea, which has moved from its high growth phase during the 1970–90 period to a situation close to the Japanese one. As it is no longer an emerging country, South Korea has to cope with the economic and social problems of industrialized countries. Besides, the cultural changes are even more important in China, whose challenges are partly different, as major reforms enabled the financial system to open during the last 30 years. Moreover, the country promoted individual financial success, but now also has to face key social and ageing issues, whose cultural consequences are impacting the younger generations (Lee and Peterson 2000). Finally, the differences between investors' expectations and the characteristics of equity markets should be put into perspective with other possible investments (money market, bond markets, real estate market) and the regulation (taxes, opening level of the economy, share of bank financing compared market financing).

Regarding the momentum effect, the auto-regression coefficients of daily returns on the three markets are worth mentioning. The coefficient is 0.0379 for Japan, 0.0180 for Korea and 0.00051 for China. These values differ from those of Nivoix and Gupta (2014), who found a larger autocorrelation in the Chinese market and a higher shock-responsive volatility over the short period 2006–2010.

Our results therefore indicate that the tendency towards autocorrelation of daily returns, and thus to some extent to mimicry, is weaker in China than in Japan and Korea. We did not intend to compare the various cultural dimensions in order to identify which one would best describe reality, but one theory has implications that are closer to the characteristics of equity markets. Indeed, Hofstede's model undoubtedly provides the most accurate understanding of the relationship between cultural dimensions and financial behavior. His focus on individual behavior matches with the specific decisions of investors in the markets, whatever their degree of mimicry. It shows a stronger acceptance of risk in China and a more pronounced search for profitability. As China is now beginning to experience a maturity phase already reached by the other two countries, it will be interesting to analyse whether the behavior of investors is changing towards that of Korea and Japan. Financial convergence would then happen, despite some divergence between the cultural characteristics of the Chinese market. Since Korea is in an intermediate position between the other two countries, it is interesting to study whether the future will show more economic similarities between the three countries.

9.4. Conclusion

This study investigated the relationship between cultural dimensions and the stock market patterns in three Asian countries. Our results show that whereas Chinese investors should be attracted by low risk and return markets on a cultural viewpoint, they experience a booming and higher risk and return stock market than the two neighboring countries. This does not converge with the trends we noticed, except the mimicry tendency of China, which could be perceived through a high kurtosis. Nevertheless, we pointed out that the tendency towards autocorrelation of daily returns, and thus to some extent to mimicry, is weaker in China than in Japan and South Korea. Meanwhile, as we could anticipate, the results for South Korea are between those of Japan and China for most of its patterns, i.e. risk taking, return and mimicry.

Considering the various cultural dimensions we used, Hofstede's model undoubtedly provides the most accurate understanding of the relationship between cultural dimensions and financial behavior. Its focus on individual behavior helps to understand the decisions of investors in the markets. It shows a stronger acceptance of risk in China and a more pronounced search for profitability, while the propension to take risk and require high returns is smaller in Japan, and the figures are intermediate for South Korea. In the long run, a financial convergence between the three countries could take place at the same time as, in China, some divergence between the cultural characteristics and the financial patterns of the market.

It is worth indicating that the empirical part of this research has two limits. First, the socio-cultural variables are qualitative and difficult to measure, even when the theoretical works on this topic are homogeneous. Second, as the relationships that have been pointed out are in three countries located in the same part of the world, a comparison with other cultural areas, Asian or not, would be insightful.

9.5. References

Chai, D.S., Jeong, S., Kim, J., Kim, S., Hamlin, R.G. (2016). Perceived managerial and leadership effectiveness in a Korean context: An indigenous qualitative study. *Asia Pacific Journal of Management*, 33(3), 789–820.

Chen, Y., Dou, P.Y., Rhee, S.G., Truong, C., Veeraraghavan, M. (2015). National culture and corporate cash holdings around the world. *Journal of Banking and Finance*, 50, 1–18.

Chui, A.C.W., Lloyd, A.E., Kwok, C.C.Y. (2002). The determination of capital structure: Is national culture a missing piece to the puzzle? *Journal of International Business Studies*, 33, 99–127.

Chui, A.C.W., Kwok, C.C.Y., Zhou, G. (2016). National culture and the cost of debt. *Journal of Banking and Finance*, 69, 1–19.

Dang, T.L., Faff, R., Luong, H., Nguyen, L. (2019). Individualistic cultures and crash risk. *European Financial Management*, 2563, 622–654.

Eun, C.S., Wang, L., Xiao, S.C. (2015). Culture and R^2. *Journal of Financial Economics*, 115, 283–303.

Griffin, D., Guedhami, O., Kwok, C.C.Y. (2017). National culture: The missing country-level determinant of corporate governance. *Journal of International Business Studies*, 48(6), 740–762.

Hofstede, G. (1980). *Culture's Consequences: International Differences in Work-Related Values*. Sage Publications, Beverly Hills, CA.

Hofstede, G. (2001). *Culture's Consequences: Comparing Values, Behavior, Institutions and Organizations across Nations*. Sage Publications, Beverly Hills, CA.

Ingelhart, R. (1997). *Modernization and Postmodernization: Cultural, Economic and Political Change in 43 Societies*. Princeton University Press, Princeton, NJ.

Kwok, C.C.Y. and Tadesse, S. (2006). National cultural and financial systems. *Journal of International Business Studies*, 37(2), 227–247.

Lavezzolo, S., Rodriguez-Luesma, C., Elvira, M.M. (2018). National culture and financial systems: The conditioning role of political context. *Journal of Business Research*, 85, 60–72.

Lee, S.M. and Peterson, S.J. (2000). Culture, entrepreneurial orientation, and global competitiveness. *Journal of World Business*, 35(4), 401–416.

Li, Y. and Zahra, S.A. (2012). Formal institutions, culture and venture capital activity: A cross-country analysis. *Journal of Business Venturing*, 27, 95–111.

Li, K., Griffin, D., Yue, H., Zaho, L. (2013). How does culture influence corporate risk-taking? *Journal of Corporate Finance*, 23, 1–22.

Nivoix, S. and Gupta, P. (2014). Analyse comparée des caractéristiques économétriques de trois marchés des actions en Asie : Chine, Inde et Japon. *La Revue des Sciences de Gestion*, 266, 75–87, March–April.

Schwartz, S.H. (1992). Universals in the content and structure of values: Theory and empirical tests in 20 countries. *Advances in Experimental Social Psychology*, 25, 1–65.

Schwartz, S.H. (2006). A theory of cultural value orientations: Explication and applications. *Comparative Sociology*, 5(2–3), 137–182.

Shao, L., Kwok, C.C.Y., Zhang, R. (2013). National culture and corporate investment. *Journal of International Business Studies*, 4467, 745–763.

Trompenaars, F. (1994). *Riding the Waves of Culture*. Nicholas Brealey, London.

Trompenaars, F. and Hampden-Turner, C. (2000). *Building Cross-Cultural Competence*. Yale University Press, London.

10

Geo-economics and Geopolitics of Power Balance: Insights from the China-Iran-Pakistan Alliance

China's ability to secure its energy needs will play a vital role in consolidating its geo-economic and geopolitical rise. In addition, the Asian economy needs to ensure access to other natural resources, ranging from agricultural, metals and minerals, in its quest for *"high-quality"* growth. Countries that cannot secure their energy supply and ensure sustainable access to natural resources, combined with political instability, face a considerable reduction in the avenues that enhance national, political and economic power. These are significant areas of concern for China, as they act as essential barriers on its journey to become the world's first economic power and to its ambition to increase its regional economic and political dominance.

The China-Iran-Pakistan Alliance plays a significant role in Beijing's ambition to secure its natural resource needs. Both of the Middle Eastern countries have been identified as strategic locations in China's ambition to revive its ancient Silk Road. The challenges ahead are paramount to China's future, as the One Belt One Road Initiative is closely connected to countries affected by significant economic and political uncertainty amidst growing regional and international frictions, especially with the United States of America.

Chapter written by Lucía MORALES, Daniel RAJMIL and Bernadette ANDREOSSO-O'CALLAGHAN.

For a color version of all the figures in this chapter, see www.iste.co.uk/morales/connectivity.zip

10.1. Introduction

China's ambition to revive the silk road of ancient Roman times and its aspiration to reconnect to the world's economy was confirmed by President Xi Jinping in the fall of 2013. President Xi unveiled a comprehensive and complex strategic framework that brought together a focused and ambitious plan to expand China's regional and global trade connections in order to gain global geopolitical influence. The Chinese authorities are seeking to sustain the country's pre-2008 economic performance, as the 2008 global economic and financial mayhem represented a breakpoint for the nation's economic development. Since 1978, when China began its reforms to open up its economy, GDP growth rates have reflected a transition towards a fast-growing economy that averaged almost 10% year-on-year. These solid and high economic growth rates have translated into significant improvements in the educational and health sector and had positive spillover effects on poverty reduction (World Bank 2021b). However, the country's economic development started to dwindle towards the end of the 2000s, and it has aligned with what is considered as a *"more normal type of growth"*. The Chinese economy has shifted from high to medium-high growth rates, and the economic slowdown is undeniable (Hui 2022; World Bank 2021a, 2021b). As the country is progressing with its economic adjustment, Chinese leader Xi Jinping has started to use a new term: *"high-quality"* economic growth, to refer to the economic adjustment that the country's economic model is facing. President Xi has indicated that China has entered a new era, transitioning from rapid growth to *"high-quality development"* (China's State Council Information Office 2021). In addition, the idea of high-quality growth was highlighted in China's 14th Five Year Plan, mapping out the country's political and economic priorities throughout 2025, and stressing the need: *"to achieve higher quality, more efficiency, more fairness, and more sustainable and safer development"* (UNDP 2021b). The fast-growing economy has reached its limits, flagging the need for changes that enable a more sustainable economic growth and development strategy.

The new *"high-quality"* economic growth vision underlines the importance of a people-centered approach that aligns with innovation, coordination, more environmental-friendly, open, and inclusive development. The challenges ahead are quite significant, as China's opening up to the world consisted of an economic developmental model sustained by resource-intensive manufacturing, exports, a heavy reliance on coal to fuel its energy needs, cheap labor and a plethora of distorting competitive practices. However, to achieve high-quality growth, a report from the World Bank signals the imperative need for economic rebalancing. In particular, the transition should seek the *"rebalancing from external to domestic demand, from traditional investment and industry to consumption and services, from the state to markets and the private sector, and from a high to a low-carbon economy"* (World Bank 2021b). While the Chinese economy enjoyed fast levels of growth for almost three decades – contributing to reducing poverty levels and to nurturing the development of the middle-class – it has also created significant imbalances on the economic, social, and environmental fronts. In parallel, Chinese demographic trends reveal that the country has aged significantly, with only Japan aging faster than China.

Such imbalanced demographics represent a serious concern for the Chinese authorities due to the need for young human capital that meets the requirements of a fast-aging population. Therefore, China's demographics are posing significant challenges to the sustainability of its labour market (World Population Review 2022). Some of the more inherent challenges faced by the labor market have emerged because of the Chinese authorities' former controversial sex-selective abortion approach sustained by its one-child policy. The one child-policy has resulted in a ratio of 120 boys for every 100 girls and a birth rate of 1.4 children per woman. The outcome of the policy has led to a negative impact on the replacement rate of 2.1 children per woman, resulting in a negative effect on population growth with the expectation that China's population will start to decline after 2030. Figure 10.1 below shows the significant decline experienced by birth rates and the consolidation of a downward trend in the 15–29 age band as well as a growing trend as the population ages – as reflected in the 60–69 and 70–89 age bands – indicating that China's population is aging very fast. Such a rapid adjustment translates into significant economic concerns as China's low birth rate and a fast-aging population could undermine its future economic development. The country is confronted with a future inability to replenish the needs of the labor market, compounded by the economic, financial, social, and environmental challenges that the Government is already immersed in.

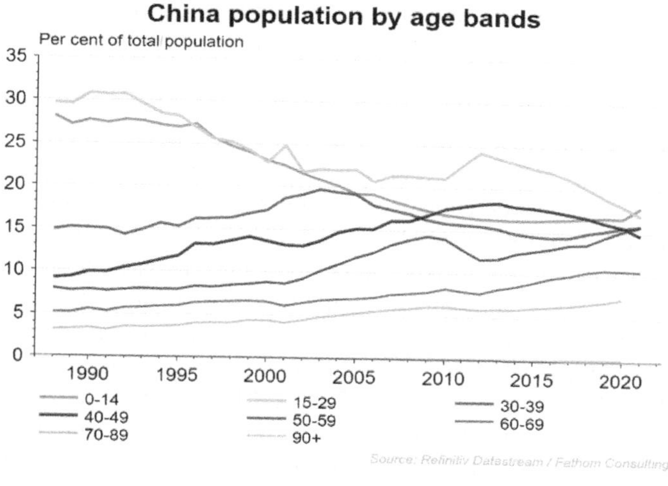

Figure 10.1. *Evolution of China's population*

In the background of a challenging economic, environmental and demographic landscape, this chapter explores how China's economic interests are defining its role at the international level and in the Asian region. In particular, this chapter will devote some special attention to our understanding of the connection to two specific countries, Pakistan and Iran, and their alliance with China. The analysis seeks to offer insights into China's rising power and how it might be challenged due to conflicting dynamics, high risks, and increasing levels of uncertainty surrounding the chosen economic corridor. The China-Pakistan-Iran alliance is characterized by every country being at different stages of global geopolitical power, national interests, political instabilities, and divergence in terms of economic development. We aim to offer insights that add value to our understanding of regional economic and political dynamics and their implications for China's ambition to become the world's first economy. To understand the challenges associated with the alliance, we start the discussions by examining China's economic challenges; we progress with the presentation of some insights on the globalization process and its implications, and we then turn our discussion towards the analysis of the China-Iran-Pakistan alliance. The chapter concludes by offering some final remarks and several critical insights on power balance dynamics.

10.2. China's economic challenges

Over the past decade, China has faced significant challenges in adjusting and in reactivating its economy due to the need to identify new drivers for growth that enable a transition towards a more defined market economy. The new approach requires that the economy reorients towards higher-end manufacturing services and that it shifts from a heavily invested economy towards incentivizing domestic consumption. In addition, the international community continues to challenge the Asian giant due to an economic model that is not environmentally friendly.

China's energy model remains heavily reliant on fossil fuels, thus representing a serious challenge to compliance with the UN economic "carbon neutrality" objectives for 2050 (UN 2020). According to the United Nations Secretary General, the 2015 Paris Agreement on climate change introduced the basic guidelines to help world economies to move towards "carbon neutrality" in a context where climate indicators are worsening (UN 2020). China has pledged to reach "carbon neutrality" before 2060. Therefore, the Chinese authorities need to identify new economic drivers in a framework that integrates economic sustainability, energy efficiency and challenging demographical trends as it seeks to address the legacies of its previous developmental path (World Bank 2021a, 2021b). China's efforts to comply with the challenges posed by pollution include accelerating a low-carbon transition and climate technology innovation (US Department of State 2021). However, from the environmental viewpoint, coal remains the primary source of concern as, historically, it has been the country's bedrock in its path to development. Current data indicates that approximately two-thirds of China's economy remains fuelled by coal (ChinaPower 2022; PhysOrg 2022; DataStream 2022). While the country has made some improvements to reduce its coal dependency, the reduction in coal consumption is insufficient to counteract the damaging effects of pollution. Figure 10.2 below depicts an extraordinary adjustment from a peak of coal consumption of around 90% of total energy consumption in the mid-1990s, to a dependence of approximately 65% in 2020. However, current events suggest that the country is finding it extremely difficult to break its umbilical cord to coal, as the Chinese authorities keep referring to it as a vital source to ensuring continuous and uninterrupted growth. Therefore, coal remains a critical player in China's economic recovery process during the post-pandemic era and it will do so in the years to come.

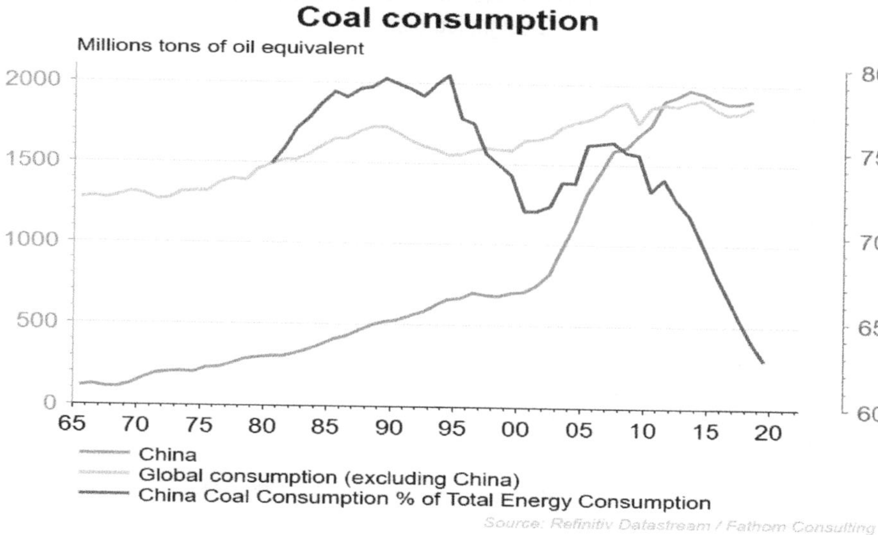

Figure 10.2. *China's coal consumption*

In October 2021, Premier Li Keqiang chaired a high-level meeting, where the nexus between stable energy supply and economic growth was stressed (State Council of the People's Republic of China 2021). According to a report from Carbon Brief (2022) and news reported by a significant number of media outlets (Bloomberg 2022; CNBC 2021), Beijing has *"doubled down on fossil fuels"* amid increasing fears of a global energy crisis that is consolidating, and that could lead to the accentuation of a long-term mismatch between energy supply and demand and/or of disrupted distribution networks. The National Bureau of Statistics of China (2022) reported a worrying increase in China's coal production of approximately 10.3% year on year in the first two months of 2022, as shown in Figure 10.3, reaching 690 million tons of raw coal production in February 2022. The Chinese authorities have taken a stance that emphasizes the need to focus on energy security issues with coal production emerging as a critical player. Consequently, Beijing's decision to increase coal production and enhance its imports to address power shortages has led to a significant increase in CO_2 emissions, in stark contradiction to the proclaimed official environmental goals. According to Global Carbon Atlas (2022), approximately 70% of the country's carbon dioxide emissions in 2020 were linked to coal. At the global level, the move towards more environmentally friendly business activities in alignment with the United Nations Sustainability Goals (UN SDGs) was, on the main, successful until the unfolding events of the Russia-Ukraine crisis.

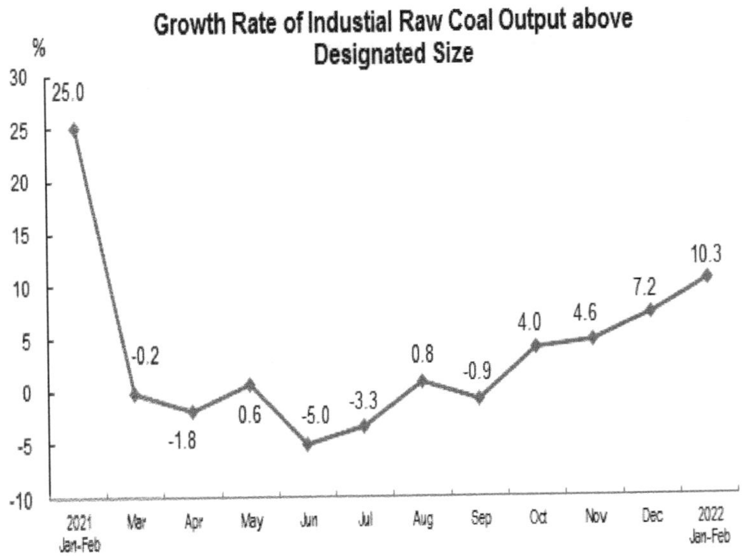

The proclaimed goals of the UN 2030 Agenda for Sustainable Development have indeed been further challenged by the disruption of oil and gas supplies resulting from the Russia-Ukraine conflict since February 2022. These recent events show how coal is becoming an easy substitute for gas and oil, and how the environmental dimension takes second place in the case of major energy supply disruptions. Clearly, economic and business interests emerge as being more prominent when compared to the need for environmental compliance, and the environmental agenda seems to be *the* adjustment variable *par excellence*, at least in some very specific cases.

Undoubtedly, China has entered a new phase of economic growth and development. Initially, the term used to explain the transition was *"a new normal"*, which has been widely employed to refer to different processes requiring some level of adjustment. In the case of Chinese economic growth, what we are witnessing is the country's economic deceleration. But, what does a *"new normal"* mean, and what is its significance? Since the Global Economic and Financial Crisis (GEFC) outburst in 2008, the world economy has faced significant challenges aggravated and exacerbated by the SARS-Cov2[1] outbreak in 2020. What became known as a new "pandemic" evolved into a global health/economic crisis combined with an energy shock derived from the Russian and Saudi Arabia oil price war in March 2020, followed by the conflict between Russia and Ukraine in February 2022. At the time of writing, the world is still immersed in an unbalanced and inappropriate response to the health crisis that translated into a generalized slow and painful economic recovery process that has led to further inequalities between developed and less developed economies. The macroeconomic landscape has been impacted by the simultaneous occurrence of base effects, supply change disruptions, and pent-up demand (ECB 2022; Bernstein and Tedeschi 2021). Base effects are explained by growth rates that are unusually high or low. The world economy has experienced low and negative economic growth rates resulting from the economic constraints (i.e. lockdowns) imposed to attempt to manage the effects of the global health crisis, and China has not remained unscathed from lower growth trends. The second source of instability relates to global supply chain disruptions connected with severe economic activity interruptions resulting from the various economic lockdowns. This has represented a major hit to China due to its dominant position in global supply chains. More specifically, the Asian region is taking central stage, as it plays a critical role in global supply chains with a significant impact on the transport and warehousing sectors that have led to rising costs passed on to consumer prices. The third element is explained by the pent-up demand for goods and services. As the world economy adjusted and started to open up again, the recovery process has materialized in higher prices of goods and services led by the energy sector. The imposed economic lockdowns, combined with the monetary and fiscal policy response to the health crisis (Andreosso-O'Callaghan *et al.* 2021), have resulted in a situation that has created inflationary pressures worldwide. Prices have experienced significant upward adjustments, led in particular by volatile food and energy prices.

Unfortunately, the measures introduced to either control the spread of the virus and or/and to aid the economy have not been very effective. They have translated into significant human, social, economic and financial losses and costs, enhancing existing social inequalities and deepening the differences between developing countries and the world's most developed economies. From a purely economic and

1 Severe Acute Respiratory Syndrome Coronavirus 2. Note that the diffusion of SARS-Cov 1 in 2002 in China and in other parts of Asia did not cause economic lockdowns at the time.

financial perspective, a missed opportunity for debate regarding the implications of a forced economic hibernation process has resulted in severe disruptions to global supply chains and negative spillover effects severely impacting macroeconomic fundamentals.

10.3. Globalization insights and power balance

As we try to understand the meaning of a *"new normal economic growth"* path, we turn our eyes to the economic implications of the deceleration of economic growth and its potential connection to the globalization process. We seek to explore and reflect on the role played by the globalization process and the disruptive phase initiated by Deng Xiaoping when launching China's reforms and when opening-up the economy at the 1978 Third Plenum. President Xi has reiterated his commitment to China's reforms and opening up (NPC 2018). Over the past 40 years, China has experienced significant transformations from a predominantly agricultural nation to becoming the world's second-largest economy. But the emergence of China as an economic power, the consequent shift in economic activity, the rise of political conflicts, as well as regional and global tensions seems to reveal the imbalanced impact of the globalization process on the world economies. The benefits of the globalization process have been subject to severe questioning and criticism, as it has enabled some selected countries and regions to accumulate economic wealth and political power while leaving many others behind (Paidipaty and Ramos Pinto 2021; Piketty 2020; Martin *et al.* 2018).

The world has been facing increasing economic and social domestic inequalities, rising political discontent and social unrest, and China has not remained unscathed by these global trends. China's economic model has been facing significant challenges as it seems to have reached its limits without showing convincingly that it is able to deal with the problem of environmental degradation. As a result, the Chinese authorities have embarked upon a journey that seeks to rejuvenate the country's economic goals. The *"One Belt, One Road"* (OBOR), renamed as the *Belt and Road Initiative* (BRI), presented a comprehensive plan to reposition China as a major international economic and political power. The initiative integrates geostrategic ambitions with clear significance on the geo-economics front and significant implications for the world balance of power. China keeps consolidating its position as the future first economic power to the detriment of the US dominance (Johnson 2016). The BRI aims to reopen ancient trade corridors and explore additional avenues to help the country project its power as a world trade hegemon (Andreosso-O'Callaghan and Morales 2022). At the center of its economic and developmental strategy, we find a land-sea corridor. China intends to use the corridor to help reactivate inland cargo activities aiming to facilitate the transport of goods towards ASEAN (Association of Southeast Asian Nations) economies, and from there to expand to other parts of the world; this strategy would ultimately consolidate its new *"market economy"* model. The corridor is characterized by a model that integrates multiple transport connections that include railways, highways, airways, and water routes with a threefold objective: i) to enable China's access to regional and global markets, as Chinese goods can be transported to relevant ports and distributed to the rest of the world economies. At the same time, the corridor can be used to import goods to the Chinese market, helping to enhance Chinese trade operations; ii) the route is grounded on a multimodal network that seeks to bring cost-efficiency and hassle-free operations to its customers; iii) the route aims to bring balanced economic development in China as part of the country's strategy to foster the development of its western provinces that have lagged behind in terms of economic achievements (China Daily 2021).

The trade corridor is helping China's western provinces to become more involved in international economic cooperation and it is assisting the country in its economic recovery process. The transition of an economic model that is more connected to regional economies in Southeast-Asia can act as a bridge to the global economic market and help promote the economic recovery needed in the post-pandemic era. China is interested in promoting socio-economic activity to boost and increase connections between China and regional economic players and expand its reach towards the global economy. The corridor connects over 100 countries and reaches over 300 ports worldwide, with the Chongqing municipality identified as the center of operations for the corridor (Government of China 2021). In addition, the BRI represents a significant strategic approach for China to secure its access to natural resources, enhance the country's dominant position in the global supply chains, and expand and consolidate its global position. At this point, it is of interest to understand the significance of Pakistan and Iran for China as countries that offer access to natural resources and are located in a geographically strategic position opening wider opportunities to gain geopolitical and geo-economic power. Iran connects the Indian subcontinent to the Mediterranean Sea, while Pakistan is the bridge between South Asia and West Asia. The sections that follow explore the importance of Pakistan and Iran as China seeks to grow and increase its position globally (Hanson 2021).

10.4. China-Pakistan-Iran trilateral cooperation

The objectives of the BRI are very ambitious, and the potential for its success is very uncertain; there is no doubt that the initiative has been and will continue to be surrounded by significant controversies. As an example, we can consider the trilateral cooperation between China and its regional allies, Pakistan and Iran. The trilateral cooperation is emerging and consolidating as an imbalanced power relationship (Rajmil *et al.* 2021; Raza 2019). At the early stages of the cooperation, it is rather clear that China's global ambition and aspirations impact on how the Asian region is repositioning itself in the international context, leading to significant implications in geopolitics and geo-economics dynamics. If successfully implemented, the BRI plan, commonly referred to as the String of Pearls, would enable China to find a maritime Silk Road along the Indian Ocean Region (Ashraf 2017). In addition, the renewed importance that energy policies and coal consumption will play is also present in the ambitious projects for the CPEC (China-Pakistan Economic Corridor) region. The CPEC importance goes beyond merely establishing economic bridges between the two countries as it aims to develop a further connectivity between China and Pakistan with the potential aim of integrating other sub-regions of Asia that could play a key role in improving the area's economic and strategic environment (Ahmad *et al.* 2020).

As hinted at above, and given the current conflictual and disruptive context, the world economy is struggling to transition towards environmentally-friendly energies. The year 2022 is witness to significant inflationary pressures emerging from the energy and food sectors, as well as from global supply chain disruptions particularly since the global health crisis. Moreover, the recent Glasgow COP 26 meeting of November 2021 did not lead to a much needed agreement and it finished instead with more divergences than international political unity. The Glasgow meeting made very little progress; Arora and Mishra (2021) argue that even though zero-emission vehicles to promote "greener" transport and deforestation where debated, the evaluation of the conference meeting demonstrates that the targets have not been achieved and that, overall, the "roadmap" is not very clear.

The CPEC will be, without doubt, a double measure project: i) it offers signs of the real Chinese energy policy shift, and in addition, ii) it contributes to understanding the effectiveness of the international community pressures to curb Chinese coal consumption, domestically and abroad (Rajmil *et al.* 2020; Ramay 2016). In practical terms, this would mean empowering China and Pakistan as rising powers in the region. There are different definitions of how to delimit a rising power. According to Miller (2016), various dimensions could be considered when a nation is trying to rise and reposition itself with the aim of emerging as a great economic and political power. For example, a state can increase its military capacity to strengthen its economic power and help to delimit its globalizing interests, and exhibit internal and external recognition of its changing status (Miller 2016). When looking at broader aspects of the geopolitics of the region and when examining how China is positioning itself, both China and Pakistan would fit into Miller's definition as both countries have been actively building their military-economic capabilities and looking outwards across regions (Iftekhar and Zhan 2020).

On the one hand, China is taking a central stage, as the Chinese authorities shape the country's regional policy guided by geo-economics with substantial implications for economic development and the balance of the region's economic power that will contribute to defining the future of Asian International affairs. Political and economic joint interests have brought together these countries by developing significant links to China's economic corridor with its energy projections. As has been explained above, the Chinese Government is seeking to address domestic and international pressures derived from its over-reliance on coal as its primary energy resource, in parallel with the sharp decline in economic growth rates experienced since the 2008 GEFC (Rajmil *et al.* 2021). On the other hand, Pakistan is immersed in geopolitical instability caused by its relations with its neighbors India and Afghanistan, thus creating a constant pole of tension that challenges its economic development and that adds to its ongoing relationship with Iran. In addition, China-Pakistan and, by extension, Iran all conform to a complicated triangle that can be connected to Pakistan's long-standing rivalry with India and Iran's protracted antagonism against the USA (Khan 2014).

To understand the complexities of these three countries' alliance, it is important to first demark the geopolitical challenges that these countries face amidst regional unrest and second to explore the economic benefits of their partnership. First, we examine the China-Pakistan Economic Corridor and how it could become a profitable option for both countries in the years to come in the face of current events. Moreover, the study uses and explores the effects through the China-Pakistan economic corridor to offer critical insight into the economic corridors' value and relevance as enablers of strategic growth and economic development in a context of significant instability and conflict (Ogunlana 2006). Shared geopolitical and geo-economic interests have solidified the links of China's economic corridor, in particular with regard to energy projections in the Pakistani and Iranian economies with potential spillover effects to neighboring countries. The Chinese Government seeks to address domestic and international pressures derived from its over-reliance on coal as its primary energy resource, and Iran could contribute to addressing China's energy security issues (Rajmil *et al.* 2021).

The discussions presented in the following sections offer insights into Pakistan's geopolitical and geo-economic perspectives linked to China's interests. Pakistan's geopolitical and geo-economic joint interests are also considered in combination with the role of Iran in the alliance.

10.5. Pakistan's vital role in the CPEC and regional stability

For decades, Pakistan's geopolitical instability has been concomitant with the lack of economic opportunities in the country, which has hindered and limited its internal economic development and, to some extent, its regional leadership. With the emergence of the CPEC project, a new geopolitical and geo-economic path to achieve new infrastructure and internal development was opened to the country through China's investment. One of Pakistan's main internal challenges is related to the underdevelopment of its economy, which is also related to the enormous weight of its informal economy and to the related difficulties in quantifying its contribution to the country's GDP. Historically, informality has been a constant factor when looking at Pakistan's economy. For example, a study by Aslam (1998) found that over a 30-year period, between 1960 and 1990, the informal economy grew to nearly 75% of GDP, based on the log ratio of cash in circulation to foreign currency. Similarly, Khan and Khalil (2018) found that between 2007 and 2008, informal economic growth reached 91% of the country's economic weight. In this context, the emergence of laws and forms behind the CPEC project has brought about enormous social, economic and political changes, opening up new opportunities for the future. However, despite the economic deficiencies experienced by the country, the ongoing conflict between Pakistan and its neighbor India is probably one of the biggest challenges that the CPEC is facing and it highlights the complexity of international cooperation and its future success. The roots of the Indo-Pakistani conflict can be traced back to 1947 when India's partition led to two independent dominion states (India and Pakistan). Conflict studies, along with the geopolitical reality of the sub-Indian continent, have shown the evolution of the conflict between Pakistan and India, which is often simplified to the mere dispute for the Kashmir region. As stated by Behera (2016) *"conventional understanding of this conflict remains emblematically tied to the territorial and ideological parameters, which suggests the dispute is rooted solely in the idea that a Muslim-majority state had its fate determined by a Hindu maharaja, that Pakistan – the 'homeland' of the subcontinent's Muslims – is incomplete without Kashmir's inclusion"*. However, it should not be forgotten that the two countries have lived in periods of relative calm. Accordingly, most International Relations scholars will argue that the two countries follow a frozen conflict relations dynamic (Sumit *et al.* 2019). China has historically seen Pakistan as a possible ally while India has played a much more complex role in China's regional stability. In other words, for more than half a century, the geopolitics of South-Asia have been shaped by a triangular relationship between India, Pakistan and China. This different series of inter-state conflicts resulted in two basic and enduring security structures, one rooted in the partition of India and the ensuing Indo-Pakistani war (the "1947 Structure"), and the other in persistent and often confrontational sexual Sino-Indian relations, including a border conflict in 1962 ("1962 Structure") (Smith 2003). Nowadays, the CPEC corridor also seems to go into the same direction, as Beijing's growing relationship with Islamabad, and the presence of the Chinese navy in the region enable China's influence to expand into the Indic Ocean (ibid). In this complex triangle of interests between the three countries, some initial signals on the potential response from Beijing regarding future armed conflicts between India and Pakistan will be guided by the Chinese authorities aiming to protect national interests can be suggested. This implies that in any power of balance game, the South-Asian military balance of power is neither pro-India nor pro-Pakistan; it has always been pro-China (Malik 2003).

With the historical geopolitical conflict of the three countries in mind, it is much easier to understand a shared geo-economic interest of both China and Pakistan in seeking Afghanistan's stability. Moreover, when looking into Pakistan and Iran, the shared Muslim identity of the countries helped in the designing of their common foreign policy towards Afghanistan and in portraying it as a neighboring ally. However, the sentiment was often not met with the same reciprocity within Afghan political elites (Javaid 2020). Regardless of public opinion attitudes towards its neighbor country, as a matter of fact Pakistan has been investing in building ties with its neighboring country. For example, it has promoted the completion of the Torkham-Jalalabad Road and the contribution to the Jinnah Hospital Complex, amongst other actions that include funding scholarships for thousands of Afghan students. This strategy seemed to be successful on economic terms, and Afghanistan has become the market for Pakistani exports (ibid). However, the ascension to power of the Taliban in August 2021 could endanger the CPEC project as well as the geo-economic projections that Pakistan and China have for their shared projects and infrastructure, which are very much in need of geopolitical stability in Afghanistan. Perhaps this could be the ultimate reason why Pakistan has been shifting its public diplomacy efforts towards recognizing the Taliban regime and warning that failure to engage with Afghanistan's new government will doom its citizens (Foreign Policy 2021). In the same line, Chinese leaders met in October 2021 along with other Pakistani, Iranian, and Russian delegates with Taliban representatives in Qatar, hinting at a possible alignment that will probably push for the regime, and that might help in terms of bringing some level of political stability to the region.

10.6. Energy and natural resources as a binding element for China's geo-economics aspirations

Pakistan has been facing a deep crisis in its power sector. For decades, it has experienced a shortage of electricity and natural gas, which has led to the country's mandatory load shedding policy (Aized and Al 2017). In addition to this electricity supply deficit, the country lacks appropriate energy modeling tools and expertise to integrate energy planning and energy policy formulation (Valasai *et al.* 2017). According to estimations and recent studies such as the one published by Mirza *et al.* (2019), Pakistan will experience an increase of approximately 41% of its aggregate energy consumption in 2030 compared to its 2013 level. The results from the study indicate that CPEC related economic activities will boost energy consumption by approximately 48% and 57% by 2030 from its 2013 level under moderate and advanced scenarios, respectively (Mirza *et al.* 2019). Consequently, the CPEC is projected as an energy policy safeguard for the country's economic growth and developmental projections. It also means that energy resources are not the critical element for China's interest in Pakistan.

China has gradually become a global economic actor and investor, especially during the recent Trump period. In contrast to the former US Administration's approach that shifted towards inward interest in alignment with protectionism, President Xi Jinping's administration has looked towards international cooperation and regional leadership, and continues to consolidate its deep reform and internationalization process (NPC 2018). Overall, China intends to present the BRI project as a *"win-win"* inter-state cooperation (Liu and Dunford 2016). Knowing that China needs a growing infrastructure to succeed in its geopolitical ambition to influence Asian affairs directly, the connection between the development of adequate infrastructure emerges as a guideline for the countries' political agendas. Infrastructure is critical as part of the logistical chain as it is fundamental to enable the transportation of goods for the international, regional, and domestic markets (Larkin 2013). However, this *"win-win development"* has several limitations considering that not all partner countries to the Chinese plans have the same institutional framework as China. This becomes more crucial to understand and portray the future influence of China's development model on those countries, as in the case of Pakistan. Pakistan will be influenced in its domestic settings regarding its economy, institutions, and socio-political environment. These settings have already been impacted by the idea of a development model based on a friendly partnership with China under the CPEC scheme that can be an indicator of the inherent challenges of the BRI project (Shah 2018).

The minerals sector has supported a variety of countries in their search for economic development, as natural resources exploitation contributes to improving international trade dynamics, enables the creation of employment, and acts as an enhancer of economic growth and income levels (Hussain Shah 2018). Pakistan has immense mineral reserves that include coal, gold, copper, bauxite, mineral salt, chromite, and iron ore. It also possesses a significant range of mines for various precious and semi-precious minerals, including ruby, topaz, and emeralds. However, the lack of appropriate infrastructure, human capital, and technologies represent a major hindrance to the development of the sector, in combination with a lack of access to mines, industrial zones, and low levels of investment. The connection to China can be found in China's economic growth and its strong demand for mineral commodities and in particular in its increasing demand for major minerals that include bauxite, chromium copper, iron, lead, manganese, nickel, oil, and potash. The country is reliant on imports to meet its needs. The Chinese Government is interested in developing the CPEC to enable transport cost efficiency and accessibility to Pakistan natural resources that will contribute to consolidating the country's dominance in global supply chains (Pui-Kwan 2013; Hanson 2021). Agriculture is the most significant economic sector in Pakistan, contributing approximately 25% of GDP and accounting for half of the employed labor force. The main crops are wheat, cotton, rice, sugarcane and maize, with commodities like pulses, onions, potatoes, chillies, and tomatoes gaining economic importance (Pakistan Bureau of Statics 2022). On the other hand, oil and gas reserves are not significant, but they are a strength for Iran accounting for 9.5% of the world's total oil reserves. According to the EIA (2021), estimated natural gas reserves are very significant as Iran was the third-largest natural gas producer in the world in 2019 just behind Russia. Iran ranks as the world's third-largest and second-largest reserve holder of oil and natural gas, respectively, in 2020, revealing the significant interest of China in these two countries that are a combination of geostrategic positions and availability of a different range of most desired natural resources.

10.7. Pakistan's shift from geopolitics to geo-economics

Pakistan is located in southern Asia and connects South-Asia, West-Asia, and Central-Asia with the Gwadar Port, identified as a critical transportation route regarding the CPEC. In addition, the Jinnah International Airport is an important location for cargo flights (Raza 2020). Economic diplomacy emerges as a critical element in how Pakistan is trying to position its relationship with China as the two countries' cooperation has grown over the years. Pakistan's geographic position places the country as a major player within China's BRI ambition and amidst the US-China rivalry with very important implications for the Asian region, particularly when safeguarding Pakistan's political and economic interests. As such, Pakistan is reassessing its role and reconsidering its geostrategic approach by shifting from geopolitics towards a more focused approach to strategic competition. Unfortunately, current world dynamics defined by rising levels of conflict and economic uncertainty severely impact on how global powers might contribute to undermining world peace and where economic interests dominate the agenda. These are critical aspects that need to be considered when trying to maximize economic well-being and nations' own interests (Ozkizilcik 2022). On the other hand, Pakistan's geographic position needs to be considered carefully as its neighbors Afghanistan, Iran, China, and India are positioning the country in a strategic location that brings opportunities to its economic development, but it is also affected by serious challenges due to the political and economic uncertainty and ongoing conflicts that define regional dynamics. Pakistan is critical for China, as it plays a paramount role in Beijing's BRI due to its strategic location and, in particular, its access to the sea is associated with the goals of the Maritime Route which is a vital element for China's geopolitical ambitions. Concurrently, Pakistan's alignment with Chinese interests is also fuelled by their bitter past with the USA and growing feelings of abandonment from the American administration during critical times. The Pakistani detachment and resentment towards the USA have increased due to the neglect of its crucial role during the post 9/11 period. It had further become more complicated as a result of the American approach towards Afghanistan during the summer of 2021 when the US army exited the country after more than 20 years of intervention, leaving it in the hands of the Taliban regime. The US Administration has sent a clear message indicating that Pakistan might not represent a strategic location for the USA anymore. The US withdrawal from Afghanistan has led to an economic and humanitarian crisis affecting the Afghani population, with more than 1.45 million Afghan refugees being hosted by Pakistan. After the takeover, Afghanistan is at risk of near-universal poverty, with up to 97% of the population at risk of sinking below the poverty line in 2021, representing adverse severe spillover effects on the economy of Pakistan (Rajmil *et al.* 2022; UN 2022; UNDP 2021a; The Guardian 2021). Furthermore, and in line with the United Nations Secretary-General concerns:

> "[...] without action, lives will be lost, and despair and extremism will grow" – António Guterres (UN Secretary General, January 2022).

The economic implications are enormous, as the economic collapse of Afghanistan could lead to a massive exodus of people fleeing the country with significant consequences for Pakistan. The country already hosts a substantial number of Afghan refugees, compounded by a delicate economic situation and hands-off approach of the international community. According to Mahbouba Serah, an executive director of the Afghan's Women Skills and Development Center, the international community's hasty exit in August 2021 has clearly undermined two decades of hard work for equality, human rights, inclusive governance, peace, and security with a significant human and economic impact, as the country has been left with a collapsed banking system, rising food prices and the loss of jobs that have contributed to exacerbating the country's brain drain and that have significantly impacted on women's ability to be able to work outside their homes and restricted girls from their right to education (UN 2022). Furthermore, Pakistan is also affected by the impact of the global health pandemic, the ongoing challenges associated with environmental degradation and its economic externalities, the deterioration of its economy, the rising conflicts within the Asian region, and the unfolding events of the Russian-Ukrainian crisis. Undoubtedly, the region's economic and political instability is on the rise, representing significant challenges to the potential success of China's OBOR ambition.

10.8. Iran's role in the alliance

Unsurprisingly, Iran is of significant interest to China because of its natural resources and key geopolitical role for both central Asia and the Middle-East regions. The country's oil fields are its primary strategic resource, but apart from petroleum, Iran is rich in other natural resources such as for example natural gas, coal, chromium, copper, iron ore, lead manganese, zinc, and sulfur (OPEC 2022). In addition, the country is the route to connect the Indian subcontinent and the Mediterranean Sea, but due to its size and complex topography, there are major geographical and economic challenges that prevent the successful development, exploitation, and commercialization of its resources (Rajput 2020; WorldView 2011). On the other hand, in March 2021, Iran and China signed a Strategic Cooperation Agreement seeking to increase trade relations over the next 25 years. Since then, China has increased oil imports from Iran and has offered rhetorical support for the Iranian position against the US (Figueroa 2022; Bloomberg 2021). In addition, the Russia-Ukraine crisis has clearly reminded the world that it is heavily reliant on fossil fuels, and since oil is Iran's most strategic resource, the country is benefiting from a renewed interest emerging from Beijing. The Persian Gulf provides the largest petroleum resources worldwide (Northrup 2013). As illustrated in Figure 10.4, Iran is one of the world's major oil reserve holders.

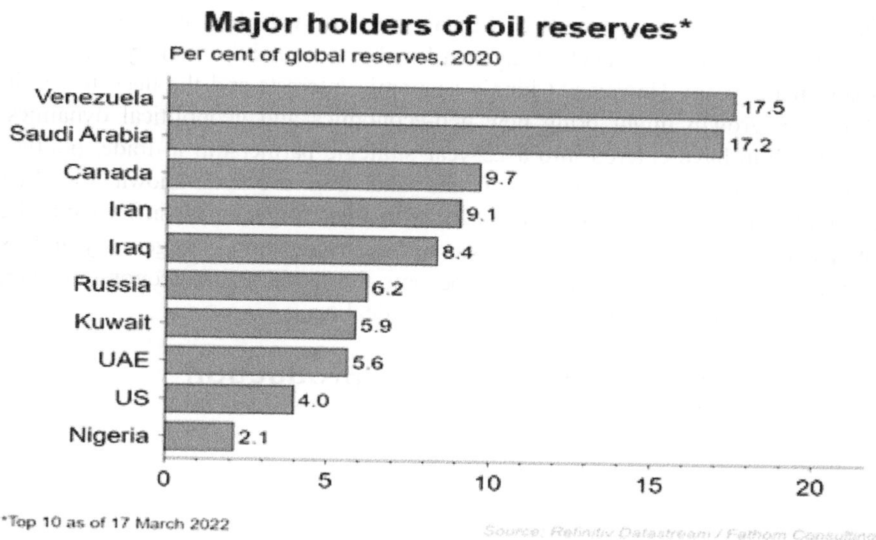

Figure 10.4. *World oil reserves*

Moreover, global pressure to move towards energy models that are less dependent on coal resources are mounting, and this might lead to a significant global shift from coal towards oil and gas, reinforcing the global dependency on fossil fuels. At this point, it is of interest that we acknowledge the reality of the world economies, as renewable energies are not yet representing a real alternative to the world's less-developed economies that need cheap and accessible energy resources. Furthermore, the world's most developed economies are also heavily dependent on fossil fuels and have not designed and deployed the required infrastructure to enable the transition towards "green" energy. In addition, and as clearly exhibited by economic dynamics in the post-SARS-Cov2 era and as exacerbated by global uncertainty on energy markets amplified by the Russian war with Ukraine, fossil fuels do remain a strategic energy resource. Consequently, shifting pressures towards the oil and gas market as countries seek to impose more bans on coal consumption are expected.

The current reality is thus that the world economy is not yet ready to embrace a dramatic "green" energy transition due to obstructions posed by the lack of appropriate infrastructure and investments. Within the constraints of an energy market that is heavily reliant on fossil fuels, Iran offers some interesting opportunities to China as it seeks to transition towards a less coal-dependent model while progressing with a more energy-sustainable model. Iran is considered to be one of the world's major players in the oil market as it holds the fourth-largest oil reserves, in addition to being the fourth-largest oil producer in the Middle-East region, as illustrated in Figure 10.5. China's oil trade with Iran is a clear case of significant uncertainty, as sanctions against Iran have limited the country's access to Iranian oil for years. However, China's economic interests and the need to regain high-quality growth might bring new geo-economics and geopolitical dynamics. China and Iran have entered into a 25-year strategic partnership in trade, politics, culture, and security. In addition, China and Iran are well-known for their confrontational relationships with the USA, with a growing Chinese influence in the East-Asian region creating significant worries regarding the US hegemony and its ability to react to China's ambitions to become the world's first economic power, while the US is viewed as a mature economy in decline.

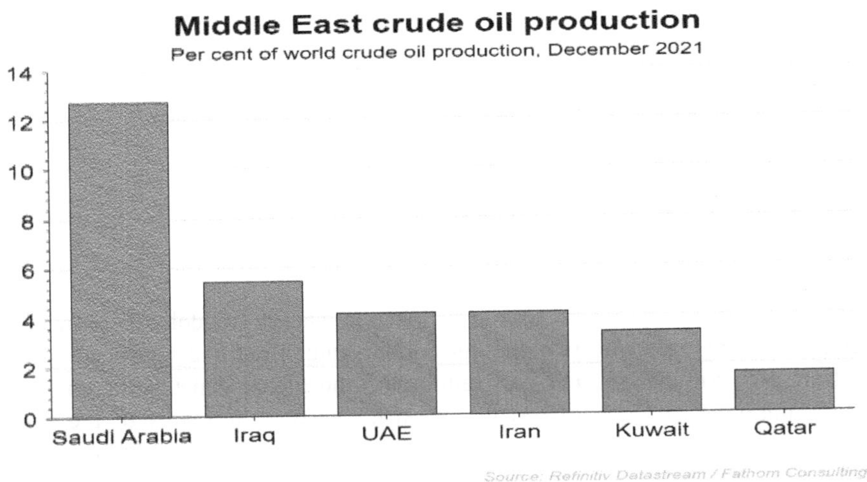

Figure 10.5. *Iran's oil production within the Middle East*

China is the largest buyer of Iranian crude oil (EIA 2021), registering an increase in Chinese oil imports of crude oil towards the end of 2021. Figure 10.6 illustrates the rise in Iranian oil production amidst rising international conflicts. Iranian oil exports focus on the Chinese market, positioning China as a reliable and irreplaceable trade partner for Iran with a significant dominance of slightly above 50% of oil exports, as illustrated in Figure 10.7 (China Briefing 2021).

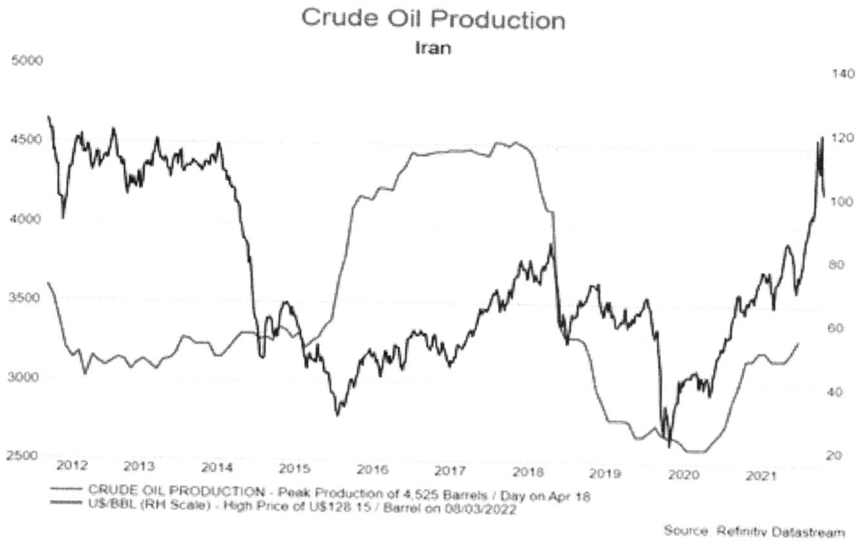

Figure 10.6. *Oil prices and Iran's oil production*

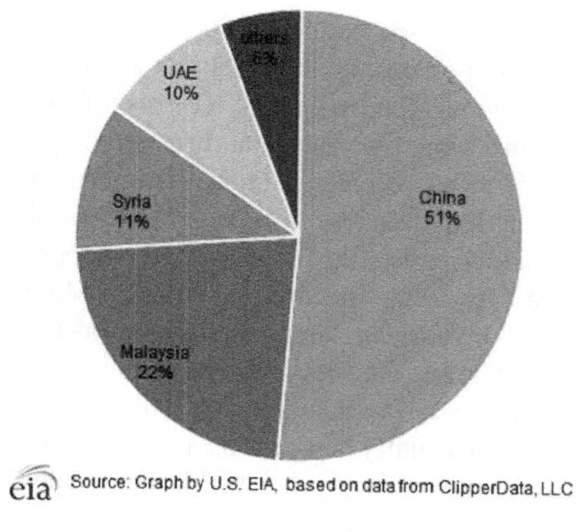

Figure 10.7. *Iran's crude oil and condensate exports by destination, 2020*

China's trade relationship with Iran can be traced back to the dates of the ancient Silk Road in the first century BCE (China Briefing 2021). Officially, China and Iran have engaged in economic cooperation since 1937, and since then, bilateral diplomatic relationships have remained steady, mainly due to China's interests in Iranian's natural resources. The two countries have kept bilateral trade relationships despite the sanctions placed on Iran by the international community. Recent developments indicate that the two countries are willing to move on with their economic cooperation despite the restrictions. Moreover, the conflict between Russia and Ukraine might help to consolidate a more active agenda between the two countries, without forgetting that Beijing has warned of a *"hugely risky"* 25-year deal as China's growing interest in Iran is raising concerns among countries that are hostile to Tehran's regime (Wang 2021; The New York Times 2021).

10.9. Conclusion

China's ability to secure its energy needs will play a vital role in consolidating its economic rise along with its capability to increase its geopolitical power. The country's dependency on foreign resources such as energy and basic raw materials acts as a deterrent towards achieving economic development and political gains as this dependency has significant leverage effects on policy options available to the government. Countries that cannot secure their energy supply and cannot offer political stability face a considerable reduction in the avenues that contribute to cultivating and enhancing national political and economic power. These are significant areas of concern for China, as they act as serious barriers on its journey to becoming the world's first economic power. The Chinese authorities are attempting to reactivate and redefine an economic model that has reached its limits and that needs to be profoundly reformed as the country seeks to consolidate its rise. After decades of enjoying fast-economic growth, the country is facing a dilemma, as it needs to transition from an economic model that has inflicted significant damage on its environment due to its reliance on coal. The manufacturing sector accounts for two-thirds of the country's energy needs, mainly covered by burning coal plants, and its dependency on coal to fuel economic growth is undeniable. In addition, China's energy landscape has for decades shifted towards foreign countries that are politically unstable and characterized by complex topographies that represent a major challenge in accessing needed resources. Moreover, underdeveloped infrastructure, lack of investment, an unqualified workforce and high levels of corruption, to name but a few, contribute to questioning the potential success of the country's OBOR or BRI initiative. China is left with a legacy dominated by energy needs based on coal as the country has become a major importer of coal even though it holds the third-largest reserves in the world. The country is positioned as the world's largest emitter of carbon dioxide and it thus urgently needs to secure access to alternative and stable energy sources. The country's demographics are not helping either, as the Chinese population is aging fast, and its fertility rate has dropped below the 2.1 replacement level. As the country is facing significant domestic challenges, we cannot forget the international dimension currently marked by rising levels of political and economic uncertainty. Due to the need to find new economic growth drivers, President Xi Jinping launched the OBOR initiative in 2013 to revive its connectivity to the world economy. However, the challenges are significant due to its dependency on other economies. As an example, we have considered the geopolitical complexities associated with the instability of the Pakistan-Iran partnership.

Finally, as the world witnesses the unfolding of different armed conflicts, it becomes clear that the humanitarian crises emerging from these armed conflicts are over shadowed by the dominance of the economic and business agenda led by energy market dynamics; the China, Pakistan and Iran triangle is clearly one of the main priorities of the world's economy, with China playing a pivotal role in the relationship.

10.10. References

Ahmad, P. and Singh, B. (2017). Sino-Pakistan friendship, changing South Asian geopolitics and India's post-Obama options. *South Asia Research*, 37(2), 133–146.

Ahmad, R., Mi, H., Fernald, L.W. (2020). Revisiting the potential security threats linked with the China–Pakistan Economic Corridor (CPEC). *Journal of the International Council for Small Business*, 1(1), 64–80.

Ahmed, Z. and Shahram, A. (2020). Pakistan caught between Iran and Saudi Arabia. *Contemporary South Asia*, 28(3), 336–350. DOI: 10.1080/09584935.2020.1779181.

Aized T., Shahid M., Bhaffti, AM., Saleeem, M., Anandarajah, G. (2018). Energy security and renewable energy policy analysis of Pakistan. *Renewable and Sustainable Energy Reviews*, 284: 155–169. DOI: http://dx.doi.org/10.1016/j.rser.2017.05.254.

Akhter, M. (2018). Geopolitics of the belt and road: Space, state, and capital in China and Pakistan. In *Logistical Asia*, Neilson B., Rossiter N., Samaddar R. (eds). Palgrave Macmillan, Singapore. DOI: 10.1007/978-981-10-8333-4_11.

Andreosso-O'Callaghan, B. and Morales, L. (2022). China's economic connectivity to the world economy. *F1000Research*, 11(317) [Online]. Available at: https://f1000research.com/articles/11-317.

Andreosso-O'Callaghan, B., Moon, W., Sohn, W. (2021). *Economic Policy and the Covid-19 Crisis – The Macroeconomic Response in the US, Europe and East Asia*. Routledge, London.

Ashraf, J. (2017). String of pearls and China's emerging strategic culture. *Strategic Studies*, 37(4), 166–181. DOI: 10.2307/48537578

Arora, N.K. and Mishra, I. (2021). COP26: More challenges than achievements. *Environmental Sustainability*, 4, 585–588.

Behera, N.C. (2016). The Kashmir conflict: Multiple fault lines. *Journal of Asian Security and International Affairs*, 3(1), 41–63. DOI: https://doi.org/10.1177/2347797015626045.

Bernstein, J. and Tedeschi, E. (2021). Pandemic prices: Assessing inflation in the months and years ahead. *The White House Written Materials* [Online]. Available at: https://www.whitehouse.gov/cea/written-materials/2021/04/12/pandemic-prices-assessing-inflation-in-the-months-and-years-ahead/.

Bloomberg News (2021). China ramps up Iran oil purchases after getting new quotas [Online]. Available at: https://www.bloomberg.com/news/articles/2021-12-16/china-teapots-boost-iran-oil-imports-after-getting-new-quotas#:~:text=USD%2Fbbl.&text=China%20ramped%20up%20its%20buying,to%20market%20intelligence%20firm%20Kpler.

Bloomberg News (2022). Faced with turmoil, China turns to its old reliable – Coal [Online]. Available at: https://www.bloomberg.com/news/articles/2022-03-14/china-doubles-down-on-coal-endangering-climate-goals.

CarbonBrief (2022). China Briefing, March 17 2022: Beijing “doubling down on fossil fuels”; China’s CO2 emissions increase; coal production growth [Online]. Available at: https://www.carbonbrief.org/china-briefing-17-march-2022-beijing-doubling-down-on-fossil-fuels-chinas-co2-emissions-increase-coal-production-growth.

China Briefing (2021). China and Iran: Bilateral trade relationship and future outlook [Online]. Available at: https://www.china-briefing.com/news/china-and-iran-bilateral-trade-relationship-and-future-outlook/.

China Daily (2021). ASEAN trade corridor to help develop Western areas [Online]. Available at: https://www.chinadaily.com.cn/a/202101/20/WS600782c2a31024ad0baa3bf3.html.

ChinaPower (2022). How is China’s energy footprint changing? [Online]. Available at: https://chinapower.csis.org/energy-footprint/.

CNBC (2021). China’s coal imports in October nearly double from a year ago [Online]. Available at: https://www.cnbc.com/2021/11/08/chinas-coal-imports-in-october-nearly-doubled-from-a-year-ago.html.

CSIS (2020). How is China’s energy footprint changing? [Online]. Available at: https://chinapower.csis.org/energy-footprint/.

ECB (2021). Supply chain disruptions and the effects on the global economy. *ECB Economic Bulletin*, Issue 8 [Online]. Available at: https://www.ecb.europa.eu/pub/economic-bulletin/focus/2022/html/ecb.ebbox202108_01~e8ceebe51f.en.html.

ECB (2022). Account of the monetary policy meeting of the Governing Council of the European Central Bank held in Frankfurt am Main on Wednesday and Thursday, 2–3 February [Online]. Available at: https://www.ecb.europa.eu/press/accounts/2022/html/ecb.mg220303~7ac13bacbe.en.html.

EIA (2021). Iran executive summary [Online]. Available at: https://www.eia.gov/international/analysis/country/irn.

Figueroa, W. (2021). China-Iran Relations: The myth of massive investment. *The Diplomat* [Online]. Available at: https://thediplomat.com/2021/04/china-iran-relations-the-myth-of-massive-investment/.

Global Carbon Atlas (2022). Fossil fuels emissions [Online]. Available at: http://www.globalcarbonatlas.org/en/CO2-emissions.

Government of China (2021). Land-sea trade corridor connects 106 countries, regions. *The State Council, The People's Republic of China* [Online]. Available at: http://english.www.gov.cn/news/internationalexchanges/202107/22/content_WS60f8bf5ec6d0df57f98dd5ed.html.

Hanson, E. (2021). Winning without war: Chinese supremacy in global supply chains. *The Strategy Bridge Organisation* [Online]. Available at: https://thestrategybridge.org/the-bridge/2021/6/29/winning-without-war-chinese-supremacy-in-global-supply-chains.

Hui, M. (2022). What China means when it says it wants "high-quality" GDP growth. *Quartz* [Online]. Available at: https://qz.com/2119395/what-china-means-by-high-quality-economic-growth/.

Hussain Shah, S.A. (2018). Strategy for mineral sector development in Pakistan. Planning Commission of Pakistan. Ministry of Planning, Development and Reform. Government of Pakistan [Online]. Available at: chrome-extension://efaidnbmnnnibpcajpcglclefindmkaj/viewer.html?pdfurl=https%3A%2F%2Fwww.pc.gov.pk%2Fuploads%2Fpub%2FFIRST_05_PAGES_STRATEGY_FOR_MINERAL_SECTOR_DEVELOPMENT_IN_PAKISTAN.pdf&clen=471976&chunk=true.

Iftikhar, M. and Zhan, J.V. (2020). The geopolitics of China's overseas port investments: A comparative analysis of Greece and Pakistan. *Geopolitics*, 27(3), 826–851. DOI: 10.1080/14650045.2020.1832473.

Khan, M. (2014). Pakistan-Iran-China triangle: A game changer in the region? *Dialogue*, 9(2), 116–138.

Kugelman, M. (2021). Pakistan pitches the Taliban regime to the world. *Foreign Policy* [Online]. Available at: https://foreignpolicy.com/2021/09/30/pakistan-afghanistan-support-taliban-regime-legitimacy/ [Accessed November 2021].

Javaid, P. (2020). Analyzing the dynamics of Pakistan-Afghanistan relations: Past and present. *South Asian Studies*, 31(1).

Johnson, C.K. (2016). President Xi Jinping's "Belt and Road" Initiative. A practical assessment of the Chinese Communist Party's Roadmap for China's global resurgence. A report of the CSIS Freeman Chair in China Studies. *Center for Strategic and International Studies (CSIS)* [Online]. Available at: https://www.csis.org/analysis/president-xi-jinping%E2%80%99s-belt-and-road-initiative.

Larkin, B. (2013). The politics and poetics of infrastructure. *Annu. Rev. Anthropol.* 42, 327–343 [Online]. Available at: www.annualreviews.org.

Malik, M. (2003). The China factor in the India-Pakistan conflict. *The US Army War College Quarterly: Parameters*, 33(1), 8.

Martin, R., Tyler, P., Storper, M., Evenhuis, E., Glasmeier, A. (2018). Globalisation at a critical juncture? *Cambridge Journal of Regions and Society*, 11, 3–16.

McKinsey Global Institute (2017). China's role in the next phase of globalisation. April 2017 discussion paper [Online]. Available at: https://www.mckinsey.com/featured-insights/china/chinas-role-in-the-next-phase-of-globalization.

Miller, M.C. (2016). The role of beliefs in identifying rising powers. *The Chinese Journal of International Politics*, 9(2), 211–38. DOI:10.1093/cjip/pow006.

Mirza, F.M., Fatima, N., Ullah, K. (2019). Impact of China-Pakistan economic corridor on Pakistan's future energy consumption and energy saving potential: Evidence from sectoral time series analysis. *Energy Strategy Reviews*, 25, 34–46.

National Bureau of Statistics of China (2022). Energy production from January to February 2022 [Online]. Available at: http://www.stats.gov.cn/english/PressRelease/202203/t20220317_1828823.html.

New York Times (2021). China, with $400 billion Iran deal, could deepen influence in Mideast [Online]. Available at: https://www.nytimes.com/2021/03/27/world/middleeast/china-iran-deal.html.

NPC (2018). 40 years of China's reform and opening up. A great revolution that has changed the destiny of the Chinese nation and influence the world. *National People's Congress of China*, (4), 1–48 [Online]. Available at: http://www.npc.gov.cn/zgrdw/npc/zgrdzz/site1/20190403/00016cd0abbd1e0e6af60a.pdf.

OPEC (2021). Iran facts and figures. Annual statistical bulletin [Online]. Available at: https://www.opec.org/opec_web/en/about_us/163.htm#:~:text=Apart%20from%20petroleu%2C%20the%20country's,national%20currency%20is%20the%20rial.

Ozkilzilcik, O. (2022). The limits of Pakistan's strategic pivot to geoeconomics [Online]. Available at: https://www.trtworld.com/opinion/the-limits-of-pakistan-s-strategic-pivot-to-geoeconomics-53779.

Paidipaty, P. and Ramos Pinto, P. (2020). Revisiting the "Great Levelling": The limits of Piketty's capital and ideology for understanding the rise of late 20th century inequality. *The British Journal of Sociology*, 72(1), Special Issue: Debating Thomas Piketty's Capital and Ideology, 52–68.

Pakistan Bureau of Statistics (2022). Agriculture Statics. *Government of Pakistan* [Online]. Available at: https://www.pbs.gov.pk/.

Piketty, T. (2020). *Capital and Ideology*. Harvard University Press, Cambridge, MA.

Pui-Kwan, T. (2013). Mineral Yearbook China. Accessed through US Department of Interior US Geological Survey (USGS).

Ramay, S.A. (2016). China Pakistan economic corridor: A Chinese dream being materialized through Pakistan. *Sustainable Development Policy Institute* [Online]. Available at: http://www.jstor.org/stable/resrep02843.

Rajmil, D., Morales, L., Andreosso-O'Callaghan, B. (2020). China's ecological civilization: Geopolitical and geoeconomic insights? In *Sustainable Development and Energy Transition in Europe and Asia*, Andreosso-O'Callaghan, B., Dzever, S., Jaussaud, J., Taylor, R (eds). ISTE Ltd, London and Wiley, New York.

Rajmil, D., Morales, L., Andreosso-O'Callaghan, B. (2021). How realistic is the China–Pakistan–Iran economic corridor? *Asian Journal of Comparative Politics*, 6(4), 405–420. DOI: https://doi.org/10.1177/20578911211041403.

Rajput, V. (2020). Iran: The game changer in the geopolitics and security algorithm of Middle East. *Diplomatist* [Online]. Available at: https://diplomatist.com/2020/04/28/iran-the-game-changer-in-the-geopolitics-and-security-algorithm-of-middle-east/.

Raza, S.F. (2020). Geo-strategic importance of Pakistan [Online]. Available at: https://www.economy.pk/geo-strategic-importance-of-pakistan/.

Shah, A.R. (2018). How does China–Pakistan economic corridor show the limitations of China's "One Belt One Road" model. *Asia & the Pacific Policy Studies*, 5(2), 378–385.

Smith, P. (2013). The tilting triangle: Geopolitics of the China–India–Pakistan relationship. *Comparative Strategy*, 32(4), 313330. DOI: 10.1080/01495933.2013.821850.

State Council Information Office (2021). Xi Jinping on China's high-quality development. *The People's Republic of China* [Online]. Available at: http://english.scio.gov.cn/m/topnews/2021-08/03/content_77670307.htm.

The Guardian (2021). Afghan at risk of near-universal poverty, UN report warns [Online]. Available at: https://www.theguardian.com/global-development/2021/sep/09/afghans-risk-near-universal-poverty-un.

UN (2020). Carbon neutrality by 2050: The world's most urgent mission [Online]. Available at: https://www.un.org/sg/en/content/sg/articles/2020-12-11/carbon-neutrality-2050-the-world%E2%80%99s-most-urgent-mission.

UN (2022). With Afghanistan "Hanging by a Thread", Security Council delegates call on Taliban to tackle massive security, economic concerns, respect women's equal rights. *United Nations Meetings Coverage and Press Releases* [Online]. Available at: https://www.un.org/press/en/2022/sc14776.doc.htm.

UNDP (2021a). New UN Development Programme Emergency Initiative to Support Afghan People in Need [Online]. Available at: https://www.af.undp.org/content/afghanistan/en/home/presscenter/pressreleases/2021/ABADEI.html.

UNDP (2021b). Issue Brief – China's 14th Five-Year Plan [Online]. Available at: https://www.cn.undp.org/content/china/en/home/library/environment_energy/issue-brief---china-s-14th-five-year-plan.html.

US Department of State (2021). US-China Joint Glasgow Declaration on Enhancing Climate Action in the 2020s. Media MNote, Office of the Spokesperson. November 10 [Online]. Available at: https://www.state.gov/u-s-china-joint-glasgow-declaration-on-enhancing-climate-action-in-the-2020s/.

Wang, A. (2021). China warned 25-year deal with Iran is "hugely risky" despite hope it will boost influence in Middle East. *South China Morning Post* [Online]. Available at: https://www.scmp.com/news/china/diplomacy/article/3127672/china-warned-25-year-deal-iran-hugely-risky-despite-hope-it?module=perpetual_scroll_0&pgtype=article&campaign=3127672.

Weidong, L. and Dunford, M. (2016). Inclusive globalization: Unpacking China's Belt and Road Initiative. *Area Development and Policy*, 1(3), 323–340. DOI: 10.1080/23792949.2016.1232598.

World Bank (2021a). The World Bank in China [Online]. Available at: https://www.worldbank.org/en/country/china/overview#1.

World Bank (2021b). Structural reforms can ease China's transition to high-quality growth: Report [Online]. Available at: https://www.worldbank.org/en/news/press-release/2021/12/22/structural-reforms-can-ease-china-s-transition-to-high-quality-growth-report.

World Population Review (2022) China's population [Online]. Available at: https://worldpopulationreview.com/countries/china-population.

WorldView (2011). The geopolitics of Iran: Holding the center of a mountain fortress [Online]. Available at: https://worldview.stratfor.com/article/geopolitics-iran-holding-center-mountain-fortress.

11

The New Silk Road, EU-China Connectivity and Global Logistics Crisis: Nordic Perspective to the Eurasian Land Bridge Rail Routes[1]

This chapter explores the New Silk Road rail transports between Northern Europe and China. Taking Nordic countries as an exemplary case, the purpose is to investigate the impact of Europe-China connectivity policies and the contemporary global logistics disruption on the development of Finnish rail routes to China. The focus is on the evolvement of two connections, their usage by Finnish and other Nordic firms, and the possible extensions of the routes in the Nordics and in Asia. Drawing from a news review, expert interviews and company data, it has been found that both connections have benefited from policy support, whereas one has been able to capitalize on the recent global maritime transport crisis and the increased demand for Europe-China rail transports.

11.1. Introduction

The European Union (EU) has recently launched its new Global Gateway strategy, introduced in December 2021 by the Commission and the High Representative (EC 2021). The aim of the EU's Global Gateway is to enhance digital, energy and transport links and to strengthen health, education and research

Chapter written by Erja KETTUNEN and Claes G. ALVSTAM.

1 Kettunen is grateful to the Foundation for Economic Education, Finland, for financial support for the study.

systems across the world with investments of up to 300 billion EUR by year 2027. Since transport and infrastructure are at the core of the plan, the strategy responds to the Belt and Road Initiative (BRI) launched by China in 2013. The so-called New Silk Road of China's BRI has included infrastructure development for land and sea trade routes between China and Europe, Asia and the Middle East (e.g. Frankopan 2018; Wei and Sheng 2018; Dunford and Liu 2019; Alvstam 2020). Other countries, such as the United States and Japan have introduced similar large-scale infrastructure investment programs. Therefore, the EU's Global Gateway is not only a comprehensive policy program, but also a response to global infrastructure diplomacy (Karjalainen 2022). It is also a response to current difficulties in supply chains and global logistics systems due to the Covid-19 pandemic (Buckley 2020; Mouritz 2020) that have led to disruptions in maritime container transports and a consequent growth in railway transports in Europe-China trade. Railway transports were already supported by China's BRI policy before the pandemic and there have been attempts at a joint Europe-China connectivity policy, but the recent geopolitical tensions may have changed the situation. As the EU's Global Gateway embraces the development of tangible infrastructure for transporting globally traded goods over air, sea, and land, it is relevant in the foreseeable logistics situation amidst the pandemic, cuts in global value chains, and tense geopolitics. The first step of the strategy was to launch an EU-Africa investment package in February 2022, whereas the actions concerning transports and trade with Asia remain to be seen.

This chapter investigates rail transportations from Northern Europe to China along the landbound New Silk Road. After the launch of the BRI, these rail routes along the Eurasian Land Bridge have shortened Europe-China transport times to ca. two weeks compared to sea transports that typically take four to eight weeks. We take the perspective of the Nordics and focus on rail routes from Finland to China and their relevance and extensions to other Nordic countries and to broader Asia. Two connections from Finland, i.e. Kouvola-Xi'an and Helsinki-Hefei, were opened in 2017 and 2018, respectively, and have been used for transporting exports and imports between the countries. The location of Finland as the northernmost start-point of the rail routes from Europe has an impact on the potential demand, speed, and contents of the cargo transported compared to other European start-points. The operation of all routes has been affected by local, national and international policies and the problems in maritime transportations that may increase the need for rail transports.

Therefore, our aim is to explore the impact of the connectivity policies and global logistics disruption on rail transports from Finland to China along the Eurasian Land Bridge. Reflecting on the different modes of transport in Europe-China trade, the empirical focus is on the development of these transportations and their relevance to Finnish and potentially other Nordic companies. The study leans on data from news sources, interviews, press releases, and logistics portals mainly from Finland. We find specific effects of both the local-global policy framework and the disruption of global logistics systems, and analyze these in the Finnish case.

Geographically, the case provides a particularly good example of how rail-borne traffic can serve as an alternative to the maritime route between Europe and East Asia. The location of Finland in the northernmost part of Europe and the Baltic Sea, far from the main sea routes, gives the longest sea distance and transit time in maritime transport to China. At the same time, Finland's location offers one of the shortest distances in railway transport among all European countries, particularly to and from the northern parts of China. Finnish railroads have the same rail track width as those in Russia and Kazakhstan along the route, requiring only one reloading on the way, in contrast to the narrower rail gauge in Western Europe that requires two reloadings. This is a further advantage regarding the time and cost of rail transports from Finland.

The chapter continues as follows. We first review the development of different transport modes in Europe-Asia trade and the policies for Europe-China connectivity as a framework for the study, and identify a research gap concerning the impact of the policies and global logistics disruption on the rail transports between Finland and China. Second, we present the data and method of this study, and third, continue by presenting our findings on Finnish rail connections to China regarding their development, specificities and future outlook. We conclude with discussion on the results of the study.

11.2. Europe-China connectivity and the geography of transportations

The idea of developing rail routes through Eurasia is not new, as there had been many efforts to improve the railway connections between Europe and China since the early 1990s. However, the rapid development of global maritime container transport, its low price and easy availability strengthened the dominance of sea freight and lessened the potential for competitive rail transports until 2020. We outline these developments in Europe-China transports next.

11.2.1. *Modes of transport in Europe-China trade*

Almost all international trade in goods has for a long time been transported by sea. Sea transport grew rapidly since the 1980s thanks to developments in container traffic and technical improvements in ships and terminals. By 2019, over 90% of global trade volume was carried by sea, and the volume of global maritime trade was 11,076 million tons, up from the 3,704 million tons in 1980 (UNCTAD 2020). The growth of sea transportations and the parallel decrease in the price of sea freight made the world economy dependent on seaborne trade. This led to the maritime shipping industry gaining a monopoly on transportation of large volumes of cargo between continents (Levinson 2016; Petersson *et al.* 2019).

However, while maritime transport is the cheapest, it is also the slowest and most unreliable mode of transport as to the accuracy of delivery times. Air transport is the fastest, more reliable and safer, and also the most expensive mode of transport typically used for valuable or perishable products or time-sensitive freight carried over long distances, and its carrying capacity is limited as to the weight and volume of the delivery. Rail transport lays in between the two when it comes to the cost and speed of the delivery. It is more energy-efficient per carried unit and distance, and not directly dependent on oil. Since transportations cause significant greenhouse gas emissions within supply chains (Eng-Larsson and Kohn 2012), companies may consider freight issues more closely than before (Rogerson *et al.* 2014). Rail transportations may grow in the future, supported by public awareness on sustainable development (Pomfret 2019).

In Europe-Asia transportations, the main connection is the shipping route through the Suez Canal. Given that eight of the world's nine biggest ports are located in Asia and one in Europe (Anwar 2020), seaborne transportations have accounted for 96% of the Europe-Asia trade volume and 61% of the trade value (Rodemann and Templar 2014). When it comes to trade between Europe and China, the figures are slightly different. By trade value, the share of sea transport has been slightly higher (64%), whereas air transport has accounted for 28%, road transport for 6% and rail transport for only 2% of trade value in 2016 (Hillman 2018). The uneven shares of the different transport modes in pre-Covid-19 times have been explained by two factors: the frequency of operations and freight rates. While railway operators have offered weekly departures between Europe and China, maritime transport operators from Chinese seaports have typically offered daily departures. Maritime freight rates have been very low compared to rail freight, as the average sea freight rate between Shanghai and Europe more than halved in 2010–2018 (UNCTAD 2019). According to World Container Index, the global sea freight rate for a 40 feet container ranged at around 1,500 USD up to spring 2020. However, the rates started to increase in summer 2020 and grew ten-fold in a year for Shanghai-Europe routes, reaching 15,000 USD in autumn 2021 and settling at around 13,000 USD in spring 2022 (Drewry 2021; 2022). The soaring freight rates were due to the revival of Chinese exports in 2020 and the continuing stagnation of exports in other parts of the world, which led to a lack of sea containers in Chinese ports (FT 2021). The containers were left empty in other parts of the world, which in turn increased the demand for other transport modes in global trade.

These developments further emphasize the question of location, as sea transport between China and Finnish ports takes much longer compared to the main European ports, such as Rotterdam. Sea transport has also become somewhat slower due to global logistics disruption. In spring 2022, the container route between Shanghai and Rotterdam took 28–34 days depending on the number of port callings along the route, whereas Shanghai-Helsinki took 42–52 days (Maersk 2022). The difference in rail transit times depends strongly on the location of the departure and arrival ports. For example, the container sea route between the Northeastern Chinese city Dalian and Rotterdam takes about 44 days, while Dalian-Helsinki takes 52–60 days (Maersk 2022), and the railway connection between Helsinki and major port cities in China takes ca. 15–19 days (Nurminen Logistics 2022). As the other Nordic countries, particularly Sweden and Norway, are also located far from main maritime hubs in Europe but close to Finland, there may be time and cost advantages for exporters in using Finnish rail connections to China.

11.2.2. *Policy initiatives and the development of railway connectivity*

During the last decade, various initiatives and policies have been introduced to develop transport infrastructure and connectivity. The EU's Global Gateway is the most recent initiative to invest in global infrastructure development by 2027, and its actions will take shape in the years to come. As a joint initiative, the EU and China aimed to improve connectivity between the regions by establishing the EU-China Connectivity Platform in 2015. The intention was to look for synergies between the EU's Trans-European Transport Network (TEN-T) and China's BRI and identify sustainable railway-based transport corridors between the two regions. A number of transport infrastructure projects were suggested in both China and Eastern Europe (EC 2022); however, with little concrete results so far.

In contrast, the launch of the BRI and the associated development of rail infrastructure had contributed to increasing the quality and reliability and cutting off transit time in Europe-China rail transportations. Being an overall transport infrastructure project, the BRI is not only about railways, but also concerns ports, pipelines, and roads — by which countries have become connected in new ways that are expected to have major effects on international trade (Brakman *et al.* 2019). The BRI has been a means for China to ensure the imports of energy and the exports of goods by land in case maritime routes were closed, but also to ensure the functioning of its maritime transport by investing in ports around the world. The geographical coverage of the BRI has expanded, and it covers 145 countries in Asia, Pacific, Europe and Africa by late 2021 (EBRD 2020; FIFS 2021).

In rail infrastructure, the opening of several routes through Kazakhstan as a shorter alternative to the traditional Trans-Siberian route, in addition to infrastructure development in China's interior, have significantly improved freight transport capacity within China (Yang and McCarthy 2013; Kettunen 2019; Alvstam 2020). Investment in better reloading terminals at the borders between China and Kazakhstan and between Belarus and Poland have decreased the average transit time by rail between Central Europe and Eastern China from about 36 days in 2006 to 12–18 days within a decade (Hillman 2018). Therefore, the use of Europe-China rail transportations grew before the pandemic as a result of China's policy to develop the routes. The connections had grown since the early 2000s (Hilmola *et al.* 2021), and European companies were increasingly interested in using container block train transports between Europe and China, and further motivated by China's financial support for using the routes.

The first regular connections in rail freight services were opened between Leipzig/Wackersdorf and Shenyang in 2010, followed by Duisburg-Chongqing in 2012, Zhengzhou-Hamburg in 2013, and Madrid-Yiwu and Poland-Suzhou in 2014 (Ruppik 2015). The connections were operated by European and Chinese service providers, such as DB Schenker Rail Automotive, YuXinOu (Chongqing) Logistics joint venture, Trans Eurasia Logistics, InterRail Services, and the Chinese ZIH (Zhengzhou International Hub Development and Construction Co., Ltd). The speed of rail transportations increased and became an advantage compared to maritime transports. For example, the transit time of DHL's service from Xi'an to Neuss/Hamburg was cut to just 10–12 days (Love 2020).

However, the rail freight volumes are still small compared to maritime transports. The capacity of container trains running through the Eurasian continent is ca. 100 TEUs[2] (Pieriegud 2019), which, although being more than the capacity of airplanes or trucks (ca. two TEUs), is far less than the capacity of ultra large container vessels, over 23,000 TEUs (WMN 2019). Before the current logistics disruption, it was estimated that the potential throughput of rail connections would remain only a small fraction, 1–2% of the maritime transport in Europe-China trade (Rastogi and Arvis 2014). Nowadays the expectations are somewhat higher although rail transportations will likely never replace sea transport in global trade.

Rail transports are challenged by technical inhibitors such as differences in rail gauge (track width) along the rail routes between Europe and China (Rodemann and Templar 2014). The containers must be moved from one train to another at the borders of Kazakhstan, Russia and Belorussia that have a different gauge from China and Western Europe. Another problem has been the negative image of the Eurasian rail freight regarding safety and security. The possibility of theft, loss, damage, and corruption is high when transportation involves many handling

2 TEU is a measure for capacity in container transportation and stands for "twenty-foot equivalent unit" based on a 20-foot (6.1 metres) long standard-sized intermodal container.

operations (Witlox and Vandaele 2005). The functioning of the rail routes is thus affected by the different railway systems (e.g. Griffiths 2017; Kuester 2017; Griffiths 2019) and the institutional environments of the countries along the route.

When it comes to Finnish rail connections to China, the potential seems evident yet we do not find many analyses, as prior research is relatively scarce. In the early 2000s, this route was not extensively used by Nordic firms, although some growth was expected (Hilmola and Szekely 2006; Hilmola *et al.* 2010). Concerning different route options between Kouvola and China, the one through Kazakhstan gave a shorter lead time, a supply chain cost advantage and a better catchment area of Chinese consumers compared to the Trans-Siberian Railway (Hilmola *et al.* 2018). However, using railways for imports to the Nordics was challenging due to the required sea and road links to Sweden, Denmark and Norway, which led to a cost disadvantage (Hilmola *et al.* 2018). The studies offer interesting results that call for further research. In particular, we observe a lack of research on the current use of Finnish rail connections to China by Finnish and other Nordic firms. This is even more relevant because of the contemporary global logistics situation where supply chains have been cut and maritime transports challenged.

Therefore, we explore the contemporary Finnish rail connections to China and focus on their development, relevance and future outlook. We discuss the opening and operation of the connections and the impact of policies and global logistics disruption on the present state of the transports.

11.2.3. *Data and method of the study*

The data for the study was gathered mainly from news materials and press releases, and complemented with expert interviews and company data covering a timeframe of 2014–2022. The main material was collected from publicly available online sources, including newspaper articles, professional magazine articles, exporting companies' press releases, logistics providers' press releases, and industry webpages and portals, most of which are in Finnish. The method of gathering the online material was to use the Google search engine with keywords such as "Kiina" (China), "juna" (train), and "kontti" (container). Altogether, 40 pieces were found relevant and selected for analysis, 33 of which are in Finnish and seven in English. The news sources include outputs from Finland's major media houses, such as the Finnish broadcasting company YLE, Finnish commercial broadcasting company MTV3, major newspapers, and logistics news portals.

Four personal interviews were conducted in 2020–2021 and further information was obtained from a logistics webinar in 2022 to complement the data. The interviewees included trade policy officers from the EU and Finland, the managing director of a Finnish importing company, and a scholar. The semi-structured interviews lasted ca. one hour and dealt with the development of the connections, the policies of the EU, Finland and China, and the global logistics situation. Interviews were tape-recorded and careful notes were made on each interview. The webinar presentation was given by the managing director of a logistics service provider in an event organized by the Finnish Chamber of Commerce in March 2022. The interviews and the company presentation are anonymized for citations for confidentiality.

Data from these sources was examined using the method of qualitative content analysis. The method is suitable for studying emerging themes and concepts from text data, such as news pieces and press releases. For the analysis, the text material was coded, i.e., statements from the text were grouped into categories according to key phrases, such as "Logistics service providers", "The Helsinki connection", or "Companies using rail transport". This was done manually, and it resulted in a document of 17 pages (5,500 words). The statements were arranged under the codes, and new codes were created for relevant information as the work proceeded. Contradicting information was analyzed to come up with an interpretation of the facts, whereas parallel findings from different sources were considered to strengthen the evidence.

In the following empirical section of the paper, we present a narrative of the development of Finnish rail connections to China and elaborate on the impacts of connectivity policies and global logistics disruption on their current state. References to the news sources are given in the text marked with "#" preceding the reference (for example, #Kaleva 2017) to distinguish them from other references. The list of the news sources is presented separately in the References. References to interviews and the company presentation are numbered for citations (for example, Interview#1).

11.3. Finnish rail transport routes to China along the Eurasian Land Bridge

11.3.1. *Before the regular connections*

A few years before the opening of the Kouvola and Helsinki connections, there had been some sporadic rail transportations from Eastern Finnish border station Niirala to China. Located close to the city of Joensuu, Niirala is the only international border station of the North Karelia province. The exported items included pulp and timber, typical Finnish forestry industry products. In May 2015, Stora Enso, the Finnish-Swedish producer of board, biomaterials and paper delivered pulp from its Finnish mill by railway through Russia to Korla, close to

Urumqi in Xinjiang province in Northwestern China. Later in the same year, high level discussions were held for state level cooperation in the operation of the route. The Finnish and Russian customs, the state railways and provincial authorities were jointly negotiating on future cooperation to develop rail transportations from Finland to China (#Karjalainen 2015).

In 2017, there was similarly a transportation of pulp bales from Stora-Enso's pulp mill Enocell in Uimaharju, North Karelia province. The train carried 50 containers that were 40 feet each, amounting to a total length of 800 meters, and set off in November 2017 from Niirala border station. This was the first whole train transportation operated by Nurminen Logistics along the route through Russia and Kazakhstan to central China and was estimated to take ca. 10–12 days. Nurminen Logistics is one of Finland's oldest and largest private logistics service operators specialized in transports to Russia, the Baltic states, and China. The delivery was carried out in cooperation with Russian, Kazakhstani and Chinese collaborators; for example, the containers were owned by a Chinese company. It was further estimated that the route may be suitable for the exports of metal and food products to China and the imports of seasonal products from China (#Lundén 2017). Nurminen Logistics was using its terminal in Niirala for the loading of the cargo. The terminal had sufficient rail capacity and was located close to the border station at a logistically central place for the export industries in Eastern Finland (#Vali 2017).

At the time, Nurminen Logistics was developing the Niirala connection to China and was planning to operate one full train a month on this route. The company was ready to invest in this location in case there was further demand for the trains bound to China. The expected deliveries would consist of mass products such as pulp, paper, timber and mechanical engineering products, and the train would be filled with one type of product to ease bureaucracy on the Chinese side (#Kämppi 2017). However, the deliveries from Niirala discontinued afterwards, and in 2019, Nurminen Logistics sold its local terminals to Tohmajärvi municipality and Cemagro Oy, a fertilizer producer company (#Nurminen Logistics 2019). Since then, Nurminen Logistics has operated the Helsinki route and has used the Vainikkala border station facing the Russian Buslovskaya station in its transportations between Finland and China.

11.3.2. *The start of regular transports*

Two main Finnish connections to China, from Kouvola in Southeast Finland and from the capital city Helsinki, were opened concurrently in the late 2010s. This was based on local initiatives to benefit from China's policy that supported the development and use of Europe-China rail routes; it was not part of Finland's or the EU's policy (Interview#1).

The first regular container train connection was opened from Kouvola to Xi'an in 2017. It was initiated by the city of Kouvola and its development corporation Kouvola Innovation Oy, with funding from the EU to build a new intermodal logistics terminal that would combine different transport modes. The loading and forwarding on the Finnish side were operated by Kouvola Cargo Handling. Transportation along the route was operated by its international partners Kazakhstan Railways' freight company KTZ Express (#Kaleva 2017) and later the Russian TransContainer, and since spring 2019, by a Russian-Kazakhstani service provider Logbox (#Tahkokorpi 2019). The plan for the new terminal was based on Kouvola being the only locality in Finland with a rail-and-road terminal that is part of the European TEN-T core network (#Suominen 2017; #Anteroinen 2018). The plan implies that cargo trains as long as 1100 meters could enter the terminal for unloading and reloading.

The first container train set off from Kouvola to Xi'an in early November 2017 with high media visibility. The train had 41 containers carrying timber, mechanical engineering products, working clothes, and components for shipbuilding. It was operated by the Kazakhstan state railways' representative in the Nordic countries, Unytrade Oy. The return trip was planned for late November and was to carry electronics from China to Finland (#Niemi 2017). The second delivery from Kouvola set off in mid-December, and the third, in late December, was operated by a new international partner, the Russian logistics company TransContainer. This was a whole-train transportation of one product, timber from Versowood, Finland's largest private sawn timber producer. The delivery was carried along the Trans-Siberian route with estimated arrival to China in two weeks. The length of the train was ca. 800 meters and it carried 41 containers filled with ca. 2,000 m^3 of sawn timber (#Versowood 2017). However, at the time, most Finnish timber exports to China were transported by sea to China's coastal regions and then delivered landbound to inland locations.

Altogether, in 2018, in 24 trains departed from Kouvola to Xi'an as claimed by Unytrade (#Skön 2019a,b). Many of the containers were however half-empty and were thus carrying "a lot of air". According to Unytrade, this was due to the decline in the price of pulp and the deteriorating economic situation in China (#Skön 2019a). In 2019 only five trains set off to China[3] and Kouvola Innovation reported about the change of the operator after KTZ Express stopped deliveries in spring 2019 and there was no traffic for a few months. The new operator was the Russian-Kazakhstani service provider Logbox, and regular transportations were to be started

3 Information on the number of departing trains in 2019 differs between the sources: while #Tahkokorpi (2019) reported five trains until mid-2019, #Tanskanen & Väisänen (2020) reported three for the whole year.

again in October on a monthly basis (#Tahkokorpi 2019). However, the connection seems to have faded since then, and there is no information on transportations from Kouvola to China since 2020.

In the meantime, the Helsinki-Hefei route was opened in 2018 as the second regular connection from Finland to China. It was developed by the private service provider Nurminen Logistics located in the Helsinki Vuosaari harbor. The company had signed a letter of intent in 2014 for operating the route to China in cooperation with UTLC, a joint-venture of the Russian, Kazakhstan and Belarusian state railways. The connection would run from Helsinki via Kazakhstan and was expected to shorten the transport time from 80 days by sea to 20 days by rail (#Cision 2014; #Hämäläinen 2019). The Vuosaari cargo harbor is connected to Finland's interior by a railroad for transports of freight, such as pulp from mills in different parts of Finland.

The regular deliveries were started in late November 2018 by an incoming container train from China to the Helsinki Vuosaari terminal. The first cargo train from Helsinki to Hefei departed in early December and was expected to take 14 days. These were not whole-train transportations for one customer company, but open for all companies to book space in the containers. Nurminen Logistics and their representative in China provided all logistics services, including forwarding, loading and door-to-door transportation (#Leino 2018).

In 2019, the Helsinki connection became established for regular rail container service with departures offered every two weeks. Altogether 26 container trains did a return trip to China, with transport time shortened to 14 days. The service provider Nurminen Logistics was content with the functioning of the route through Kazakhstan and Russia and considered that the deliveries were punctual and reliable (#Calcus 2019). In spring 2020, the trains were sold out as factories in China were opened after the Chinese New Year and the first lockdown of the Covid-19 pandemic, and both air and maritime transports had been disrupted. Therefore, the demand for rail transports increased significantly among Finnish exporters and importers, and the trains were fully booked several weeks in advance. The length of trains was increased to almost one kilometer, the maximum length that railway yards can accommodate. While operating a biweekly service of 26 departures in both directions in 2020, the goal of Nurminen Logistics was to have a weekly connection to China, as their customers had asked for additional trains for the route (#Tanskanen and Väisänen 2020).

The development of the two Finland-China rail connections was affected by public sector policies on connectivity, as well as the global logistics disruption. We discuss these two explanations for the current state of the connections next.

11.3.3. *The impact of the connectivity policies*

Both the Kouvola and Helsinki connections have used the route that runs through Russia and Kazakhstan and was partly developed with BRI loans. The length of the Kouvola-Xi'an route is over 8,000 km and the Helsinki-Hefei route passing through Xi'an is over 9,000 km. The whole route is electrified, and Kazakhstan for example has invested massively in its border terminals, electric engines, and electric railways. The connection benefits from the same track width all the way from Finland to the Chinese border – an advantage compared to the routes that start from other European countries (#MTV 2017).

The opening of both the Kouvola and Helsinki connections was spurred by China's BRI policy to financially support the use of the Eurasian Land Bridge rail transport (Interview#2). This support was granted by China to increase trade with Europe and it lowered the freight prices close to those in maritime shipping (van Leijen 2019; EUCCC 2020). Therefore, the price paid by European operators may have halved and enabled profitable container train transportations (#Skön 2019a). The number of Europe-China railway connections increased rapidly, but also led to problems and less profitable business, such as in Kouvola. The development of the Kouvola connection was heavily grounded on public funding both from the Kouvola city, the EU and China. The support led to nearly empty trains moving between the regions, which resulted in a change in China's policy to tighten the regulations for the support in 2018 (van Leijen 2018; #Skön 2019a,b). It appears that China took away this support altogether in 2020 and the freight price was increased by 60–70% (Interview#3).

Despite this change, the city of Kouvola was investing heavily to build Finland's longest loading platform for the new intermodal terminal (#Tanskanen and Väisänen 2020). The platform would accommodate trains of up to 1100 meters of length – although the longest trains do not need this capacity yet – in a terminal that would combine different modes of transport. The construction of the terminal was estimated to cost 40 million euros, of which the EU funding covered almost eight million euros (#Skön 2019b). The city of Kouvola expected the terminal to be ready by 2023 (#Kouvola 2019).

Originally, the Kouvola-China connection was planned to serve not only Finnish firms, but also other Nordic and European companies (#Rönkkö 2017). This was seemingly also one basis for getting public funding for the development of the terminal. In 2017, the representatives of Unytrade and Kouvola Innovation had expected that ca. 75% of the containers coming from China would continue from Kouvola to other Nordic countries and to Central Europe. This option was also marketed to companies, as the route from China to Germany was said to be very busy and stuck already (#Rönkkö 2017). Kouvola Innovation stated they had negotiated cooperation agreements to serve Swedish and Norwegian companies by offering a connection between North Europe and Asia, and they were also ready to help the companies to locate in Kouvola (#Anteroinen 2018). However, there is no evidence on the realization of these plans.

Geographically, the location of Kouvola is ideal as a logistics hub for eastbound traffic, with its rail connections in many directions including Finland's main pulp mills, whereas Helsinki's location is better for attracting traffic e.g. from Sweden with reloading directly in the port area. It seems that the Kouvola connection did not find an adequate customer base in Finland let alone in China. According to Kouvola Innovation, it was hard to receive cargo from Xi'an and they could not do much about it. The core problem appears to be the lack of experience in international logistics and in doing business in China. The development of the connection was heavily supported by public funding and the negotiations on establishing the route and its marketing were taken care of by civil servants of the city (#Skön 2019a,b) who potentially lack business networks and the competence needed for profitable international business. Therefore, the development of the Kouvola connection appears more of an urban development project than a transport project. In the recent past, the city had also been a location for a China Center and "used to have good relations with China", whereas the current cargo terminal has mostly served Finland's trade with Russia (Interview#2).

11.3.4. *The impact of the pandemic and global logistics disruption*

According to data, in comparison, the Helsinki connection has expanded and has benefited from the increased demand for rail transport due to the global pandemic and the logistics disruption. It is operated by a long-established service provider Nurminen Logistics, a listed company founded in 1886 that has a wide cooperation network, a growing client base, and experience in international operations. The company had an agent in China to sell freight to Finland and was able to offer a regular connection for the transportations since the beginning (#Skön 2019a).

The increased demand has also led to diversification of the products transported and geographical extensions of the connection both in the Nordics, China and in broader Asia. In early 2020, Nurminen Logistics planned for the transporting of foodstuffs, and a train from Helsinki was prepared to carry a trial consignment of food in special cooled cars that became possible after Russia removed sanctions on the through transports of foodstuffs (#Lukkari 2020). However, the delivery was not realized due to bureaucratic problems in the Russian border controls and in import permits to China (Interview#1). The trains instead carried industrial accessories and pulp to China, and returning trains brought components for Finnish manufacturing industries, as well as healthcare accessories, such as respirator masks needed for the

Covid-19 pandemic. According to Nurminen Logistics, some of their customers wanted to permanently switch from air freight to rails, as the transit time for container trains had markedly shortened (#Tanskanen and Väisänen 2020).

The company was also interested in serving other Nordic countries and stated that customers in the Nordics were pushing the logistics sector to renew faster, and that the company wanted to develop more optimized solutions for consumers in different countries (#Vali 2019). In autumn 2020, Nurminen Logistics began cooperation with Narvik harbor to transport salmon from Norway to China in the future. The Russia route was the only option to transport frozen goods; this was not possible through Kazakhstan (Interview#1). However, these transports were not realized and instead, new routes were opened from Helsinki to Chongqing, Suzhou, Ningbo and Jinan (#Nurminen Logistics 2021a). The company started to operate whole-train transportations to some locations in China for single customers according to demand, and the connection to Chongqing became very active with weekly departures in spring 2021. A new connection was opened from the Finnish Kotka harbor to China, with two to three monthly departures in both directions (#Nurminen Logistics 2021b,c), as well as a further connection via the Trans-Siberian Railway to Japan and Korea with an export delivery of a large Swedish firm to Yokohama (#Osto&Logistiikka 2021). Earlier, the rail route from Korea had not been viable compared to maritime transports (Interview#4). In late 2021 Nurminen Logistics disclosed new cooperation with Swedish operators to offer container block train services to China, and as a milestone, it brought the millionth container from Chongqing to Helsinki carrying car components, retail equipment, and consumer goods (#Nurminen Logistics 2021d,e).

The Helsinki connection has managed to overcome the problems with the global container situation. While most of Europe had an excess number of containers in domestic harbors and a lack of containers for incoming imports from China, Finland lacked containers mostly for the exports to North America (Ojala *et al.* 2021) and later also in the eastward direction. The Helsinki connection started to operate incoming freight from China bound to Central Europe in late 2021. As the maritime shipping crisis had led to ships waiting for access to harbors, and transports were transferred to railways, traffic jams were growing in Europe-China rail routes and in European rail cargo terminals (#Tanskanen 2021).

The Helsinki connection has continued to operate in the geopolitically tense situation at the time of writing in spring 2022. Direct container ship routes were opened from Helsinki to Sweden, and a cooperation agreement with the Kazakh State Railways was signed to develop the Trans-Caspian International Transport Route. The route starts from China and Southeast Asia and runs through Kazakhstan, Azerbaijan and Georgia to Central Europe (#Nurminen Logistics 2022a,b). With the foreseeable problems in maritime transportation and the possible further development of rail connections, transit through Eurasia may still double or triple (Interview#3). China is expected to continue investing in railways due to the constant threat of military conflict in the South China Sea (Interview#3). The sanctions on Russia after its military offensive in Ukraine in spring 2022 did not instantly affect the Finland-China deliveries because the cargo is only handled at the end-points and the customers are from the West and from China (Presentation#1). However, the situation may quickly change due to developments in global and regional geopolitics.

In summary, the Helsinki connection has been able to capitalize on the global changes in logistical systems. The route extension to Sweden and the planned one to Norway may further increase the demand for rail transports between Finland and China in case the main route continues to operate.

11.4. Conclusion

We explored the development of container train transportations between Finland and China from the perspective of Finnish and other Nordic firms. The aim was to investigate the impact of European and Chinese connectivity policies and the global logistics crisis on the development of the northernmost regular rail transport connections from Europe to China. We found that the two regular connections from Finland – i.e. Kouvola-Xi'an and Helsinki-Hefei – benefited from the Chinese BRI policy and its financial support for Europe-China rail transports. Whereas the Kouvola connection then faded due to problems in managing international cooperation. The Helsinki connection was able to seize the business potential caused by the Covid-19 pandemic and the resulting global maritime logistics disruption and has grown continuously up to spring 2022.

This study contributes to prior research by narrating "the tale of two routes", their origins, development, rationales, the products transported and the extensions of the routes. The developments are explained both by policies and the radical changes in global logistics systems due to Covid-19 that strongly affected the freight prices, not foreseen in the former cheap sea freight context (cf. Brakman *et al.* 2019; Pomfret 2019; Buckley 2020). Local policies were found decisive in the Kouvola case, whereas China's BRI policy has supported all Europe-China routes, and the Helsinki case indicates how a rail logistics operator seizes a business opportunity resulting from disruption in global maritime shipping. While the Kouvola connection has seemingly suffered from a lack of logistics business experience and relevant international connections, the Helsinki connection is operated by an established private logistics service provider with a long experience in international transportations and the needed cooperation network abroad. Another difference between the two is related to a geographical dimension. The developers of the

Kouvola connection are bound to this particular location and focus on developing the planned intermodal terminal in the city, whereas Nurminen Logistics is an agile operator that can move and operate a network in several locations. Therefore, two different rationales appear to be directing the development in the two locations: an urban development rationale in Kouvola, compared to a logistics business rationale in Helsinki.

The products transported have included Finnish exports of engineering and forest industries such as mechanical engineering products, components for shipbuilding, pulp, paper, and industrial accessories. Returning trains have brought electronics, components for Finnish manufacturing industries, healthcare accessories, car components, and consumer goods. Since China is Finland's biggest trade partner outside the EU and Finnish firms are dependent on imports of components from China, rail transports have been crucial in ensuring the functioning of supply chains. In addition, some of the production networks have been relocated back to Europe and domestic supply chains have been recreated.

Available data showed that the Finland-China rail connections have mainly been used by Finnish exporters and importers, but have also appeared to become relevant to other Nordic companies, and the Helsinki connection has recently been extended with sea routes to Sweden. The use of sea routes is based on the geography of the region: with the exception of Northern Norway that can be accessed by rail through Finland and Sweden, major cities in the Nordic countries are more easily accessed by sea, either directly from global maritime routes or from the Baltic Sea.

It is likely that the global logistics system will continue to suffer from the maritime transport crisis, which will further increase the need for rail transports. Yet the impact of geopolitics is hard to foresee in the current politically tense situation, where the connections between Europe and China, as well as broader Asia, are challenged.

11.5. References

Alvstam, C.G. (2020). Belts and roads: The geopolitics and transport geography of the China–European seaborne trade. In *Geographies of Maritime Transport*, Wilmsmeier, G. and Monios, J. (eds). Edward Elgar, Cheltenham.

Anwar, S.T. (2020). Global strategy gone astray: Maersk's big box boats and the world shipping industry. *Thunderbird International Business Review*, 62(2), 183–196.

Brakman, S., Frankopan, P., Garretsen, H., van Marrewijk, C. (2019). The New Silk Roads: An introduction to China's belt and road initiative. *Cambridge Journal of Regions, Economy and Society*, 12, 3–16.

Buckley, P.J. (2020). China's belt and road initiative and the Covid-19 crisis. *Journal of International Business Policy*, 3(3), 311–314.

Drewry (2021). World Container Index – 8 April 21 [Online]. Available at: https://www.drewry.co.uk/supply-chain-advisors/supply-chain-expertise/world-container-index-assessed-by-drewry [Accessed 15 April 2021].

Drewry (2022). World Container Index – 10 Mar 22 [Online]. Available at: https://www.drewry.co.uk/supply-chain-advisors/supply-chain-expertise/world-container-index-assessed-by-drewry [Accessed 14 March 2022].

Dunford, M. and Liu, W. (2019). Chinese perspectives on the belt and road initiative. *Cambridge Journal of Regions, Economy and Society*, 12(1), 145–167.

EBRD (2020). Belt and Road Initiative (BRI) [Online]. Available at: https://www.ebrd.com/what-we-do/belt-and-road/overview.html [Accessed 14 March 2022].

EC (2021). Global gateway: Up to €300 billion for the European Union's strategy to boost sustainable links around the world. Press release, European Commission, 1 December [Online]. Available at: https://ec.europa.eu/commission/presscorner/detail/en/ip_21_6433 [Accessed 9 March 2022].

EC (2022). The EU-China Connectivity Platform. *European Commission, Mobility and Transport* [Online]. Available at: https://transport.ec.europa.eu/transport-themes/international-relations/eu-china-connectivity-platform_en [Accessed 17 March 2022].

Eng-Larsson, F. and Kohn, C. (2012). Modal shift for greener logistics – The shipper's perspective. *International Journal of Physical Distribution & Logistics Management*, 42(1), 36–59.

EUCCC (2020). The road less travelled. European Involvement in China's Belt and Road Initiative [Online]. Available at: https://www.europeanchamber.com.cn/en/publications-archive/762/The_Road_Less_Travelled_European_Involvement_in_China_s_Belt_and_Road_Initiative [Accessed 14 April 2022].

FIFS (2021). Countries of the Belt and Road Initiative (BRI) [Online]. Available: https://greenfdc.org/countries-of-the-belt-and-road-initiative-bri [Accessed 14 March 2022].

Frankopan, P. (2018). *The New Silk Roads — The Present and Future of the World.* Bloomsbury Publishing, London.

FT (2021). China's exporters hit by global shortage of shipping containers. *Financial Times*, 1 March [Online]. Available at: https://www.ft.com/content/71818164-9f74-48ad-af10-88c3acf30190 [Accessed 20 April 2021].

Griffiths, R.T. (2017). *Revitalising the Silk Road: China's Belt and Road Initiative.* HIPE Publications, Leiden.

Griffiths, R.T. (2019). *The New Silk Road: Challenge and Response.* HIPE Publications, Leiden.

Hillman, J.E. (2018). The rise of China-Europe railways. *Centre for Strategic and International Studies* [Online]. Available at: https://www.csis.org/analysis/rise-china-europe-railways.

Hilmola, O.-P. and Szekely, B. (2006). Logistics development in Finnish and Swedish companies with respect of Russia and four Asian countries: Traffic flow and warehousing analysis from current situation and likely development trends. Research report 175, Lappeenranta University of Technology, Lappeenranta.

Hilmola, O.-P., Ujvari, S., Torkkeli, M., Lorentz, H., Andersson, T. (2010). From Northern Europe to Russia and Asia, and vice versa: Traffic flow analysis – Current situation and development trends. *International Journal of Logistics Systems and Management*, 6(2), 205–217.

Hilmola, O.-P., Henttu, V., Panova, Y. (2018). Development of Asian Landbridge from Finland: Current state and future prospects. *22nd Cambridge International Manufacturing Symposium*, 27–28 September, University of Cambridge.

Hilmola, O.-P., Li, W., Panova, Y. (2021). Development status and future trends for Eurasian container land bridge transport. *Logistics*, 5(1), 18 [Online]. Available at: https://doi.org/10.3390/logistics5010018.

Karjalainen, T. (2022). The EU's Global Gateway. Building connectivity as a policy. FIIA Working Paper 127, The Finnish Institute of International Affairs, Helsinki.

Kettunen, E. (2019). The one belt one road initiative and the changing multi-scalar governance of trade in China. In *Mapping China's One Belt One Road Initiative*, Li, X. (ed.). Palgrave Macmillan, Cham.

Kuester, F. (2017). The New Silk Road – The vision of an interconnected Eurasia. *Combined Transport Magazine*, 10 January [Online]. Available: https://combined-transport.eu/the-new-silk-road-obor [Accessed 22 May 2020].

Laporte, G., Ghiani, G., Musmanno, R. (2013). *Introduction to Logistics Systems Management*, 2nd edition. John Wiley & Sons, Chichester.

van Leijen, M. (2018). Only fully loaded trains to depart from China. *Rail Freight*, 23 October [Online]. Available at: https://www.railfreight.com/beltandroad/2018/10/23/only-fully-loaded-trains-to-depart-from-china/ [Accessed 22 May 2020].

van Leijen, M. (2019). Chinese subsidies for the New Silk Road on a decline. *Rail Freight*, 1 October [Online]. Available at: https://www.railfreight.com/specials/2019/10/01/chinese-subsidies-for-the-new-silk-road-on-a-decline/ [Accessed 22 May 2020].

Levinson, M. (2016). *The Box: How the Shipping Container Made the World Smaller and the World Economy Bigger*, 2nd edition. Princeton University Press, Princeton, NJ.

Love, A. (2020). Inside DHL's new rail freight service between China and Germany. *Railway Technology*, 3 March [Online]. Available at: https://www.railway-technology.com/features/rail-freight-from-china-to-europe/ [Accessed 22 May 2020].

Maersk (2022). Schedules [Online]. Available at: https://www.maersk.com/schedules/ [Accessed 15 March 2022].

Mouritz, F. (2020). Implications of the Covid-19 pandemic on China's belt and road initiative. *Connections*, 19(2), 115–124.

Nurminen Logistics (2022). China–Northern Europe Railway Connection [Online]. Available at: https://www.nurminenlogistics.com/services/china-northern-europe-railway-connection/ [Accessed 15 March 2022].

Ojala, L., Paimander, A., Kairinen, I. (2021). Konttikuljetusten ajankohtaisselvitys. Toimeksiantaja: Huoltovarmuuskeskus, Helsinki. [Report on current container transports; in Finnish].

Petersson, N., Tenold, S., White, N. (2019). Shipping and globalization in the post-war era: Contexts, companies, connections. In *Shipping and Globalization in the Post-War Era: Contexts, Companies, Connections*, Petersson, N., Tenold, S., White, N. (eds). Palgrave Macmillan, Cham.

Pieriegud, J. (2019). Analysis of the potential of the development of rail container transport market in Poland. Final report, European Commission, DG for Regional and Urban *Policy*, Publications Office of the European Union, Luxembourg.

Pomfret, R. (2019). Eurasian Land Bridge: Linking regional value chains along the New Silk Road. *Cambridge Journal of Regions, Economy and Society*, 12, 45–56.

Rastogi, C. and Arvis, J.-F. (2014). The Eurasian connection. Supply-chain efficiency along the modern Silk Route through Central Asia. *The World Bank*, Washington, D.C.

Rodemann, H. and Templar, S. (2014). The enablers and inhibitors of intermodal rail freight between Asia and Europe. *Journal of Rail Transport Planning & Management*, 4(3), 70–86.

Rogerson, S., Andersson, D., Johansson, M.I. (2014). Influence of context on the purchasing process for freight transport services. *International Journal of Logistics Research and Applications*, 17(3), 232–248.

Ruppik, D. (2015). Growing business on the steel Silk Road. *Railway Gazette International*, 171(3), 44–47.

UNCTAD (2019). Review of maritime transport. *United Nations Conference for Trade and Development*, Geneva.

UNCTAD (2020). Review of maritime transport. *United Nations Conference for Trade and Development*, Geneva.

Wei, H. and Sheng, Z. (2018). Logistics connectivity considering import and export for Chinese inland regions in the 21st-century maritime Silk Road by dry ports. *Maritime Policy and Management*, 45(1), 53–70.

Witlox, F. and Vandaele, E. (2005). Determining the monetary value of quality attributes in freight transportation using a stated preference approach. *Transportation Planning and Technology*, 28(2), 77–92.

WMN (2019). MSC: Third 23,000 TEU boxship named in Bremerhaven. *World Maritime News*, 18 September [Online]. Available at: https://worldmaritimenews.com/archives/283386/msc-third-23000-teu-boxship-named-in-bremerhaven/ [Accessed 18 April 2022].

Yang, J. and McCarthy, P. (2013). Multi-modal transportation investment in Kazakhstan: Planning for trade and economic development in a post-soviet country. *Procedia – Social and Behavioral Sciences*, 96(6), 2105–2114.

Interviews and company presentation

Interview#1. Desk Officer on China, Finnish Ministry of Foreign Affairs, 10 December 2020 via Zoom.

Interview#2. Economic Affairs Adviser, European External Action Service, 12 February 2021 via Zoom.

Interview#3. Professor of Logistics, Finland, 25 February 2021 via Zoom.

Interview#4. Managing Director of a Finnish importer, 30 September 2021 via Zoom.

Presentation#1. Managing Director of a logistics service provider, 9 March 2022 webinar.

News pieces used in the empirical section

#Anteroinen, S. (2018). Railgate Finland rokkaa! Konttijuna kulkee Kiinaan kahdessa viikossa, kun laivalla siihen menisi kaksi kuukautta. *Kauppalehti*, 8 November [Online]. Available at: https://studio.kauppalehti.fi/studiovieras/railgate-finland-rokkaa.

#Calcus (2019). Säännöllinen raideyhteys kappaletavaralle Suomen ja Kiinan välille. *Calcus News* [Online]. Available at: https://news.calcus.com/nurminen-logistics/.

#Cision (2014). Uusi yhteistyö logistiikassa lyhentää kuljetusmatkaa Suomesta Kiinaan 60 päivällä. *Cision News*, 28 August [Online]. Available at: https://news.cision.com/fi/nurminen-logistics/r/uusi-yhteistyo-logistiikassa-lyhentaa-kuljetusmatkaa-suomesta-kiinaan-60-paivalla,c9683898.

#Hämäläinen, J. (2019). Helsingistä alkoi kulkea suora juna Kiinaan – yhteydestä haaveillaan jokaviikkoista. *Helsingin Uutiset*, 2 October [Online]. Available at: https://www.helsinginuutiset.fi/paikalliset/1201164.

#Kaleva (2017). Konttijunaliikenne Kouvolasta Kiinaan alkaa huomenna – yhteinen raideleveys Venäjän kanssa nopeuttaa rahdin kulkua. *Kaleva*, 9 November [Online]. Available at: https://www.kaleva.fi/uutiset/talous/konttijunaliikenne-kouvolasta-kiinaan-alkaa-huomenna-yhteinen-raideleveys-venajan-kanssa-nopeuttaa-rahdin-kulkua/775805/.

#Kämppi, M-L. (2017). Jättijuna puksuttanut Siperian halki Kiinaan – vientiyritykset miettivät matkan hintaa. *Yle uutiset*, 4 December [Online]. Available at: https://yle.fi/uutiset/3-9946329.

#Karjalainen (2015). Suomi ja Venäjä kehittävät yhdessä rautatiekuljetuksia Venäjän läpi Kiinaan. *Karjalainen*, 19 November [Online]. Available at: https://www.karjalainen.fi/uutiset/uutis-alueet/maakunta/item/90657.

#Kouvola (2019). Konttijunayhteys Kiinaan vakiintunut. *Kouvolan kaupunki*, 21 May [Online]. Available at: https://www.kouvola.fi/ajankohtaiset/konttijunayhteys-kiinaan-vakiintunut/.

#Leino, H. (2018). Rahti Kiinaan 14 päivässä. *Port of Helsinki*, 13 December [Online]. Available at: https://www.portofhelsinki.fi/verkkolehti/rahti-kiinaan-14-paivassa.

#Lukkari, E. (2020). Nurminen veisi Kiinan junalla elintarvikkeita. *Osto & Logistiikka*, 31 March [Online]. Available at: https://www.ostologistiikka.fi/kategoriat/kuljetukset/nurminen-veisi-kiinan-junalla-elintarvikkeita.

#Lundén, K. (2017). 50 konttia Uimaharjun sellua lähti aamujunassa Kiinaan. Rahtihinta nelinkertainen? *Maaseudun tulevaisuus*, 22 November [Online]. Available at: https://www.maaseuduntulevaisuus.fi/talous/artikkeli-1.214473.

#Mäki, E. (2019). Vuosaaresta Kiinaan kulkee suora junayhteys. *Helsingin Sanomat*, 6 October [Online]. Available at: https://www.hs.fi/kaupunki/art-2000006263302.html.

#MTV (2017). Silkkitie-rautatieyhteys Kiinasta Kouvolaan on avautumassa. *MTV uutiset*, 4 August [Online]. Available at: https://www.mtvuutiset.fi/artikkeli/silkkitie-rautatieyhteys-kiinasta-kouvolaan-on-avautumassa/6525302#gs.5w305x.

#Niemi, P. (2017). Ensimmäinen tavarajuna lähti Kouvolasta Kiinaan – historiallisella ensimatkalla mittaa 8 000 kilometriä. *Yle uutiset*, 10 November [Online]. Available at: https://yle.fi/uutiset/3-9919969.

#Nurminen Logistics (2019). Nurminen Logistics manages real estate property. Stock exchange release, 19 June [Online]. Available at: https://www.nurminenlogistics.com/stock-exchange-releases/nurminen-logistics-manages-real-estate-property/.

#Nurminen Logistics (2021a). Nurminen Logistics avaa kolme uutta junareittiä Kiinasta Suomeen. Press release, 20 January [Online]. Available at: https://www.nurminenlogistics.fi/uutiset/5322/.

#Nurminen Logistics (2021b). Uudet Juna-aikataulut on julkaistu. 10 March [Online]. Available at: https://www.nurminenlogistics.fi/uutiset/uudet-juna-aikataulut-on-julkaistu/.

#Nurminen Logistics (2021c). The Trans-Siberian route is stabilizing – Second train transportation to Japan, Vietnam, and Singapore. 17 May [Online]. Available at: https://www.nurminenlogistics.com/news/the-trans-siberian-route-is-stabilizing-second-train-transportation-to-japan-vietnam-and-singapore/.

#Nurminen Logistics (2021d). Nurminen Logistics Plc, NTEX AB and Stena Rederi, have signed a letter of intent to jointly increase their current co-operation and offer China container block train services. Press release, 13 December [Online]. Available at: https://www.nurminenlogistics.com/press-releases/nurminen-logistics-plc-ntex-ab-and-stena-rederi-have-signed-a-letter-of-intent-to-jointly-increase-their-current-co-operation-and-offer-china-container-block-train-services/.

#Nurminen Logistics (2021e). Container number 1 million from China via Russia to Europe in Nurminen Logistics container train. Press release, 14 December [Online]. Available at: https://www.nurminenlogistics.com/press-releases/container-number-1-million-from-china-via-russia-to-europe-in-nurminen-logistics-container-train/.

#Nurminen Logistics (2022a). Direct container ship from Helsinki to Sweden opens up new business opportunities. 27 January [Online]. Available at: https://www.nurminenlogistics.com/news/direct-container-ship-from-helsinki-to-sweden-opens-up-new-business-opportunities/.

#Nurminen Logistics (2022b). Nurminen Logistics Services Oy and Kazakh State Railways (KTZE) agreed on the commercialization of the Trans-Caspian International Transport Route between China and Europe. Press release, 16 March [Online]. Available at: https://www.nurminenlogistics.com/press-releases/nurminen-logistics-services-oy-and-kazakh-state-railways-ktze-agreed-on-the-commercialization-of-the-trans-caspian-international-transport-route-between-china-and-europe/.

#Osto&Logistiikka (2021). Nurminen Logisticsille uusia junayhteyksiä Aasiaan [Online]. Available at: https://www.ostologistiikka.fi/kategoriat/kuljetukset/nurminen-logisticsille-uusia-junayhteyksia-aasiaan.

#Pekkarinen, S. (2018). Ensimmäinen pelkästään sahatavaraa sisältävä juna Suomesta Kiinaan pääsi perille: Matkaa yli 8000 kilometriä. *Yle uutiset*, 16 January [Online]. Available at: https://yle.fi/uutiset/3-10024590.

#Railwaypro (2014). Nurminen Logistics (Finland) signed a cooperation agreement with UTLC. 23 September [Online]. Available at: https://www.railwaypro.com/wp/nurminen-logistics-finland-signed-a-cooperation-agreement-with-utlc/.

#Rönkkö, J. (2017). Kouvolan Kiina-yhteys kiinnostaa myös Keski-Euroopassa – Yhden kontin rahti Kiinaan on noin 4 000 euroa. *Kouvolan Sanomat*, 3 October [Online]. Available at: https://kouvolansanomat.fi/uutiset/lahella/0b1daacf-aae0-486f-af63-7d7e46f441bc.

#Skön, K. (2019a). Kouvolasta rakennettiin suora junayhteys Kiinaan – Kiinan valtio maksoi niin paljon tukea, että raiteilla kannatti kuljettaa liki tyhjiä kontteja. *MOT Yle*, 2 December [Online]. Available at: https://yle.fi/aihe/artikkeli/2019/12/02/kouvolasta-rakennettiin-suora-junayhteys-kiinaan-kiinan-valtio-maksoi-niin.

#Skön, K. (2019b). Kovan onnen kiskot Kouvolasta Kiinaan: Käsikirjoitus. *MOT Yle*, 2 December [Online]. Available at: https://yle.fi/aihe/artikkeli/2019/12/02/kovan-onnen-kiskot-kouvolasta-kiinaan-kasikirjoitus.

#Suominen, E. (2017). Junalla Kiinaan. *Konepörssi*, 28 September [Online]. Available at: https://koneporssi.com/kuljetuskalusto/junalla-kiinaan/.

#SVKK (2018). Nurminen Logistics myi venäläisen tytäryhtiönsä. *Suomalais-venäläinen kauppakamari*, 31 October [Online]. Available at: https://www.svkk.fi/uutishuone/nurminen-logistics-myi-venalaisen-tytaryhtionsa/.

#Tahkokorpi, M. (2019). Kouvolasta on lähtenyt Kiinaan tänä vuonna vasta viisi tavarajunaa – syynä operaattorin vaihtuminen. *Yle uutiset*, 20 August [Online]. Available at: https://yle.fi/uutiset/3-10929562.

#Tanskanen, J. (2021). Joululahjat ja muut verkkotilaukset seisovat nyt Keski-Euroopan rautateillä – pian raideruuhkaa puretaan tuomalla konttijunia Suomen satamiin. *Yle uutiset*, 18 October [Online]. Available at: https://yle.fi/uutiset/3-12147792.

#Tanskanen, J. and Väisänen, R. (2020). Konttijunat ovat nyt monille yrityksille ainoa keino saada tavara liikkumaan – junarahti Kiinan ja Suomen välillä ennätysvilkasta. *Yle uutiset*, 6 April [Online]. Available at: https://yle.fi/uutiset/3-11294355.

#TS (2017). Silkkitie-rautatieyhteys Kiinasta Suomeen on avautumassa. *Turun Sanomat*, 4 August [Online]. Available at: https://www.ts.fi/uutiset/kotimaa/3604871/Silkkitierautatieyhteys+Kiinasta+Suomeen+on+avautumassa.

#Turunen, J. (2017). Kolmas konttijuna vei kuusta Kiinaan – Kouvolasta lähteneestä kuljetuksesta vastaa venäläinen rahtiyritys. *Kouvolan Sanomat*, 28 December [Online]. Available at: https://kouvolansanomat.fi/uutiset/lahella/b9e54cce-70ad-49c9-a300-f55d4301aa3e.

#Turunen, A. (2018). Uusi silkkitie. *Voima*, 21 November [Online]. Available at: https://voima.fi/artikkeli/2018/uusi-silkkitie/.

#Vali, K. (2017). Nurminen Logistics järjestää kokojunakuljetuksen Suomesta Kiinaan. *Rautatieuutiset*, 22 November [Online]. Available at: http://www.rautatieuutiset.uutisparkki.com/wp/?p=1099.

#Vali, K. (2019). Nurminen Logisticsin Kiinan junan toinen toimintavuosi on käynnistynyt. *Rautatieuutiset*, 25 November [Online]. Available at: http://www.rautatieuutiset.uutisparkki.com/wp/?p=1799.

#Varova (2018). Uusi reittivaihtoehto Kiinan rautatiekuljetuksiin. *Kauppalehti*, 13 November [Online]. Available at: https://studio.kauppalehti.fi/studiovieras/varova-uusi-reittivaihtoehto-kiinan-rautatiekuljetuksiin.

#Versowood (2017). Ensimmäinen sahatavaraa täynnä oleva junakuljetus lähtee kohti Kiinaa. *Versowood News*, 22 December [Online]. Available at: https://www.versowood.fi/fi/konserni/uutiset-ja-tapahtumat/ensimmainen-sahatavaraa-taynna-oleva-junakuljetus-lahtee-kohti-kiinaa.

Conclusion

The overall objective of this edited book has been to offer critical insights into the current debate on connectivity during times of crisis. The world is gradually emerging from the Covid-19 pandemic which, in addition to the obvious international health crisis, has brought about significant disruptions in social and economic life. One of the critical lessons learned from all this is that connectivity matters. Central to this are innovation, investment, and technology – factors critical to economic recovery and a shift towards a more environmentally friendly approach to development while, at the same time, ensuring that the world stays connected. The global health crisis has revealed that more than ever before, ubiquitous connectivity underpinned by cutting-edge innovation and digital transformation are vital tools to ensure that things keep running remotely from an industrial, social and economic perspective.

We hope the themes addressed in this book provide the reader with a better understanding of complexity and different aspects of industrial connectivity in times of crisis.

Sam DZEVER

List of Authors

Claes G. ALVSTAM
University of Gothenburg
Sweden

Bernadette ANDREOSSO-O'CALLAGHAN
University of Limerick
Republic of Ireland
and
Ruhr University Bochum
Germany

Bart CAMBRÉ
Antwerp Management School
and
University of Antwerp
Belgium

Thi Ngoc DAO
Technological University Dublin
Republic of Ireland

Sam DZEVER
Institut Mines-Télécom Business School
LITEM – University of Paris-Saclay
Evry
France

Jana-Larissa GRZESZKOWIAK
Ruhr University Bochum
Germany

Fabian HÄNLE
Antwerp Management School
and
University of Antwerp
Belgium

Erja KETTUNEN
University of Turku
Finland

Junshi LI
University of Limerick
Republic of Ireland

Lucía MORALES
Technological University Dublin
Republic of Ireland

Sophie NIVOIX
University of Poitiers
France

Clare O'MAHONY
Technological University Dublin
Republic of Ireland

Vít PÁSZTO
Moravian Business College Olomouc
Czech Republic

Daniel RAJMIL
University Oberta de Catalunya
Barcelona
Spain

Louis-Caleb REMANDA
University of Paris-Saclay
France

Serge REY
University of Pau and Pays de l'Adour
France

Qin TANG
Ruhr University Bochum
Germany

Robert TAYLOR
University of Sheffield
UK

Stefanie WEIL
Antwerp Management School
and
University of Antwerp
Belgium

Yin XU
Central University of Finance
and Economics
Beijing
China

Miroslava ZAVADSKA
Moravian Business College Olomouc
Czech Republic

Jarmila ZIMMERMANNOVÁ
Moravian Business College Olomouc
Czech Republic

Index

F, G

H, I

K, L, M

N, O, P

Q, R

S

T, U

Other titles from

iSTE

in

Innovation, Entrepreneurship and Management

2022

AOUINAÏT Camille
Open Innovation Strategies (Smart Innovation Set – Volume 39)

BOUCHÉ Geneviève
Productive Economy, Contributory Economy: Governance Tools for the Third Millennium (Innovation and Technology Set – Volume 15)

HELLER David
Valuation of the Liability Structure by Real Options (Modern Finance, Management Innovation and Economic Growth Set – Volume 5)

MATHIEU Valérie
A Customer-oriented Manager for B2B Services: Principles and Implementation

NOËL Florent, SCHMIDT Géraldine
Employability and Industrial Mutations: Between Individual Trajectories and Organizational Strategic Planning (Technological Changes and Human Resources Set – Volume 4)

DE SAINT JULIEN Odile
The Innovation Ecosystem as a Source of Value Creation: A Value Creation Lever for Open Innovation (Diverse and Global Perspectives on Value Creation Set – Volume 4)

SALOFF-COSTE Michel
Innovation Ecosystems: The Future of Civilizations and the Civilization of the Future (Innovation and Technology Set – Volume 14)

VAYRE Emilie
Digitalization of Work: New Spaces and New Working Times (Technological Changes and Human Resources Set – Volume 5)

ZAFEIRIS Konstantinos N, SKIADIS Christos H, DIMOTIKALIS Yannis, KARAGRIGORIOU Alex, KARAGRIGORIOU-VONTA Christina
Data Analysis and Related Applications 1: Computational, Algorithmic and Applied Economic Data Analysis (Big Data, Artificial Intelligence and Data Analysis Set – Volume 9)
Data Analysis and Related Applications 2: Multivariate, Health and Demographic Data Analysis (Big Data, Artificial Intelligence and Data Analysis Set – Volume 10)

2021

ARCADE Jacques
Strategic Engineering (Innovation and Technology Set – Volume 11)

BÉRANGER Jérôme, RIZOULIÈRES Roland
The Digital Revolution in Health (Health and Innovation Set – Volume 2)

BOBILLIER CHAUMON Marc-Eric
Digital Transformations in the Challenge of Activity and Work: Understanding and Supporting Technological Changes (Technological Changes and Human Resources Set – Volume 3)

BUCLET Nicolas
Territorial Ecology and Socio-ecological Transition (Smart Innovation Set – Volume 34)

DIMOTIKALIS Yannis, KARAGRIGORIOU Alex, PARPOULA Christina, SKIADIS Christos H
Applied Modeling Techniques and Data Analysis 1: Computational Data Analysis Methods and Tools (Big Data, Artificial Intelligence and Data Analysis Set - Volume 7)
Applied Modeling Techniques and Data Analysis 2: Financial, Demographic, Stochastic and Statistical Models and Methods (Big Data, Artificial Intelligence and Data Analysis Set – Volume 8)

DISPAS Christophe, KAYANAKIS Georges, SERVEL Nicolas, STRIUKOVA Ludmila
Innovation and Financial Markets (Innovation between Risk and Reward Set – Volume 7)

ENJOLRAS Manon
Innovation and Export: The Joint Challenge of the Small Company (Smart Innovation Set – Volume 37)

FLEURY Sylvain, RICHIR Simon
Immersive Technologies to Accelerate Innovation: How Virtual and Augmented Reality Enables the Co-Creation of Concepts (Smart Innovation Set – Volume 38)

GIORGINI Pierre
The Contributory Revolution (Innovation and Technology Set – Volume 13)

GOGLIN Christian
Emotions and Values in Equity Crowdfunding Investment Choices 2: Modeling and Empirical Study

GRENIER Corinne, OIRY Ewan
Altering Frontiers: Organizational Innovations in Healthcare (Health and Innovation Set – Volume 1)

GUERRIER Claudine
Security and Its Challenges in the 21st Century (Innovation and Technology Set – Volume 12)

HELLER David
Performance of Valuation Methods in Financial Transactions (Modern Finance, Management Innovation and Economic Growth Set – Volume 4)

LEHMANN Paul-Jacques
Liberalism and Capitalism Today

SOULÉ Bastien, HALLÉ Julie, VIGNAL Bénédicte, BOUTROY Éric, NIER Olivier
Innovation in Sport: Innovation Trajectories and Process Optimization (Smart Innovation Set – Volume 35)

UZUNIDIS Dimitri, KASMI Fedoua, ADATTO Laurent
Innovation Economics, Engineering and Management Handbook 1: Main Themes
Innovation Economics, Engineering and Management Handbook 2: Special Themes

VALLIER Estelle
Innovation in Clusters: Science–Industry Relationships in the Face of Forced Advancement (Smart Innovation Set – Volume 36)

2020

ACH Yves-Alain, RMADI-SAÏD Sandra
Financial Information and Brand Value: Reflections, Challenges and Limitations

ANDREOSSO-O'CALLAGHAN Bernadette, DZEVER Sam, JAUSSAUD Jacques, TAYLOR Robert
Sustainable Development and Energy Transition in Europe and Asia (Innovation and Technology Set – Volume 9)

BEN SLIMANE Sonia, M'HENNI Hatem
Entrepreneurship and Development: Realities and Future Prospects (Smart Innovation Set – Volume 30)

CHOUTEAU Marianne, FOREST Joëlle, NGUYEN Céline
Innovation for Society: The P.S.I. Approach (Smart Innovation Set – Volume 28)

CORON Clotilde
Quantifying Human Resources: Uses and Analysis
(Technological Changes and Human Resources Set – Volume 2)

CORON Clotilde, GILBERT Patrick
Technological Change
(Technological Changes and Human Resources Set – Volume 1)

CERDIN Jean-Luc, PERETTI Jean-Marie
The Success of Apprenticeships: Views of Stakeholders on Training and Learning (Human Resources Management Set – Volume 3)

DELCHET-COCHET Karen
Circular Economy: From Waste Reduction to Value Creation
(Economic Growth Set – Volume 2)

DIDAY Edwin, GUAN Rong, SAPORTA Gilbert, WANG Huiwen
Advances in Data Science
(Big Data, Artificial Intelligence and Data Analysis Set – Volume 4)

DOS SANTOS PAULINO Victor
Innovation Trends in the Space Industry
(Smart Innovation Set – Volume 25)

GASMI Nacer
Corporate Innovation Strategies: Corporate Social Responsibility and Shared Value Creation
(Smart Innovation Set – Volume 33)

GOGLIN Christian
Emotions and Values in Equity Crowdfunding Investment Choices 1: Transdisciplinary Theoretical Approach

GUILHON Bernard
Venture Capital and the Financing of Innovation
(Innovation Between Risk and Reward Set – Volume 6)

LATOUCHE Pascal
Open Innovation: Human Set-up
(Innovation and Technology Set – Volume 10)

LIMA Marcos
Entrepreneurship and Innovation Education: Frameworks and Tools (Smart Innovation Set – Volume 32)

MACHADO Carolina, DAVIM J. Paulo
Sustainable Management for Managers and Engineers

MAKRIDES Andreas, KARAGRIGORIOU Alex, SKIADAS Christos H.
Data Analysis and Applications 3: Computational, Classification, Financial, Statistical and Stochastic Methods
(Big Data, Artificial Intelligence and Data Analysis Set – Volume 5)
Data Analysis and Applications 4: Financial Data Analysis and Methods
(Big Data, Artificial Intelligence and Data Analysis Set – Volume 6)

MASSOTTE Pierre, CORSI Patrick
Complex Decision-Making in Economy and Finance

MEUNIER François-Xavier
Dual Innovation Systems: Concepts, Tools and Methods
(Smart Innovation Set – Volume 31)

MICHAUD Thomas
Science Fiction and Innovation Design (Innovation in Engineering and Technology Set – Volume 6)

MONINO Jean-Louis
Data Control: Major Challenge for the Digital Society
(Smart Innovation Set – Volume 29)

MORLAT Clément
Sustainable Productive System: Eco-development versus Sustainable Development (Smart Innovation Set – Volume 26)

SAULAIS Pierre, ERMINE Jean-Louis
Knowledge Management in Innovative Companies 2: Understanding and Deploying a KM Plan within a Learning Organization
(Smart Innovation Set – Volume 27)

2019

AMENDOLA Mario, GAFFARD Jean-Luc
Disorder and Public Concern Around Globalization

BARBAROUX Pierre
Disruptive Technology and Defence Innovation Ecosystems
(Innovation in Engineering and Technology Set – Volume 5)

DOU Henri, JUILLET Alain, CLERC Philippe
Strategic Intelligence for the Future 1: A New Strategic and Operational Approach
Strategic Intelligence for the Future 2: A New Information Function Approach

FRIKHA Azza
Measurement in Marketing: Operationalization of Latent Constructs

FRIMOUSSE Soufyane
Innovation and Agility in the Digital Age
(Human Resources Management Set – Volume 2)

GAY Claudine, SZOSTAK Bérangère L.
Innovation and Creativity in SMEs: Challenges, Evolutions and Prospects
(Smart Innovation Set – Volume 21)

GORIA Stéphane, HUMBERT Pierre, ROUSSEL Benoît
Information, Knowledge and Agile Creativity
(Smart Innovation Set – Volume 22)

HELLER David
Investment Decision-making Using Optional Models
(Economic Growth Set – Volume 2)

HELLER David, DE CHADIRAC Sylvain, HALAOUI Lana, JOUVET Camille
The Emergence of Start-ups
(Economic Growth Set – Volume 1)

HÉRAUD Jean-Alain, KERR Fiona, BURGER-HELMCHEN Thierry
Creative Management of Complex Systems
(Smart Innovation Set – Volume 19)

LATOUCHE Pascal
Open Innovation: Corporate Incubator
(Innovation and Technology Set – Volume 7)

LEHMANN Paul-Jacques
The Future of the Euro Currency

LEIGNEL Jean-Louis, MÉNAGER Emmanuel, YABLONSKY Serge
Sustainable Enterprise Performance: A Comprehensive Evaluation Method

LIÈVRE Pascal, AUBRY Monique, GAREL Gilles
Management of Extreme Situations: From Polar Expeditions to Exploration-Oriented Organizations

MILLOT Michel
Embarrassment of Product Choices 2: Towards a Society of Well-being

N'GOALA Gilles, PEZ-PÉRARD Virginie, PRIM-ALLAZ Isabelle
Augmented Customer Strategy: CRM in the Digital Age

NIKOLOVA Blagovesta
The RRI Challenge: Responsibilization in a State of Tension with Market Regulation
(Innovation and Responsibility Set – Volume 3)

PELLEGRIN-BOUCHER Estelle, ROY Pierre
Innovation in the Cultural and Creative Industries
(Innovation and Technology Set – Volume 8)

PRIOLON Joël
Financial Markets for Commodities

QUINIOU Matthieu
Blockchain: The Advent of Disintermediation

RAVIX Joël-Thomas, DESCHAMPS Marc
Innovation and Industrial Policies
(Innovation between Risk and Reward Set – Volume 5)

ROGER Alain, VINOT Didier
Skills Management: New Applications, New Questions
(Human Resources Management Set – Volume 1)

SAULAIS Pierre, ERMINE Jean-Louis
Knowledge Management in Innovative Companies 1: Understanding and Deploying a KM Plan within a Learning Organization
(Smart Innovation Set – Volume 23)

SERVAJEAN-HILST Romaric
Co-innovation Dynamics: The Management of Client-Supplier Interactions for Open Innovation
(Smart Innovation Set – Volume 20)

SKIADAS Christos H., BOZEMAN James R.
Data Analysis and Applications 1: Clustering and Regression, Modeling-estimating, Forecasting and Data Mining
(Big Data, Artificial Intelligence and Data Analysis Set – Volume 2)
Data Analysis and Applications 2: Utilization of Results in Europe and Other Topics
(Big Data, Artificial Intelligence and Data Analysis Set – Volume 3)

UZUNIDIS Dimitri
Systemic Innovation: Entrepreneurial Strategies and Market Dynamics

VIGEZZI Michel
World Industrialization: Shared Inventions, Competitive Innovations and Social Dynamics
(Smart Innovation Set – Volume 24)

2018

BURKHARDT Kirsten
Private Equity Firms: Their Role in the Formation of Strategic Alliances

CALLENS Stéphane
Creative Globalization
(Smart Innovation Set – Volume 16)

CASADELLA Vanessa
Innovation Systems in Emerging Economies: MINT – Mexico, Indonesia, Nigeria, Turkey
(Smart Innovation Set – Volume 18)

CHOUTEAU Marianne, FOREST Joëlle, NGUYEN Céline
Science, Technology and Innovation Culture
(Innovation in Engineering and Technology Set – Volume 3)

CORLOSQUET-HABART Marine, JANSSEN Jacques
Big Data for Insurance Companies
(Big Data, Artificial Intelligence and Data Analysis Set – Volume 1)

CROS Françoise
Innovation and Society
(Smart Innovation Set – Volume 15)

DEBREF Romain
Environmental Innovation and Ecodesign: Certainties and Controversies
(Smart Innovation Set – Volume 17)

DOMINGUEZ Noémie
SME Internationalization Strategies: Innovation to Conquer New Markets

ERMINE Jean-Louis
Knowledge Management: The Creative Loop
(Innovation and Technology Set – Volume 5)

GILBERT Patrick, BOBADILLA Natalia, GASTALDI Lise,
LE BOULAIRE Martine, LELEBINA Olga
Innovation, Research and Development Management

IBRAHIMI Mohammed
Mergers & Acquisitions: Theory, Strategy, Finance

LEMAÎTRE Denis
Training Engineers for Innovation

LÉVY Aldo, BEN BOUHENI Faten, AMMI Chantal
Financial Management: USGAAP and IFRS Standards
(Innovation and Technology Set – Volume 6)

MILLOT Michel
Embarrassment of Product Choices 1: How to Consume Differently

PANSERA Mario, OWEN Richard
Innovation and Development: The Politics at the Bottom of the Pyramid
(Innovation and Responsibility Set – Volume 2)

RICHEZ Yves
Corporate Talent Detection and Development

SACHETTI Philippe, ZUPPINGER Thibaud
New Technologies and Branding
(Innovation and Technology Set – Volume 4)

SAMIER Henri
Intuition, Creativity, Innovation

TEMPLE Ludovic, COMPAORÉ SAWADOGO Eveline M.F.W.
Innovation Processes in Agro-Ecological Transitions in Developing Countries
(Innovation in Engineering and Technology Set – Volume 2)

UZUNIDIS Dimitri
Collective Innovation Processes: Principles and Practices
(Innovation in Engineering and Technology Set – Volume 4)

VAN HOOREBEKE Delphine
The Management of Living Beings or Emo-management

2017

AÏT-EL-HADJ Smaïl
The Ongoing Technological System
(Smart Innovation Set – Volume 11)

BAUDRY Marc, DUMONT Béatrice
Patents: Prompting or Restricting Innovation?
(Smart Innovation Set – Volume 12)

BÉRARD Céline, TEYSSIER Christine
Risk Management: Lever for SME Development and Stakeholder Value Creation

CHALENÇON Ludivine
Location Strategies and Value Creation of International Mergers and Acquisitions

CHAUVEL Danièle, BORZILLO Stefano
The Innovative Company: An Ill-defined Object
(Innovation between Risk and Reward Set – Volume 1)

CORSI Patrick
Going Past Limits To Growth

D'ANDRIA Aude, GABARRET Inés
Building 21st Century Entrepreneurship
(Innovation and Technology Set – Volume 2)

DAIDJ Nabyla
Cooperation, Coopetition and Innovation
(Innovation and Technology Set – Volume 3)

FERNEZ-WALCH Sandrine
The Multiple Facets of Innovation Project Management
(Innovation between Risk and Reward Set – Volume 4)

FOREST Joëlle
Creative Rationality and Innovation
(Smart Innovation Set – Volume 14)

GUILHON Bernard
Innovation and Production Ecosystems
(Innovation between Risk and Reward Set – Volume 2)

HAMMOUDI Abdelhakim, DAIDJ Nabyla
Game Theory Approach to Managerial Strategies and Value Creation
(Diverse and Global Perspectives on Value Creation Set – Volume 3)

LALLEMENT Rémi
Intellectual Property and Innovation Protection: New Practices and New Policy Issues
(Innovation between Risk and Reward Set – Volume 3)

LAPERCHE Blandine
Enterprise Knowledge Capital
(Smart Innovation Set – Volume 13)

LEBERT Didier, EL YOUNSI Hafida
International Specialization Dynamics
(Smart Innovation Set – Volume 9)

MAESSCHALCK Marc
Reflexive Governance for Research and Innovative Knowledge
(Responsible Research and Innovation Set – Volume 6)

MASSOTTE Pierre
Ethics in Social Networking and Business 1: Theory, Practice and Current Recommendations
Ethics in Social Networking and Business 2: The Future and Changing Paradigms

MASSOTTE Pierre, CORSI Patrick
Smart Decisions in Complex Systems

MEDINA Mercedes, HERRERO Mónica, URGELLÉS Alicia
Current and Emerging Issues in the Audiovisual Industry
(Diverse and Global Perspectives on Value Creation Set – Volume 1)

MICHAUD Thomas
Innovation, Between Science and Science Fiction
(Smart Innovation Set – Volume 10)

PELLÉ Sophie
Business, Innovation and Responsibility
(Responsible Research and Innovation Set – Volume 7)

SAVIGNAC Emmanuelle
The Gamification of Work: The Use of Games in the Workplace

SUGAHARA Satoshi, DAIDJ Nabyla, USHIO Sumitaka
Value Creation in Management Accounting and Strategic Management: An Integrated Approach
(Diverse and Global Perspectives on Value Creation Set –Volume 2)

UZUNIDIS Dimitri, SAULAIS Pierre
Innovation Engines: Entrepreneurs and Enterprises in a Turbulent World (Innovation in Engineering and Technology Set – Volume 1)

2016

BARBAROUX Pierre, ATTOUR Amel, SCHENK Eric
Knowledge Management and Innovation (Smart Innovation Set – Volume 6)

BEN BOUHENI Faten, AMMI Chantal, LEVY Aldo
Banking Governance, Performance And Risk-Taking: Conventional Banks Vs Islamic Banks

BOUTILLIER Sophie, CARRÉ Denis, LEVRATTO Nadine
Entrepreneurial Ecosystems (Smart Innovation Set – Volume 2)

BOUTILLIER Sophie, UZUNIDIS Dimitri
The Entrepreneur (Smart Innovation Set – Volume 8)

BOUVARD Patricia, SUZANNE Hervé
Collective Intelligence Development in Business

GALLAUD Delphine, LAPERCHE Blandine
Circular Economy, Industrial Ecology and Short Supply Chains (Smart Innovation Set – Volume 4)

GUERRIER Claudine
Security and Privacy in the Digital Era (Innovation and Technology Set – Volume 1)

MEGHOUAR Hicham
Corporate Takeover Targets

MONINO Jean-Louis, SEDKAOUI Soraya
Big Data, Open Data and Data Development (Smart Innovation Set – Volume 3)

MOREL Laure, LE ROUX Serge
Fab Labs: Innovative User (Smart Innovation Set – Volume 5)

PICARD Fabienne, TANGUY Corinne
Innovations and Techno-ecological Transition
(Smart Innovation Set – Volume 7)

2015

CASADELLA Vanessa, LIU Zeting, DIMITRI Uzunidis
Innovation Capabilities and Economic Development in Open Economies
(Smart Innovation Set – Volume 1)

CORSI Patrick, MORIN Dominique
Sequencing Apple's DNA

CORSI Patrick, NEAU Erwan
Innovation Capability Maturity Model

FAIVRE-TAVIGNOT Bénédicte
Social Business and Base of the Pyramid

GODÉ Cécile
Team Coordination in Extreme Environments

MAILLARD Pierre
Competitive Quality and Innovation

MASSOTTE Pierre, CORSI Patrick
Operationalizing Sustainability

MASSOTTE Pierre, CORSI Patrick
Sustainability Calling

2014

DUBÉ Jean, LEGROS Diègo
Spatial Econometrics Using Microdata

LESCA Humbert, LESCA Nicolas
Strategic Decisions and Weak Signals

2013

HABART-CORLOSQUET Marine, JANSSEN Jacques, MANCA Raimondo
VaR Methodology for Non-Gaussian Finance

2012

DAL PONT Jean-Pierre
Process Engineering and Industrial Management

MAILLARD Pierre
Competitive Quality Strategies

POMEROL Jean-Charles
Decision-Making and Action

SZYLAR Christian
UCITS Handbook

2011

LESCA Nicolas
Environmental Scanning and Sustainable Development

LESCA Nicolas, LESCA Humbert
Weak Signals for Strategic Intelligence: Anticipation Tool for Managers

MERCIER-LAURENT Eunika
Innovation Ecosystems

2010

SZYLAR Christian
Risk Management under UCITS III/IV

2009

COHEN Corine
Business Intelligence

ZANINETTI Jean-Marc
Sustainable Development in the USA

2008

CORSI Patrick, DULIEU Mike
The Marketing of Technology Intensive Products and Services

DZEVER Sam, JAUSSAUD Jacques, ANDREOSSO Bernadette
Evolving Corporate Structures and Cultures in Asia: Impact of Globalization

2007

AMMI Chantal
Global Consumer Behavior

2006

BOUGHZALA Imed, ERMINE Jean-Louis
Trends in Enterprise Knowledge Management

CORSI Patrick *et al.*
Innovation Engineering: the Power of Intangible Networks

Printed and bound by CPI Group (UK) Ltd, Croydon, CR0 4YY
16/09/2026
14963076-0005